COLLINS·LONGMAN
ATLAS
for Secondary Schools

Editorial Adviser
Richard Kemp
County Adviser for Humanities
Buckinghamshire

Copyright © Collins-Longman Atlases 1987, 1989, 1991, 1992

First edition published 1987
Reprinted 1987 (twice), 1988, 1989 (twice), 1990, 1991

Second edition published 1992

Maps copyright Collins-Longman Atlases, except those on pages
12 - 23 and 26 - 27 which are licenced to Collins-Longman Atlases
and are derived from databases © Bartholomew Times,
a division of HarperCollins Publishers

HarperCollins Publishers
PO Box
Glasgow
G4 0NB

Longman Group UK Ltd
Longman House
Burnt Mill
Harlow
Essex
CM20 2JE

Printed in Scotland

Photographic Credits
Colorific Photo Library Ltd.
The Environmental Picture Library
The J. Allan Cash Photolibrary
V. Miles
Picturepoint
M. Simpson
University of Dundee
Zefa Picture Library

Contents

4   Symbols

REFERENCE MAPS

Relief and physical features

▲ 8848   Spot height (metres)

⋈   Pass

☐   Permanent ice cap

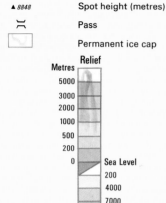

Relief and physical names   *ALPS*   *Zaïre Basin*   *Nicobar Islands*   *Mt. Cook*

Water features

   Submarine contour

• 11034   Ocean depth (metres)

Reef

River

Intermittent river

Falls/Dam

Gorge

Canal

   Lake/Reservoir

   Intermittent lake

Marsh/Swamp

Water names   *PACIFIC OCEAN*   *Red Sea*   *Lake Erie*   *Amazon*

Communications

Tunnel ═══   Railway

Tunnel ┄┄┄   Road

┄ ┄ ┄   Proposed road/desert track

✈   Main airport

Administration

─────   International boundary

─ ─ ─   Undefined or disputed boundary

─·─·─   Internal boundary

◪ ◉ ◎ ⊙   National capitals

Country name   CHILE   Internal division   IOWA   Territorial admin.   *(Fr.)*

Settlement

◪ **Dhākā**

◉ **Khulna**   City and town
                    symbols in
◎ Imphal   order of size.

⊙ Thimbu

MAP SYMBOLS

Symbols are used on a map to show the location of features such as roads, rivers and towns. The meaning of each symbol used on the map is explained in the key.

Map symbols often look like the features they represent. The colour of a symbol may also provide a clue to its meaning. The importance of a feature might be shown by the size of the symbol, the size of the printing or the thickness of the line.

Many maps in this atlas use the same symbols: the meanings of these symbols are shown on this page. Where different colours or symbols are used, their meaning is explained in a key next to the map.

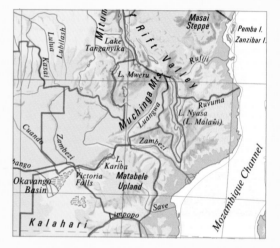

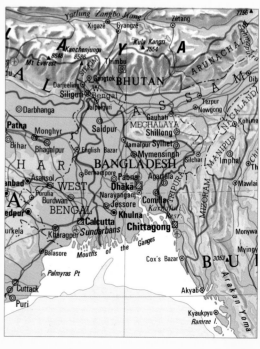

To draw a map of the world, or of a part of the world, the real area has to be reduced in size, or scaled down, to fit onto the map sheet or atlas page. The **scale** of any map therefore tells us precisely how much the real area has been reduced in size.

To use a map to work out the size of areas or distances on the real ground, we need to refer to the scale of that particular map. Map scales can be shown in several ways:

As a **linear scale** — a horizontal line is marked off in units which show how the real ground distances are represented on the map, as in the example below.

As a **statement of scale** — the linear scale above would be written as *1 cm to 1 km*. This means that 1 cm on the map represents 1 km on the real ground.

As a **representative fraction** — for example the scale shown above would be *1:100 000*. This means that every 1 unit of measurement on the map represents 100 000 units on the real ground.

As the scale becomes smaller the amount of real ground that can be fitted onto the map becomes larger. But in making the scale smaller, the accuracy of the map, and the detail it can show, have to be reduced.

The four examples on this page show what happens when the map scale is made smaller. As the scale decreases from the top to the bottom of the page, the details shown on the maps become less precise and more generalised.

On Map A, at a scale of *1:1 000 000*, the Isle of Wight is shown as a county of England, and detail of roads, the location of towns and relief is clearly shown. It is possible to distinguish bays and inlets around the coast.

On Map B, at a scale of *1:4 000 000*, a larger area of the south of England is shown. Thus the coastline of the Isle of Wight has been generalised, and there are few details about the island other than its name.

On Map C, at a scale of *1:16 000 000*, it is possible to show the whole of England and part of the mainland of Europe. The coastline of the Isle of Wight is very generalised, and the island is no longer named.

On Map D, at a scale of *1:85 000 000*, all of Europe can be shown, but the Isle of Wight is represented only by a small dot. At this small scale it is impossible to show any detail of the actual shape of the island, but its location is marked.

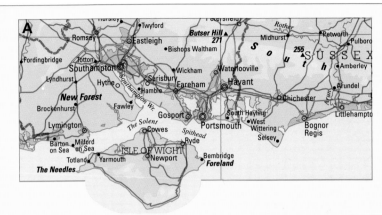

The scale of this map is 1:1 000 000 or 1cm represents 10 km

The scale of this map is 1:4 000 000 or 1cm represents 40 km

The scale of this map is 1:16 000 000 or 1cm represents 160 km

The scale of this map is 1:85 000 000 or 1cm represents 850 km

Lines of latitude and longitude are imaginary lines drawn around a globe or on maps of the whole, or part of the world. Like the grid lines on Ordnance Survey maps they can be used to locate a place accurately.

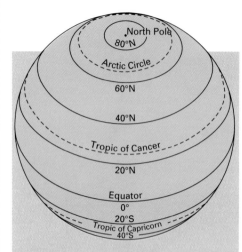

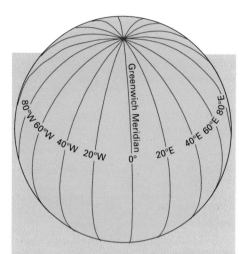

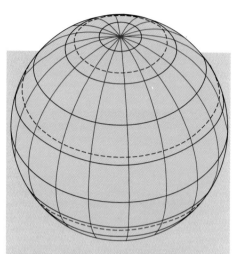

LATITUDE

Lines of **latitude** (or *parallels*) are drawn parallel to the Equator. They are numbered in **degrees** either *north* or *south* of the Equator.
The Equator is numbered 0°, the North Pole 90°N and the South Pole 90°S.

Other important lines of latitude are the Tropic of Cancer (23 1/2°N) and the Tropic of Capricorn (23 1/2°S), the Arctic Circle (66 1/2°N) and the Antarctic Circle (66 1/2°S).

LONGITUDE

Lines of **longitude** (or *meridians*) are drawn from the North Pole to the South Pole. The prime meridian, numbered 0°, runs through the Greenwich Observatory in London and is called the Greenwich Meridian. Lines of longitude are numbered in **degrees** either *east* or *west* of the Greenwich Meridian. The 180° line of longitude, exactly opposite the Greenwich Meridian on the other side of the globe, is the International Date Line.

THE EARTH'S GRID SYSTEM

When lines of latitude and longitude are drawn on a globe or map they form a grid. By using a combination of a place's latitude and longitude that place can be accurately located on the globe or map.

To be really accurate each degree of latitude and longitude can be divided into smaller units called **minutes**. There are 60 minutes in one degree. For example the location of Moscow is 55° 45' north of the Equator, and 37° 42' east of the Greenwich Meridian – this latitude and longitude reference is usually shortened to 55 45N 37 42E.

THE HEMISPHERES

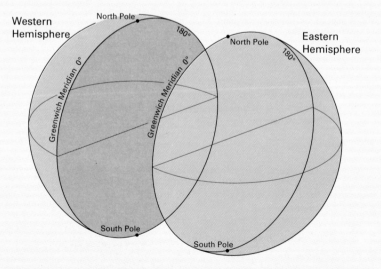

By splitting the globe along the line of the Equator the earth can be divided into two halves, called the Northern and Southern **hemispheres**. If the globe is divided into two from the North Pole to the South Pole, along the 0° and 180° lines of longitude, the halves are called the Eastern Hemisphere and the Western Hemisphere.

© Collins <> Longman Atlases

An atlas map of the world shows the whole world on the flat surface of the page. Yet in reality the earth is actually a sphere. This means that a system has to be used to turn the round surface of the earth into a flat map of the world, or part of the world. This cannot be done without some distortion – on a map some parts of the world have been stretched, other parts have been compressed. A system for turning the globe into a flat map is called a **projection**.

There are many different projections, each of which distorts different things to achieve a flat map. Correct area, correct shape, correct distances or correct directions can be achieved by a projection; but, by achieving any of these things the others have to be distorted. When choosing the projection to use for a particular map it is important to think which of these things it is most important to have correct.

The maps below illustrate four types of world projections, including some of those used in this atlas.

WORLD MAP PROJECTIONS

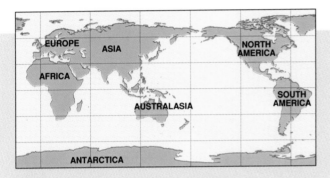

Plate Carrée projection – Pacific-centred

The Plate Carrée projection is used for many of the world maps in this atlas. The version shown here is 'Pacific-centred'. In other words the flat map has been drawn with the Pacific Ocean at its centre. For people living in countries around the Pacific, such as Australia and Japan , this is a more useful way of mapping the world.

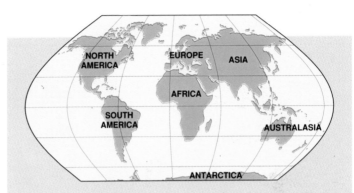

Winkel projection

The Winkel projection is an equal-area projection. Equal-area projections are useful for world maps where it is important to show the correct relative sizes of continental areas. The Winkel projection has curved meridians (lines of longitude), which help to suggest the spherical nature of the earth.

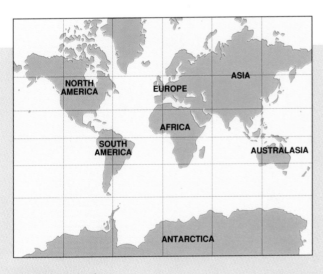

Mercator projection

The Mercator projection was once one of the most commonly used. Its advantage is that it avoids distorting land shapes. To do this, however, it has to show areas near the poles larger than they should be. For example, the island of Greenland near the North Pole seems larger than Australia, when in fact the opposite is true. The projection is useful for navigation as directions can be plotted as straight lines.

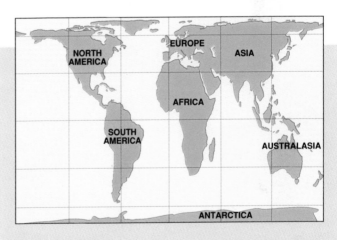

Peter's projection

The aim of Peter's projection is to show the correct size of the continents in relation to each other. To achieve this the projection has to distort the shapes of the continents. Compared with other world maps the land near the equator may appear to have been stretched in a north/south direction. One reason for showing the world like this has been to emphasise the size of the countries of the poorer, developing world.

ORKNEY ISLANDS

SHETLAND ISLANDS

Scale 1:4 000 000

0   50   100   150 km

Conic Projection

© Collins ○ Longman Atlases

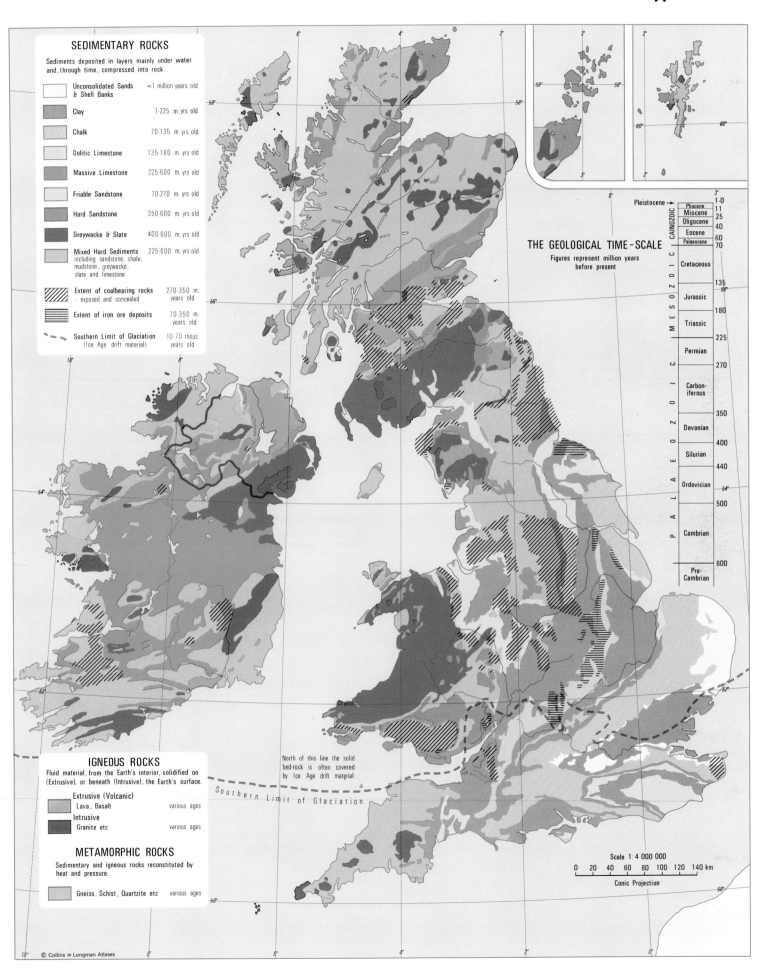

SEDIMENTARY ROCKS

Sediments deposited in layers mainly under water and, through time, compressed into rock.

	Unconsolidated Sands & Shell Banks	<1 million years old
	Clay	1-225 m. yrs old
	Chalk	70-135 m. yrs old
	Oolitic Limestone	135-180 m. yrs old
	Massive Limestone	225-600 m. yrs old
	Friable Sandstone	70-270 m. yrs old
	Hard Sandstone	350-600 m. yrs old
	Greywacke & Slate	400-600 m. yrs old
	Mixed Hard Sediments including sandstone, shale, mudstone, greywacke, slate and limestone	225-600 m. yrs old
	Extent of coalbearing rocks - exposed and concealed	270-350 m. years old
	Extent of iron ore deposits	70-350 m. years old
	Southern Limit of Glaciation (Ice Age drift material)	10-70 thous. years old

THE GEOLOGICAL TIME-SCALE

Figures represent million years before present

Pleistocene →

CAINOZOIC	Pliocene	1-0
	Miocene	11
	Oligocene	25
	Eocene	40
		60
	Palaeocene	70
MESOZOIC	Cretaceous	
		135
	Jurassic	
		180
	Triassic	
		225
	Permian	
		270
PALAEOZOIC	Carboniferous	
		350
	Devonian	
		400
	Silurian	
		440
	Ordovician	
		500
	Cambrian	
		600
	Pre-Cambrian	

North of this line the solid bed-rock is often covered by Ice Age drift material.

Southern Limit of Glaciation

IGNEOUS ROCKS

Fluid material, from the Earth's interior, solidified on (Extrusive), or beneath (Intrusive), the Earth's surface.

	Extrusive (Volcanic) Lava, Basalt	various ages
	Intrusive Granite etc	various ages

METAMORPHIC ROCKS

Sedimentary and igneous rocks reconstituted by heat and pressure.

	Gneiss, Schist, Quartzite etc	various ages

Scale 1:4 000 000

0 20 40 60 80 100 120 140 km

Conic Projection

© Collins ◇ Longman Atlases

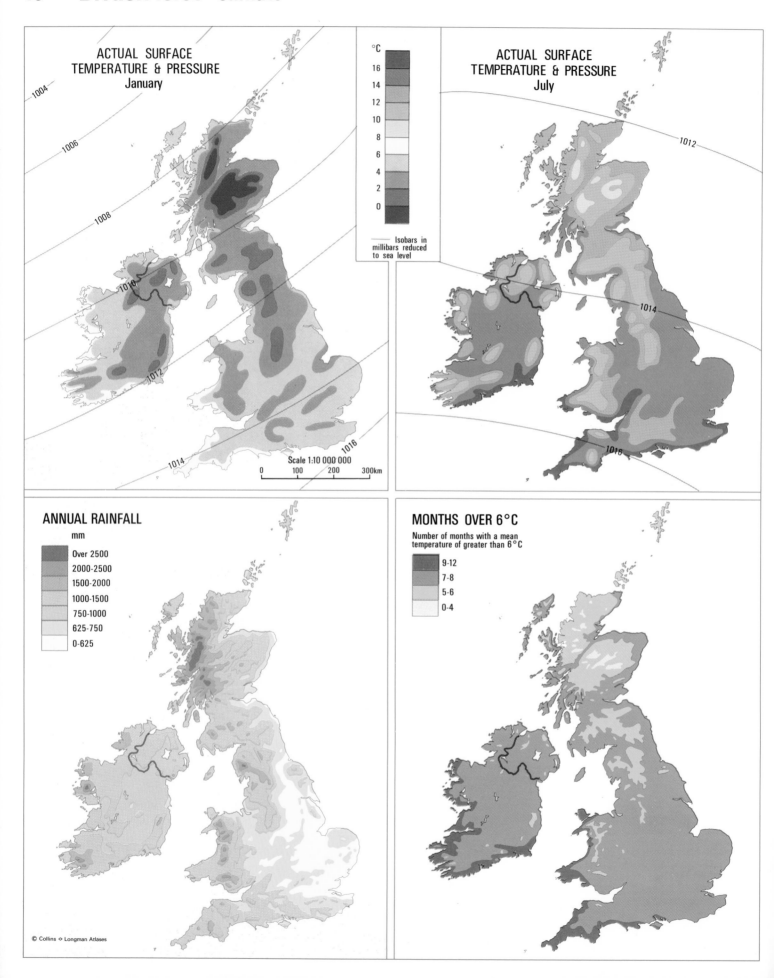

ACTUAL SURFACE TEMPERATURE & PRESSURE
January

1004
1006
1008
1010
1012
1014
1016

°C
16
14
12
10
8
6
4
2
0

Isobars in millibars reduced to sea level

Scale 1:10 000 000
0   100   200   300km

ACTUAL SURFACE TEMPERATURE & PRESSURE
July

1012
1014
1016

ANNUAL RAINFALL

mm

Over 2500
2000-2500
1500-2000
1000-1500
750-1000
625-750
0-625

MONTHS OVER 6°C

Number of months with a mean temperature of greater than 6°C

9-12
7-8
5-6
0-4

© Collins ◇ Longman Atlases

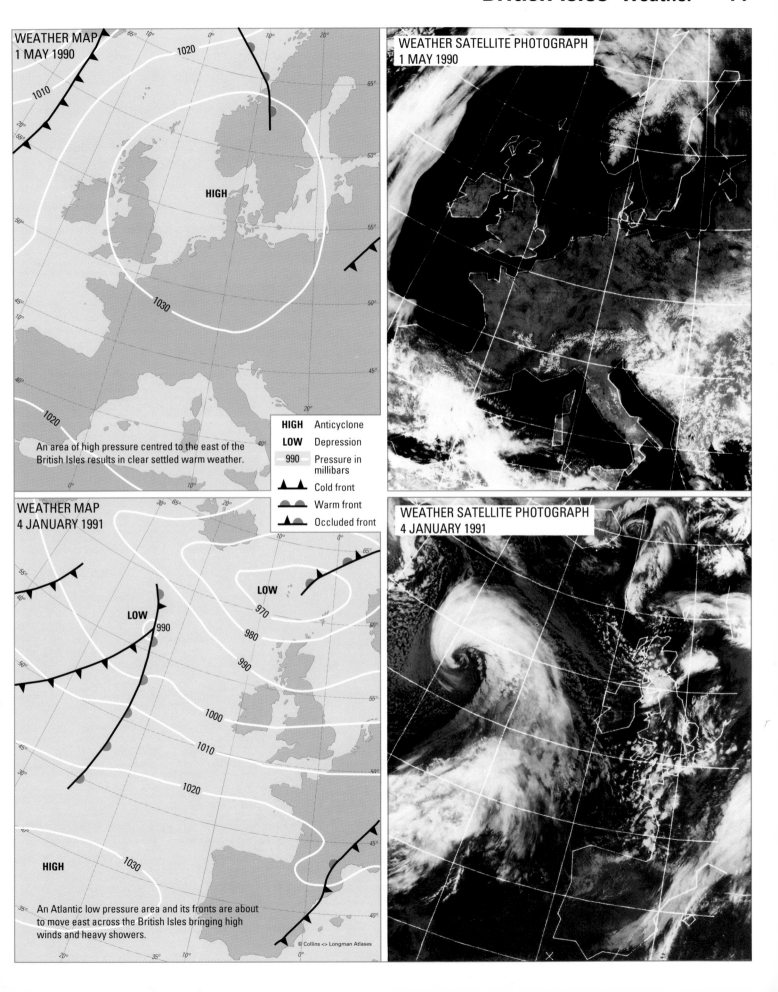

WEATHER MAP
1 MAY 1990

1020

1010

1030

1020

HIGH

An area of high pressure centred to the east of the British Isles results in clear settled warm weather.

HIGH	Anticyclone
LOW	Depression
990	Pressure in millibars
▲▲	Cold front
●●	Warm front
▲●▲●	Occluded front

WEATHER SATELLITE PHOTOGRAPH
1 MAY 1990

WEATHER MAP
4 JANUARY 1991

LOW

970
980
990

LOW
990

1000

1010

1020

1030

HIGH

An Atlantic low pressure area and its fronts are about to move east across the British Isles bringing high winds and heavy showers.

© Collins ◇ Longman Atlases

WEATHER SATELLITE PHOTOGRAPH
4 JANUARY 1991

CLIMATE GRAPHS

POPULATION 1961 - 89

	1961	1971	1981	1989
TOTAL	3 712 000	4 111 800	4 381 300	4 652 400
MALES	1 796 000	1 989 900	2 117 200	2 247 000
FEMALES	1 916 000	2 121 900	2 264 100	2 405 400
LIVE BIRTHS	60 500	61 700	50 400	58 300
DEATHS	46 200	50 700	54 400	56 300
NATURAL INCREASE	14 300	11 000	-4 000	2 000

EMPLOYMENT 1989

- Agriculture, forestry & fishing
- Energy
- Manufacturing
- Construction, transport & communications
- Other services

Total employed: 1 754 100
Males employed: 920 300
Females employed: 833 800

ETHNIC GROUPS 1987-89

All Ethnic Groups — White — Ethnic minority population

Ethnic Minority Population — West Indian & African | Indian, Pakistani & Bangladeshi | Other

MIGRATION 1989

Inflow
Total Inflow: 10 500

Outflow
Total Outflow: 16 500

Origin / Destination of migrants
- Old Commonwealth
- New Commonwealth
- European Community
- USA
- Rest of the World

Climate graph locations: Cheltenham, Weston-super-Mare, Bude, Bournemouth, Plymouth, Penzance, St. Mary's

CHELTENHAM Height 65 metres
WESTON-SUPER-MARE Height 9 metres
BOURNEMOUTH Height 42 metres
BUDE Height 15 metres
PLYMOUTH Height 27 metres
PENZANCE Height 19 metres
ST MARY'S Height 48 metres

© Collins <> Longman Atlases

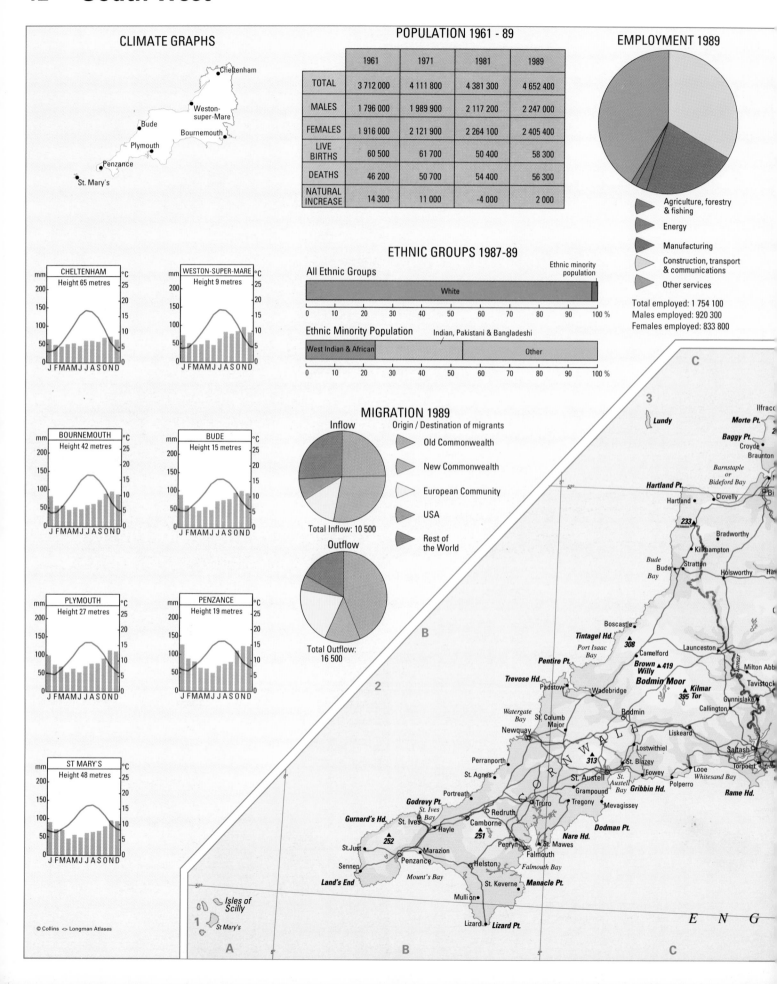

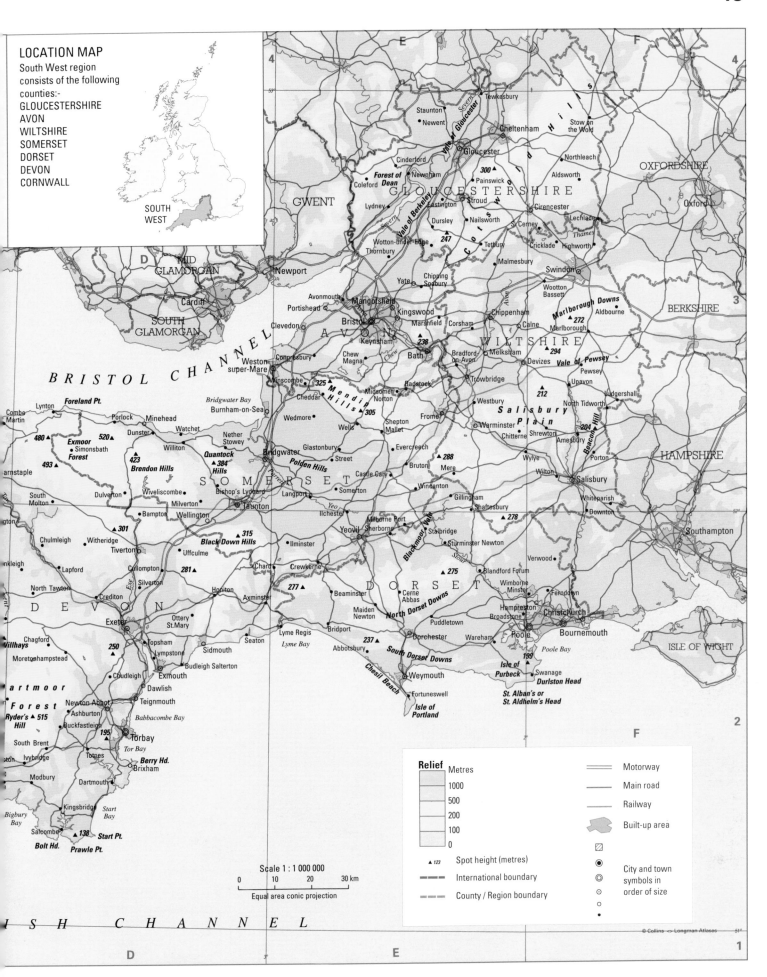

LOCATION MAP

South West region
consists of the following
counties:-
GLOUCESTERSHIRE
AVON
WILTSHIRE
SOMERSET
DORSET
DEVON
CORNWALL

SOUTH
WEST

Relief

Metres
1000
500
200
100
0

▲ 123 Spot height (metres)

– – – International boundary

– – – County / Region boundary

═══ Motorway

─── Main road

─── Railway

Built-up area

◉ City and town
◎ symbols in
◦ order of size
∘
•

Scale 1 : 1 000 000

0   10   20   30 km

Equal area conic projection

© Collins ◇ Longman Atlases

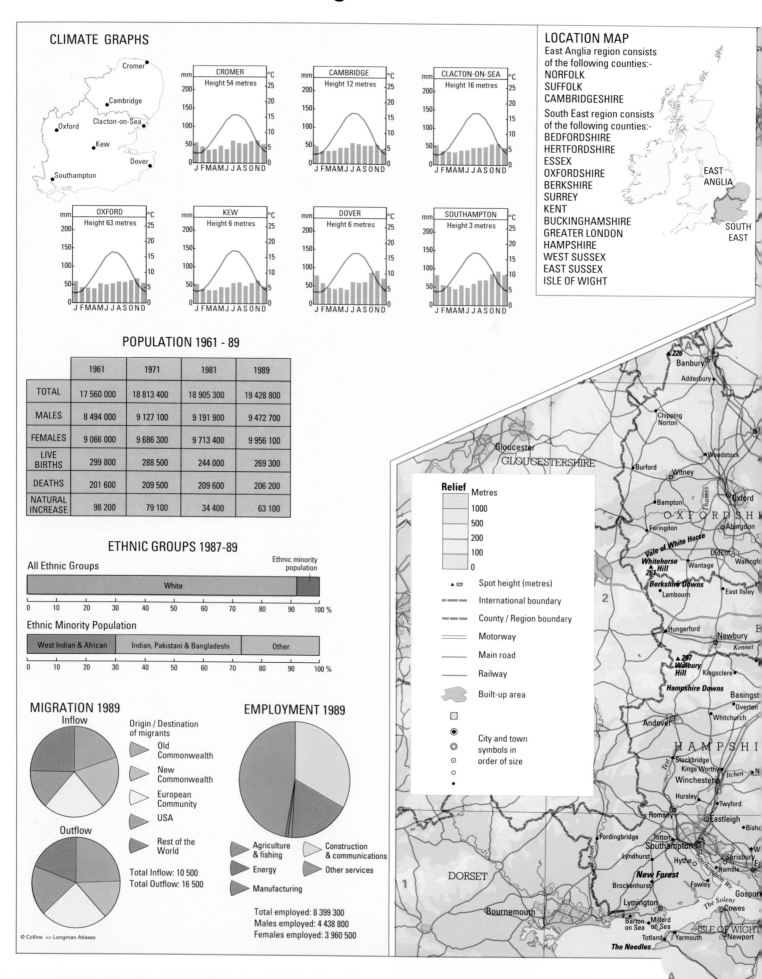

CLIMATE GRAPHS

CROMER
Height 54 metres

CAMBRIDGE
Height 12 metres

CLACTON-ON-SEA
Height 16 metres

OXFORD
Height 63 metres

KEW
Height 6 metres

DOVER
Height 6 metres

SOUTHAMPTON
Height 3 metres

LOCATION MAP

East Anglia region consists
of the following counties:-
NORFOLK
SUFFOLK
CAMBRIDGESHIRE

South East region consists
of the following counties:-
BEDFORDSHIRE
HERTFORDSHIRE
ESSEX
OXFORDSHIRE
BERKSHIRE
SURREY
KENT
BUCKINGHAMSHIRE
GREATER LONDON
HAMPSHIRE
WEST SUSSEX
EAST SUSSEX
ISLE OF WIGHT

EAST
ANGLIA

SOUTH
EAST

POPULATION 1961 - 89

	1961	1971	1981	1989
TOTAL	17 560 000	18 813 400	18 905 300	19 428 800
MALES	8 494 000	9 127 100	9 191 900	9 472 700
FEMALES	9 066 000	9 686 300	9 713 400	9 956 100
LIVE BIRTHS	299 800	288 500	244 000	269 300
DEATHS	201 600	209 500	209 600	206 200
NATURAL INCREASE	98 200	79 100	34 400	63 100

ETHNIC GROUPS 1987-89

All Ethnic Groups

White

Ethnic minority population

0 10 20 30 40 50 60 70 80 90 100 %

Ethnic Minority Population

West Indian & African   Indian, Pakistani & Bangladeshi   Other

0 10 20 30 40 50 60 70 80 90 100 %

MIGRATION 1989

Inflow

Outflow

Origin / Destination
of migrants
- Old Commonwealth
- New Commonwealth
- European Community
- USA
- Rest of the World

Total Inflow: 10 500
Total Outflow: 16 500

EMPLOYMENT 1989

- Agriculture & fishing
- Energy
- Manufacturing
- Construction & communications
- Other services

Total employed: 8 399 300
Males employed: 4 438 800
Females employed: 3 960 500

© Collins ◇ Longman Atlases

Relief   Metres
1000
500
200
100
0

▲ 123   Spot height (metres)

International boundary

County / Region boundary

Motorway

Main road

Railway

Built-up area

City and town
symbols in
order of size

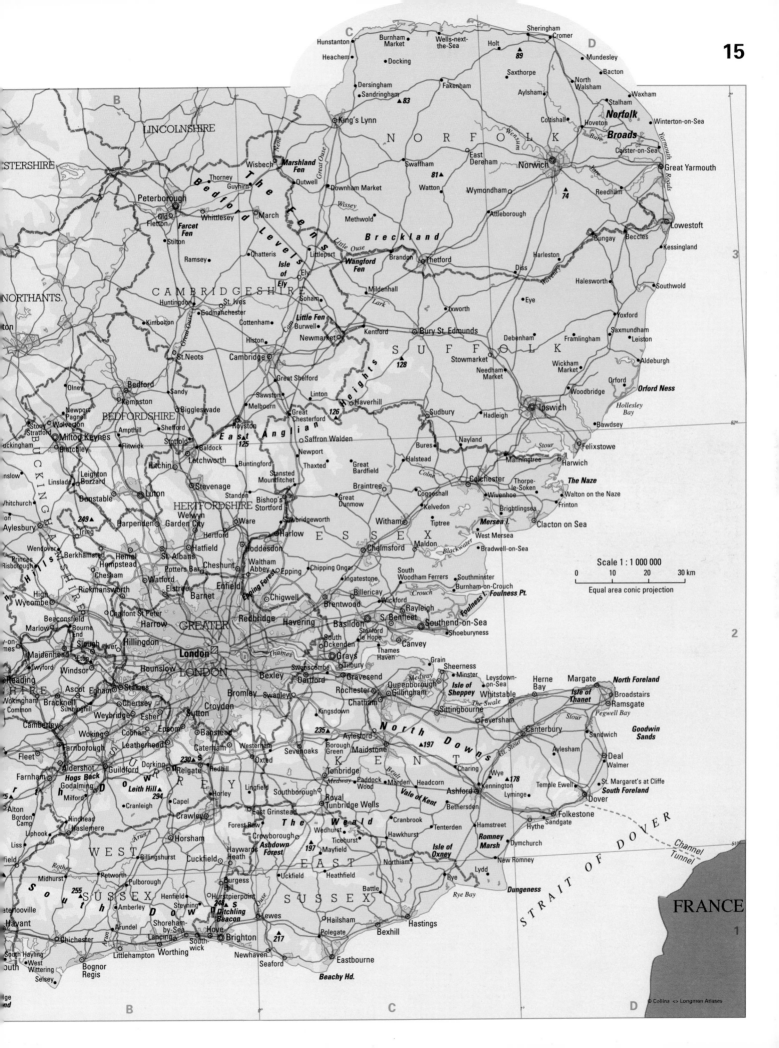

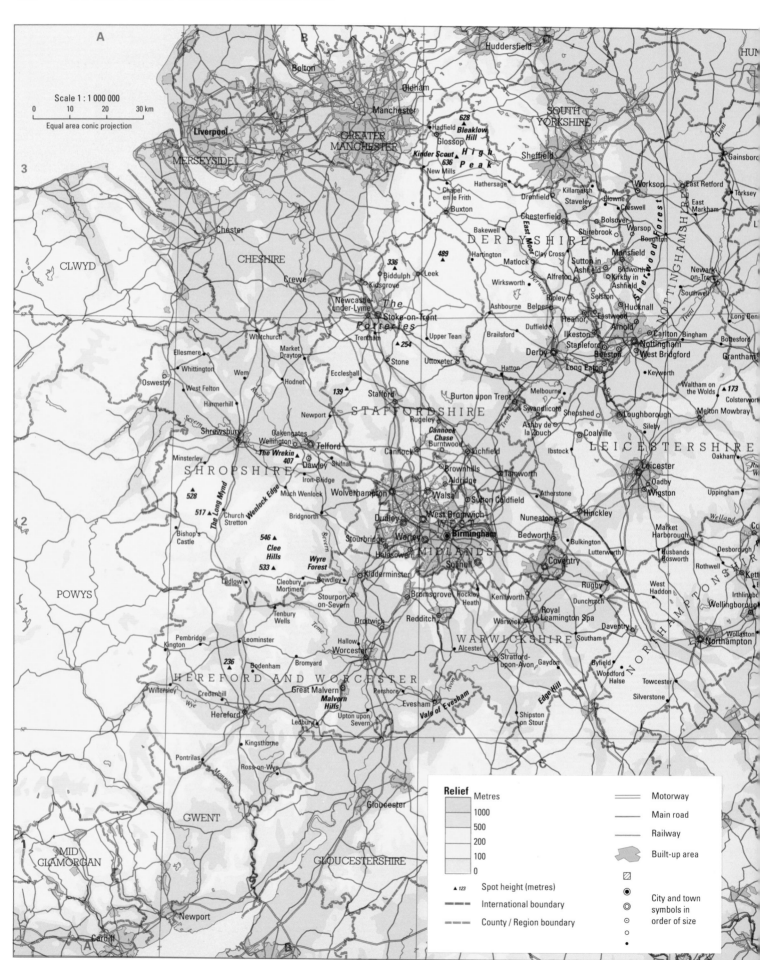

Scale 1 : 1 000 000

0   10   20   30 km

Equal area conic projection

Relief

Metres

1000
500
200
100
0

▲ *123*   Spot height (metres)

– ·– ·–   International boundary

– ·– ·–   County / Region boundary

═══   Motorway

───   Main road

───   Railway

Built-up area

◉ ◎ ⊙ ○ •   City and town symbols in order of size

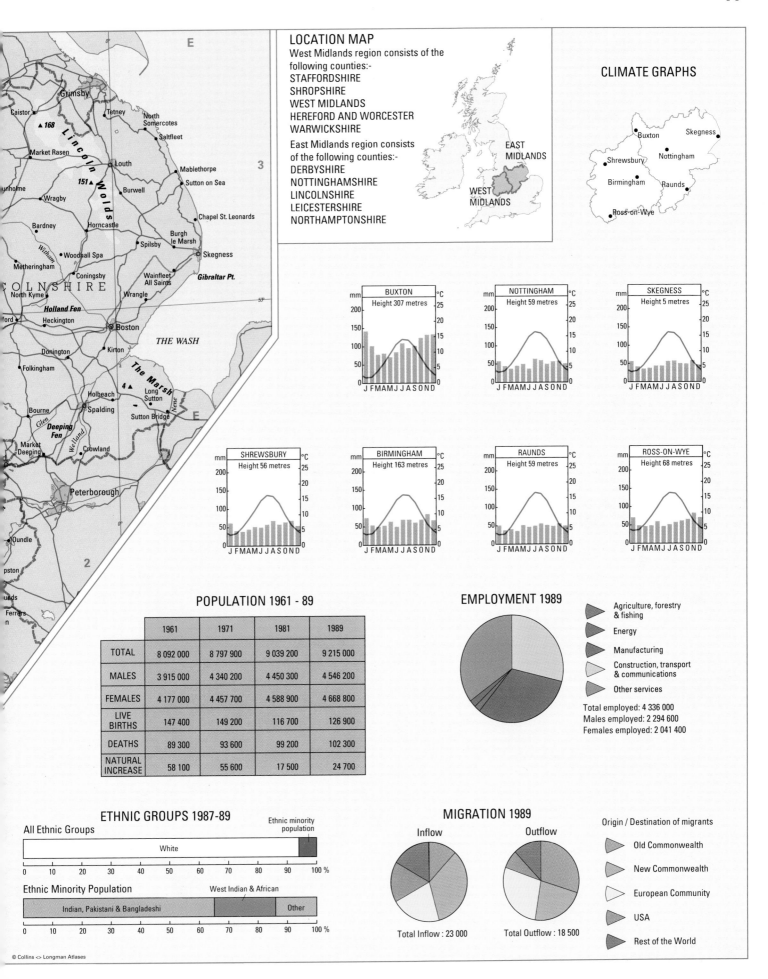

LOCATION MAP

West Midlands region consists of the following counties:-
STAFFORDSHIRE
SHROPSHIRE
WEST MIDLANDS
HEREFORD AND WORCESTER
WARWICKSHIRE

East Midlands region consists of the following counties:-
DERBYSHIRE
NOTTINGHAMSHIRE
LINCOLNSHIRE
LEICESTERSHIRE
NORTHAMPTONSHIRE

EAST MIDLANDS

WEST MIDLANDS

CLIMATE GRAPHS

BUXTON — Height 307 metres
NOTTINGHAM — Height 59 metres
SKEGNESS — Height 5 metres
SHREWSBURY — Height 56 metres
BIRMINGHAM — Height 163 metres
RAUNDS — Height 59 metres
ROSS-ON-WYE — Height 68 metres

POPULATION 1961 - 89

	1961	1971	1981	1989
TOTAL	8 092 000	8 797 900	9 039 200	9 215 000
MALES	3 915 000	4 340 200	4 450 300	4 546 200
FEMALES	4 177 000	4 457 700	4 588 900	4 668 800
LIVE BIRTHS	147 400	149 200	116 700	126 900
DEATHS	89 300	93 600	99 200	102 300
NATURAL INCREASE	58 100	55 600	17 500	24 700

EMPLOYMENT 1989

- Agriculture, forestry & fishing
- Energy
- Manufacturing
- Construction, transport & communications
- Other services

Total employed: 4 336 000
Males employed: 2 294 600
Females employed: 2 041 400

ETHNIC GROUPS 1987-89

All Ethnic Groups

White — Ethnic minority population

0 10 20 30 40 50 60 70 80 90 100 %

Ethnic Minority Population

Indian, Pakistani & Bangladeshi — West Indian & African — Other

0 10 20 30 40 50 60 70 80 90 100 %

MIGRATION 1989

Inflow

Outflow

Total Inflow : 23 000
Total Outflow : 18 500

Origin / Destination of migrants
- Old Commonwealth
- New Commonwealth
- European Community
- USA
- Rest of the World

© Collins <> Longman Atlases

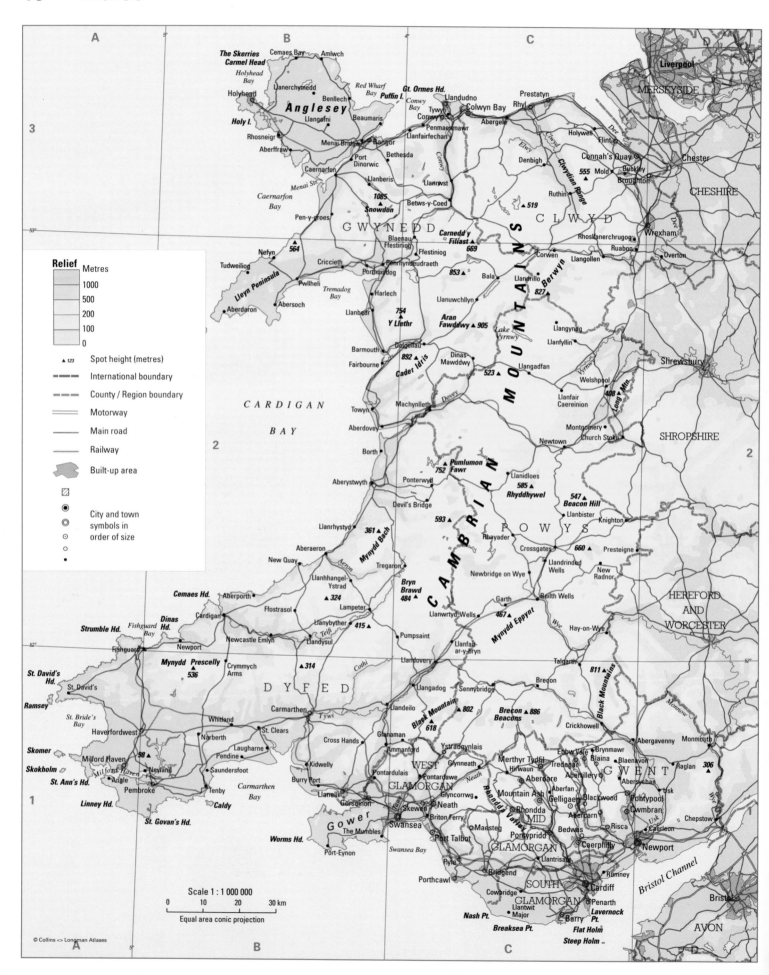

Relief

Metres

1000
500
200
100
0

▲ 123   Spot height (metres)

International boundary

County / Region boundary

Motorway

Main road

Railway

Built-up area

● City and town
◉ symbols in
⊙ order of size
○
•

Scale 1 : 1 000 000

0   10   20   30 km

Equal area conic projection

© Collins <> Longman Atlases

LOCATION MAP

Wales consists of the following counties:-

GWYNEDD
CLWYD
DYFED
POWYS
WEST GLAMORGAN
MID GLAMORGAN
SOUTH GLAMORGAN
GWENT

WALES

CLIMATE GRAPHS

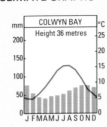

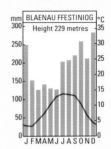

BLAENAU FFESTINIOG
Height 229 metres

COLWYN BAY
Height 36 metres

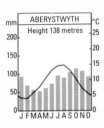
ABERYSTWYTH
Height 138 metres

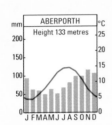
ABERPORTH
Height 133 metres

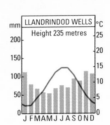
LLANDRINDOD WELLS
Height 235 metres

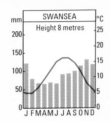
SWANSEA
Height 8 metres

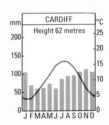
CARDIFF
Height 62 metres

POPULATION 1961 - 89

	1961	1971	1981	1989
TOTAL	2 635 000	2 740 300	2 813 400	2 873 100
MALES	1 275 000	1 328 500	1 365 000	1 393 500
FEMALES	1 360 000	1 411 800	1 448 400	1 479 600
LIVE BIRTHS	44 900	43 100	35 800	38 000
DEATHS	33 700	34 800	35 000	35 100
NATURAL INCREASE	11 200	8 300	800	2 900

ETHNIC GROUPS 1987-89

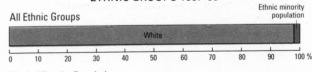

All Ethnic Groups — White — Ethnic minority population

Ethnic Minority Population — West Indian & African — Indian, Pakistani & Bangladeshi — Other

MIGRATION 1989

Inflow

Outflow

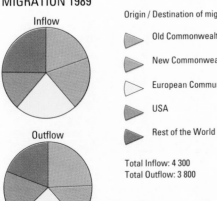

Origin / Destination of migrants
- Old Commonwealth
- New Commonwealth
- European Community
- USA
- Rest of the World

Total Inflow: 4 300
Total Outflow: 3 800

EMPLOYMENT 1989

- Agriculture, forestry & fishing
- Energy
- Manufacturing
- Construction, transport & communications
- Other services

Total employed: 986 700
Males employed: 521 700
Females employed: 465 000

© Collins <> Longman Atlases

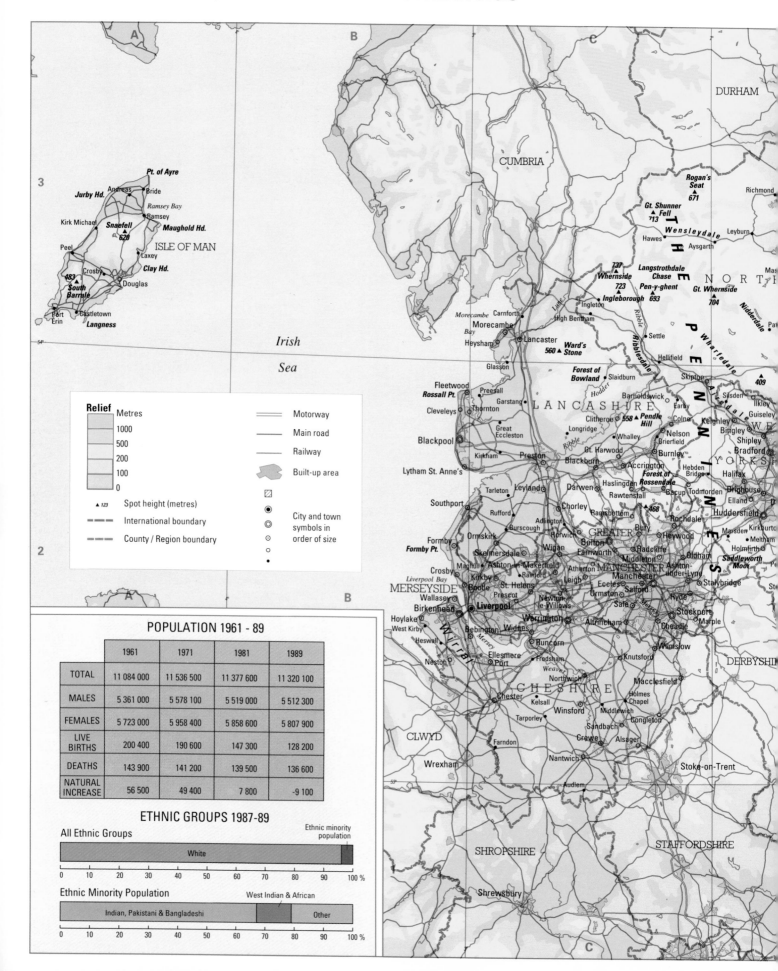

Relief

Metres
- 1000
- 500
- 200
- 100
- 0

▲ 123 Spot height (metres)

– – – International boundary

– – – County / Region boundary

Motorway

Main road

Railway

Built-up area

City and town symbols in order of size

POPULATION 1961 - 89

	1961	1971	1981	1989
TOTAL	11 084 000	11 536 500	11 377 600	11 320 100
MALES	5 361 000	5 578 100	5 519 000	5 512 300
FEMALES	5 723 000	5 958 400	5 858 600	5 807 900
LIVE BIRTHS	200 400	190 600	147 300	128 200
DEATHS	143 900	141 200	139 500	136 600
NATURAL INCREASE	56 500	49 400	7 800	-9 100

ETHNIC GROUPS 1987-89

All Ethnic Groups

White | Ethnic minority population

0 10 20 30 40 50 60 70 80 90 100 %

Ethnic Minority Population

West Indian & African

Indian, Pakistani & Bangladeshi | Other

0 10 20 30 40 50 60 70 80 90 100 %

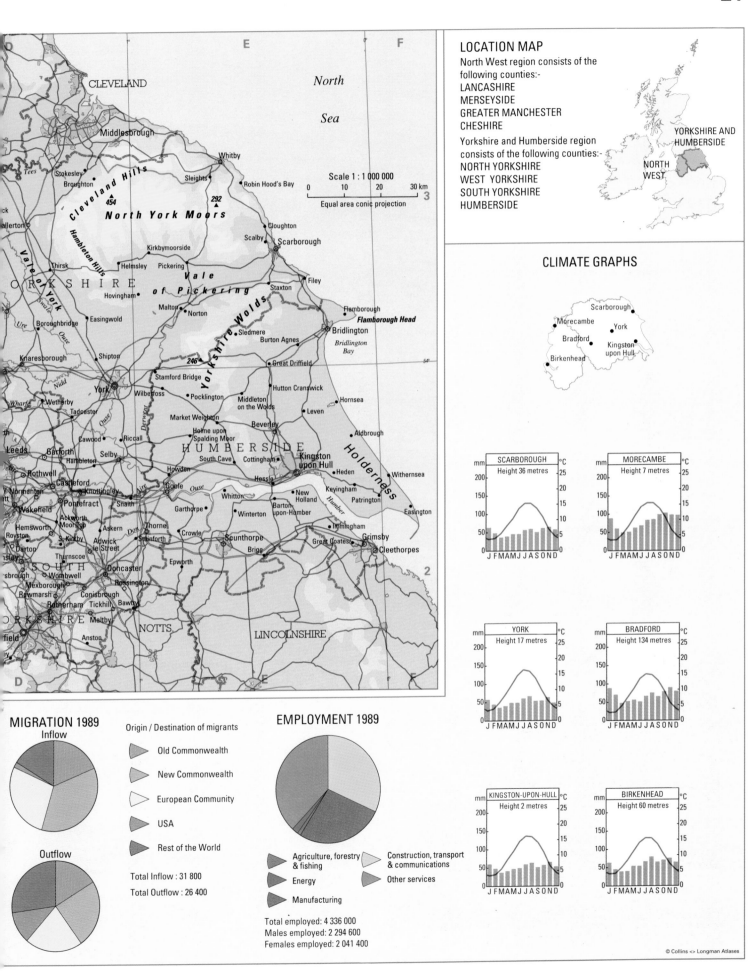

LOCATION MAP

North West region consists of the following counties:-
LANCASHIRE
MERSEYSIDE
GREATER MANCHESTER
CHESHIRE

Yorkshire and Humberside region consists of the following counties:-
NORTH YORKSHIRE
WEST YORKSHIRE
SOUTH YORKSHIRE
HUMBERSIDE

YORKSHIRE AND HUMBERSIDE
NORTH WEST

Scale 1 : 1 000 000
0   10   20   30 km
Equal area conic projection

CLIMATE GRAPHS

Scarborough
Morecambe
York
Bradford
Kingston upon Hull
Birkenhead

SCARBOROUGH — Height 36 metres
MORECAMBE — Height 7 metres
YORK — Height 17 metres
BRADFORD — Height 134 metres
KINGSTON-UPON-HULL — Height 2 metres
BIRKENHEAD — Height 60 metres

MIGRATION 1989

Inflow
Outflow

Origin / Destination of migrants

- Old Commonwealth
- New Commonwealth
- European Community
- USA
- Rest of the World

Total Inflow : 31 800
Total Outflow : 26 400

EMPLOYMENT 1989

- Agriculture, forestry & fishing
- Energy
- Manufacturing
- Construction, transport & communications
- Other services

Total employed: 4 336 000
Males employed: 2 294 600
Females employed: 2 041 400

© Collins <> Longman Atlases

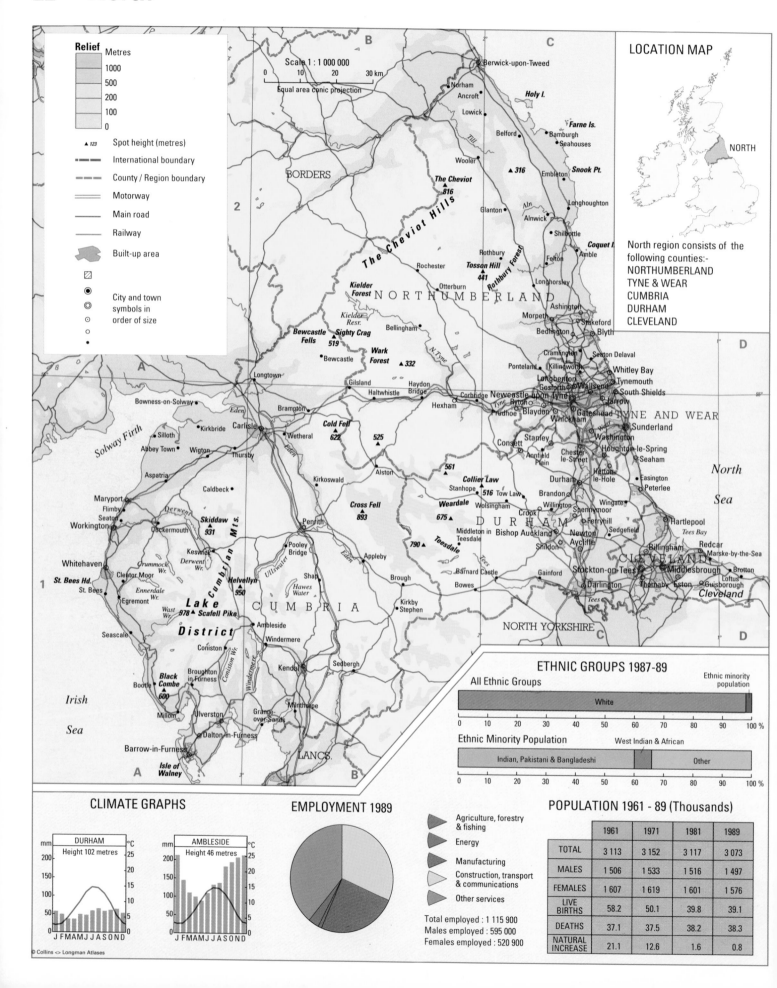

LOCATION MAP

NORTH

North region consists of the following counties:-
NORTHUMBERLAND
TYNE & WEAR
CUMBRIA
DURHAM
CLEVELAND

Relief

Metres
1000
500
200
100
0

▲123　Spot height (metres)

International boundary

County / Region boundary

Motorway

Main road

Railway

Built-up area

City and town symbols in order of size

Scale 1 : 1 000 000

Equal area conic projection

ETHNIC GROUPS 1987-89

All Ethnic Groups

White — Ethnic minority population

0　10　20　30　40　50　60　70　80　90　100 %

Ethnic Minority Population

Indian, Pakistani & Bangladeshi — West Indian & African — Other

0　10　20　30　40　50　60　70　80　90　100 %

CLIMATE GRAPHS

DURHAM — Height 102 metres

AMBLESIDE — Height 46 metres

EMPLOYMENT 1989

- Agriculture, forestry & fishing
- Energy
- Manufacturing
- Construction, transport & communications
- Other services

Total employed : 1 115 900
Males employed : 595 000
Females employed : 520 900

POPULATION 1961 - 89 (Thousands)

	1961	1971	1981	1989
TOTAL	3 113	3 152	3 117	3 073
MALES	1 506	1 533	1 516	1 497
FEMALES	1 607	1 619	1 601	1 576
LIVE BIRTHS	58.2	50.1	39.8	39.1
DEATHS	37.1	37.5	38.2	38.3
NATURAL INCREASE	21.1	12.6	1.6	0.8

© Collins ◇ Longman Atlases

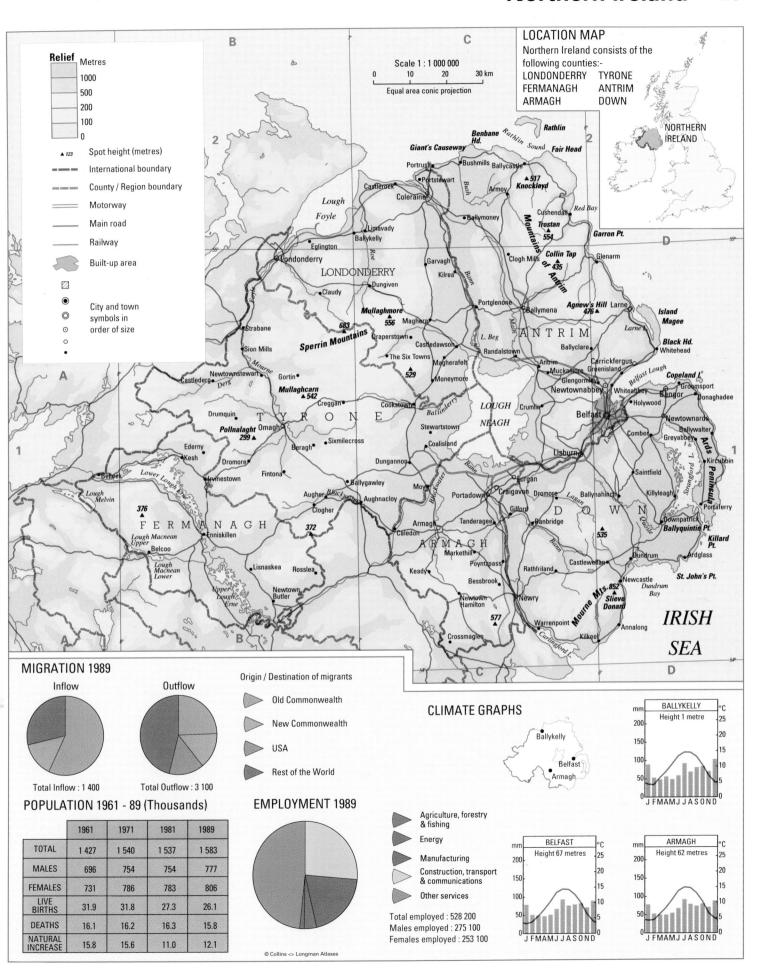

Relief

Metres
- 1000
- 500
- 200
- 100
- 0

▲ 123 Spot height (metres)

International boundary

County / Region boundary

Motorway

Main road

Railway

Built-up area

City and town symbols in order of size

Scale 1 : 1 000 000

0 10 20 30 km

Equal area conic projection

LOCATION MAP

Northern Ireland consists of the following counties:-

LONDONDERRY   TYRONE
FERMANAGH   ANTRIM
ARMAGH   DOWN

NORTHERN IRELAND

MIGRATION 1989

Inflow   Outflow

Origin / Destination of migrants

- Old Commonwealth
- New Commonwealth
- USA
- Rest of the World

Total Inflow : 1 400   Total Outflow : 3 100

POPULATION 1961 - 89 (Thousands)

	1961	1971	1981	1989
TOTAL	1 427	1 540	1 537	1 583
MALES	696	754	754	777
FEMALES	731	786	783	806
LIVE BIRTHS	31.9	31.8	27.3	26.1
DEATHS	16.1	16.2	16.3	15.8
NATURAL INCREASE	15.8	15.6	11.0	12.1

EMPLOYMENT 1989

- Agriculture, forestry & fishing
- Energy
- Manufacturing
- Construction, transport & communications
- Other services

Total employed : 528 200
Males employed : 275 100
Females employed : 253 100

CLIMATE GRAPHS

Ballykelly

Belfast

Armagh

BALLYKELLY
Height 1 metre

BELFAST
Height 67 metres

ARMAGH
Height 62 metres

© Collins <> Longman Atlases

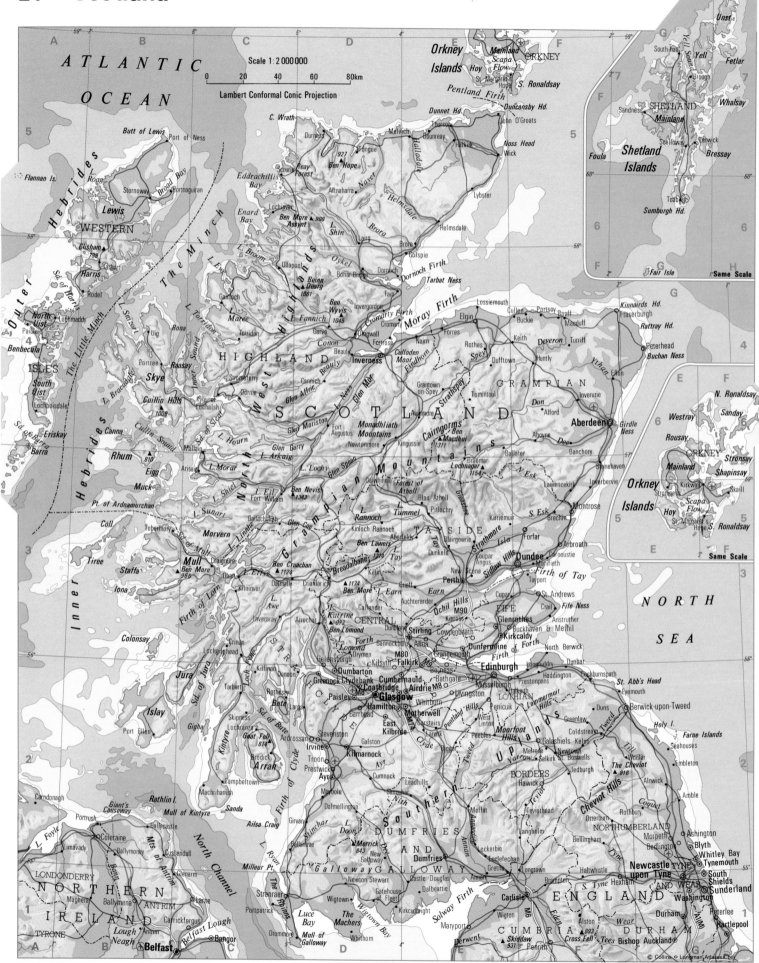

Scale 1:2 000 000

0   20   40   60   80km

Lambert Conformal Conic Projection

© Collins · Longman Atlases Coll

LOCATION MAP

Scotland consists of the following regions:-

SHETLAND ISLANDS
ORKNEY ISLANDS
WESTERN ISLES
HIGHLAND
GRAMPIAN
TAYSIDE
CENTRAL
FIFE
STRATHCLYDE
LOTHIAN
BORDERS
DUMFRIES & GALLOWAY

CLIMATE GRAPHS

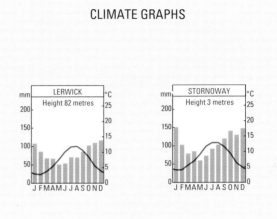

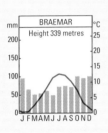

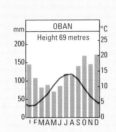

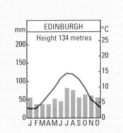

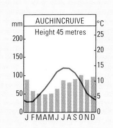

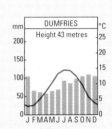

POPULATION 1961 - 89

	1961	1971	1981	1989
TOTAL	5 184 000	5 235 600	5 180 200	5 090 700
MALES	2 485 000	2 515 700	2 494 900	2 460 400
FEMALES	2 699 000	2 719 900	2 685 300	2 630 300
LIVE BIRTHS	101 200	86 700	69 100	63 500
DEATHS	63 900	61 600	63 800	65 000
NATURAL INCREASE	37 300	25 100	11 000	-1 500

ETHNIC GROUPS 1987-89

All Ethnic Groups

Ethnic minority population

White

0 10 20 30 40 50 60 70 80 90 100 %

Ethnic Minority Population

West Indian & African

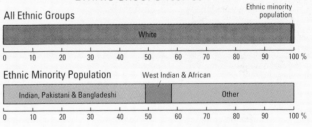

Indian, Pakistani & Bangladeshi   Other

0 10 20 30 40 50 60 70 80 90 100 %

MIGRATION 1989

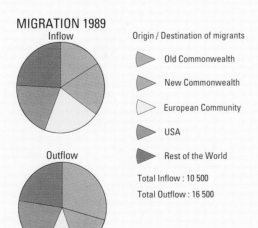

Inflow

Outflow

Origin / Destination of migrants

Old Commonwealth

New Commonwealth

European Community

USA

Rest of the World

Total Inflow : 10 500

Total Outflow : 16 500

EMPLOYMENT 1989

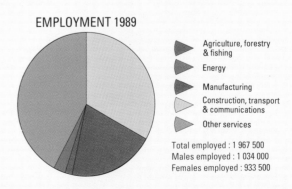

Agriculture, forestry & fishing

Energy

Manufacturing

Construction, transport & communications

Other services

Total employed : 1 967 500
Males employed : 1 034 000
Females employed : 933 500

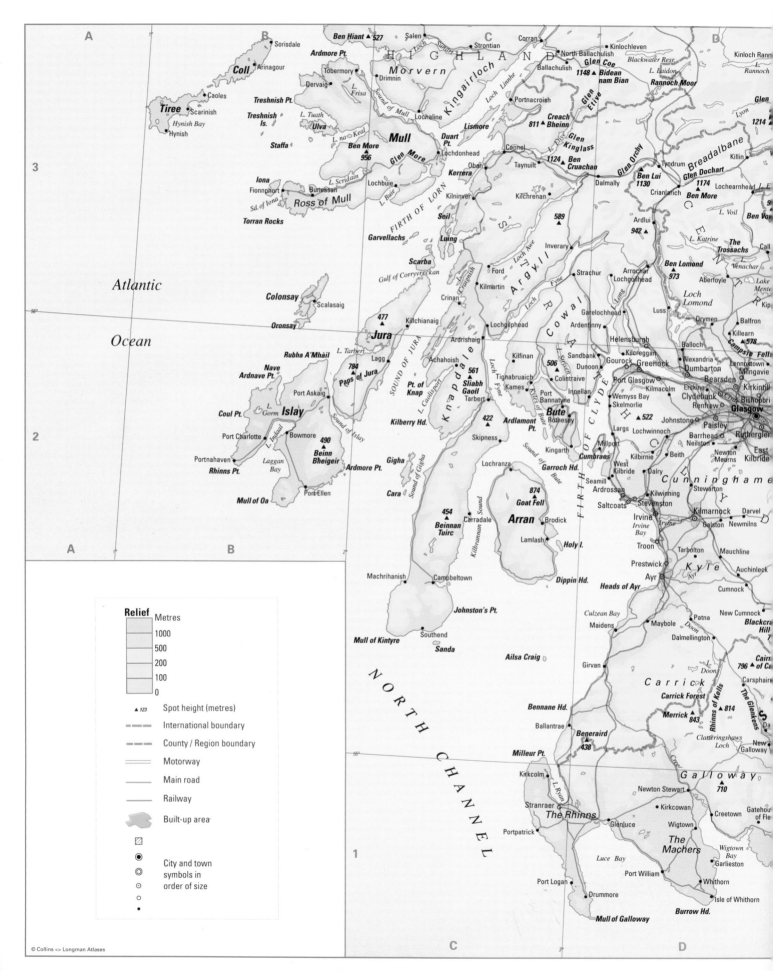

Relief
Metres
1000
500
200
100
0

▲ 123 Spot height (metres)

– – – – International boundary

– – – – County / Region boundary

―――― Motorway

――――― Main road

――――― Railway

    Built-up area

◉
◎ City and town
○ symbols in
○ order of size
·

© Collins <> Longman Atlases

Scale 1 : 1 000 000

0   10   20   30 km

Equal area conic projection

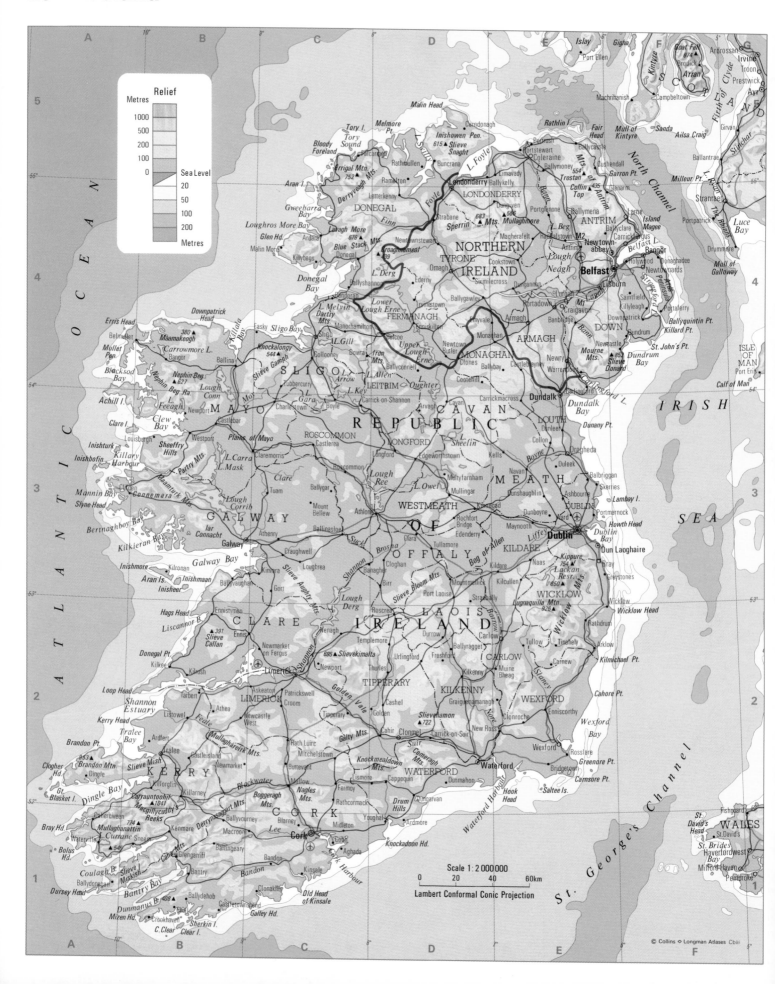

Relief

Metres
1000
500
200
100
0
Sea Level
20
50
100
200
Metres

Scale 1:2 000 000

0   20   40   60km

Lambert Conformal Conic Projection

© Collins ◊ Longman Atlases Cbiii

ORKNEY

SHETLAND

WESTERN ISLES

HIGHLAND

GRAMPIAN

• Stornoway

• Inverness

• Aberdeen

SCOTLAND
9 Regions
3 Island Authorities
53 Districts

International boundary
National boundary
County or region boundary
Historic counties in Northern Ireland
Former metropolitan county
Greater London
• Administrative headquarters (those underlined contain the offices of more than one county)

The local government boundaries for England & Wales shown on this map were officially approved by an Act of Parliament in October 1972, and those for Scotland and Northern Ireland in October 1973. The sub-division of Counties and Regions is not shown.

In 1986 the executive powers of the Metropolitan Counties were taken over by joint boards and agencies made up of representatives from the Metropolitan Districts and central government.

TAYSIDE
• Dundee
CENTRAL
FIFE
• Stirling
• Glenrothes
• Edinburgh
STRATHCLYDE
• Glasgow
LOTHIAN
• Newtown St Boswells
BORDERS

NORTHERN IRELAND
1 Region
26 Districts

DONEGAL
• Lifford
Londonderry
Antrim
Tyrone
• Belfast
Fermanagh
Monaghan
Down
Sligo
LEITRIM
CAVAN
• Monaghan
Armagh
• Cavan
LOUTH
• Dundalk

MAYO
• Castlebar
ROSCOMMON
Carrick-on-Shannon
• Longford
LONGFORD
• Roscommon
WEST MEATH
• Mullingar
MEATH
• Navan
SLIGO

GALWAY
• Galway
OFFALY
• Tullamore
• Port Laoise
LAOIS
KILDARE
• Naas
DUBLIN
• Dublin
WICKLOW
• Wicklow

CLARE
• Ennis
TIPPERARY
CARLOW
• Carlow
KILKENNY
• Kilkenny
WEXFORD

LIMERICK
• Limerick
• Clonmel
WEXFORD
• Wexford

KERRY
• Tralee
WATERFORD
• Waterford

CORK
• Cork

REPUBLIC OF IRELAND
26 Counties

ISLE OF MAN
• Douglas

NORTHUMBER-LAND
• Morpeth
• Newcastle upon Tyne
TYNE & WEAR
• Carlisle
• Durham
DURHAM
CLEVELAND
• Middlesbrough
CUMBRIA
• Northallerton
NORTH YORKSHIRE

DUMFRIES & GALLOWAY
• Dumfries

ENGLAND
39 Counties
6 Metropolitan Counties
Greater London
36 Former Metropolitan Counties
296 Non-Metropolitan Districts

LANCASHIRE
• Preston
WEST YORKSHIRE
• Wakefield
• Barnsley
SOUTH YORKSHIRE
HUMBERSIDE
• Beverley
MERSEYSIDE
• Liverpool
• Manchester
CHESHIRE
• Chester
DERBYSHIRE
• Matlock
NOTTINGHAMSHIRE
• Nottingham
LINCOLN-SHIRE
• Lincoln

Caernarfon •
GWYNEDD
• Mold
CLWYD
• Stafford
STAFFORD-SHIRE
LEICESTER-SHIRE
• Leicester
NORFOLK
• Norwich

• Shrewsbury
SHROP-SHIRE
• Birmingham
W.M.
WARWICK-SHIRE
• Warwick
NORTHAMPTONSHIRE
• Northampton
CAMBRIDGE-SHIRE
SUFFOLK
• Ipswich

WALES
8 Counties
37 Districts

POWYS
• Llandrindod Wells
HEREFORD & WORCESTER
• Worcester
GLOUCESTER-SHIRE
• Gloucester
OXFORD-SHIRE
• Oxford
BUCKINGHAMSHIRE
• Aylesbury
BEDFORD-SHIRE
• Bedford
• Cambridge
HERTFORD-SHIRE
• Hertford
ESSEX
• Chelmsford

DYFED
• Carmarthen
W. GLAMORGAN
• Swansea
MID GLAMORGAN
GWENT
• Cwmbran
S.G.
• Cardiff
AVON
• Bristol
• Reading
BERKSHIRE
GREATER LONDON
• Kingston upon Thames
SURREY
• Maidstone
KENT

REPUBLIC OF IRELAND

• Newport
WILTSHIRE
• Trowbridge
HAMPSHIRE
• Winchester
WEST SUSSEX
• Chichester
EAST SUSSEX
• Lewes

SOMERSET
• Taunton
DORSET
• Dorchester
ISLE OF WIGHT
• Newport

DEVON
• Exeter

CORNWALL
• Truro

Scale 1:4 000 000

0   50   100   150km

Conic Projection

G.M.   GREATER MANCHESTER
S.G.   SOUTH GLAMORGAN
W.M.   WEST MIDLANDS

© Collins ◇ Longman Atlases

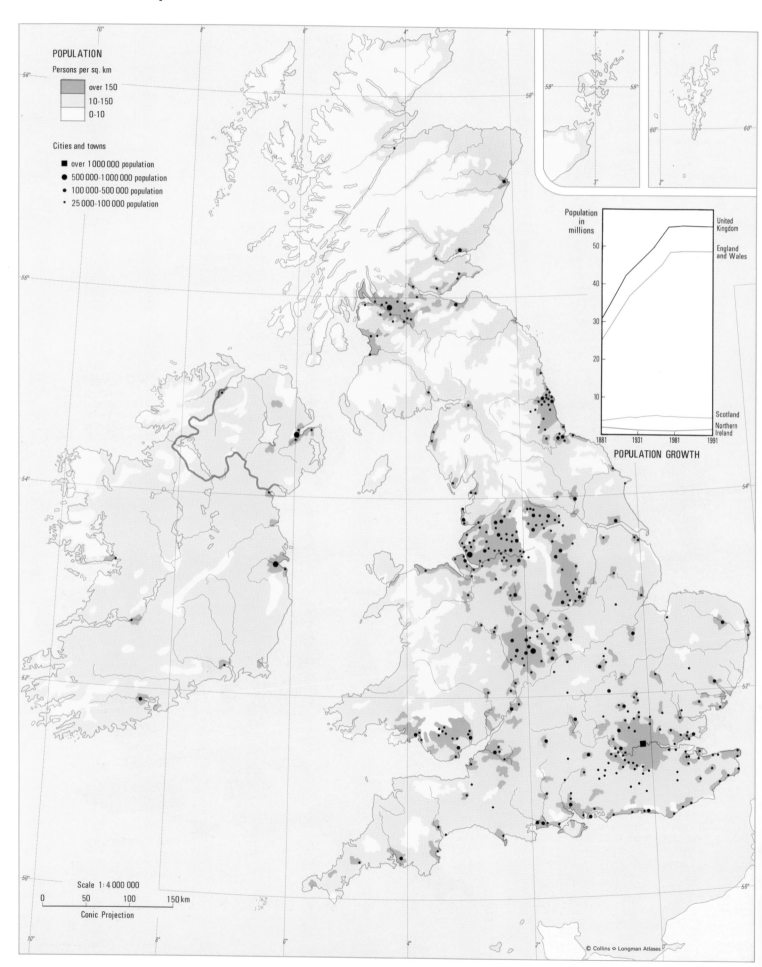

POPULATION

Persons per sq. km

over 150
10–150
0–10

Cities and towns

■ over 1 000 000 population
● 500 000–1 000 000 population
• 100 000–500 000 population
· 25 000–100 000 population

Population in millions

United Kingdom
England and Wales
Scotland
Northern Ireland

POPULATION GROWTH

Scale 1:4 000 000

0   50   100   150 km

Conic Projection

© Collins ◇ Longman Atlases

POPULATION OVER PENSION AGE, 1989
(Women aged 60 and over, men aged 65 and over.)

21% and over
20.1 - 21%
19.1 - 20%
18.1 - 19%
17.1 - 18%
16.1 - 17%
14.0 - 16%

UK average 18%

Scale 1 : 10 000 000

0   100   200   300 km

UNEMPLOYMENT RATE, JANUARY 1991

12% and over
10 - 11.9%
7 - 9.9%
4 - 6.9%
0 - 3.9%

UK average 6.9%

Scale 1 : 10 000 000

0   100   200   300 km

AGE STRUCTURE, UK AND SELECTED REGIONS - 1966, 1978, 1989

NORTHERN IRELAND

AGE GROUP

65 and over
45-64
15-44
5-14
0-4

Male 1966 Female   Male 1978 Female   Male 1989 Female

NORTH ENGLAND

AGE GROUP

65 and over
45-64
15-44
5-14
0-4

Male 1966 Female   Male 1978 Female   Male 1989 Female

SOUTH WEST ENGLAND

AGE GROUP

65 and over
45-64
15-44
5-14
0-4

Male 1966 Female   Male 1978 Female   Male 1989 Female

UNITED KINGDOM

AGE GROUP

65 and over
45-64
15-44
5-14
0-4

Male 1966 Female   Male 1978 Female   Male 1989 Female

© Collins <> Longman Atlases

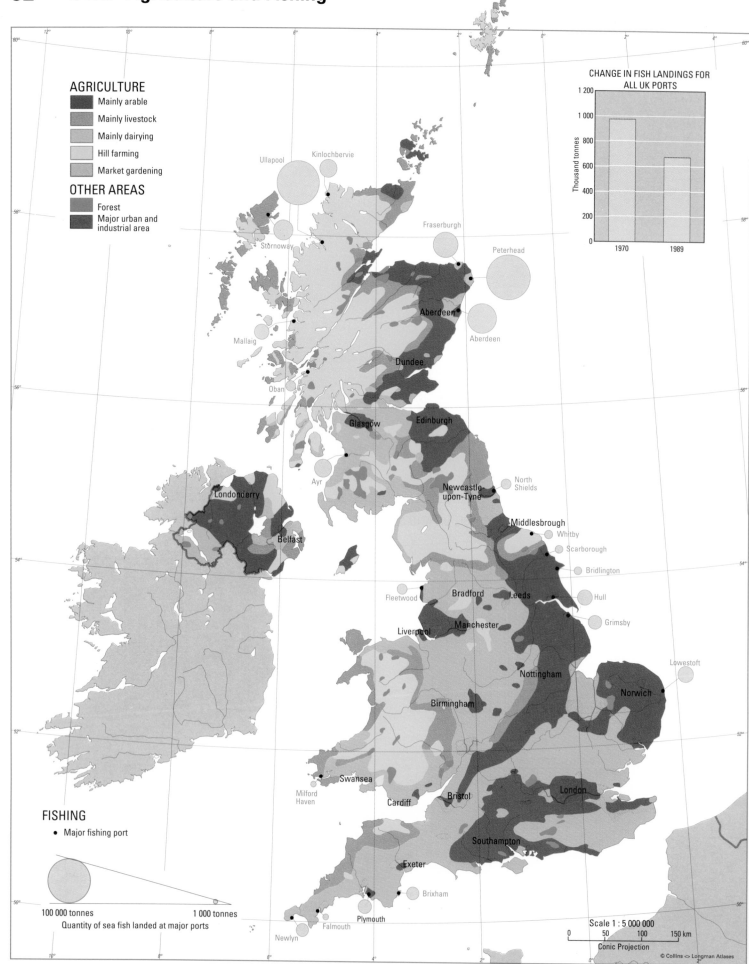

AGRICULTURE

- Mainly arable
- Mainly livestock
- Mainly dairying
- Hill farming
- Market gardening

OTHER AREAS

- Forest
- Major urban and industrial area

CHANGE IN FISH LANDINGS FOR ALL UK PORTS

Thousand tonnes

1970   1989

Ullapool
Kinlochbervie
Stornoway
Mallaig
Oban
Fraserburgh
Peterhead
Aberdeen
Aberdeen
Dundee
Glasgow
Edinburgh
Ayr
Newcastle-upon-Tyne
North Shields
Middlesbrough
Whitby
Scarborough
Bridlington
Londonderry
Belfast
Fleetwood
Bradford
Leeds
Hull
Liverpool
Manchester
Grimsby
Nottingham
Lowestoft
Birmingham
Norwich
Swansea
London
Milford Haven
Cardiff
Bristol
Southampton
Exeter
Brixham
Falmouth
Plymouth
Newlyn

FISHING

- Major fishing port

100 000 tonnes   1 000 tonnes
Quantity of sea fish landed at major ports

Scale 1 : 5 000 000
0   50   100   150 km
Conic Projection

© Collins ◇ Longman Atlases

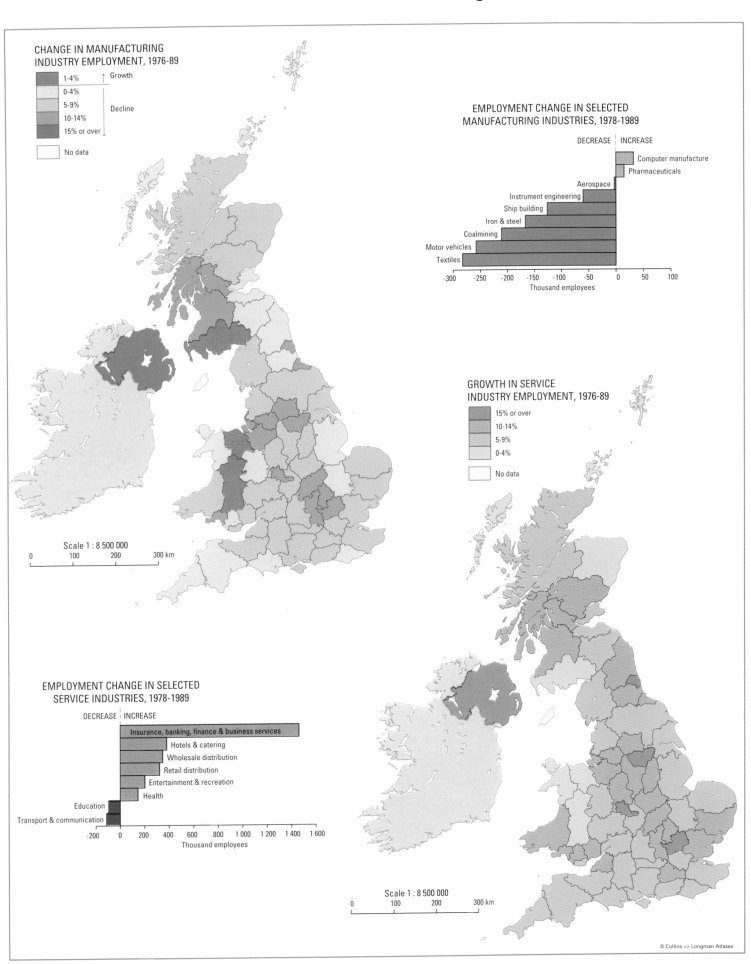

CHANGE IN MANUFACTURING INDUSTRY EMPLOYMENT, 1976-89

- 1-4% ↑ Growth
- 0-4%
- 5-9% Decline
- 10-14%
- 15% or over ↓
- No data

EMPLOYMENT CHANGE IN SELECTED MANUFACTURING INDUSTRIES, 1978-1989

DECREASE | INCREASE

Computer manufacture
Pharmaceuticals
Aerospace
Instrument engineering
Ship building
Iron & steel
Coalmining
Motor vehicles
Textiles

-300 -250 -200 -150 -100 -50 0 50 100
Thousand employees

GROWTH IN SERVICE INDUSTRY EMPLOYMENT, 1976-89

- 15% or over
- 10-14%
- 5-9%
- 0-4%
- No data

Scale 1 : 8 500 000
0 100 200 300 km

EMPLOYMENT CHANGE IN SELECTED SERVICE INDUSTRIES, 1978-1989

DECREASE | INCREASE

Insurance, banking, finance & business services
Hotels & catering
Wholesale distribution
Retail distribution
Entertainment & recreation
Health
Education
Transport & communication

-200 0 200 400 600 800 1 000 1 200 1 400 1 600
Thousand employees

Scale 1 : 8 500 000
0 100 200 300 km

© Collins <> Longman Atlases

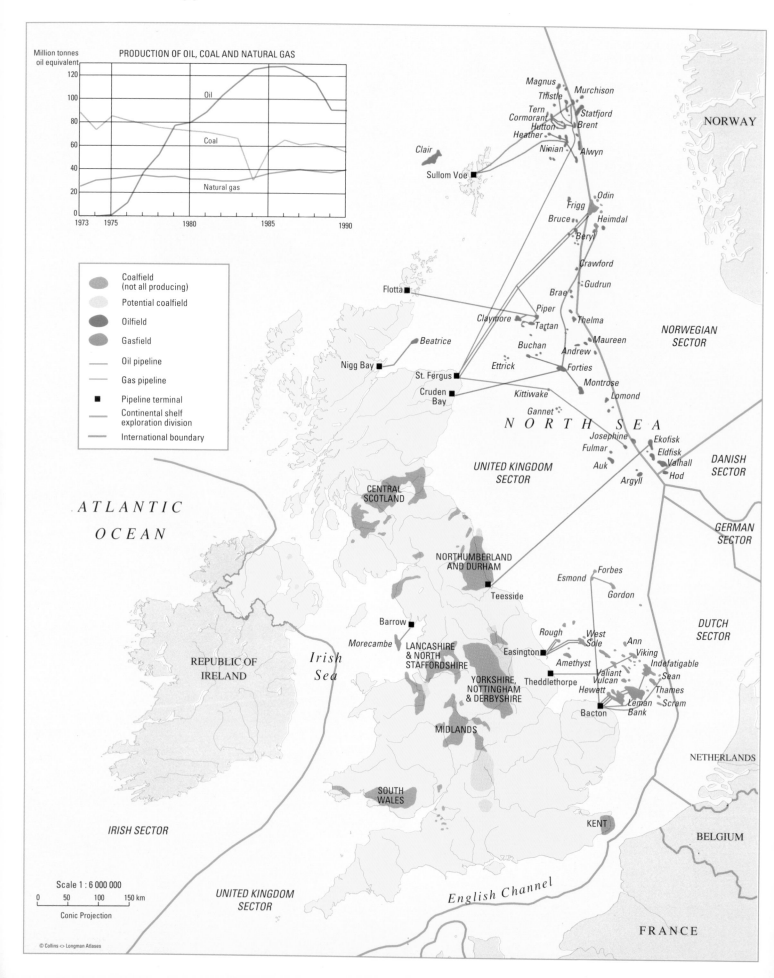

PRODUCTION OF OIL, COAL AND NATURAL GAS

Million tonnes oil equivalent

- 120
- 100
- 80
- 60
- 40
- 20

1973 1975 1980 1985 1990

Oil

Coal

Natural gas

Legend

- Coalfield (not all producing)
- Potential coalfield
- Oilfield
- Gasfield
- Oil pipeline
- Gas pipeline
- ■ Pipeline terminal
- Continental shelf exploration division
- International boundary

NORWAY

Magnus
Thistle
Murchison
Tern
Cormorant
Statfjord
Hutton
Brent
Heather
Ninian
Alwyn
Clair
Sullom Voe ■
Odin
Frigg
Bruce
Heimdal
Beryl
Crawford
Gudrun
Brae
Piper
Thelma
Claymore
Tartan
Maureen
Buchan
Andrew
Beatrice
Ettrick
Forties
NORWEGIAN SECTOR
Nigg Bay ■
St. Fergus ■
Montrose
Cruden Bay ■
Kittiwake
Lomond
Gannet
N O R T H   S E A
Josephine
Ekofisk
Fulmar
Eldfisk
UNITED KINGDOM SECTOR
Auk
Valhall
Argyll
Hod
DANISH SECTOR

Flotta ■

GERMAN SECTOR

ATLANTIC OCEAN

CENTRAL SCOTLAND

NORTHUMBERLAND AND DURHAM
Teesside

Esmond
Forbes
Gordon

DUTCH SECTOR

Barrow ■
Morecambe
Rough
West Sole
Ann
Viking
LANCASHIRE & NORTH STAFFORDSHIRE
Easington ■
Amethyst
Indefatigable
Valiant
Sean
Theddlethorpe ■
Vulcan
Thames
REPUBLIC OF IRELAND
Irish Sea
YORKSHIRE, NOTTINGHAM & DERBYSHIRE
Hewett
Scram
Bacton ■
Leman Bank

MIDLANDS

NETHERLANDS

IRISH SECTOR

SOUTH WALES

KENT

BELGIUM

Scale 1 : 6 000 000

0   50   100   150 km

Conic Projection

UNITED KINGDOM SECTOR

English Channel

FRANCE

© Collins ◇ Longman Atlases

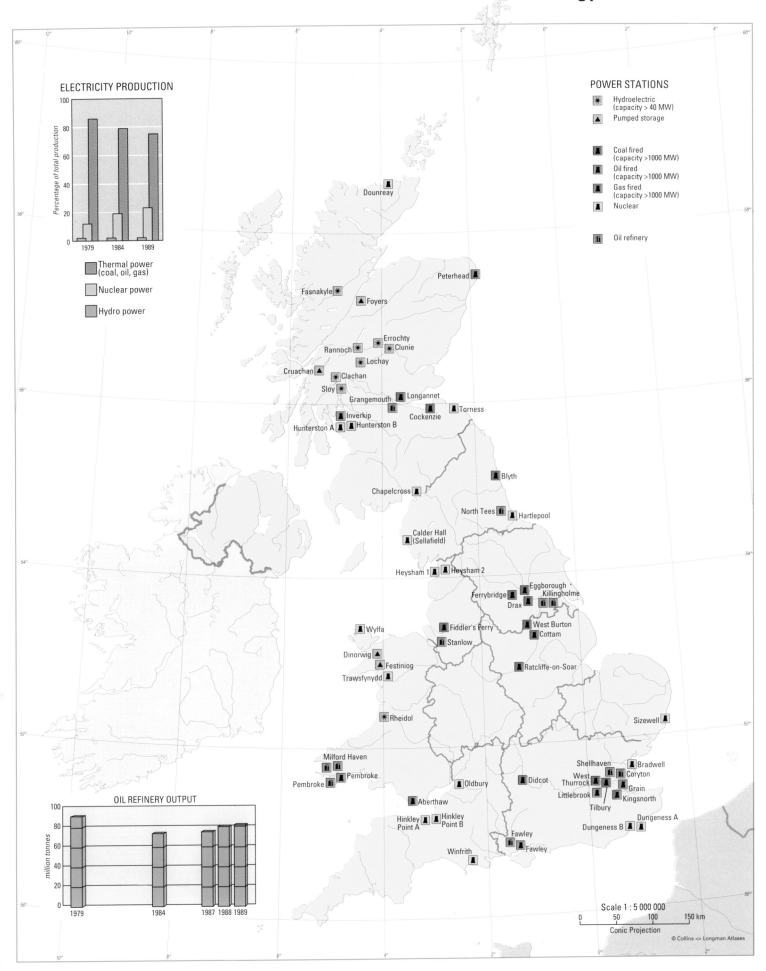

ELECTRICITY PRODUCTION

Percentage of total production

100
80
60
40
20

1979 1984 1989

Thermal power (coal, oil, gas)

Nuclear power

Hydro power

POWER STATIONS

Hydroelectric (capacity > 40 MW)

Pumped storage

Coal fired (capacity >1000 MW)

Oil fired (capacity >1000 MW)

Gas fired (capacity >1000 MW)

Nuclear

Oil refinery

Dounreay

Peterhead

Fasnakyle
Foyers

Errochty
Rannoch   Clunie
Lochay
Cruachan   Clachan
Sloy
Grangemouth Longannet
Inverkip   Cockenzie   Torness
Hunterston A Hunterston B

Blyth

Chapelcross

North Tees Hartlepool

Calder Hall (Sellafield)

Heysham 1 Heysham 2

Eggborough
Ferrybridge   Killingholme
Drax

West Burton
Wylfa   Fiddler's Ferry   Cottam
Stanlow

Dinorwig
Festiniog
Trawsfynydd   Ratcliffe-on-Soar

Rheidol   Sizewell

Milford Haven   Shellhaven   Bradwell
Pembroke   West   Coryton
Pembroke   Thurrock   Grain
Oldbury   Didcot   Littlebrook   Kingsnorth
Aberthaw   Tilbury
Dungeness A
Hinkley   Hinkley   Dungeness B
Point A   Point B
Fawley
Winfrith   Fawley

OIL REFINERY OUTPUT

million tonnes

100
80
60
40
20
0

1979   1984   1987 1988 1989

Scale 1 : 5 000 000

0   50   100   150 km

Conic Projection

© Collins <> Longman Atlases

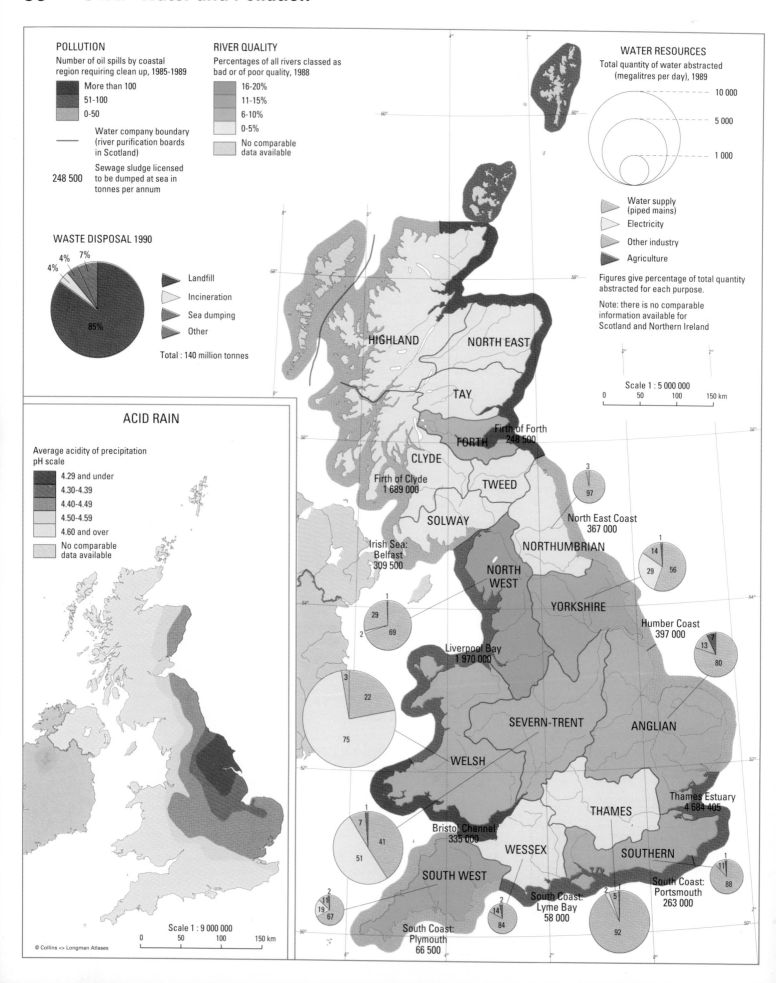

POLLUTION

Number of oil spills by coastal region requiring clean up, 1985-1989

- More than 100
- 51-100
- 0-50

Water company boundary (river purification boards in Scotland)

248 500 Sewage sludge licensed to be dumped at sea in tonnes per annum

RIVER QUALITY

Percentages of all rivers classed as bad or of poor quality, 1988

- 16-20%
- 11-15%
- 6-10%
- 0-5%
- No comparable data available

WATER RESOURCES

Total quantity of water abstracted (megalitres per day), 1989

- 10 000
- 5 000
- 1 000

- Water supply (piped mains)
- Electricity
- Other industry
- Agriculture

Figures give percentage of total quantity abstracted for each purpose.

Note: there is no comparable information available for Scotland and Northern Ireland

Scale 1 : 5 000 000
0   50   100   150 km

WASTE DISPOSAL 1990

- Landfill
- Incineration
- Sea dumping
- Other

7%
4%
4%
85%

Total : 140 million tonnes

ACID RAIN

Average acidity of precipitation pH scale

- 4.29 and under
- 4.30-4.39
- 4.40-4.49
- 4.50-4.59
- 4.60 and over
- No comparable data available

Scale 1 : 9 000 000
0   50   100   150 km

© Collins <> Longman Atlases

HIGHLAND

NORTH EAST

TAY

Firth of Forth
248 500

FORTH

CLYDE

Firth of Clyde
1 689 000

TWEED

SOLWAY

Irish Sea:
Belfast
309 500

NORTHUMBRIAN

NORTH WEST

YORKSHIRE

North East Coast
367 000

3
97

1
14
29   56

Humber Coast
397 000

7
13
80

1
29
2   69

Liverpool Bay
1 970 000

3
22
75

SEVERN-TRENT

ANGLIAN

WELSH

Bristol Channel
335 000

1
7
41
51

THAMES

Thames Estuary
4 684 405

WESSEX

SOUTHERN

South Coast:
Portsmouth
263 000

1
11
88

SOUTH WEST

2
11
19   67

South Coast:
Plymouth
66 500

2
14
84

South Coast:
Lyme Bay
58 000

2
5
92

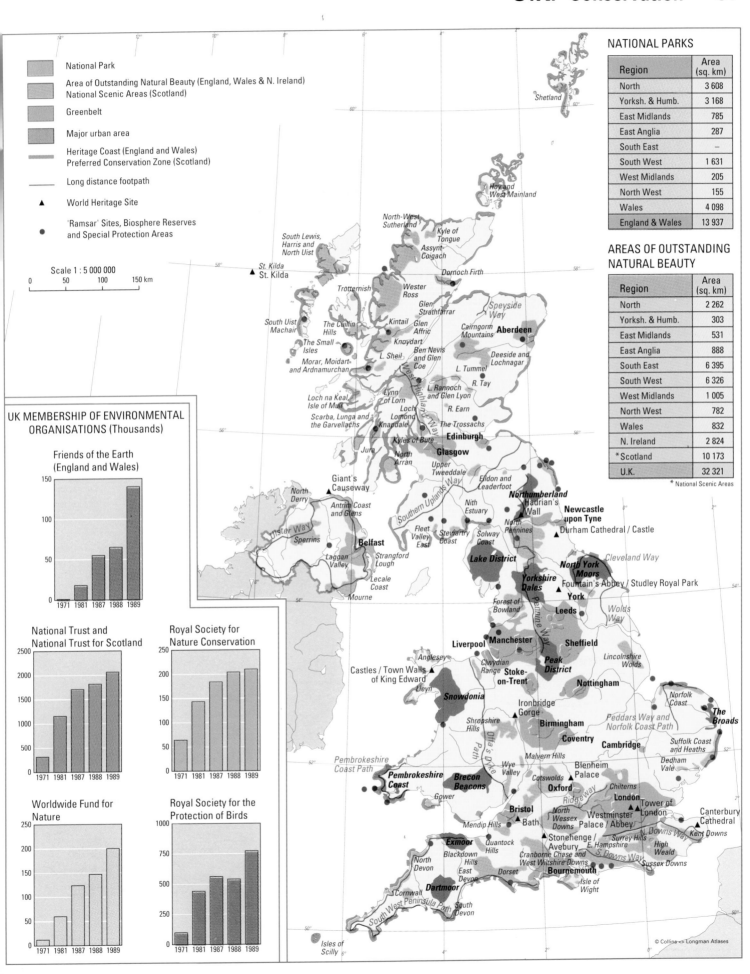

Legend:
- National Park
- Area of Outstanding Natural Beauty (England, Wales & N. Ireland)
- National Scenic Areas (Scotland)
- Greenbelt
- Major urban area
- Heritage Coast (England and Wales)
- Preferred Conservation Zone (Scotland)
- Long distance footpath
- ▲ World Heritage Site
- ● 'Ramsar' Sites, Biosphere Reserves and Special Protection Areas

Scale 1 : 5 000 000
0 50 100 150 km

NATIONAL PARKS

Region	Area (sq. km)
North	3 608
Yorksh. & Humb.	3 168
East Midlands	785
East Anglia	287
South East	–
South West	1 631
West Midlands	205
North West	155
Wales	4 098
England & Wales	13 937

AREAS OF OUTSTANDING NATURAL BEAUTY

Region	Area (sq. km)
North	2 262
Yorksh. & Humb.	303
East Midlands	531
East Anglia	888
South East	6 395
South West	6 326
West Midlands	1 005
North West	782
Wales	832
N. Ireland	2 824
*Scotland	10 173
U.K.	32 321

* National Scenic Areas

UK MEMBERSHIP OF ENVIRONMENTAL ORGANISATIONS (Thousands)

Friends of the Earth (England and Wales)
150 / 100 / 50 / 0
1971 1981 1987 1988 1989

National Trust and National Trust for Scotland
2500 / 2000 / 1500 / 1000 / 500 / 0
1971 1981 1987 1988 1989

Royal Society for Nature Conservation
250 / 200 / 150 / 100 / 50 / 0
1971 1981 1987 1988 1989

Worldwide Fund for Nature
250 / 200 / 150 / 100 / 50 / 0
1971 1981 1987 1988 1989

Royal Society for the Protection of Birds
1000 / 750 / 500 / 250 / 0
1971 1981 1987 1988 1989

© Collins ⬦ Longman Atlases

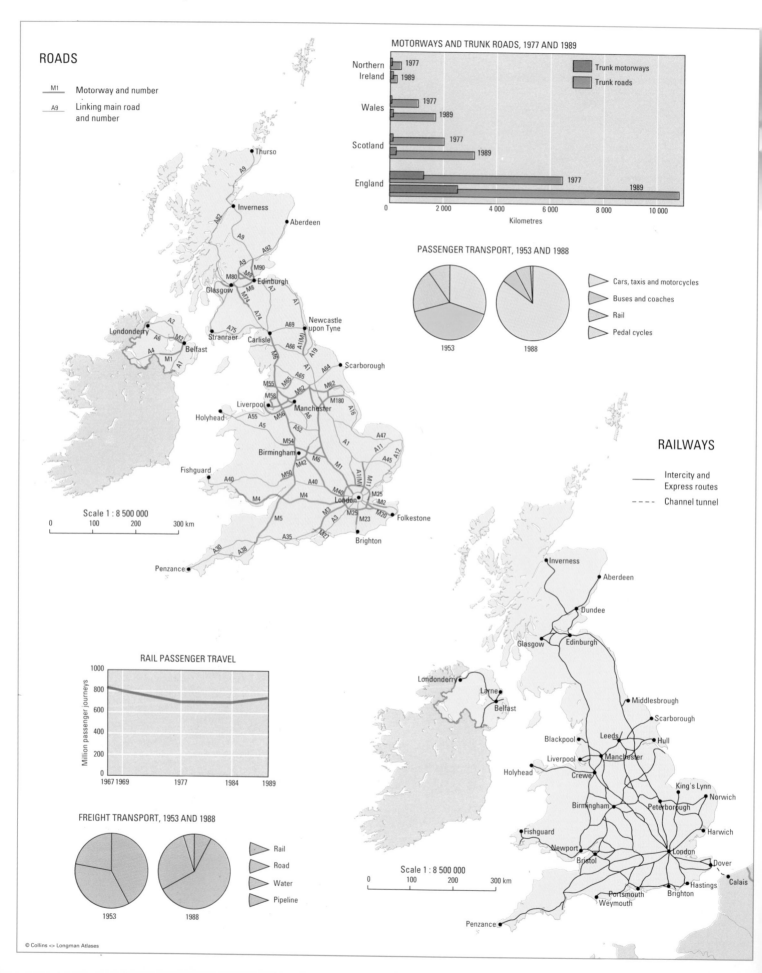

ROADS

M1 — Motorway and number

A9 — Linking main road and number

MOTORWAYS AND TRUNK ROADS, 1977 AND 1989

Trunk motorways
Trunk roads

Northern Ireland 1977 / 1989
Wales 1977 / 1989
Scotland 1977 / 1989
England 1977 / 1989

0   2 000   4 000   6 000   8 000   10 000
Kilometres

PASSENGER TRANSPORT, 1953 AND 1988

1953   1988

Cars, taxis and motorcycles
Buses and coaches
Rail
Pedal cycles

RAILWAYS

—— Intercity and Express routes

- - - Channel tunnel

Scale 1 : 8 500 000
0   100   200   300 km

RAIL PASSENGER TRAVEL

Million passenger journeys

1000
800
600
400
200
0
1967 1969   1977   1984   1989

FREIGHT TRANSPORT, 1953 AND 1988

1953   1988

Rail
Road
Water
Pipeline

Scale 1 : 8 500 000
0   100   200   300 km

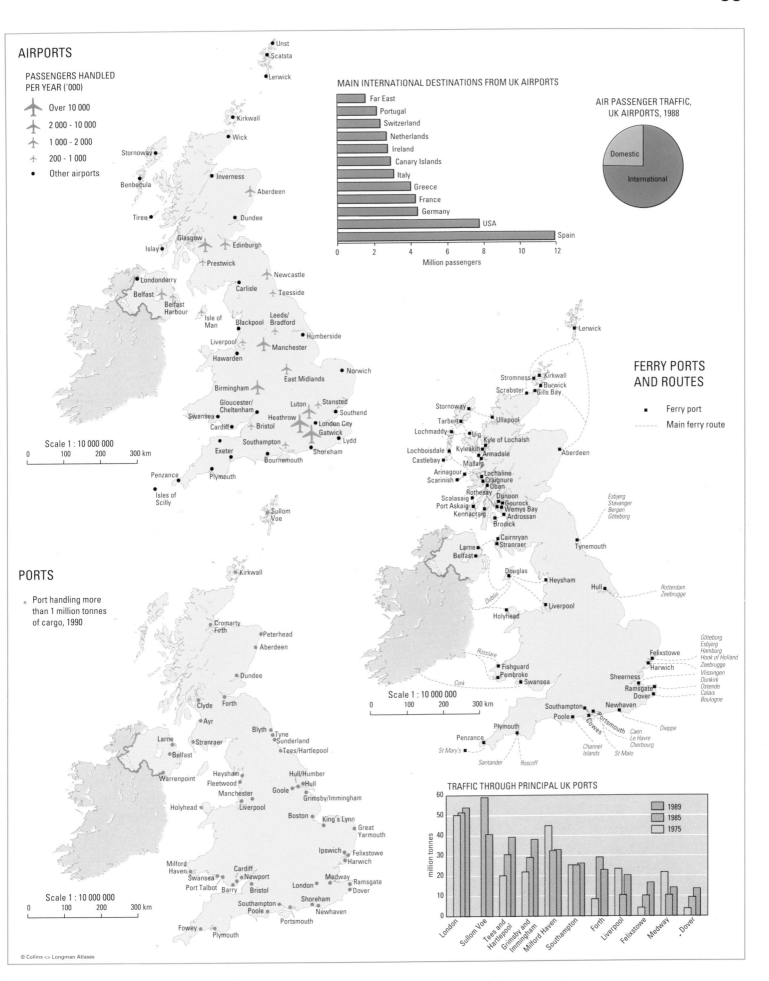

AIRPORTS

PASSENGERS HANDLED PER YEAR ('000)

- Over 10 000
- 2 000 - 10 000
- 1 000 - 2 000
- 200 - 1 000
- Other airports

Scale 1 : 10 000 000

0   100   200   300 km

MAIN INTERNATIONAL DESTINATIONS FROM UK AIRPORTS

Far East
Portugal
Switzerland
Netherlands
Ireland
Canary Islands
Italy
Greece
France
Germany
USA
Spain

0   2   4   6   8   10   12
Million passengers

AIR PASSENGER TRAFFIC, UK AIRPORTS, 1988

Domestic
International

FERRY PORTS AND ROUTES

- ■ Ferry port
- ---- Main ferry route

Scale 1 : 10 000 000

0   100   200   300 km

PORTS

- Port handling more than 1 million tonnes of cargo, 1990

Scale 1 : 10 000 000

0   100   200   300 km

TRAFFIC THROUGH PRINCIPAL UK PORTS

	1989	1985	1975

million tonnes

60
50
40
30
20
10

London
Sullom Voe
Tees and Hartlepool
Grimsby and Immingham
Milford Haven
Southampton
Forth
Liverpool
Felixstowe
Medway
Dover

© Collins ◇ Longman Atlases

Relief

Metres
5000
3000
2000
1000
500
200
Land Dep. 0 Sea Level
200
4000
7000
Metres

Scale 1:16 000 000

0   200   400   600   800 km

Conic Projection

© Collins ◇ Longman Atlases

ARCTIC

North Cape

NORWEGIAN SEA

Arctic Circle

ATLANTIC OCEAN

Straumnes
Surtsey
Snæfell 1833
Vatnajökull
Mt. Hekla 1491

Vesterålen
Lofoten
Vestfjorden
▲2123 Kebnekaise
Lapland
Inari
Muonio
Torne
Kemi

Faroe Is.

Frohavet
Storavan
Skellefte
Ume
Storsjön
Indals
Gulf of Bothnia
Oulujärvi
Kallavesi
Näsijärvi

Shetland Is.

Dovrefjell
Glittertind ▲2470
Jotunheimen
Sognefjorden
Hardangerfjorden
Lindesnes

Mjøsa
Ljusnan
Gråna
Klar
Dal
Mälaren
Vänern
Vättern
Gotland
Åland Is.
Gulf of Finland
Saaremaa
Gulf of Riga
L. Peipus

Orkney Is.
Hebrides
Moray Firth
Ben Nevis 1342
Grampian Mountains
Clyde
Firth of Forth
Southern Uplands
The Pennines

Malin Head
Galway Bay
Shannon
Wicklow Mts.
Irish Sea
Cape Clear
Snowdon 1085
Cambrian Mts.
Trent
The Wash
The Fens
Severn
Celtic Sea
St. George's Channel
Land's End
Isles of Scilly

NORTH SEA

Skagerrak
Limfjorden
Jutland
Kattegat
Zealand
Funen
Kiel Canal
Bornholm

Lagan
Öland

BALTIC SEA
Neman
Neman

Frisian Is.
IJsselmeer

EUROPE
NORTH
Vistula
Warta
Oder
Bug
Silesian Plateau
Vistula

English Channel
Channel Is.
Str. of Dover

Brittany
Seine
Marne
Meuse
Rhine
Ardennes
Mosel
Taunus
Harz Mts.
Weser
Spree
Elbe

Bay of Biscay

Loire
Vienne
Seine
Saône
Vosges
Rhône
Black Forest
Constance
Jura Mts.
L. Geneva
Mont Dore ▲1886
Massif Central
Cévennes
Rhône
Durance

Danube
Inn
Bohemian Forest
Ore Mts.
Sudeten Mts.
Gerlachovka ▲2663
Carpathian

C. Finisterre
Gironde
Garonne
Dordogne

Cantabrian Mts.
Gulf of Gascony
Iberian Mts.
Pyrénées
Pico de Aneto 3404
Ebro
Douro
Douro

Brenner Pass
Mt. Blanc ▲4807
Gross Glockner ▲3798
Mt. Rosa ▲4634
ALPS
Dolomites
Po
Adige
Drava
Sava
Danube
Tisza
Mures
Hungarian Plain
Transylvanian A
Iron Gate
Morava

Gulf of Lions
C. Creus
Ebro Delta

G. of Genoa
Ligurian Sea
Arno
Tiber
▲2914 Mt. Corno

Dinaric Alps
▲2522 Durmitor
Drina
ADRIATIC SEA
Morava
Danube
Balka

Iberian Peninsula
Tagus
Guadiana
Sierra Morena
Guadalquivir
Mulhacén 3482
Sierra Nevada

C. Roca
C. St. Vincent
Gulf of Cadiz
Str. of Gibraltar
C. Palos

Balearic Is.
Minorca
Majorca
Ibiza
C. de la Nao

Corsica
Str. of Bonifacio
Sardinia
▲1277 Vesuvius

Tyrrhenian Sea

G. of Taranto
Str. of Otranto
Corfu
Ionian Islands

Rhodope
Struma
Musala 2925
Axios
Mt. Olympus ▲2911
Mt. Ath ▲203
Pindus Mts.
Killini ▲2376
Euboea
Cyc
Aes

MEDITERRANEAN

Stromboli 926 ▲
Sicily
Mt. Etna 3340
C. Spartivento
C. Bon
C. Passero
Ionian Sea
C. Matapan
Cre

Oum er Rbia
Sebou
Rif Mts.
Cheliff
Tell Atlas
High Atlas
Chott ech Chergui
Saharan Atlas
Mejerda
Toubkal 4165

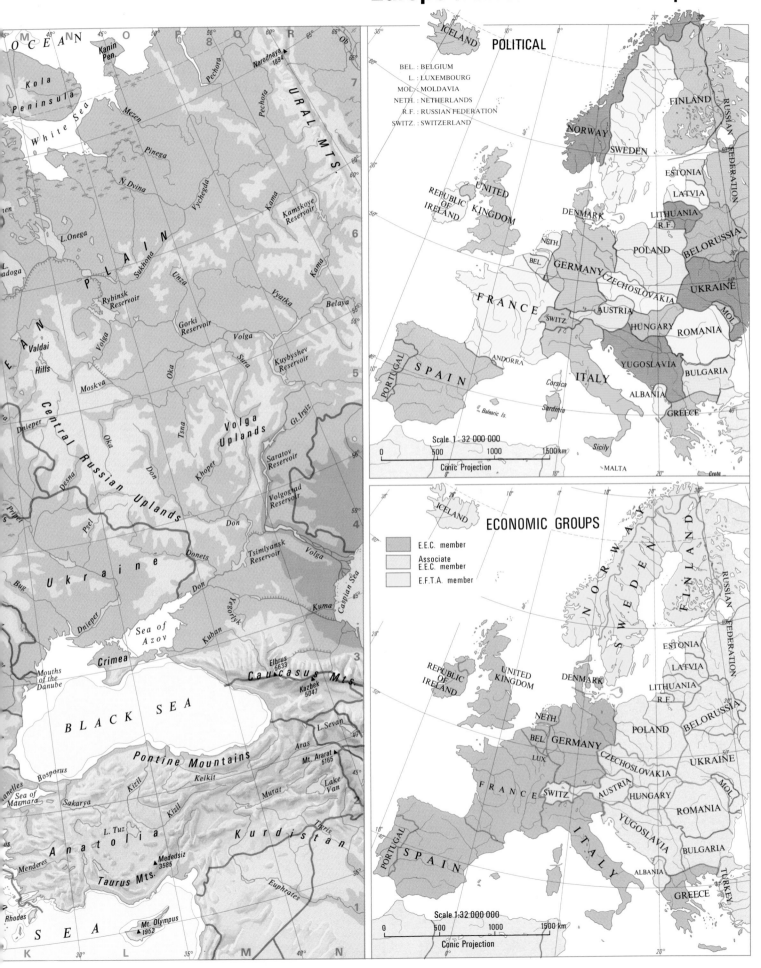

POLITICAL

BEL. : BELGIUM
L. : LUXEMBOURG
MOL. : MOLDAVIA
NETH. : NETHERLANDS
R.F. : RUSSIAN FEDERATION
SWITZ. : SWITZERLAND

Scale 1 : 32 000 000

0   500   1000   1500 km

Conic Projection

ECONOMIC GROUPS

E.E.C. member
Associate E.E.C. member
E.F.T.A. member

Scale 1:32 000 000

0   500   1000   1500 km

Conic Projection

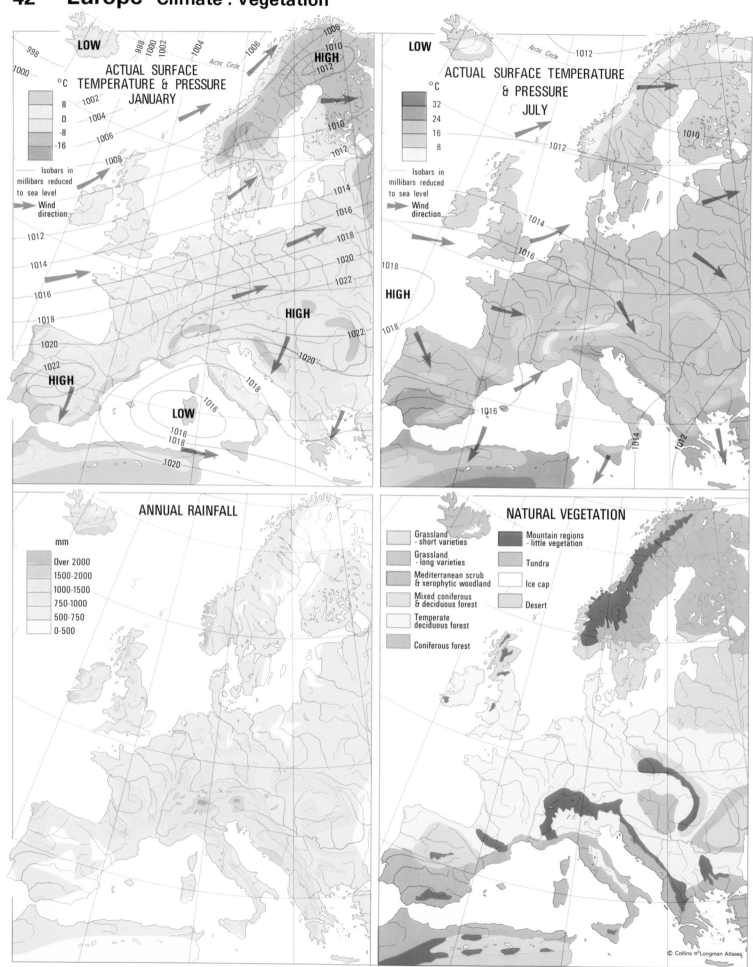

ACTUAL SURFACE TEMPERATURE & PRESSURE JANUARY

°C
8
0
-8
-16

— Isobars in millibars reduced to sea level
→ Wind direction

LOW
HIGH
HIGH
HIGH
LOW

998 1000 1002 1004 1006 1008 1010 1012 1014 1016 1018 1020 1022

Arctic Circle

ACTUAL SURFACE TEMPERATURE & PRESSURE JULY

°C
32
24
16
8

— Isobars in millibars reduced to sea level
→ Wind direction

LOW
HIGH
HIGH

1012 1010 1014 1016 1018 1014 1012

Arctic Circle

ANNUAL RAINFALL

mm

Over 2000
1500-2000
1000-1500
750-1000
500-750
0-500

NATURAL VEGETATION

Grassland - short varieties

Grassland - long varieties

Mediterranean scrub & xerophytic woodland

Mixed coniferous & deciduous forest

Temperate deciduous forest

Coniferous forest

Mountain regions - little vegetation

Tundra

Ice cap

Desert

© Collins Longman Atlases

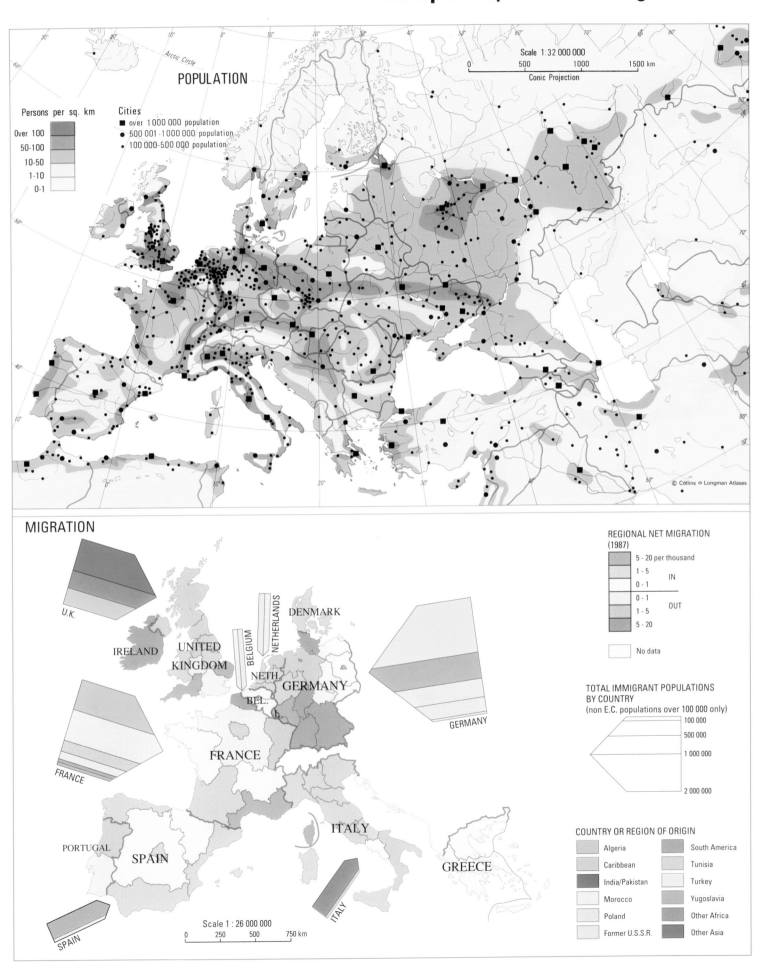

POPULATION

Scale 1:32 000 000

0   500   1000   1500 km

Conic Projection

Persons per sq. km
- Over 100
- 50-100
- 10-50
- 1-10
- 0-1

Cities
- ■ over 1 000 000 population
- ● 500 001 - 1 000 000 population
- • 100 000 - 500 000 population

Arctic Circle

© Collins ◇ Longman Atlases

MIGRATION

U.K.

IRELAND

UNITED KINGDOM

BELGIUM

NETHERLANDS

DENMARK

NETH.

GERMANY

GERMANY

BEL.

FRANCE

FRANCE

PORTUGAL

SPAIN

ITALY

GREECE

SPAIN

ITALY

Scale 1 : 26 000 000

0   250   500   750 km

REGIONAL NET MIGRATION
(1987)

5 - 20 per thousand	
1 - 5	
0 - 1	IN
0 - 1	
1 - 5	OUT
5 - 20	

No data

TOTAL IMMIGRANT POPULATIONS BY COUNTRY
(non E.C. populations over 100 000 only)

- 100 000
- 500 000
- 1 000 000
- 2 000 000

COUNTRY OR REGION OF ORIGIN

- Algeria
- Caribbean
- India/Pakistan
- Morocco
- Poland
- Former U.S.S.R.
- South America
- Tunisia
- Turkey
- Yugoslavia
- Other Africa
- Other Asia

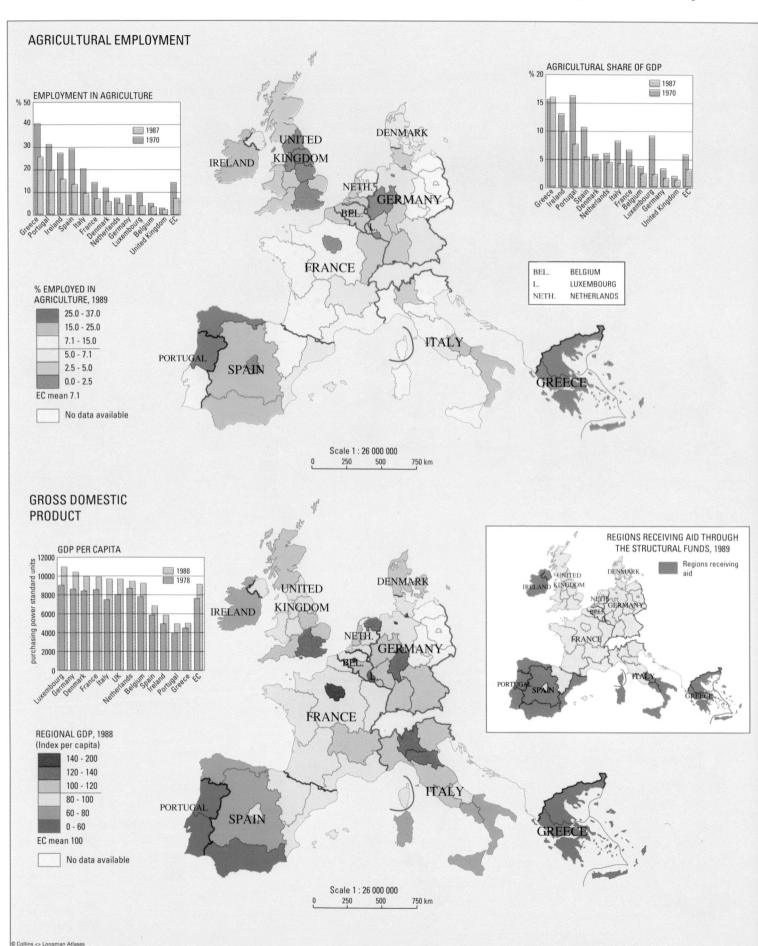

AGRICULTURAL EMPLOYMENT

EMPLOYMENT IN AGRICULTURE

% 50

- 1987
- 1970

Greece, Portugal, Ireland, Spain, Italy, France, Denmark, Netherlands, Germany, Luxembourg, Belgium, United Kingdom, EC

AGRICULTURAL SHARE OF GDP

% 20

- 1987
- 1970

Greece, Ireland, Portugal, Spain, Denmark, Netherlands, Italy, France, Belgium, Luxembourg, Germany, United Kingdom, EC

% EMPLOYED IN AGRICULTURE, 1989

- 25.0 - 37.0
- 15.0 - 25.0
- 7.1 - 15.0
- 5.0 - 7.1
- 2.5 - 5.0
- 0.0 - 2.5

EC mean 7.1

No data available

BEL.	BELGIUM
L.	LUXEMBOURG
NETH.	NETHERLANDS

Scale 1 : 26 000 000

0   250   500   750 km

GROSS DOMESTIC PRODUCT

GDP PER CAPITA

purchasing power standard units

12000

- 1988
- 1978

Luxembourg, Germany, Denmark, France, Italy, UK, Netherlands, Belgium, Spain, Ireland, Portugal, Greece, EC

**REGIONAL GDP, 1988
(Index per capita)**

- 140 - 200
- 120 - 140
- 100 - 120
- 80 - 100
- 60 - 80
- 0 - 60

EC mean 100

No data available

Scale 1 : 26 000 000

0   250   500   750 km

REGIONS RECEIVING AID THROUGH THE STRUCTURAL FUNDS, 1989

Regions receiving aid

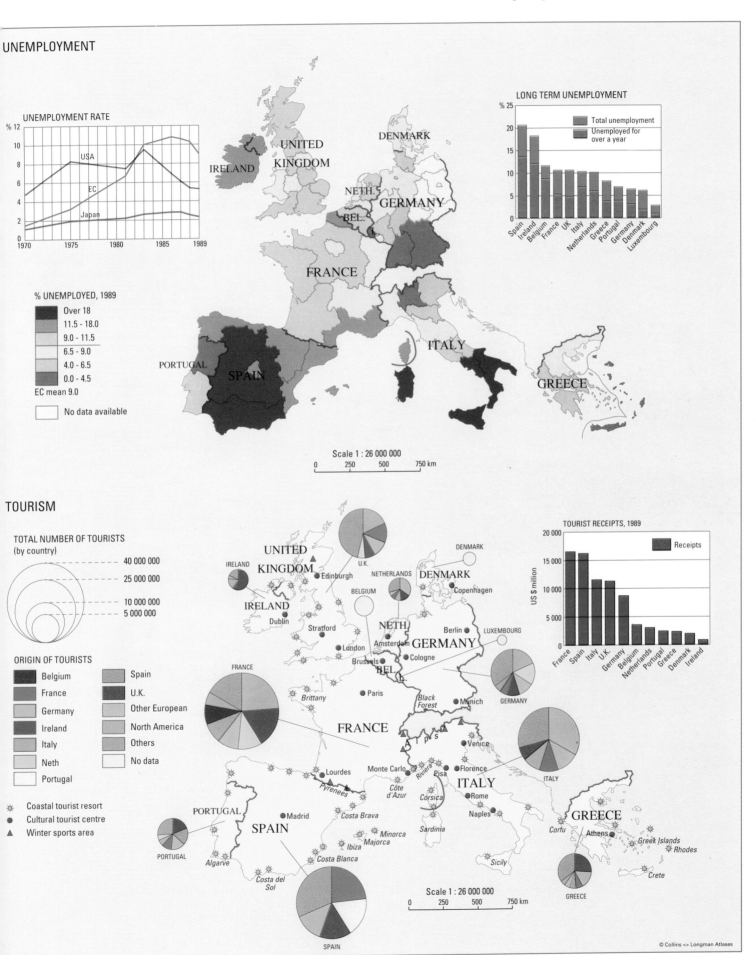

UNEMPLOYMENT

UNEMPLOYMENT RATE

USA
EC
Japan

LONG TERM UNEMPLOYMENT

Total unemployment
Unemployed for over a year

Spain Ireland Belgium France UK Italy Netherlands Greece Portugal Germany Denmark Luxembourg

% UNEMPLOYED, 1989
- Over 18
- 11.5 - 18.0
- 9.0 - 11.5
- 6.5 - 9.0
- 4.0 - 6.5
- 0.0 - 4.5
EC mean 9.0

No data available

DENMARK
UNITED KINGDOM
IRELAND
NETH.
GERMANY
BEL.
FRANCE
PORTUGAL
SPAIN
ITALY
GREECE

Scale 1 : 26 000 000
0   250   500   750 km

TOURISM

TOTAL NUMBER OF TOURISTS
(by country)
- 40 000 000
- 25 000 000
- 10 000 000
- 5 000 000

ORIGIN OF TOURISTS

Belgium
France
Germany
Ireland
Italy
Neth
Portugal

Spain
U.K.
Other European
North America
Others
No data

- ✻ Coastal tourist resort
- ● Cultural tourist centre
- ▲ Winter sports area

TOURIST RECEIPTS, 1989

Receipts
US $ million

France Spain Italy U.K. Germany Belgium Netherlands Portugal Greece Denmark Ireland

UNITED KINGDOM
IRELAND
NETHERLANDS
DENMARK
Copenhagen
U.K.
Edinburgh
BELGIUM
IRELAND
Dublin
Stratford
London
Brussels
NETH.
Amsterdam
Berlin
GERMANY
LUXEMBOURG
Cologne
FRANCE
Paris
Black Forest
Munich
GERMANY
Brittany
A l p s
Venice
FRANCE
Lourdes
Monte Carlo
Riviera
Pisa
Florence
ITALY
Pyrenees
Côte d'Azur
Corsica
Rome
ITALY
PORTUGAL
Madrid
Costa Brava
Sardinia
Naples
GREECE
SPAIN
Minorca
Majorca
Corfu
Athens
Greek Islands
Rhodes
PORTUGAL
Ibiza
Algarve
Costa Blanca
Costa del Sol
Sicily
GREECE
Crete
SPAIN

Scale 1 : 26 000 000
0   250   500   750 km

AGRICULTURE & SOILS

Heath and dune - poorest sandy soils.

Dairying on fertile alluvial soils.

Extensive livestock farming with fodder crops on poor sandy soils.

Livestock farming with cereals on fertile clay soils.

Intensive dairying and pig farming with cereals and sugar beet on fertile clay soils.

Scale 1:2 000 000
Conic Projection

© Collins · Longman Atlases

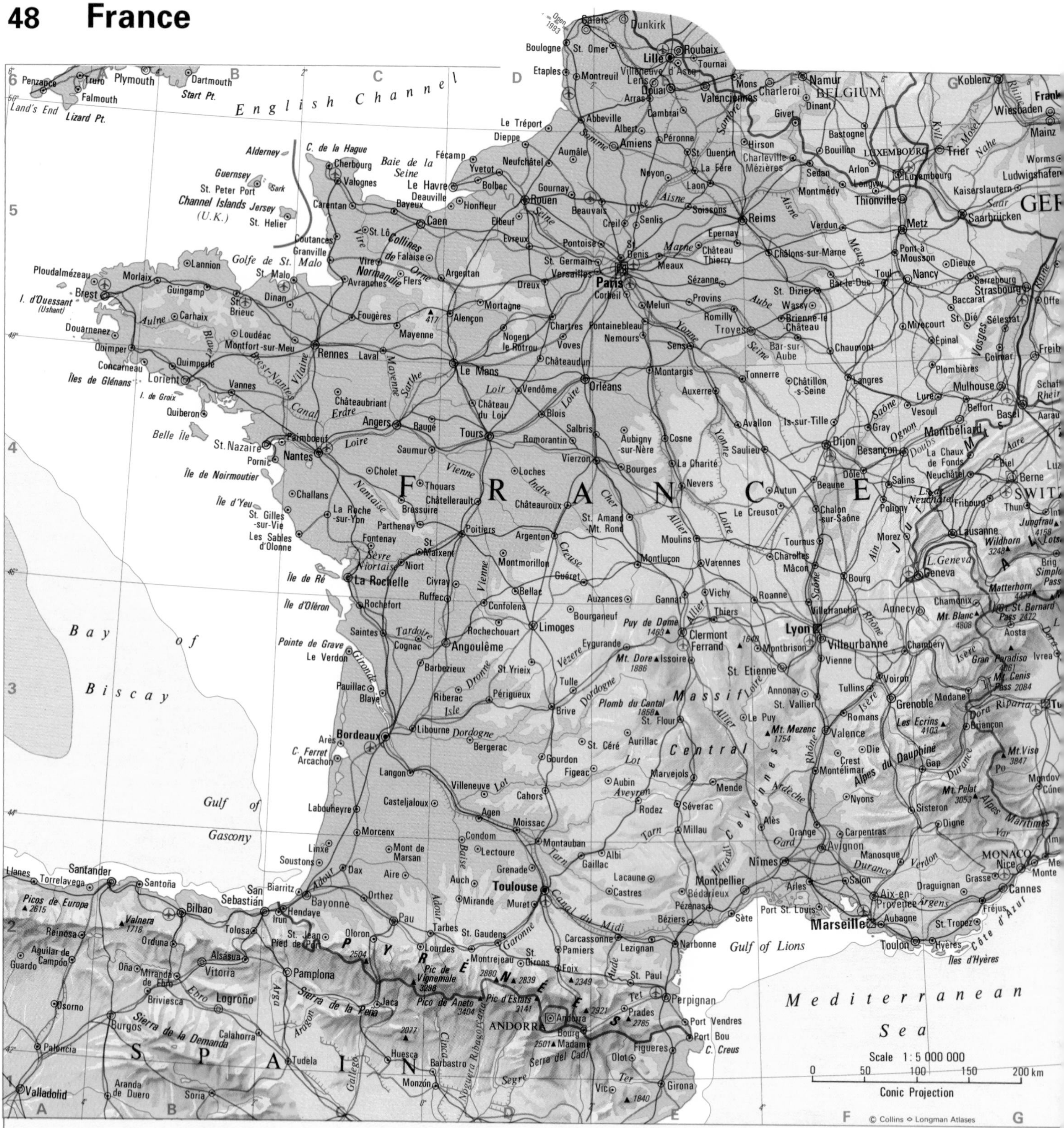

English Channel

F R A N C E

Bay of Biscay

Gulf of Gascony

SPAIN

BELGIUM

LUXEMBOURG

GERMANY

SWITZERLAND

Massif Central

Mediterranean Sea

Gulf of Lions

Scale 1 : 5 000 000

0   50   100   150   200 km

Conic Projection

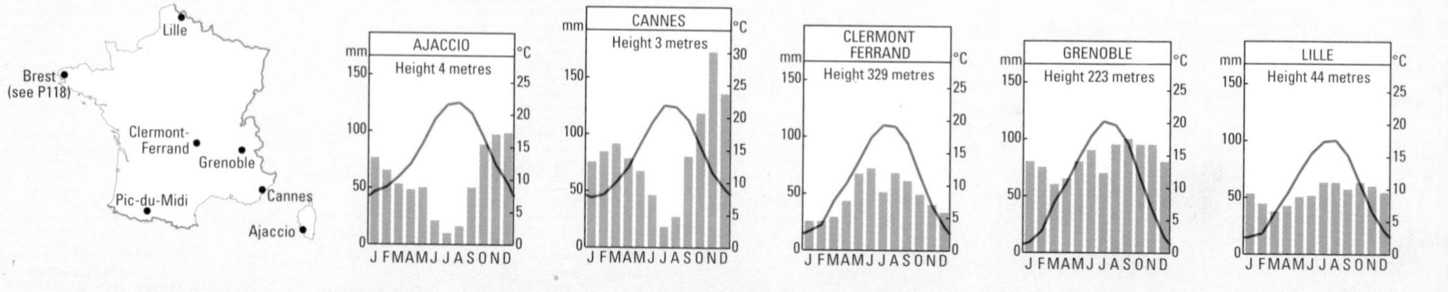

© Collins ⬦ Longman Atlases

CLIMATE GRAPHS

Lille

Brest (see P118)

Clermont-Ferrand

Grenoble

Pic-du-Midi

Cannes

Ajaccio

AJACCIO — Height 4 metres
mm / °C — J F M A M J J A S O N D

CANNES — Height 3 metres
mm / °C — J F M A M J J A S O N D

CLERMONT FERRAND — Height 329 metres
mm / °C — J F M A M J J A S O N D

GRENOBLE — Height 223 metres
mm / °C — J F M A M J J A S O N D

LILLE — Height 44 metres
mm / °C — J F M A M J J A S O N D

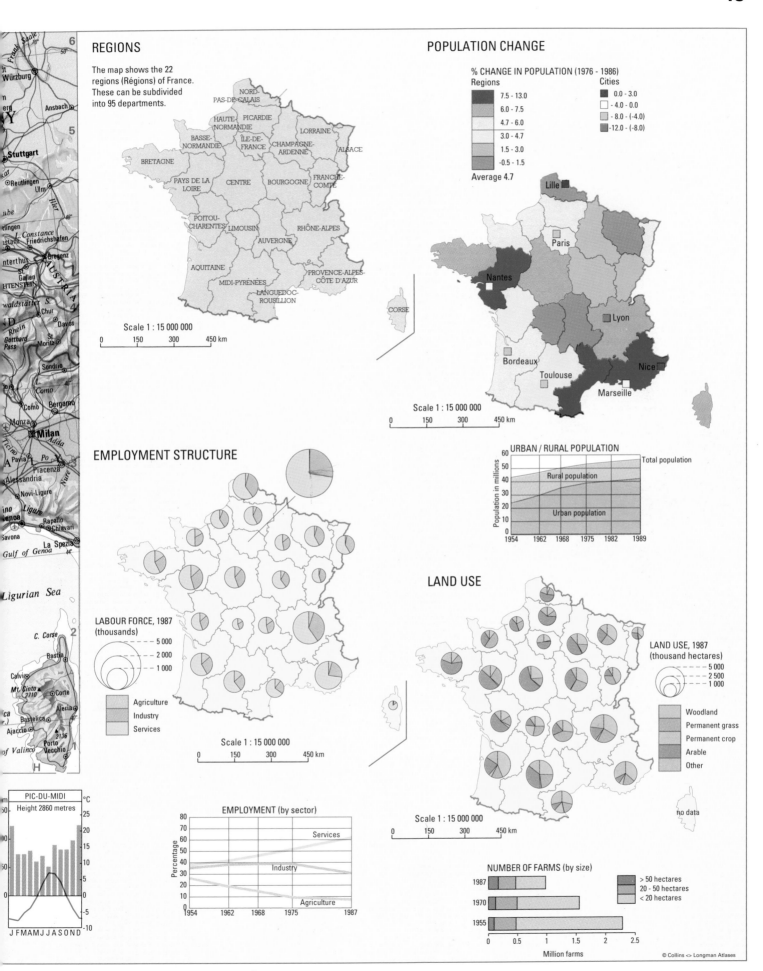

REGIONS

The map shows the 22 regions (Régions) of France. These can be subdivided into 95 departments.

NORD-PAS-DE-CALAIS
HAUTE-NORMANDIE
PICARDIE
LORRAINE
BASSE-NORMANDIE
ÎLE-DE-FRANCE
CHAMPAGNE-ARDENNE
ALSACE
BRETAGNE
PAYS DE LA LOIRE
CENTRE
BOURGOGNE
FRANCHE-COMTÉ
POITOU-CHARENTES
LIMOUSIN
RHÔNE-ALPES
AUVERGNE
AQUITAINE
MIDI-PYRÉNÉES
PROVENCE-ALPES-CÔTE D'AZUR
LANGUEDOC-ROUSILLION
CORSE

Scale 1 : 15 000 000
0   150   300   450 km

POPULATION CHANGE

% CHANGE IN POPULATION (1976 - 1986)

Regions
7.5 - 13.0
6.0 - 7.5
4.7 - 6.0
3.0 - 4.7
1.5 - 3.0
-0.5 - 1.5

Cities
0.0 - 3.0
-4.0 - 0.0
-8.0 - (-4.0)
-12.0 - (-8.0)

Average 4.7

Lille
Paris
Nantes
Lyon
Bordeaux
Toulouse
Nice
Marseille

Scale 1 : 15 000 000
0   150   300   450 km

EMPLOYMENT STRUCTURE

LABOUR FORCE, 1987 (thousands)
--- 5 000
--- 2 000
--- 1 000

Agriculture
Industry
Services

Scale 1 : 15 000 000
0   150   300   450 km

URBAN / RURAL POPULATION

Total population
Rural population
Urban population

Population in millions
60
50
40
30
20
10
0
1954 1962 1968 1975 1982 1989

LAND USE

LAND USE, 1987 (thousand hectares)
--- 5 000
--- 2 500
--- 1 000

Woodland
Permanent grass
Permanent crop
Arable
Other

no data

Scale 1 : 15 000 000
0   150   300   450 km

PIC-DU-MIDI
Height 2860 metres

°C
25
20
15
10
5
0
-5
-10

J F M A M J J A S O N D

EMPLOYMENT (by sector)

Percentage
80
70
60
50
40
30
20
10
0

Services
Industry
Agriculture

1954 1962 1968 1975 1987

NUMBER OF FARMS (by size)

1987
1970
1955

> 50 hectares
20 - 50 hectares
< 20 hectares

0   0.5   1   1.5   2   2.5
Million farms

© Collins <> Longman Atlases

CLIMATE GRAPHS

BARCELONA — Height 93 metres

FINISTERRE — Height 146 metres

MADRID — Height 660 metres

MALAGA — Height 33 metres

PAMPLONA — Height 466 metres

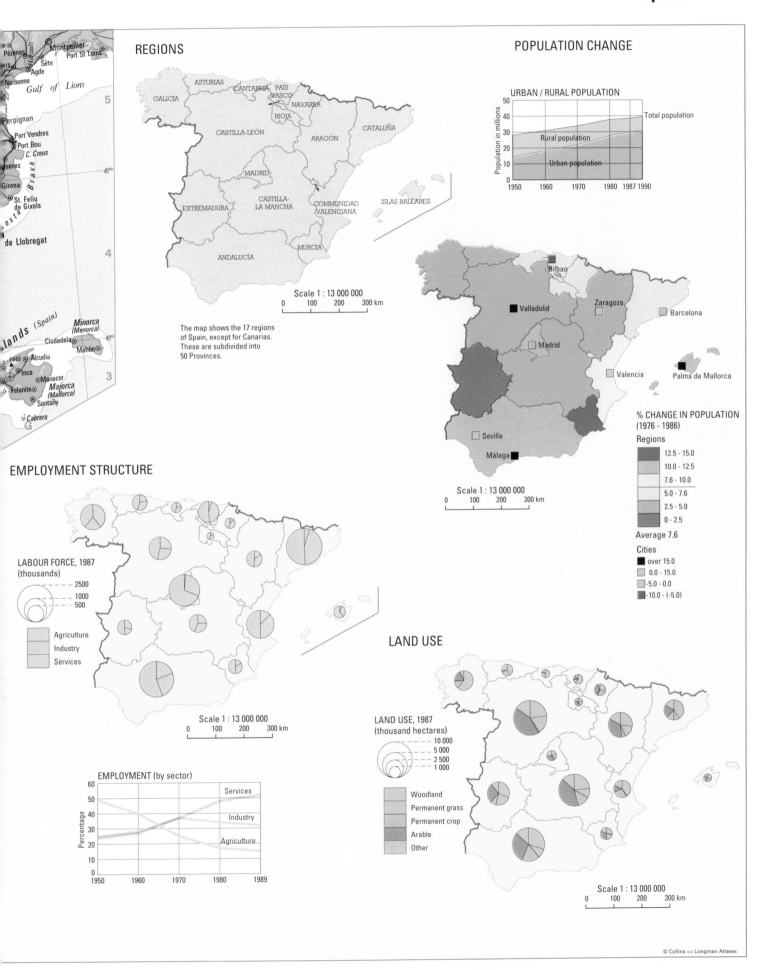

REGIONS

GALICIA
ASTURIAS
CANTABRIA PAÍS VASCO
NAVARRA
RIOJA
CASTILLA-LEÓN
ARAGÓN
CATALUÑA
MADRID
EXTREMADURA
CASTILLA-LA MANCHA
COMMUNIDAD VALENCIANA
ISLAS BALEARES
ANDALUCÍA
MURCIA

Scale 1 : 13 000 000
0   100   200   300 km

The map shows the 17 regions
of Spain, except for Canarias.
These are subdivided into
50 Provinces.

POPULATION CHANGE

URBAN / RURAL POPULATION

Population in millions

Total population
Rural population
Urban population

1950 1960 1970 1980 1987 1990

Bilbao
Valladolid
Zaragoza
Barcelona
Madrid
Valencia
Palma de Mallorca
Seville
Málaga

Scale 1 : 13 000 000
0   100   200   300 km

**% CHANGE IN POPULATION
(1976 - 1986)**
Regions
12.5 - 15.0
10.0 - 12.5
7.6 - 10.0
5.0 - 7.6
2.5 - 5.0
0 - 2.5
Average 7.6
Cities
over 15.0
0.0 - 15.0
-5.0 - 0.0
-10.0 - (-5.0)

EMPLOYMENT STRUCTURE

**LABOUR FORCE, 1987
(thousands)**
2500
1000
500

Agriculture
Industry
Services

Scale 1 : 13 000 000
0   100   200   300 km

EMPLOYMENT (by sector)

Percentage

Services
Industry
Agriculture

1950 1960 1970 1980 1989

LAND USE

**LAND USE, 1987
(thousand hectares)**
10 000
5 000
2 500
1 000

Woodland
Permanent grass
Permanent crop
Arable
Other

Scale 1 : 13 000 000
0   100   200   300 km

Montpellier
Port St Louis
Pézenas
Sète
Agde
Narbonne
Gulf of Lions
Perpignan
Port Vendres
Port Bou
C. Creus
Figueres
Girona
St. Feliu
de Gixols
Costa Brava
de Llobregat

Minorca (Spain)
(Menorca)
Ciudadela
Mahón
Alcudia
Inca
Manacor
Felanitx
Majorca (Mallorca)
Santany
Cabrera
Islands (Spain)

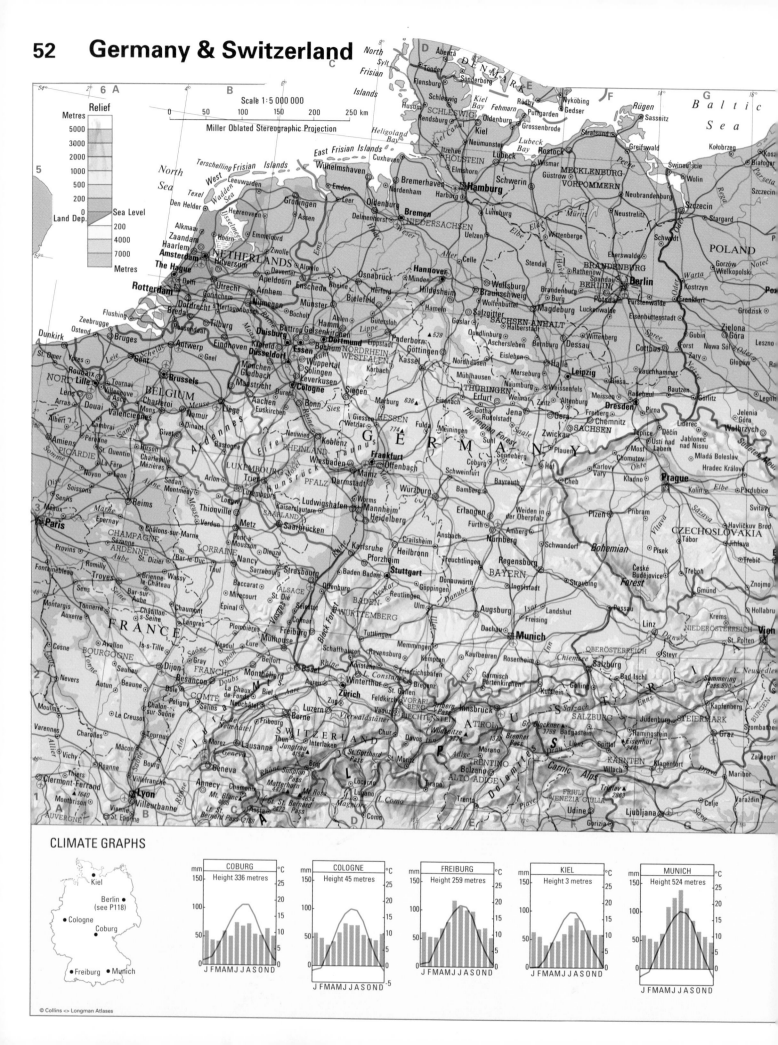

CLIMATE GRAPHS

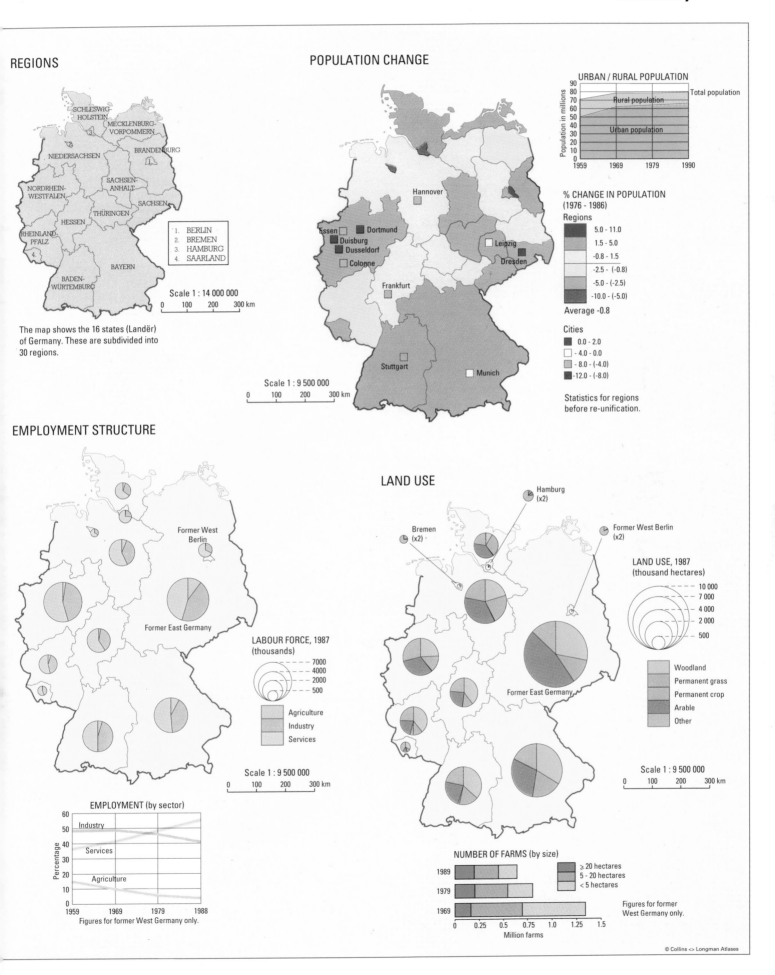

REGIONS

1. BERLIN
2. BREMEN
3. HAMBURG
4. SAARLAND

SCHLESWIG-HOLSTEIN
MECKLENBURG-VORPOMMERN
NIEDERSACHSEN
BRANDENBURG
NORDRHEIN-WESTFALEN
SACHSEN-ANHALT
SACHSEN
HESSEN
THÜRINGEN
RHEINLAND-PFALZ
BAYERN
BADEN-WÜRTEMBURG

Scale 1 : 14 000 000
0   100   200   300 km

The map shows the 16 states (Landër)
of Germany. These are subdivided into
30 regions.

POPULATION CHANGE

Hannover
Essen   Dortmund
Duisburg
Dusseldorf
Colonne   Leipzig
Dresden
Frankfurt
Stuttgart   Munich

Scale 1 : 9 500 000
0   100   200   300 km

URBAN / RURAL POPULATION

Total population
Rural population
Urban population

Population in millions
90 80 70 60 50 40 30 20 10 0
1959   1969   1979   1990

% CHANGE IN POPULATION
(1976 - 1986)

Regions
5.0 - 11.0
1.5 - 5.0
-0.8 - 1.5
-2.5 - (-0.8)
-5.0 - (-2.5)
-10.0 - (-5.0)

Average -0.8

Cities
0.0 - 2.0
-4.0 - 0.0
-8.0 - (-4.0)
-12.0 - (-8.0)

Statistics for regions
before re-unification.

EMPLOYMENT STRUCTURE

Former West Berlin
Former East Germany

LABOUR FORCE, 1987
(thousands)
7000
4000
2000
500

Agriculture
Industry
Services

Scale 1 : 9 500 000
0   100   200   300 km

EMPLOYMENT (by sector)

Industry
Services
Agriculture

Percentage
60 50 40 30 20 10 0
1959   1969   1979   1988

Figures for former West Germany only.

LAND USE

Hamburg (x2)
Bremen (x2)
Former West Berlin (x2)
Former East Germany

LAND USE, 1987
(thousand hectares)
10 000
7000
4000
2000
500

Woodland
Permanent grass
Permanent crop
Arable
Other

Scale 1 : 9 500 000
0   100   200   300 km

NUMBER OF FARMS (by size)

≥ 20 hectares
5 - 20 hectares
< 5 hectares

1989
1979
1969

0   0.25   0.5   0.75   1.0   1.25   1.5
Million farms

Figures for former
West Germany only.

REGIONS

The map shows the
20 regions (Regioni) of
Italy. These are subdivided
into 94 provinces.

VALLE D'AOSTA
PIEMONTE
LOMBARDIA
LIGURIA
TRENTINO-ALTO-ADIGE
VENETO
FRIULI-VENEZIA GIULIA
EMILIA-ROMAGNA
TOSCANA
MARCHE
UMBRIA
LAZIO
ABRUZZI
MOLISE
CAMPANIA
PUGLIA
BASILICATA
CALABRIA
SARDEGNA
SICILIA

Scale 1 : 16 000 000

0   200   400 km

Scale 1 : 5 250 000

0   50   100   150   200 km

Conic Projection

© Collins ◊ Longman Atlases

POPULATION CHANGE

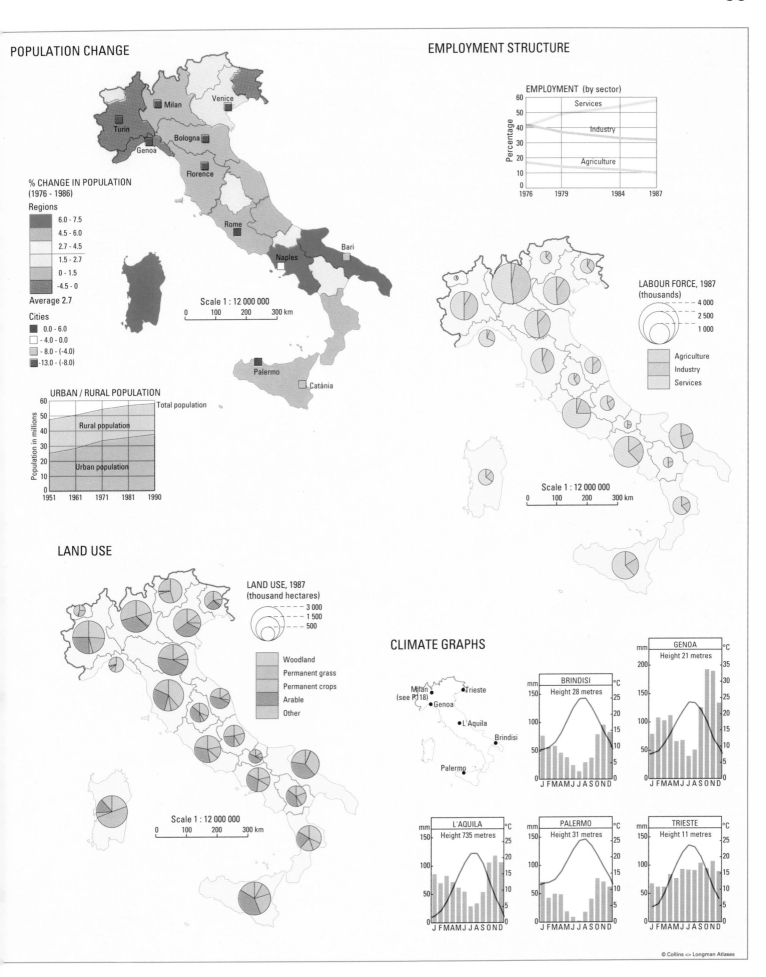

% CHANGE IN POPULATION
(1976 - 1986)
Regions

6.0 - 7.5
4.5 - 6.0
2.7 - 4.5
1.5 - 2.7
0 - 1.5
-4.5 - 0

Average 2.7

Cities

0.0 - 6.0
- 4.0 - 0.0
- 8.0 - (-4.0)
-13.0 - (-8.0)

Scale 1 : 12 000 000
0   100   200   300 km

URBAN / RURAL POPULATION

Total population
Rural population
Urban population

Population in millions
60 50 40 30 20 10 0
1951 1961 1971 1981 1990

LAND USE

LAND USE, 1987
(thousand hectares)

3 000
1 500
500

Woodland
Permanent grass
Permanent crops
Arable
Other

Scale 1 : 12 000 000
0   100   200   300 km

EMPLOYMENT STRUCTURE

EMPLOYMENT (by sector)

Percentage
60 50 40 30 20 10

Services
Industry
Agriculture

1976   1979   1984   1987

LABOUR FORCE, 1987
(thousands)

4 000
2 500
1 000

Agriculture
Industry
Services

Scale 1 : 12 000 000
0   100   200   300 km

CLIMATE GRAPHS

Milan
(see P.118)
Trieste
Genoa
L'Aquila
Brindisi
Palermo

BRINDISI
Height 28 metres
mm °C
150 25
100 20
      15
50   10
      5
J F M A M J J A S O N D

GENOA
Height 21 metres
mm °C
200 35
      30
150 25
      20
100 15
50   10
      5
J F M A M J J A S O N D

L'AQUILA
Height 735 metres
mm °C
150 25
      20
100 15
50   10
      5
J F M A M J J A S O N D

PALERMO
Height 31 metres
mm °C
150 25
      20
100 15
50   10
      5
J F M A M J J A S O N D

TRIESTE
Height 11 metres
mm °C
150 25
      20
100 15
50   10
      5
J F M A M J J A S O N D

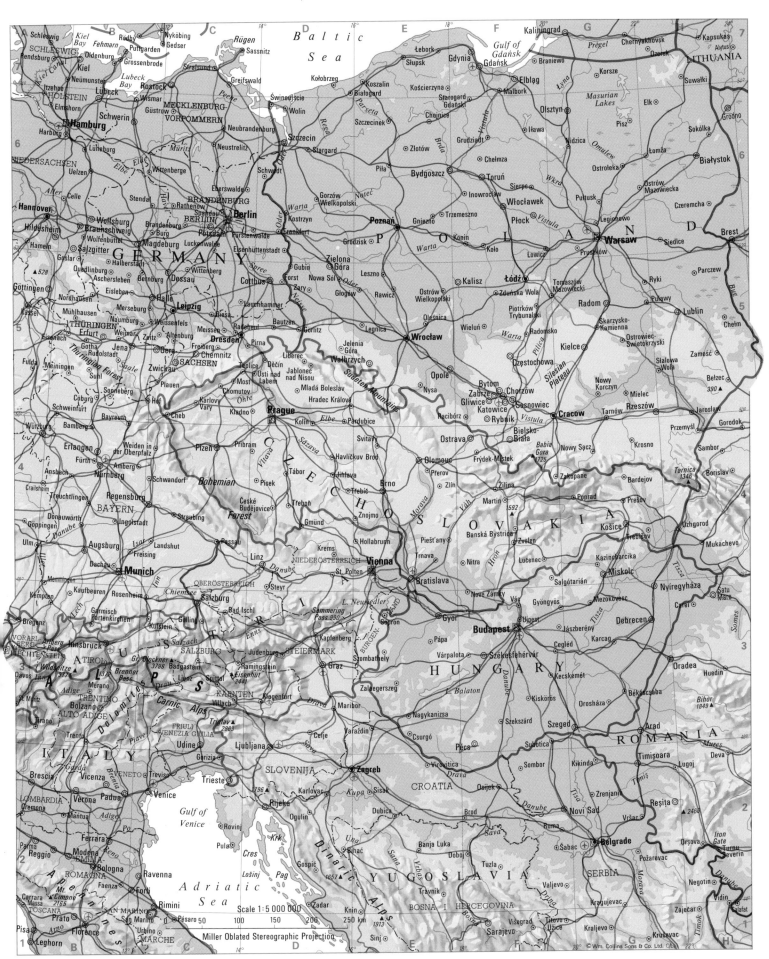

Scale 1:5 000 000

Miller Oblated Stereographic Projection

© Wm. Collins Sons & Co. Ltd. C.I.L.

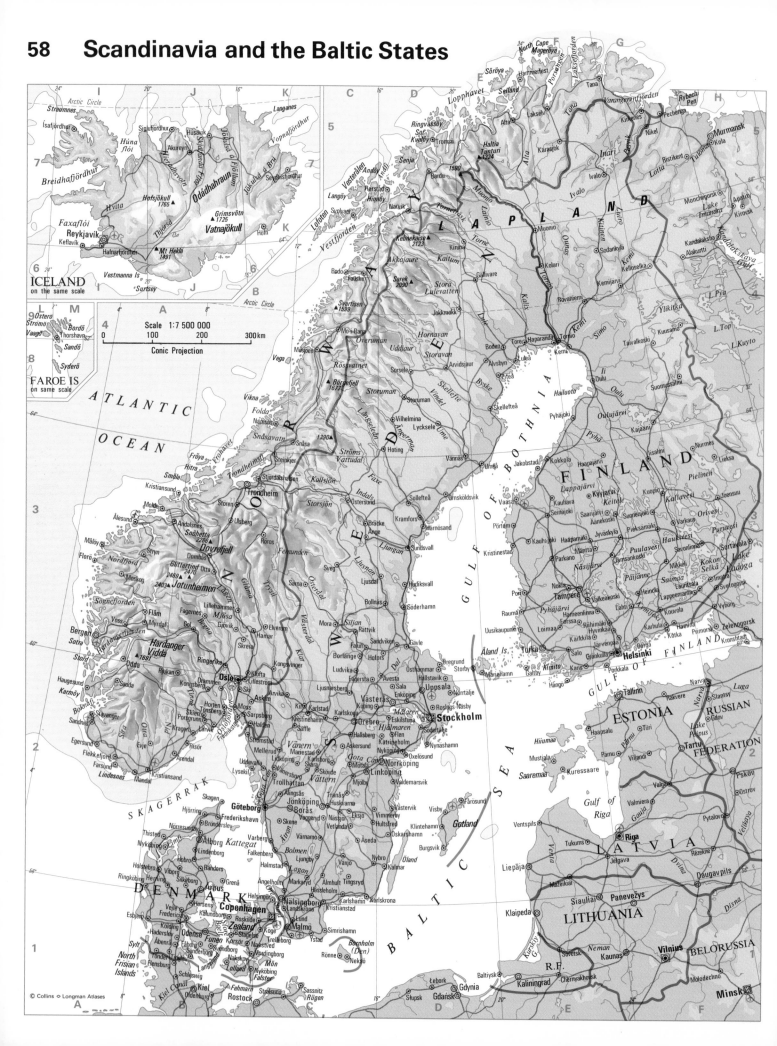

ICELAND
on the same scale

FAROE IS
on same scale

Scale 1:7 500 000

0   100   200   300km

Conic Projection

ATLANTIC OCEAN

ATLANTIC OCEAN

© Collins ◊ Longman Atlases

Relief

Metres
5000
3000
2000
1000
500
200
0
Land Dep.

Sea Level

200
4000
7000

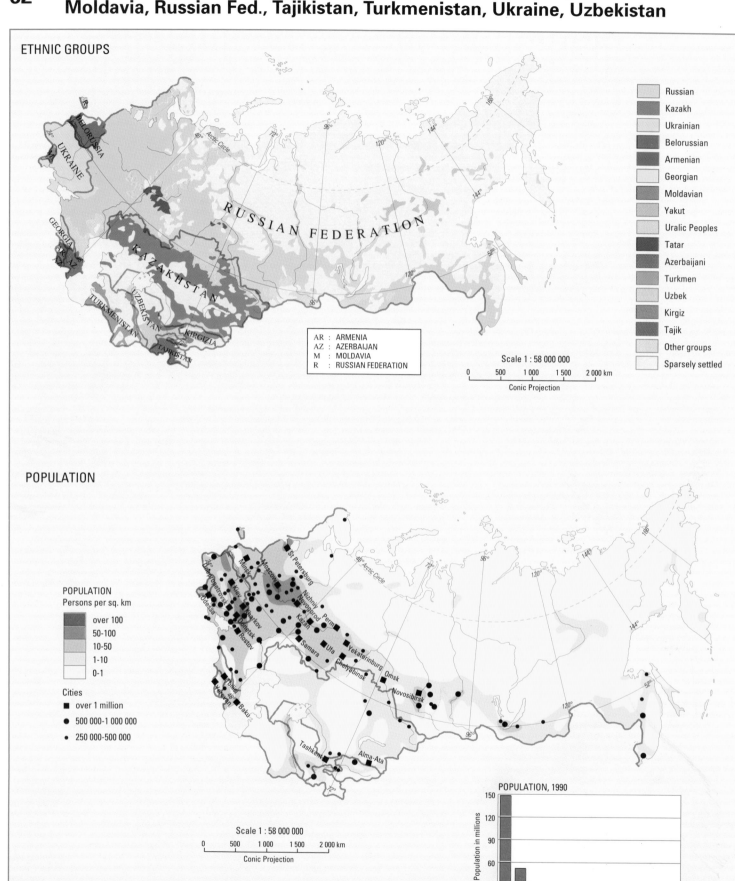

ETHNIC GROUPS

	Russian
	Kazakh
	Ukrainian
	Belorussian
	Armenian
	Georgian
	Moldavian
	Yakut
	Uralic Peoples
	Tatar
	Azerbaijani
	Turkmen
	Uzbek
	Kirgiz
	Tajik
	Other groups
	Sparsely settled

AR : ARMENIA
AZ : AZERBAIJAN
M : MOLDAVIA
R : RUSSIAN FEDERATION

Scale 1 : 58 000 000

0   500   1 000   1 500   2 000 km

Conic Projection

POPULATION

POPULATION
Persons per sq. km

	over 100
	50-100
	10-50
	1-10
	0-1

Cities
■ over 1 million
● 500 000-1 000 000
• 250 000-500 000

Scale 1 : 58 000 000

0   500   1 000   1 500   2 000 km

Conic Projection

POPULATION, 1990

Population in millions

150
120
90
60
30

Russian Federation, Ukraine, Uzbekistan, Kazakhstan, Belorussia, Azerbaijan, Georgia, Tajikistan, Kirgizia, Moldavia, Turkmenistan, Armenia

RESOURCES AND INDUSTRY

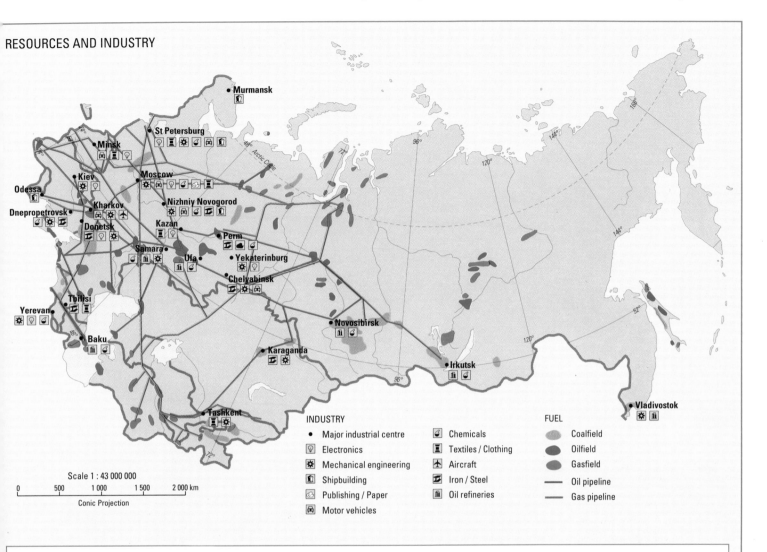

INDUSTRY

- • Major industrial centre
- Electronics
- Mechanical engineering
- Shipbuilding
- Publishing / Paper
- Motor vehicles
- Chemicals
- Textiles / Clothing
- Aircraft
- Iron / Steel
- Oil refineries

FUEL

- Coalfield
- Oilfield
- Gasfield
- Oil pipeline
- Gas pipeline

Scale 1 : 43 000 000

0   500   1 000   1 500   2 000 km

Conic Projection

FACT file

COUNTRY	POPULATION (millions)	AREA (sq. km)	CAPITAL CITY	MAJOR AGRICULTURAL PRODUCTS (1000 tonnes)	MAJOR MINERAL RESOURCES
ARMENIA	3.3	30 000	Yerevan	Vegetables, 567; Grain, 375; Fruit, 241; Grapes, 205	Copper, zinc, aluminium, molybdenum, granite, marble
AZERBAIJAN	7.1	87 000	Baku	Grain, 1 417; Cotton, 616; Grapes, 1 247; Vegetables, 880	Oil, iron, aluminium, copper, lead, zinc, precious metals
BELORUSSIA	10.3	208 000	Minsk	Grain, 6 922; Meat, 1169; Milk, 7 501; Potatoes, 7 708	Peat, rock salt
GEORGIA	5.5	70 000	Tbilisi	Grain, 714; Tea, 458; Citrus fruit, 439; Potatoes, 326; Other vegetables, 641	Manganese, oil, marble, cement
KAZAKHSTAN	16.7	2 717 000	Alma-Ata	Grain, 22 600; Potatoes, 2 300; Milk, 5 300; Vegetables, 1 400	Coal, tungsten, copper, lead, zinc, oil, manganese
KIRGIZIA	4.4	199 000	Bishkek	Grain, 1 758; Vegetables, 548; Meat, 220; Milk, 1 063	Figures not available
MOLDAVIA	4.4	34 000	Kishinev	Grain, 3 052; Sugar beet, 2 272; Grapes, 1 120; Vegetables, 1 281	Lignite, phosphorites, gypsum
RUSSIAN FED.	148.0	17 075 000	Moscow	Figures not available	Iron ore, coal, oil, gold, platinum, copper, zinc, lead, tin
TAJIKISTAN	5.3	143 000	Dushanbe	Cotton, 963; Vegetables, 556; Fruit, 208; Grapes, 178	Coal, lead, zinc, oil, uranium, radium
TURKMENISTAN	3.6	488 000	Ashkhabad	Cotton, 1 341; Grain, 435; Vegetables, 373; Grapes, 164	Oil, coal, sulphur, salt
UKRAINE	51.8	604 000	Kiev	Grain, 47 400; Sugar beet, 48 100; Milk, 24 000; Potatoes, 13 500	Coal, iron ore, salt, oil
UZBEKISTAN	20.3	447 000	Tashkent	Cotton, 5 365; Vegetables, 2 760; Grain, 2 199; Grapes, 640	Oil, coal, copper

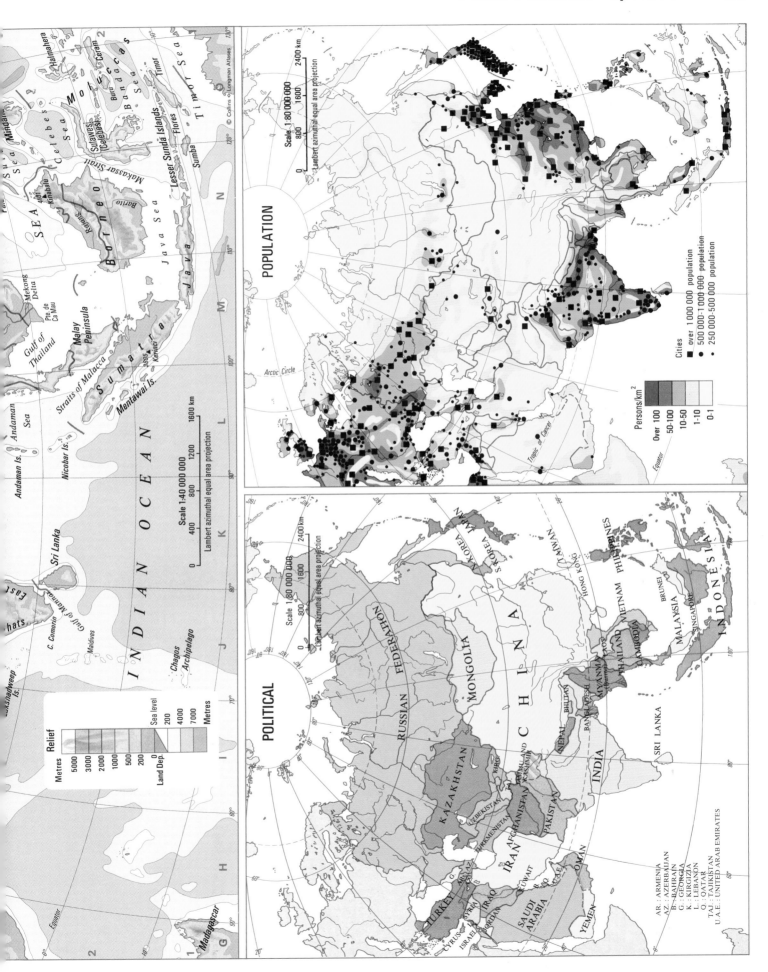

© Collins © Longman Atlases

POPULATION

Scale 1:80 000 000

Lambert azimuthal equal area projection

2400 km
1600
800
0

Arctic Circle

Tropic of Cancer

Equator

Cities

■ over 1 000 000 population
■ 500 000–1 000 000 population
● 250 000–500 000 population

Persons/km²

Over 100
50–100
10–50
1–10
0–1

POLITICAL

Scale 1:80 000 000

Lambert azimuthal equal area projection

2400 km
1600
800
0

RUSSIAN FEDERATION

MONGOLIA

KAZAKHSTAN

UZBEKISTAN

TURKMENISTAN

KIRG.

TAJ.

AFGHANISTAN

PAKISTAN

CHINA

N. KOREA

S. KOREA

JAPAN

TAIWAN

HONG KONG

NEPAL

BHUTAN

BANGLADESH

MYANMAR (Burma)

INDIA

SRI LANKA

LAOS

THAILAND

VIETNAM

CAMBODIA

PHILIPPINES

BRUNEI

MALAYSIA

SINGAPORE

INDONESIA

IRAN

IRAQ

KUWAIT

SAUDI ARABIA

OMAN

YEMEN

U.A.E.

QATAR

TURKEY

SYRIA

JORDAN

ISRAEL

LEBANON

CYPRUS

JAMMU AND KASHMIR

AR. : ARMENIA
AZ. : AZERBAIJAN
B. : BAHRAIN
G. : GEORGIA
K. : KIRGIZIA
L. : LEBANON
Q. : QATAR
TAJ. : TAJIKISTAN
U.A.E. : UNITED ARAB EMIRATES

Halmahera

Ceram

Buru

Banda Sea

Timor

Moluccas

Celebes Sea

Sulawesi (Celebes)

Makassar Strait

Kinabalu 4101

Borneo

Barito

Kapuas

Mekong Delta

Pte. de Ca Mau

Gulf of Thailand

Malay Peninsula

Sumatra

Kerinci 3805

Straits of Malacca

Mentawai Is.

Lesser Sunda Islands

Flores

Sumba

Java Sea

Java

SEA

Timor Sea

Mindanao

Banggai

Sula

Flores Sea

Andaman Is.

Andaman Sea

Nicobar Is.

Sri Lanka

Maldives

Gulf of Mannar

C. Comorin

Chagos Archipelago

Laccadive Is.

Ghats

East

INDIAN OCEAN

Scale 1:40 000 000

Lambert azimuthal equal area projection

1600 km
1200
800
400
0

Madagascar

Equator

Relief

Metres
5000
3000
2000
1000
500
200
Sea level
0
Land Dep.

Metres
200
4000
7000

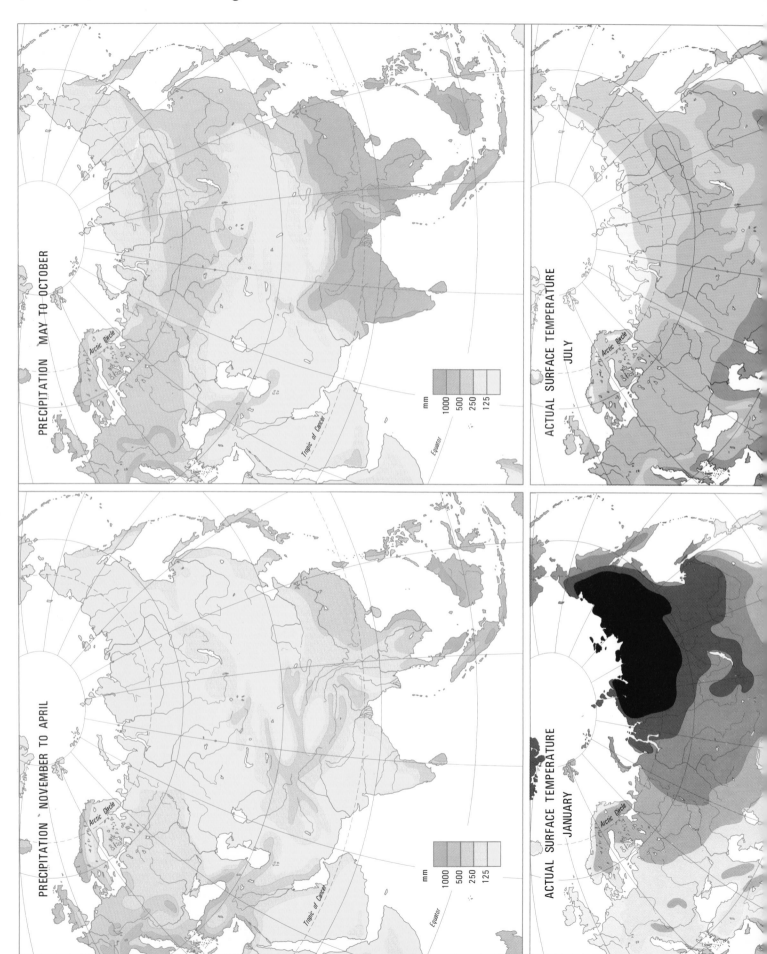

PRECIPITATION MAY TO OCTOBER

Arctic Circle

Tropic of Cancer

Equator

mm
1000
500
250
125

ACTUAL SURFACE TEMPERATURE JULY

Arctic Circle

PRECIPITATION NOVEMBER TO APRIL

Arctic Circle

Tropic of Cancer

Equator

mm
1000
500
250
125

ACTUAL SURFACE TEMPERATURE JANUARY

Arctic Circle

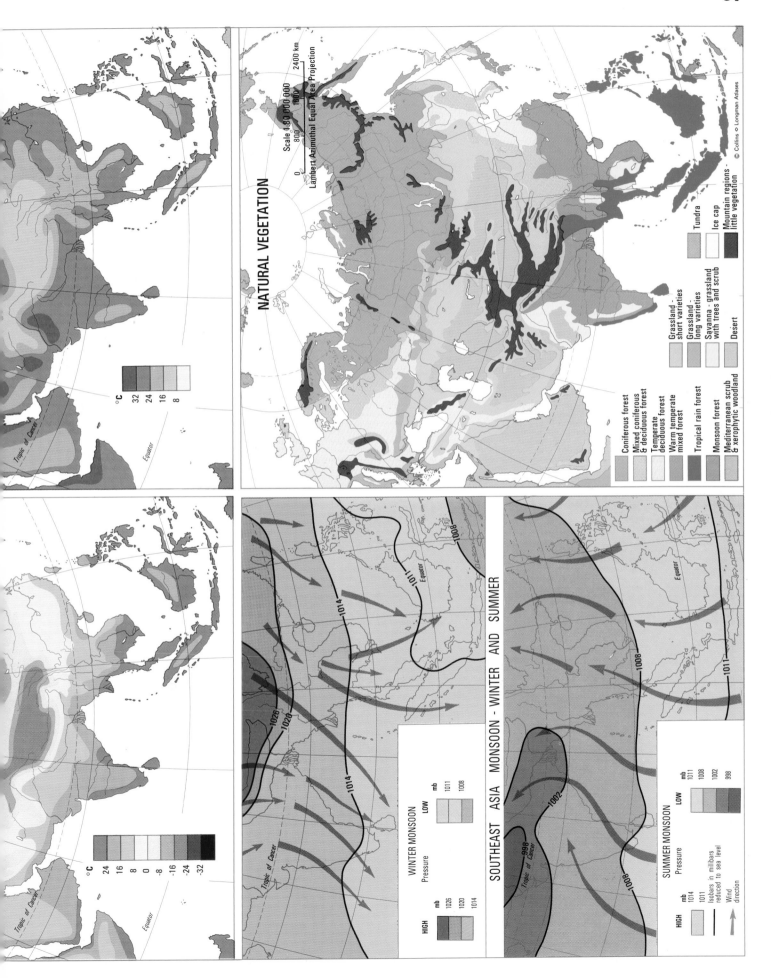

© Collins ◇ Longman Atlases

NATURAL VEGETATION

Scale 1:80 000 000

Lambert Azimuthal Equal Area Projection

0   800   1600   2400 km

Coniferous forest

Mixed coniferous & deciduous forest

Temperate deciduous forest

Warm temperate mixed forest

Tropical rain forest

Monsoon forest

Mediterranean scrub & xerophytic woodland

Grassland - short varieties

Grassland - long varieties

Savanna - grassland with trees and scrub

Desert

Tundra

Ice cap

Mountain regions - little vegetation

°C
32
24
16
8

°C
24
16
8
0
-8
-16
-24
-32

SOUTHEAST ASIA MONSOON - WINTER AND SUMMER

WINTER MONSOON

Pressure

HIGH
mb
1026
1020
1014

LOW
mb
1011
1008

1026
1020
1014
1011
1008

Tropic of Cancer

Equator

SUMMER MONSOON

Pressure

HIGH
mb
1014
1011

LOW
mb
1011
1008
1002
998

998
1002
1008
1011

Tropic of Cancer

Equator

Isobars in millibars reduced to sea level

Wind direction

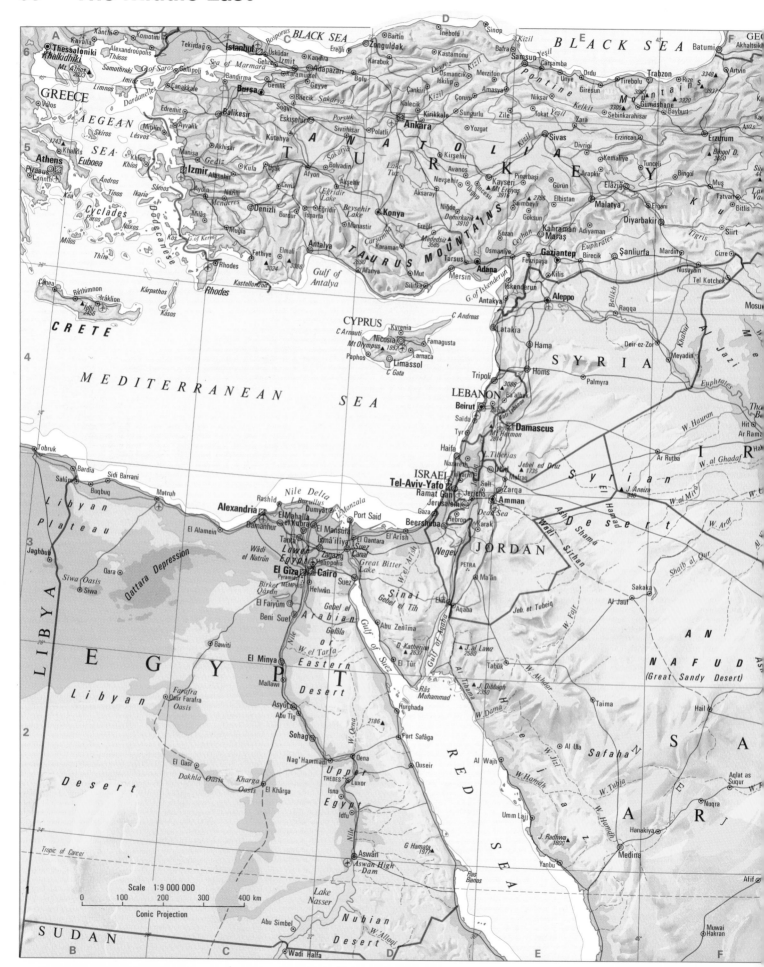

Scale 1:9 000 000

0   100   200   300   400 km

Conic Projection

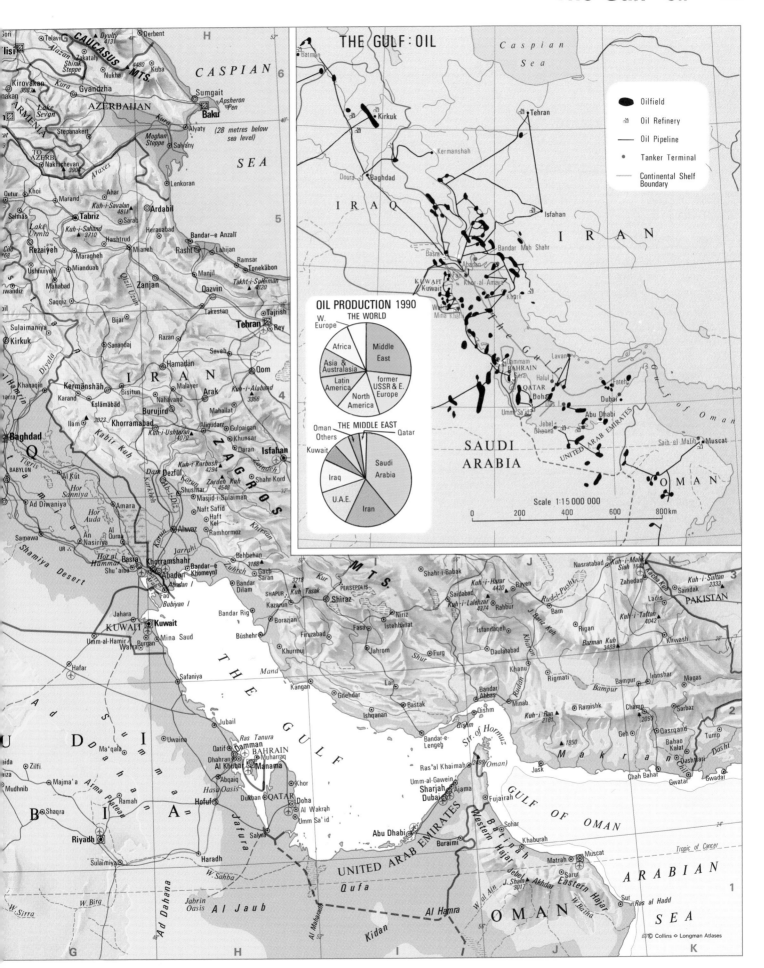

THE GULF: OIL

Legend:
- Oilfield
- Oil Refinery
- Oil Pipeline
- Tanker Terminal
- Continental Shelf Boundary

OIL PRODUCTION 1990

THE WORLD
- W. Europe
- Africa
- Asia & Australasia
- Latin America
- North America
- Middle East
- former USSR & E. Europe

THE MIDDLE EAST
- Oman
- Others
- Kuwait
- Iraq
- U.A.E.
- Iran
- Saudi Arabia
- Qatar

Scale 1:15 000 000

0   200   400   600   800 km

© Collins ◇ Longman Atlases

FACT*file* — India

Total population	796.60 million
Total area	3 288 000 sq km
GDP per head	335 US$

EMPLOYMENT

Primary	66.4%
Secondary	12.6%
Tertiary	21.0%

PRINCIPAL IMPORTS

Non-electric machinery	19.1%
Fuels / Lubricants	18.2%
Precious stones	8.9%
Iron / Steel	5.7%

PRINCIPAL EXPORTS

Precious stones / Jewellery	16.6%
Clothing	11.4%
Machinery & metal products	9.1%
Leather & products	7.3%

NATURAL RESOURCES

Coal   Iron ore   Gold   Diamonds

FACT*file* — Pakistan

Total population	105.40 million
Total area	796 095 sq km
GDP per head	350 US$

EMPLOYMENT

Primary	49.5%
Secondary	19.2%
Tertiary	31.3%

PRINCIPAL IMPORTS

Non-electric machinery	17.6%
Mineral oils	16.2%
Chemicals	9.3%
Transport equipment	8.6%

PRINCIPAL EXPORTS

Raw cotton	16.2%
Cotton yarn	13.7%
Cotton fabric	9.3%
Rice	8.6%

NATURAL RESOURCES

Coal   Iron ore   Copper   Natural Gas

FACT*file* — Bangladesh

Total population	113.34 million
Total area	143 998 sq km
GDP per head	170 US$

EMPLOYMENT

Primary	56.5%
Secondary	12.0%
Tertiary	31.5%

PRINCIPAL IMPORTS

Minerals products	15.9%
Textiles	14.2%
Vegetable products	12.4%
Base metals	11.0%

PRINCIPAL EXPORTS

Clothing	33.8%
Prawns & shrimps	11.1%
Leather & products	10.6%
Raw jute	6.6%

NATURAL RESOURCES

Natural Gas   Crude oil

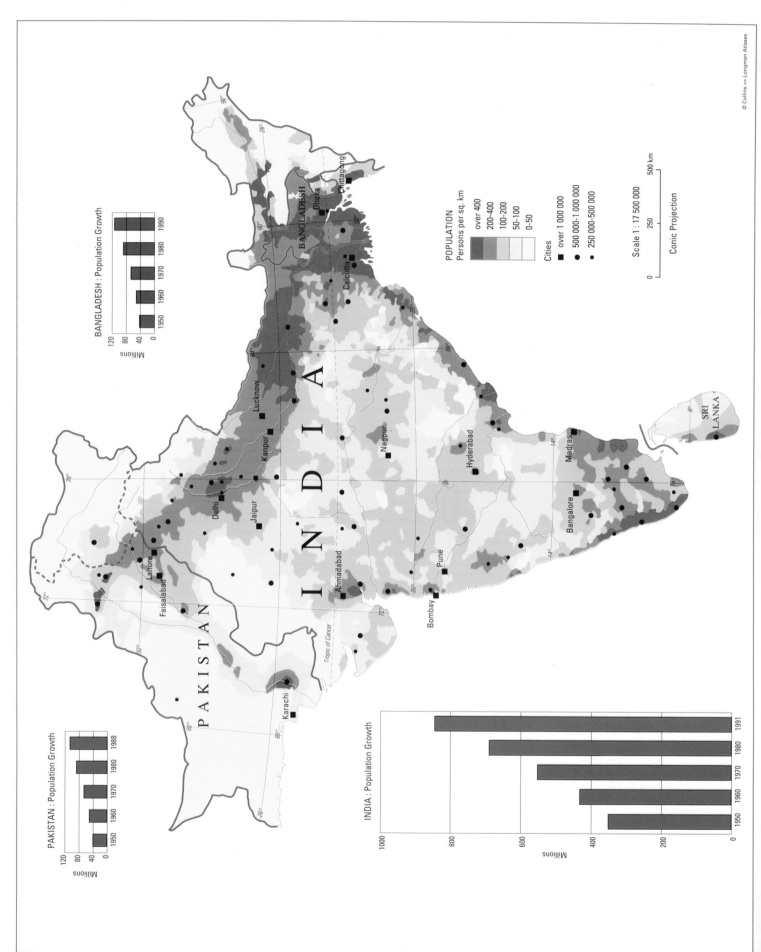

BANGLADESH : Population Growth

PAKISTAN : Population Growth

INDIA : Population Growth

POPULATION
Persons per sq. km
over 400
200-400
100-200
50-100
0-50

Cities
■ over 1 000 000
● 500 000-1 000 000
• 250 000-500 000

Scale 1 : 17 500 000
0   250   500 km
Conic Projection

© Collins ◇ Longman Atlases

BANGLADESH

Chittagong
Dhaka
Calcutta

INDIA

Lucknow
Kanpur
Delhi
Jaipur
Nagpur
Hyderabad
Madras
Bangalore
Ahmadabad
Pune
Bombay

PAKISTAN

Lahore
Faisalabad
Karachi

SRI LANKA

Tropic of Cancer

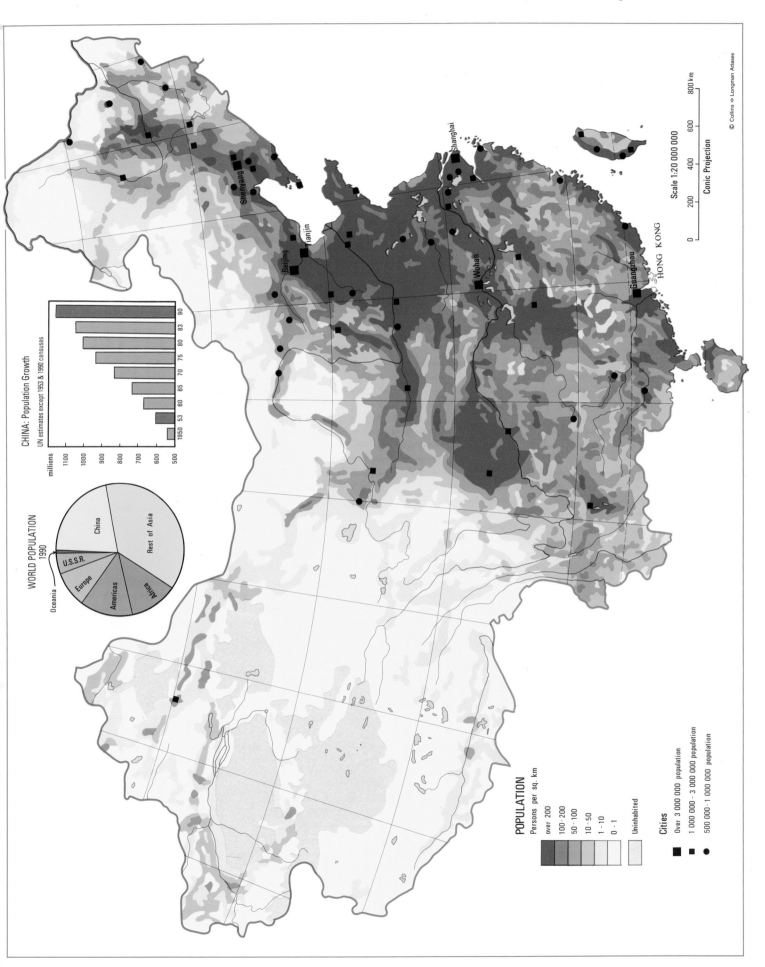

© Collins ◇ Longman Atlases

Scale 1:20 000 000

Conic Projection

| 0 | 200 | 400 | 600 | 800 km |

Shanghai

Shenyang

Tianjin

Beijing

Wuhan

Guangzhou

HONG KONG

CHINA: Population Growth
UN estimates except 1953 & 1990 censuses

millions

1100	90
1000	83
900	80
800	75
700	70
600	65
	60
	53
500	1950

WORLD POPULATION 1990

China
Rest of Asia
U.S.S.R.
Europe
Americas
Africa
Oceania

POPULATION
Persons per sq. km

- over 200
- 100 - 200
- 50 - 100
- 10 - 50
- 1 - 10
- 0 - 1
- Uninhabited

Cities

- ■ Over 3 000 000 population
- ◼ 1 000 000 - 3 000 000 population
- ● 500 000 - 1 000 000 population

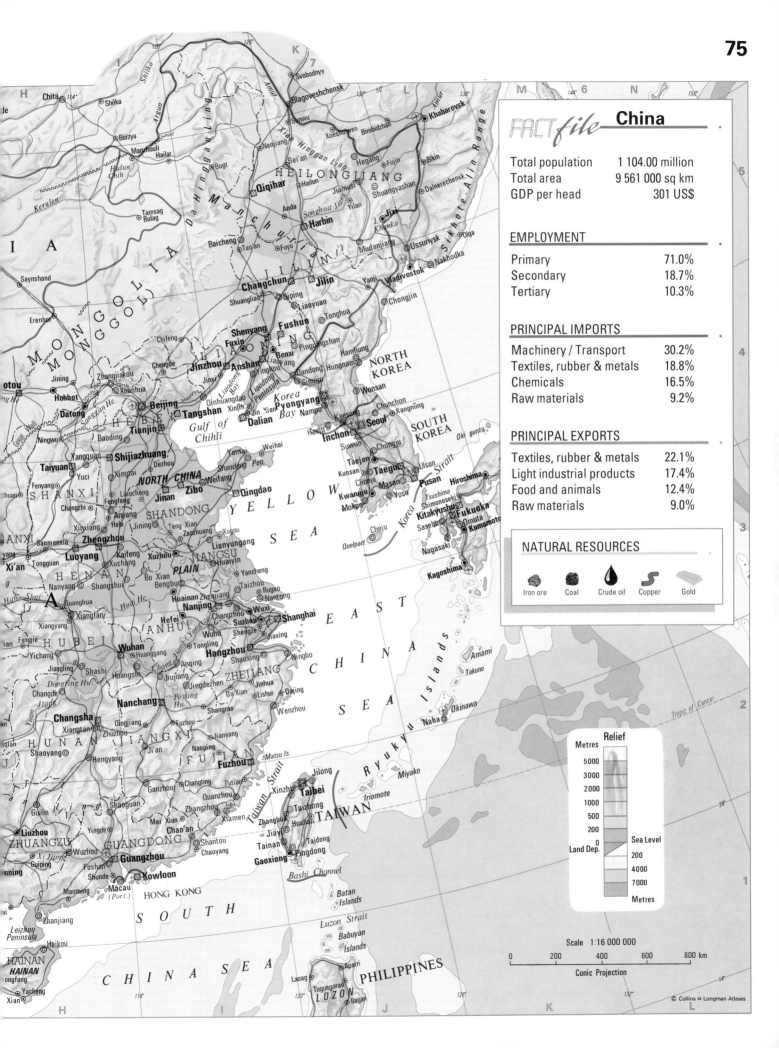

FACTfile — China

Total population	1 104.00 million
Total area	9 561 000 sq km
GDP per head	301 US$

EMPLOYMENT

Primary	71.0%
Secondary	18.7%
Tertiary	10.3%

PRINCIPAL IMPORTS

Machinery / Transport	30.2%
Textiles, rubber & metals	18.8%
Chemicals	16.5%
Raw materials	9.2%

PRINCIPAL EXPORTS

Textiles, rubber & metals	22.1%
Light industrial products	17.4%
Food and animals	12.4%
Raw materials	9.0%

NATURAL RESOURCES

Iron ore   Coal   Crude oil   Copper   Gold

Relief

Metres	
5000	
3000	
2000	
1000	
500	
200	
0	Sea Level
Land Dep.	
200	
4000	
7000	
Metres	

Scale 1:16 000 000

0   200   400   600   800 km

Conic Projection

© Collins ◇ Longman Atlases

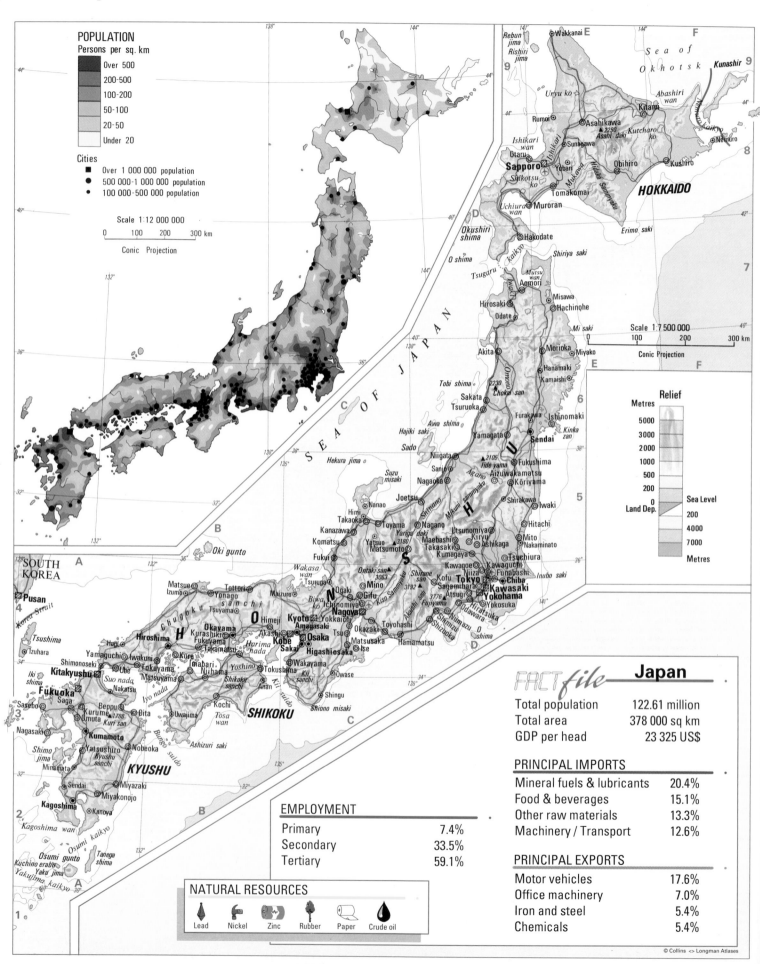

POPULATION
Persons per sq. km
- Over 500
- 200-500
- 100-200
- 50-100
- 20-50
- Under 20

Cities
- ■ Over 1 000 000 population
- ● 500 000-1 000 000 population
- • 100 000-500 000 population

Scale 1:12 000 000

0   100   200   300 km

Conic Projection

Scale 1:7 500 000

0   100   200   300 km

Conic Projection

Relief
Metres	
5000	
3000	
2000	
1000	
500	
200	
0	Sea Level
Land Dep.	200
	4000
	7000
Metres	

HOKKAIDO

Sea of Okhotsk

Kunashir

SEA OF JAPAN

SOUTH KOREA

SHIKOKU

KYUSHU

FACTfile — **Japan**

Total population	122.61 million
Total area	378 000 sq km
GDP per head	23 325 US$

PRINCIPAL IMPORTS
Mineral fuels & lubricants	20.4%
Food & beverages	15.1%
Other raw materials	13.3%
Machinery / Transport	12.6%

PRINCIPAL EXPORTS
Motor vehicles	17.6%
Office machinery	7.0%
Iron and steel	5.4%
Chemicals	5.4%

EMPLOYMENT
Primary	7.4%
Secondary	33.5%
Tertiary	59.1%

NATURAL RESOURCES
Lead   Nickel   Zinc   Rubber   Paper   Crude oil

© Collins <> Longman Atlases

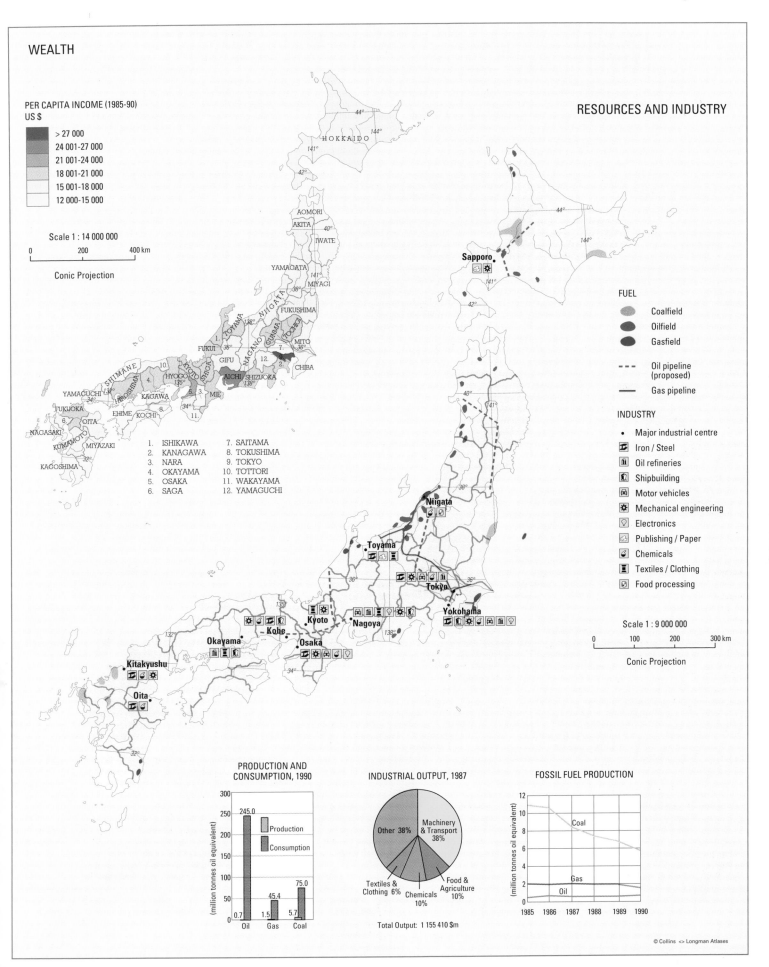

WEALTH

PER CAPITA INCOME (1985-90)
US $

> 27 000
24 001-27 000
21 001-24 000
18 001-21 000
15 001-18 000
12 000-15 000

Scale 1 : 14 000 000

0   200   400 km

Conic Projection

RESOURCES AND INDUSTRY

HOKKAIDO

Sapporo

1. ISHIKAWA
2. KANAGAWA
3. NARA
4. OKAYAMA
5. OSAKA
6. SAGA
7. SAITAMA
8. TOKUSHIMA
9. TOKYO
10. TOTTORI
11. WAKAYAMA
12. YAMAGUCHI

HOKKAIDO
AOMORI
AKITA
IWATE
YAMAGATA
MIYAGI
NIIGATA
FUKUSHIMA
TOYAMA
NAGANO
GUNMA
TOCHIGI
MITO
FUKUI
GIFU
AICHI
SHIZUOKA
CHIBA
SHIMANE
HIROSHIMA
HYOGO
KYOTO
SHIGA
MIE
YAMAGUCHI
KAGAWA
FUKUOKA
EHIME
KOCHI
OITA
NAGASAKI
KUMAMOTO
MIYAZAKI
KAGOSHIMA

Niigata
Toyama
Tokyo
Yokohama
Kyoto
Nagoya
Okayama
Kobe
Osaka
Kitakyushu
Oita

FUEL

Coalfield
Oilfield
Gasfield

- - - Oil pipeline (proposed)
——— Gas pipeline

INDUSTRY

- Major industrial centre
Iron / Steel
Oil refineries
Shipbuilding
Motor vehicles
Mechanical engineering
Electronics
Publishing / Paper
Chemicals
Textiles / Clothing
Food processing

Scale 1 : 9 000 000

0   100   200   300 km

Conic Projection

PRODUCTION AND CONSUMPTION, 1990

(million tonnes oil equivalent)

300
250 245.0
200
150
100
75.0
50 45.4
0.7 1.5 5.7

Oil   Gas   Coal

Production
Consumption

INDUSTRIAL OUTPUT, 1987

Machinery & Transport 38%
Other 38%
Textiles & Clothing 6%
Chemicals 10%
Food & Agriculture 10%

Total Output: 1 155 410 $m

FOSSIL FUEL PRODUCTION

(million tonnes oil equivalent)

12
10
8
6
4
2

Coal
Gas
Oil

1985 1986 1987 1988 1989 1990

Scale 1:15 000 000

| 0 | 200 | 400 | 600 | 800 km |

Bonne Projection

© Collins ◇ Longman Atlases

79

G

8

20°

7

15°

6

5

4

3

2

1

H · I · J · K · L

CHINA

TAIWAN

Hanoi
MACAU HONG KONG

MYANMA

Yangon

Vientiane

THAILAND

Bangkok

LAOS

VIETNAM

Andaman Is.
(India)

CAMBODIA

Phnom Penh

Manila

PHILIPPINES

BRUNEI
Bandar Seri Begawan

Kuala Lumpur

M A L A Y S I A

SINGAPORE

I N D O N E S I A

Jakarta

PAPUA NEW GUINEA

Port Moresby

A U S T R A L I A

ASEAN
(Association of South East Asian Nations)

National Capital

Scale 1:40 000 000

0   500   1000 km

TAIWAN

125°

Batan Is.

zon Strait

Babuyan Is.

C. Engaño

oag

Aparri

Tuguegarao

Ilagan

ulog
2929

Fernando

LUZON

Bayombong

aguio

upa

n Carlos

Cabanatuan

Quezon City

Manila

PHILIPPINES

San Pablo   Daet

Lucena   Naga   *Catanduanes*

indoro   Legaspi

Burias   Irosin

Bulan   Catarman

Masbate   Calbayog   *Samar*
Catbalogan   Guiuan

Panay   Iloilo   Cadiz   Tacloban   *Leyte*   C. Johnson Depth 10497

Bacolod   Cebu   Dinagat   Siargao

Negros   Bohol   Surigao

Tanjay   Tagbilaran

Dumaguete   Butuan

Dipolog   Cagayan de Oro

Ozamiz   Iligan

ala   Pagadian

Cotabato   Datu Piang   **Davao**

amboanga   *Moro Gulf*

Basilan   Datu Piang

Jolo   General Santos

Sulu Arch.

MINDANAO

Davao
Davao G.

Philippine

Trench

L E B E S

S E A

Buol   2207

omin   Kuandang

Gorontalo   1970

lf   Togian Is

Poh

ini

Peleng

Poso   Tuli   Taliabu   Obi

ESI   G. of Banggai Is.

ES   *Sula Is*

Buru

ombola   Mekongga
2790   Namlea   Ambon   *Ceram*

Kendari   Bula

Kolaka   Wowoni

of Bone

Muna   Butung

kabaena   Tukangbesi Is

kabia

SI   *Buton*

ES

Islands

es   Maumere

gapu   Ende   Alor   *Dili*

Sawu   Roti   *Timor*   1365
Nikiniki

Kupang

Karakelong   Talaud Is

Sangi

Sangihe Is

Manado   Tondano

Belang

Ternate   Jailolo
Soasiu   *Halmahera*
Weda

Molucca Sea

Tobelo

Morotai

Sonsorol

Merir

Tobi

Helen Reef

Mapia Is

Waigeo

Dampier Str   Kwoka 3000

Sorong   Klamono   Arfak 2939
Vogelkop   Wasian

Misoöl   Wasior

Kokas   Teluk Berau   Babo

Fakfak   *Teluk Irian*

Kaimana

Adi

Kokenau

M
O
L
U
C
C
A

S
E
A

CERAM SEA

Binaija 3055

Ceram

BANDA SEA

Nila

Damar

Wetar   Roma   Babar Is

Leti Is   Sermate

Jamdena   Tanimbar Is
Saumlaki   Selaru

Kai Is

Aru Is
Kobroör

Trangan

Wokam

Nila

Palau
(U.S.A)   Koror

Sorol

Ifalik

Eauripik

C a r o l i n e   I s l a n d s
(U.S. Trust Territory)

Lamotrek

P A C I F I C

O C E A N

Schouten Is   Biak
Bosnik
Mokmer   Biak   Sarmi
Japen
Serui   *Jayapura*

Manokwari

Mamberamo   Vanimo

Maprik   Wewak

Sepik

Maoke   *Range*   Angoram   Bogia

Sudirman Mts.   Jayawijaya   *PAPUA NEW*   Madang

Puntjak Jaya 5030   Mandala Pk   Wabag

Mts   4702   Laiagam   Mt Hagen

IRIAN   Mandala Pk   Goroka

JAYA   Tanahmerah   Mendi   Mt Wilhelm 4694

GUINEA   Kaiantu

Mappi   **N E W   G U I N E A**   Bululo   Lae

Okaba   Kokenau   Kikori   Baimuru   Wau

Kolepom   *Fly*   Kerema   3993

Merauke   Daru   Popondetta

C. Vals   Digoel

Gulf of Papua

Port Moresby
Kila Kila

Manus

Lorengau
Admiralty Is

Bismarck Sea

Huon Pen
Finschhafen

Relief

Metres

5000
3000
2000
1000
500
200
0   Sea Level
Land Dep.
200
4000
7000

Metres

Equator   0°

5°

Mulgrave Is   Banks I

Torres Str.

Thursday I   C. York

Prince of Wales

A R A F U R A   S E A

C o r a l   S e a

130°   135°   140°   145°

125°   130°   135°   140°

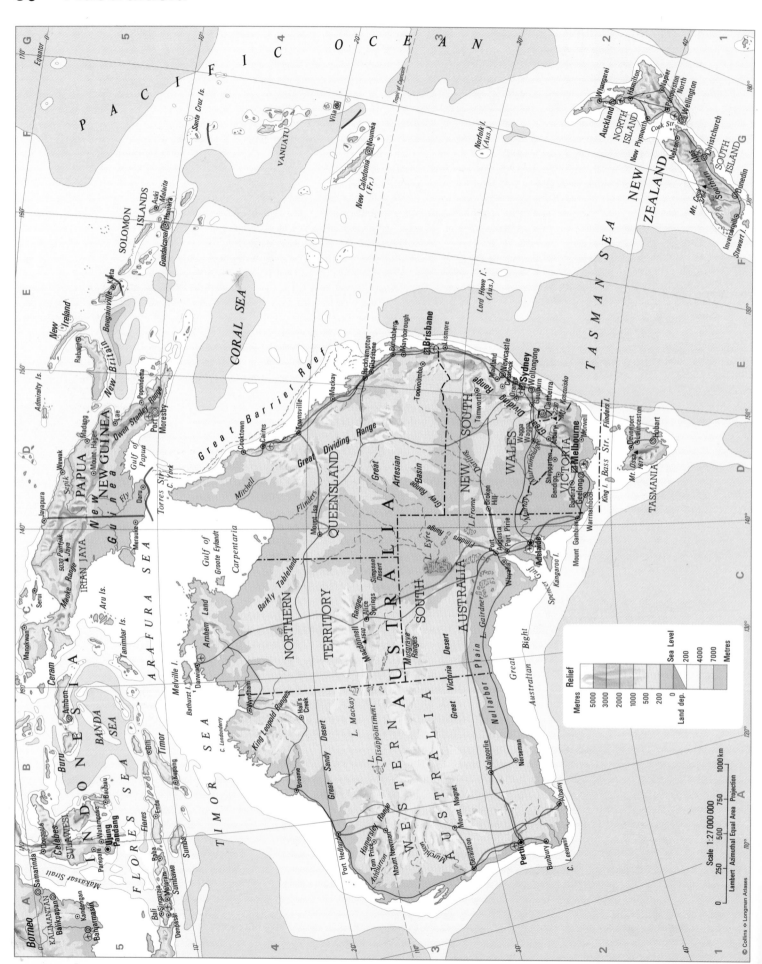

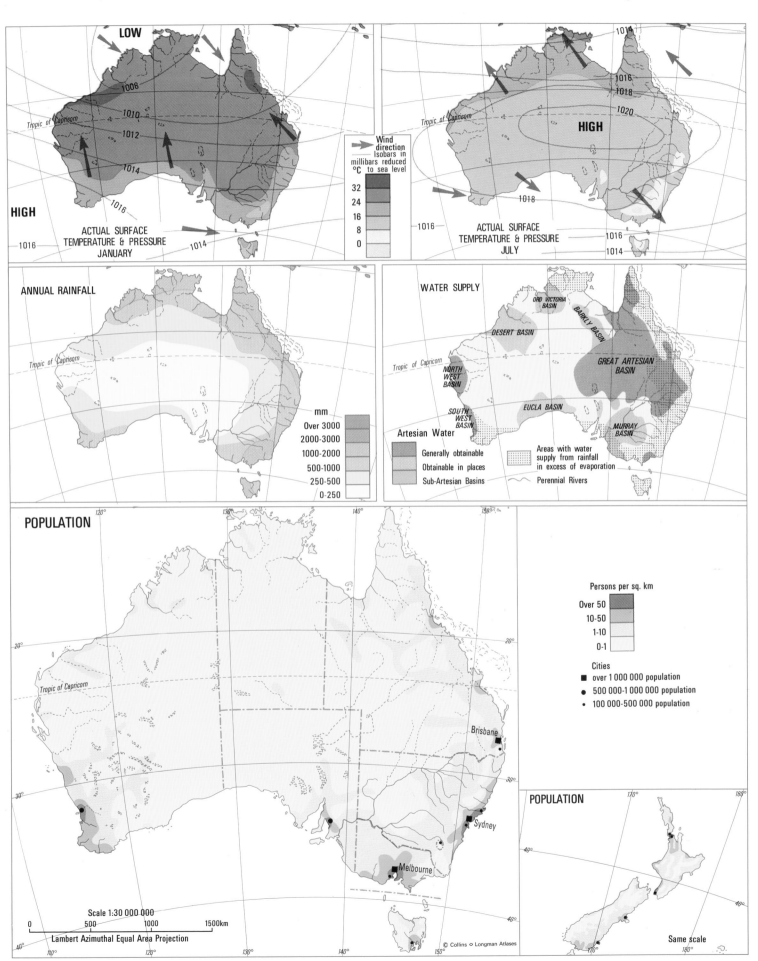

ACTUAL SURFACE TEMPERATURE & PRESSURE JANUARY

LOW

HIGH

1008
1010
1012
1014
1016

Tropic of Capricorn

Wind direction
Isobars in millibars reduced to sea level

°C
32
24
16
8
0

ACTUAL SURFACE TEMPERATURE & PRESSURE JULY

HIGH

1014
1016
1018
1020

1018
1016
1014

Tropic of Capricorn

ANNUAL RAINFALL

Tropic of Capricorn

mm
Over 3000
2000-3000
1000-2000
500-1000
250-500
0-250

WATER SUPPLY

ORD VICTORIA BASIN
DESERT BASIN
BARKLY BASIN
NORTH WEST BASIN
GREAT ARTESIAN BASIN
SOUTH WEST BASIN
EUCLA BASIN
MURRAY BASIN

Tropic of Capricorn

Artesian Water
Generally obtainable
Obtainable in places
Sub-Artesian Basins

Areas with water supply from rainfall in excess of evaporation
Perennial Rivers

POPULATION

Tropic of Capricorn

Brisbane
Sydney
Melbourne

120° 130° 140° 150°
20°
30°
40°

Persons per sq. km
Over 50
10-50
1-10
0-1

Cities
■ over 1 000 000 population
● 500 000-1 000 000 population
• 100 000-500 000 population

Scale 1:30 000 000
0   500   1500km
Lambert Azimuthal Equal Area Projection

POPULATION

170° 180°
40°

Same scale

© Collins ○ Longman Atlases

The 34 countries surrounding the Pacific Ocean and the 23 island states scattered across it have become a region of great economic and political importance. Approximately 2.4 billion people live in the region - more than half of the world's population. The region produces half of the world's total wealth (GNP) and has an abundance of natural resources, including 21% of the world's oil resources, 63% of its wool, 67% of its cotton, 87% of its natural rubber and 94% of its natural silk.

The graphs on these two pages show the importance of the trade between the major countries in the region. (The graphs show the trade between countries as a percentage of total trade for each selected country).

CANADA
Total Imports $105 965 million
Total Exports $114 845 million

U.S.A.
Total Imports $446 460 million
Total Exports $319 680 million

JAPAN
Total Imports $164 770 million
Total Exports $259 760 million

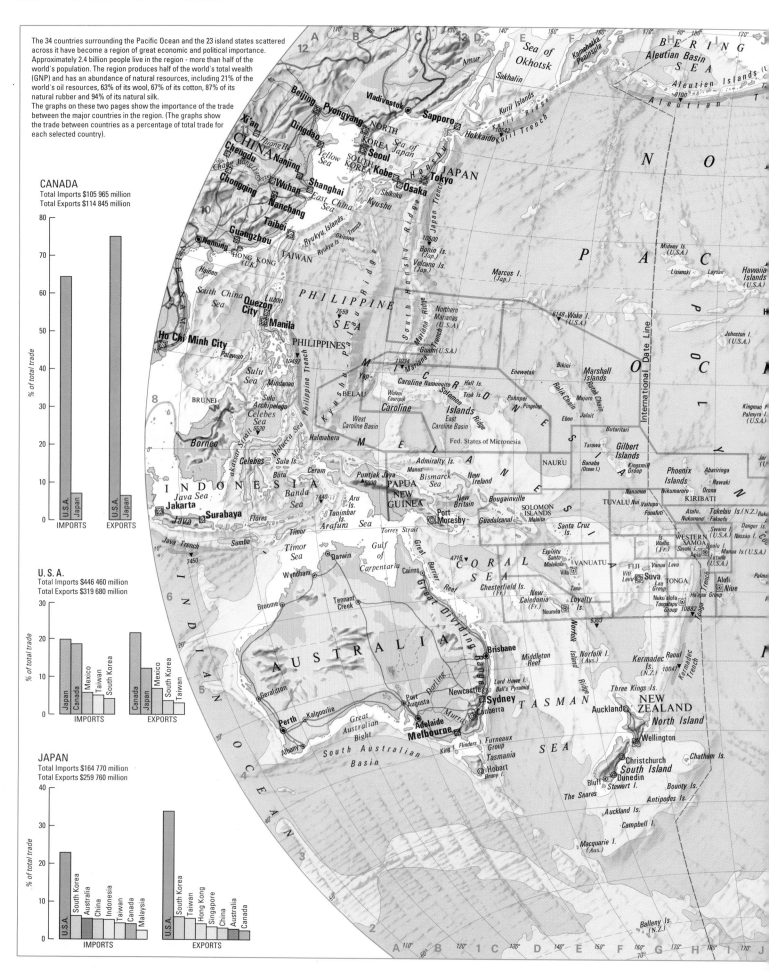

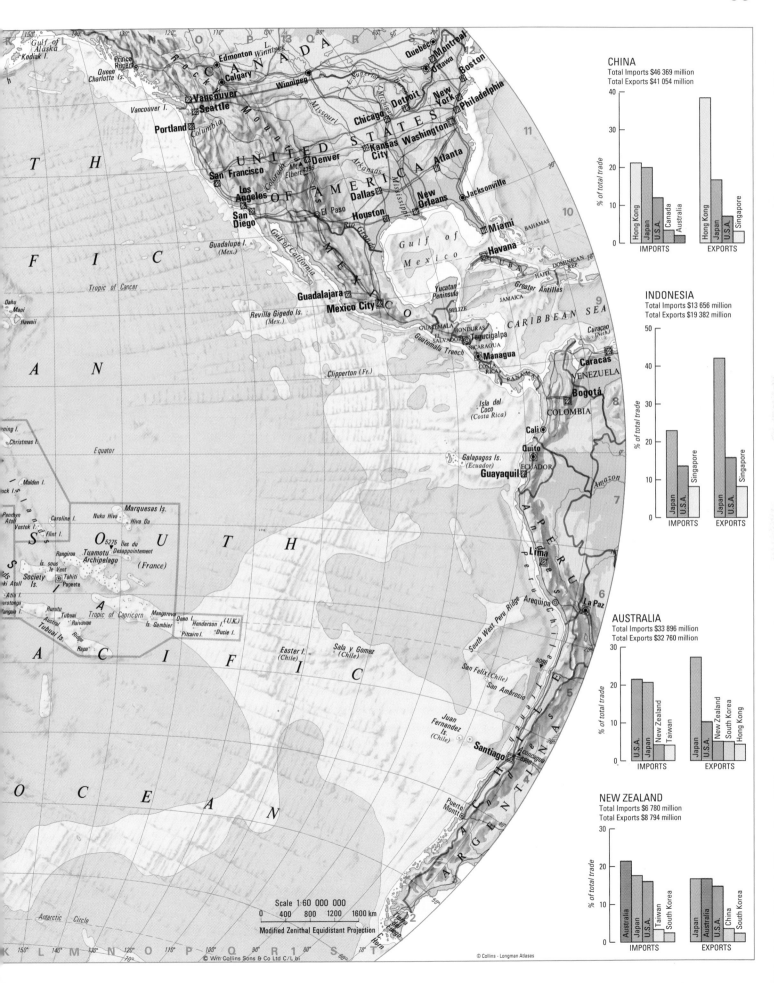

CHINA
Total Imports $46 369 million
Total Exports $41 054 million

% of total trade

IMPORTS: Hong Kong, Japan, U.S.A., Canada, Australia
EXPORTS: Hong Kong, Japan, U.S.A., Singapore

INDONESIA
Total Imports $13 656 million
Total Exports $19 382 million

% of total trade

IMPORTS: Japan, U.S.A., Singapore
EXPORTS: Japan, U.S.A., Singapore

AUSTRALIA
Total Imports $33 896 million
Total Exports $32 760 million

% of total trade

IMPORTS: U.S.A., Japan, New Zealand, Taiwan
EXPORTS: Japan, U.S.A., New Zealand, South Korea, Hong Kong

NEW ZEALAND
Total Imports $6 780 million
Total Exports $8 794 million

% of total trade

IMPORTS: Australia, Japan, U.S.A., Taiwan, South Korea
EXPORTS: Japan, Australia, U.S.A., China, South Korea

Scale 1:60 000 000
0   400   800   1200   1600 km
Modified Zenithal Equidistant Projection

© Wm Collins Sons & Co Ltd C/L bi

© Collins - Longman Atlases

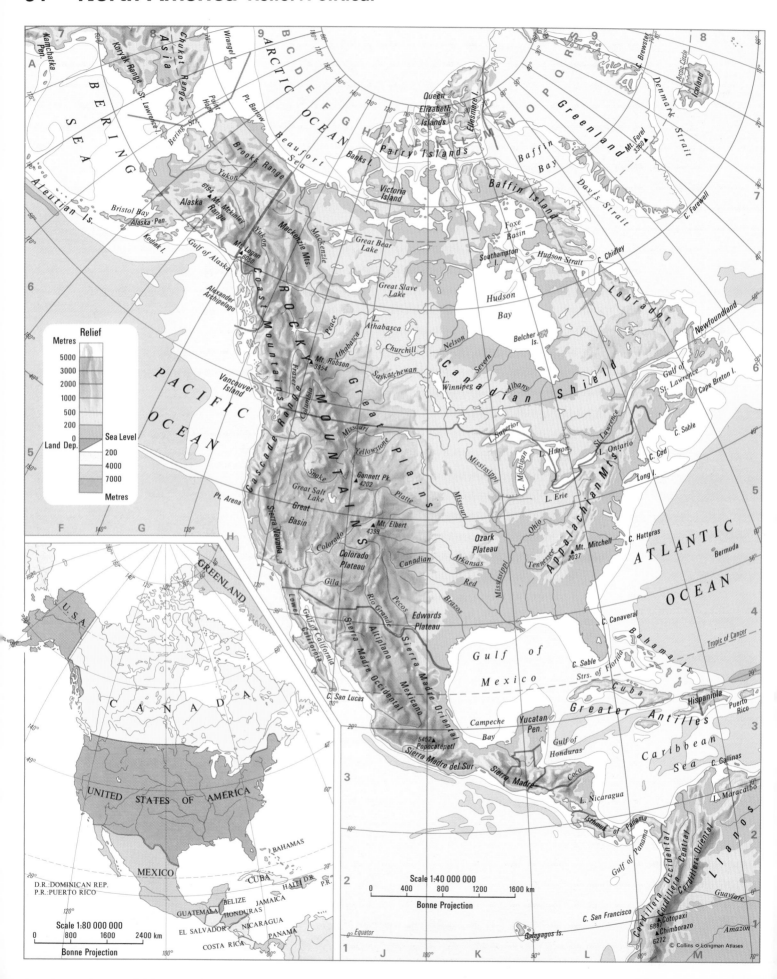

Relief
Metres
5000
3000
2000
1000
500
200
0 Sea Level
Land Dep.
200
4000
7000
Metres

BERING SEA
ARCTIC OCEAN
PACIFIC OCEAN
ATLANTIC OCEAN

Kamchatka Pen.
Koryak Range
Chukot Range
Asia
Wrangel I.
St. Lawrence I.
Bering Str.
Point Hope
Pt. Barrow
Beaufort Sea
Banks I.
Queen Elizabeth Islands
Ellesmere I.
Parry Islands
Baffin Bay
Greenland
Denmark Strait
Iceland
Mt. Forel 3360
Arctic Circle
C. Brewster

Aleutian Is.
Bristol Bay
Alaska Pen.
Kodiak I.
Gulf of Alaska
Alaska
Mt. McKinley 6194
Alaska Range
Brooks Range
Yukon
Mackenzie Mts.
Mackenzie
Great Bear Lake
Victoria Island
Baffin Island
Foxe Basin
Southampton
Hudson Strait
C. Chidley
Davis Strait
C. Farewell

Mt. Logan 6050
Coast Mountains
Alexander Archipelago
Peace
Athabasca
Great Slave Lake
L. Athabasca
Churchill
Hudson Bay
Belcher Is.
Labrador
Newfoundland

Vancouver Island
Mt. Robson 3954
Fraser
Columbia
Rocky Mountains
Saskatchewan
Nelson
Severn
Canadian Shield
Gulf of St. Lawrence
Cape Breton I.

Pt. Arena
Cascade Range
Snake
Missouri
Yellowstone
Gannett Pk. 4202
Great Plains
L. Winnipeg
Albany
L. Superior
St. Lawrence
C. Sable
C. Cod
Long I.

Sierra Nevada
Great Salt Lake
Great Basin
Colorado
Colorado Plateau
Gila
Platte
Missouri
Mississippi
L. Michigan
L. Huron
L. Ontario
L. Erie
Ohio
Appalachian Mts.
C. Hatteras
ATLANTIC OCEAN
Bermuda

Mt. Elbert 4399
Canadian
Ozark Plateau
Arkansas
Tennessee
Mt. Mitchell 2037

Lower California
Gulf of California
Sierra Madre Occidental
Rio Grande
Pecos
Red
Brazos
Edwards Plateau
C. Canaveral
Bahamas
Tropic of Cancer

C. San Lucas
Altiplano
Sierra Madre Oriental
Gulf of Mexico
C. Sable
Strs. of Florida
Cuba
Greater Antilles
Hispaniola
Puerto Rico

Mexicana
Campeche Bay
Yucatan Pen.
Gulf of Honduras
Caribbean Sea
C. Gallinas

Popocatepetl 5452
Sierra Madre del Sur
Sierra Madre
Coco
L. Nicaragua
Isthmus of Panama
Gulf of Panama
L. Maracaibo
Llanos
Cordillera Occidental
Cordillera Central
Cordillera Oriental
Guaviare

C. San Francisco
Cotopaxi 5887
Chimborazo 6272
Galapagos Is.
Equator
Amazon

Scale 1:40 000 000
0 400 800 1200 1600 km
Bonne Projection

GREENLAND
U.S.A.
CANADA
UNITED STATES OF AMERICA
MEXICO
BAHAMAS
CUBA
HAITI
D.R.
P.R.
GUATEMALA
BELIZE
JAMAICA
HONDURAS
EL SALVADOR
NICARAGUA
COSTA RICA
PANAMA

D.R.: DOMINICAN REP.
P.R.: PUERTO RICO

Scale 1:80 000 000
0 800 1600 2400 km
Bonne Projection

© Collins ◇ Longman Atlases

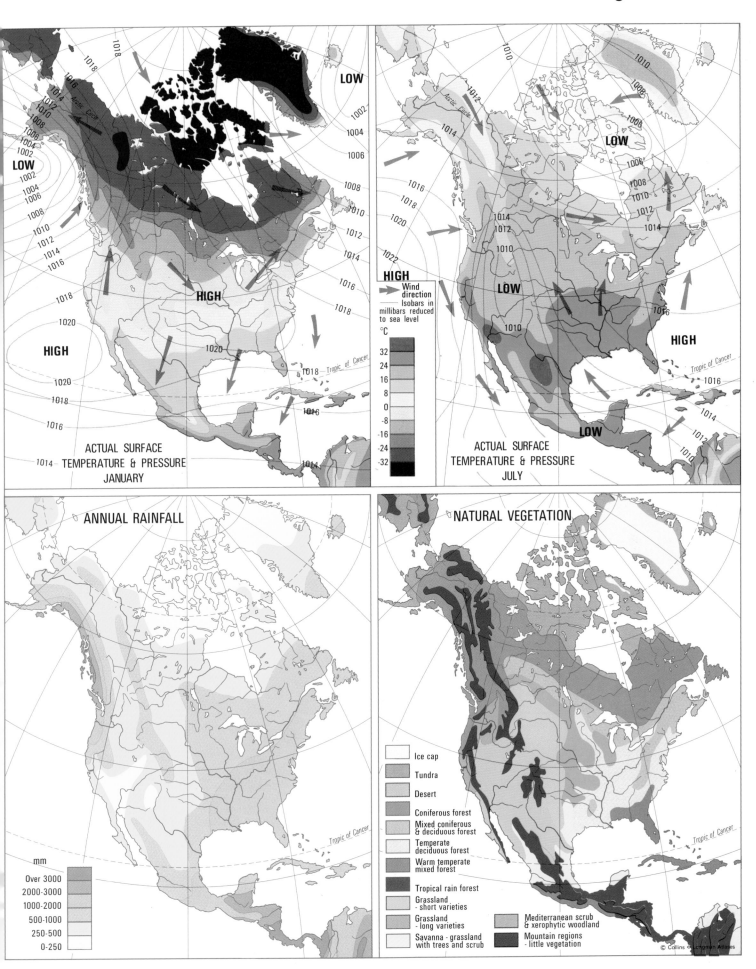

ACTUAL SURFACE TEMPERATURE & PRESSURE JANUARY

LOW
HIGH
HIGH

1018 · 1016 · 1014 · 1012 · 1010 · 1008 · 1006 · 1004 · 1002 · 1004 · 1006 · 1008 · 1010 · 1012 · 1014 · 1016 · 1018 · 1020 · 1018 · 1016 · 1020 · 1018 · 1016 · 1014

1002 · 1004 · 1006 · 1008 · 1010 · 1012 · 1014 · 1016 · 1018 · 1018 · 1016 · 1014

Arctic Circle
Tropic of Cancer

ACTUAL SURFACE TEMPERATURE & PRESSURE JULY

LOW
LOW
HIGH
LOW

1010 · 1012 · 1014 · 1008 · 1010 · 1006 · 1016 · 1018 · 1020 · 1022 · 1014 · 1012 · 1010 · 1008 · 1010 · 1012 · 1014 · 1016 · 1016 · 1014 · 1012 · 1010

Arctic Circle
Tropic of Cancer

Wind direction
Isobars in millibars reduced to sea level

°C
32
24
16
8
0
-8
-16
-24
-32

ANNUAL RAINFALL

Tropic of Cancer

mm
Over 3000
2000-3000
1000-2000
500-1000
250-500
0-250

NATURAL VEGETATION

Tropic of Cancer

Ice cap
Tundra
Desert
Coniferous forest
Mixed coniferous & deciduous forest
Temperate deciduous forest
Warm temperate mixed forest
Tropical rain forest
Grassland - short varieties
Grassland - long varieties
Savanna - grassland with trees and scrub
Mediterranean scrub & xerophytic woodland
Mountain regions - little vegetation

© Collins-Longman Atlases

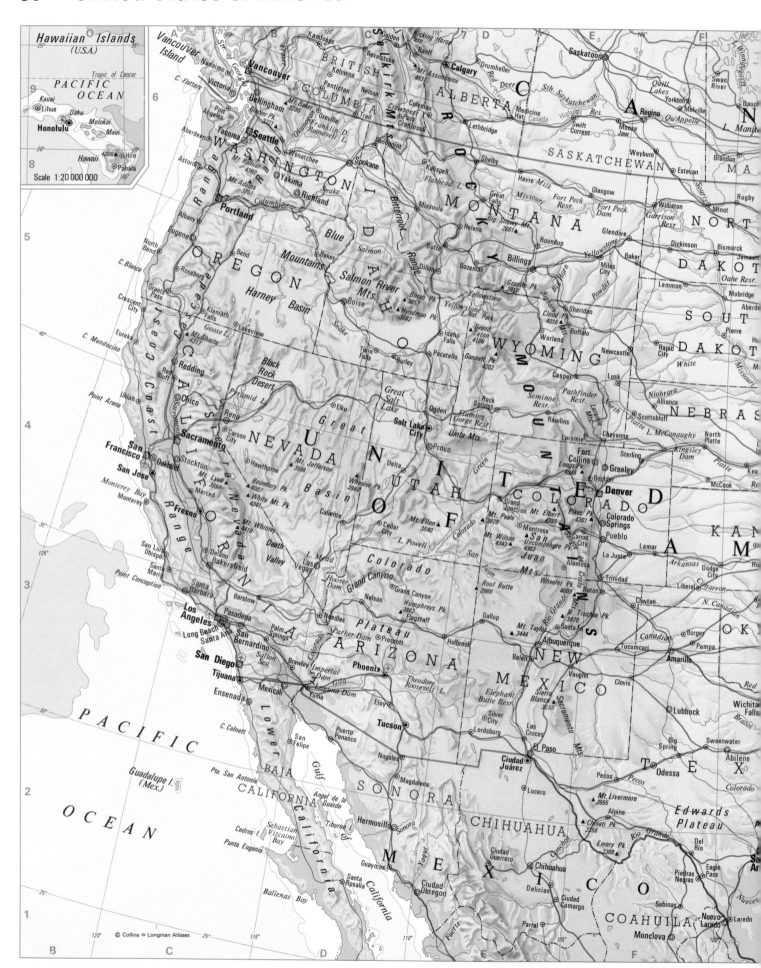

POPULATION

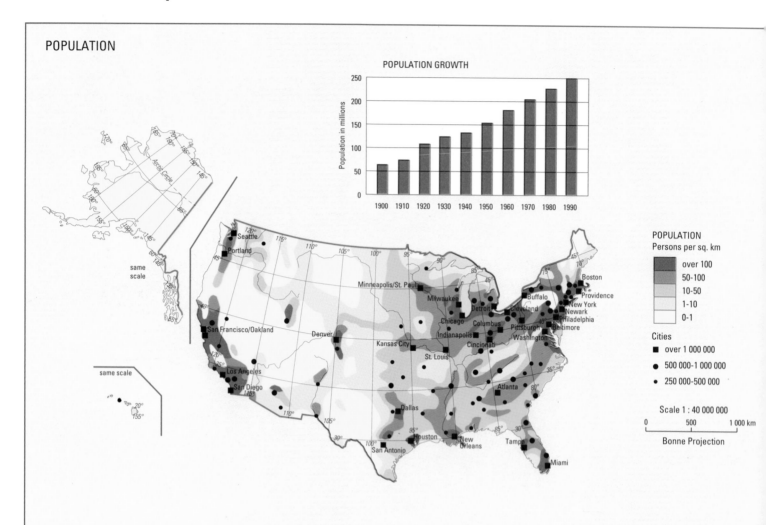

POPULATION GROWTH

POPULATION
Persons per sq. km

- over 100
- 50-100
- 10-50
- 1-10
- 0-1

Cities

- ■ over 1 000 000
- ● 500 000-1 000 000
- • 250 000-500 000

Scale 1 : 40 000 000

0   500   1 000 km

Bonne Projection

WEALTH

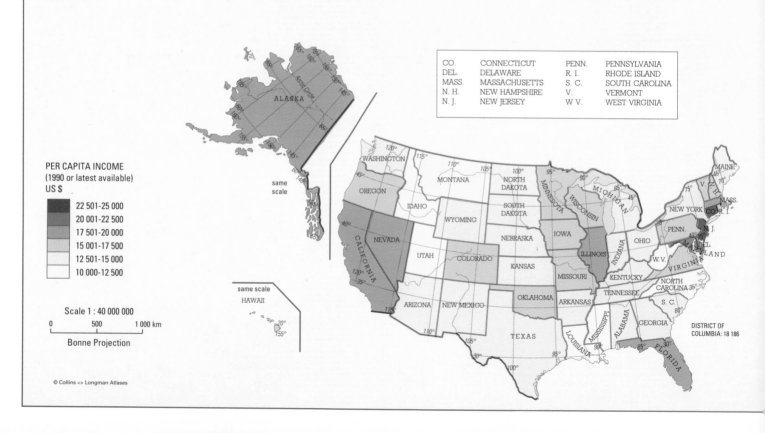

CO.	CONNECTICUT	PENN.	PENNSYLVANIA
DEL.	DELAWARE	R. I.	RHODE ISLAND
MASS.	MASSACHUSETTS	S. C.	SOUTH CAROLINA
N. H.	NEW HAMPSHIRE	V.	VERMONT
N. J.	NEW JERSEY	W V.	WEST VIRGINIA

PER CAPITA INCOME
(1990 or latest available)
US $

- 22 501-25 000
- 20 001-22 500
- 17 501-20 000
- 15 001-17 500
- 12 501-15 000
- 10 000-12 500

Scale 1 : 40 000 000

0   500   1 000 km

Bonne Projection

DISTRICT OF
COLUMBIA: 18 186

RESOURCES AND INDUSTRY

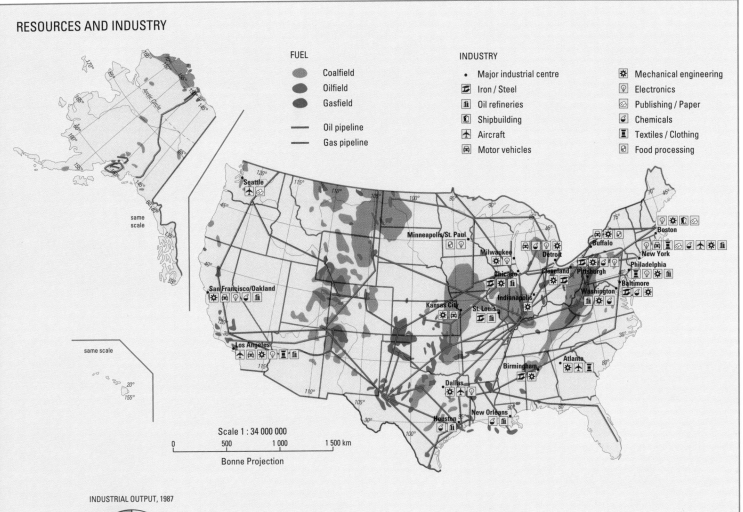

FUEL

- 🌑 Coalfield
- 🌑 Oilfield
- 🌑 Gasfield

— Oil pipeline
— Gas pipeline

INDUSTRY

- • Major industrial centre
- ⬛ Iron / Steel
- ⬛ Oil refineries
- ⬛ Shipbuilding
- ✈ Aircraft
- 🚗 Motor vehicles

- ✳ Mechanical engineering
- ⬛ Electronics
- ⬛ Publishing / Paper
- ⬛ Chemicals
- ⬛ Textiles / Clothing
- ⬛ Food processing

Scale 1 : 34 000 000

| 0 | 500 | 1 000 | 1 500 km |

Bonne Projection

INDUSTRIAL OUTPUT, 1987

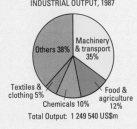

Others 38%
Machinery & transport 35%
Food & agriculture 12%
Chemicals 10%
Textiles & clothing 5%

Total Output: 1 249 540 US$m

PROVED RESERVES, 1990

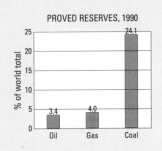

% of world total

- Oil 3.4
- Gas 4.0
- Coal 24.1

FOSSIL FUEL PRODUCTION

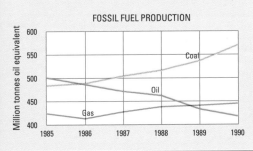

Million tonnes oil equivalent

Coal
Oil
Gas

1985 1986 1987 1988 1989 1990

FACTfile **USA**

Total population	246.33 million
Total area	9 373 000 sq km
GDP per head	19 815 US$

EMPLOYMENT

Primary	2.9%
Secondary	26.7%
Tertiary	70.4%

PRINCIPAL IMPORTS

Machinery / Transport	43.5%
Manufactured goods	29.3%
Mineral fuels & lubricants	11.1%
Foods	4.4%

PRINCIPAL EXPORTS

Machinery	29.7%
Transport equipment	14.6%
Manufactured goods	15.7%
Chemicals	10.1%

NATURAL RESOURCES

Coal   Natural Gas   Crude oil

Gold   Lead   Copper   Silver

Relief

Metres

5000
3000
2000
1000
500
200
0
Land Dep.

Sea Level

200
4000
7000

Metres

Scale 1:17 000 000

0   200   400   600   800 km

Bonne Projection

© Collins ◇ Longman Atlases

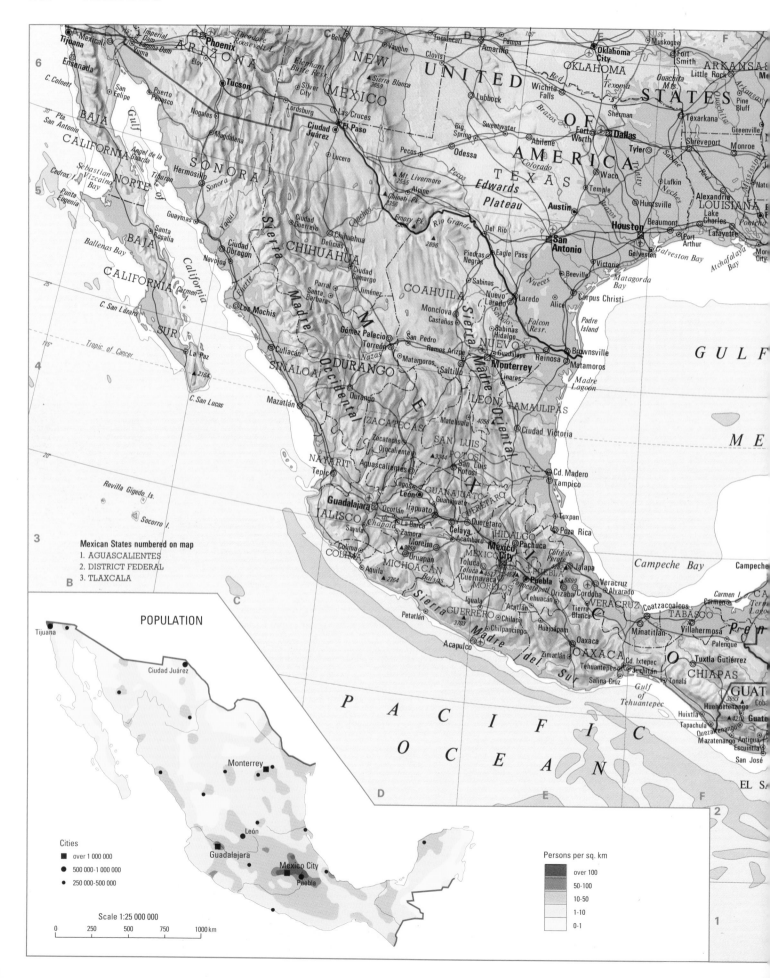

Mexican States numbered on map
1. AGUASCALIENTES
2. DISTRICT FEDERAL
3. TLAXCALA

POPULATION

Cities
■ over 1 000 000
● 500 000-1 000 000
• 250 000-500 000

Persons per sq. km
over 100
50-100
10-50
1-10
0-1

Scale 1:25 000 000

0   250   500   750   1000 km

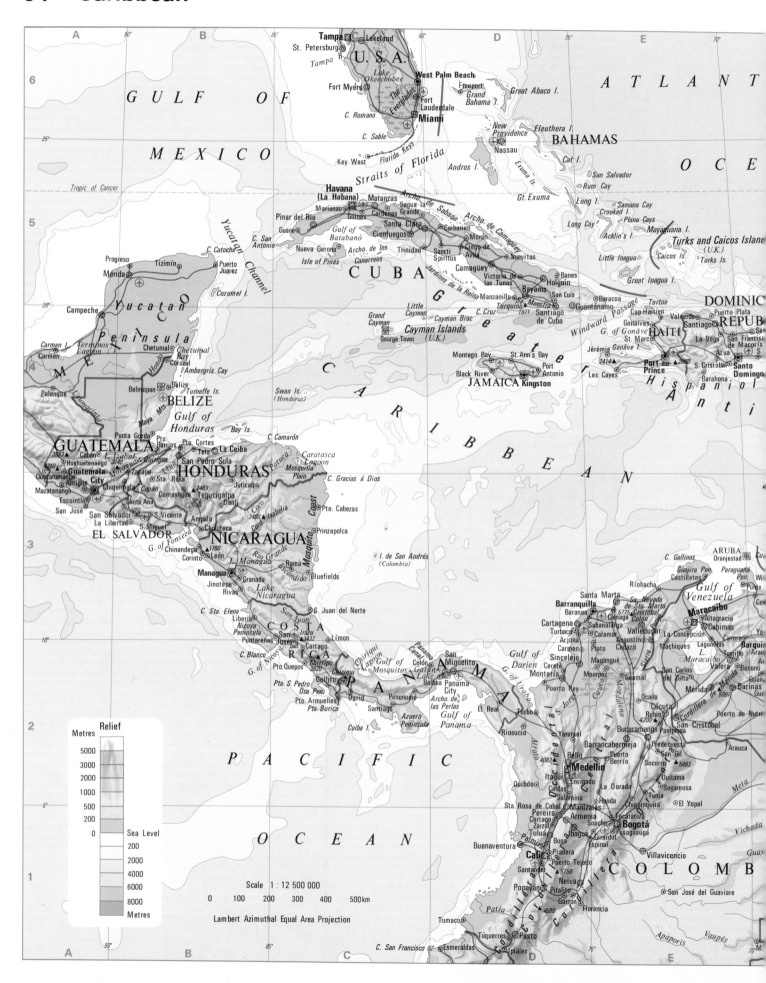

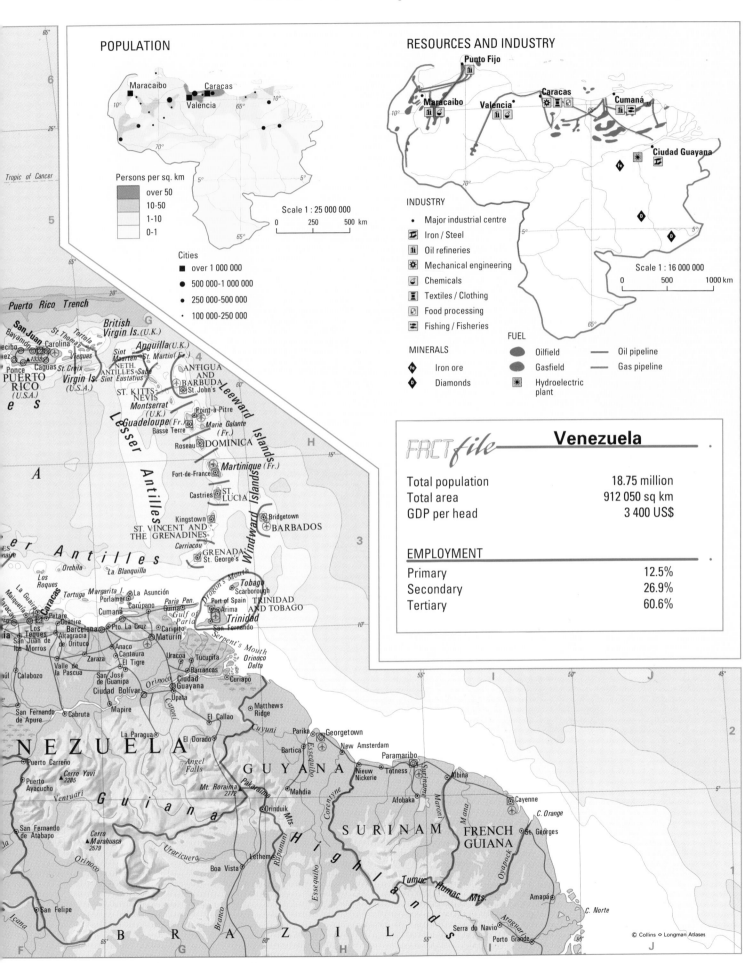

POPULATION

Persons per sq. km
- over 50
- 10-50
- 1-10
- 0-1

Scale 1 : 25 000 000

0   250   500 km

Cities
- ■ over 1 000 000
- ● 500 000-1 000 000
- • 250 000-500 000
- · 100 000-250 000

RESOURCES AND INDUSTRY

INDUSTRY
- • Major industrial centre
- Iron / Steel
- Oil refineries
- Mechanical engineering
- Chemicals
- Textiles / Clothing
- Food processing
- Fishing / Fisheries

MINERALS
- Fe Iron ore
- D Diamonds

FUEL
- Oilfield
- Gasfield
- ✳ Hydroelectric plant
- — Oil pipeline
- — Gas pipeline

Scale 1 : 16 000 000

0   500   1000 km

FACTfile — Venezuela

Total population	18.75 million
Total area	912 050 sq km
GDP per head	3 400 US$

EMPLOYMENT	
Primary	12.5%
Secondary	26.9%
Tertiary	60.6%

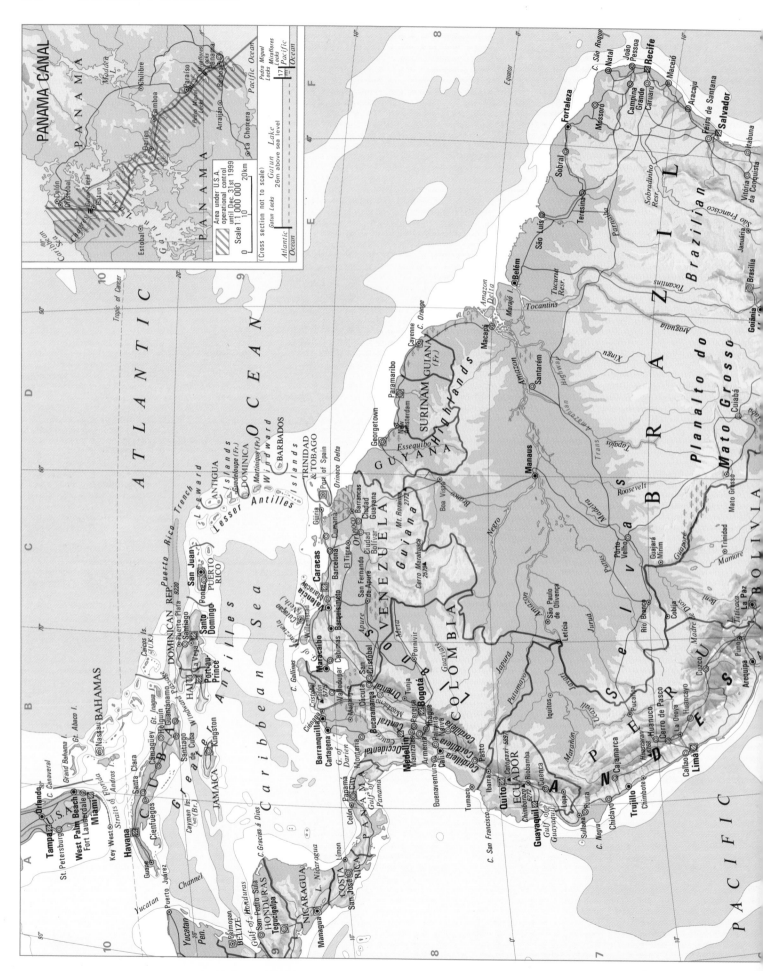

PANAMA CANAL

PANAMA

Pacific Ocean

Area under U.S.A.
operational control
until Dec. 31st 1999

Scale 1:1 000 000

(Cross section not to scale)

Gatun Locks   Gatun   Lake
26m above sea level

Pacific
Ocean

Atlantic
Ocean

0   10   20km

Pedro Miguel
Locks
Miraflores
Locks

ATLANTIC

OCEAN

PACIFIC

BAHAMAS

CUBA

JAMAICA

HAITI

DOMINICAN REP.

PUERTO RICO

Caribbean Sea

Greater Antilles

Lesser Antilles

Windward Islands

ANTIGUA

DOMINICA

BARBADOS

TRINIDAD & TOBAGO

PANAMA

COSTA RICA

NICARAGUA

HONDURAS

BELIZE

U.S.A.

COLOMBIA

VENEZUELA

GUYANA

SURINAM

GUIANA (Fr.)

Guyana Highlands

ECUADOR

PERU

BRAZIL

BOLIVIA

Planalto do Mato Grosso

Amazon

Brazilian Highlands

ANDES

Caracas

Bogotá

Lima

Quito

Guayaquil

Manaus

Belém

Fortaleza

Recife

Salvador

Georgetown

Paramaribo

Cayenne

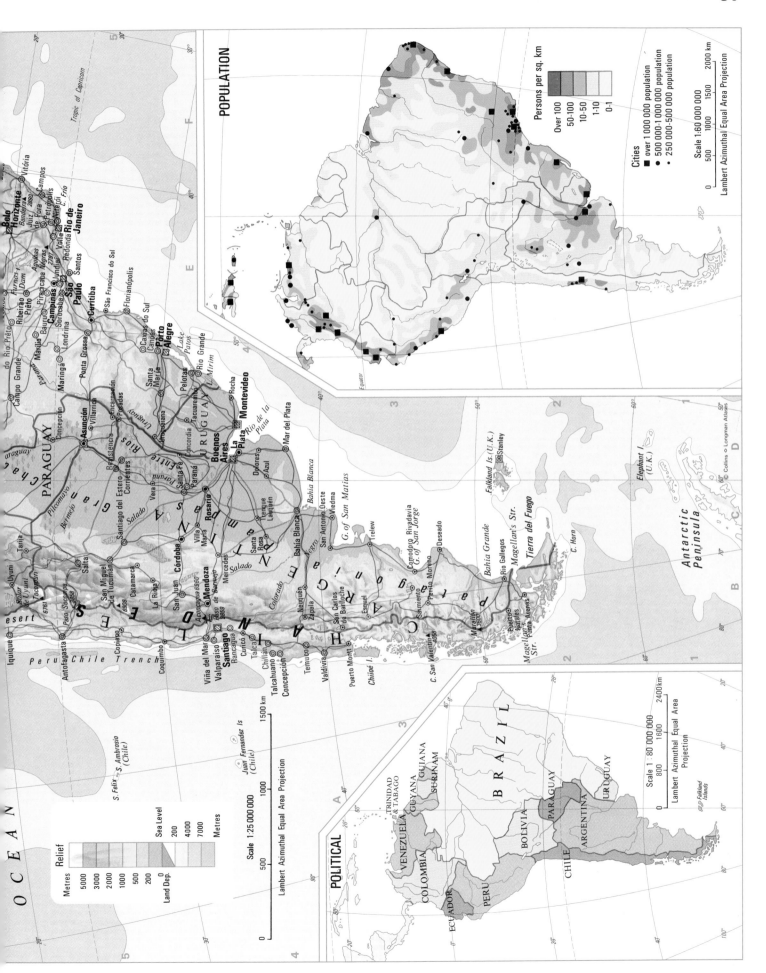

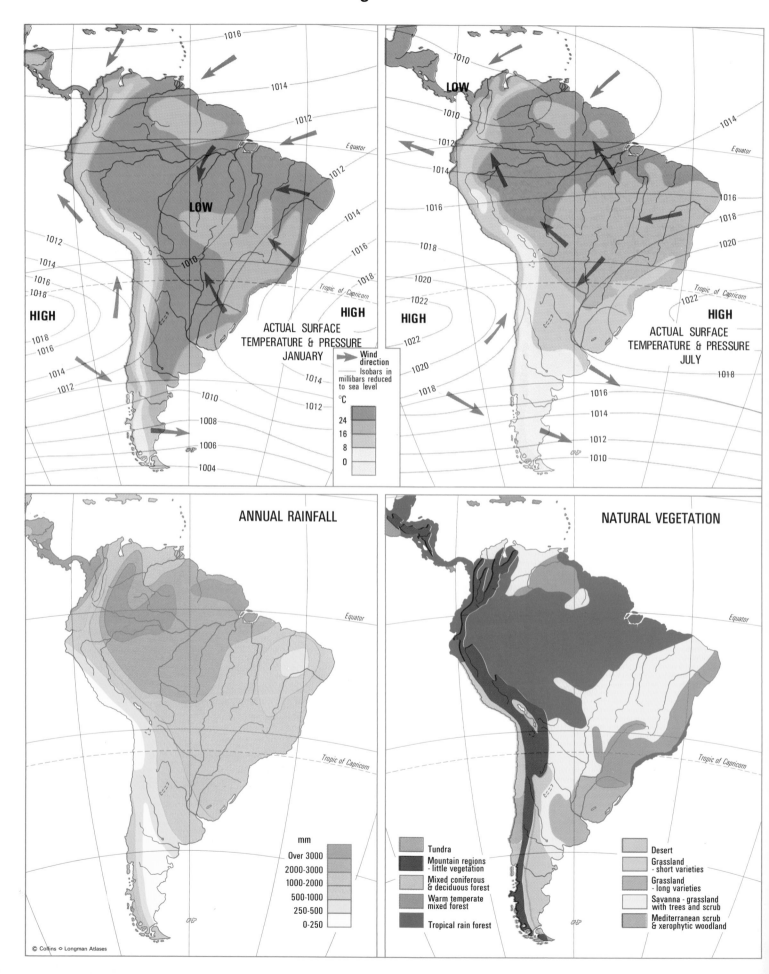

ACTUAL SURFACE TEMPERATURE & PRESSURE JANUARY

1016
1014
1012
LOW
1014
1012
1014
1016
1018
HIGH
1012
1014
1016
1018
1012
1014
1016
1012
1010
1008
1006
1004
HIGH
1018
1016
1014
1012

➤ Wind direction
Isobars in millibars reduced to sea level

°C
24
16
8
0

ACTUAL SURFACE TEMPERATURE & PRESSURE JULY

1010
LOW
1010
1012
1014
1016
1018
1020
1022
HIGH
1022
1020
1018
1014
1016
1014
1016
1018
1020
1022
Equator
Tropic of Capricorn
HIGH
1018
1016
1014
1012
1010

Equator
Tropic of Capricorn

ANNUAL RAINFALL

Equator
Tropic of Capricorn

mm
Over 3000
2000-3000
1000-2000
500-1000
250-500
0-250

NATURAL VEGETATION

Equator
Tropic of Capricorn

Tundra
Mountain regions - little vegetation
Mixed coniferous & deciduous forest
Warm temperate mixed forest
Tropical rain forest

Desert
Grassland - short varieties
Grassland - long varieties
Savanna - grassland with trees and scrub
Mediterranean scrub & xerophytic woodland

© Collins ◇ Longman Atlases

RESOURCES AND INDUSTRY

SELECTED MINERAL PRODUCTION

thousand tonnes

- Lead
- Copper
- Zinc

1970   1980   1987

MINERAL PRODUCTION
(Percentage of world total)

Zinc | rest of world
Lead | rest of world
Copper | rest of world

0   20   40   60   80   100
% world total

INDUSTRIAL OUTPUT, 1987

- Food / agriculture 24%
- Textiles / clothing 11%
- Chemicals 11%
- Machinery / transport 10%
- Other 44%

Total output 12 090 US $m

INDUSTRY

- Oil refineries
- Iron / Steel
- Mechanical engineering
- Textiles
- Publishing / Paper
- Fish processing
- Food processing

FUELS AND MINERALS

- Oilfield
- Gasfield
- Oil pipeline
- Cu Copper
- Pb Lead
- Zn Zinc
- Ag Silver

Tarala
Chiclayo
Chimbote
Paramonga
Lima
Chincha Alta
Cuzco
Arequipa

Scale 1 : 16 000 000
0   150   300   450 km

POPULATION

POPULATION
Persons per sq. km

- over 100
- 50-100
- 10-50
- 1-10
- 0-1

Cities

- over 1 million
- 500 000-1 000 000
- 250 000-500 000
- 100 000-250 000

Iquitos
Piura
Chiclayo
Trujillo
Chimbote
Callao
Lima
Cuzco
Arequipa

Scale 1 : 21 000 000
0   200   400   600 km

FACTfile **Peru**

Total population	21.26 million
Total area	1 285 000 sq km
GDP per head	2 178 US$

EMPLOYMENT

Primary	34.0%
Secondary	16.9%
Tertiary	49.1%

PRINCIPAL IMPORTS

Raw materials	48.2%
Industrial capital goods	16.0%
Machinery / Transport	6.3%

PRINCIPAL EXPORTS

Copper	22.7%
Fish products	13.6%
Zinc	9.7%

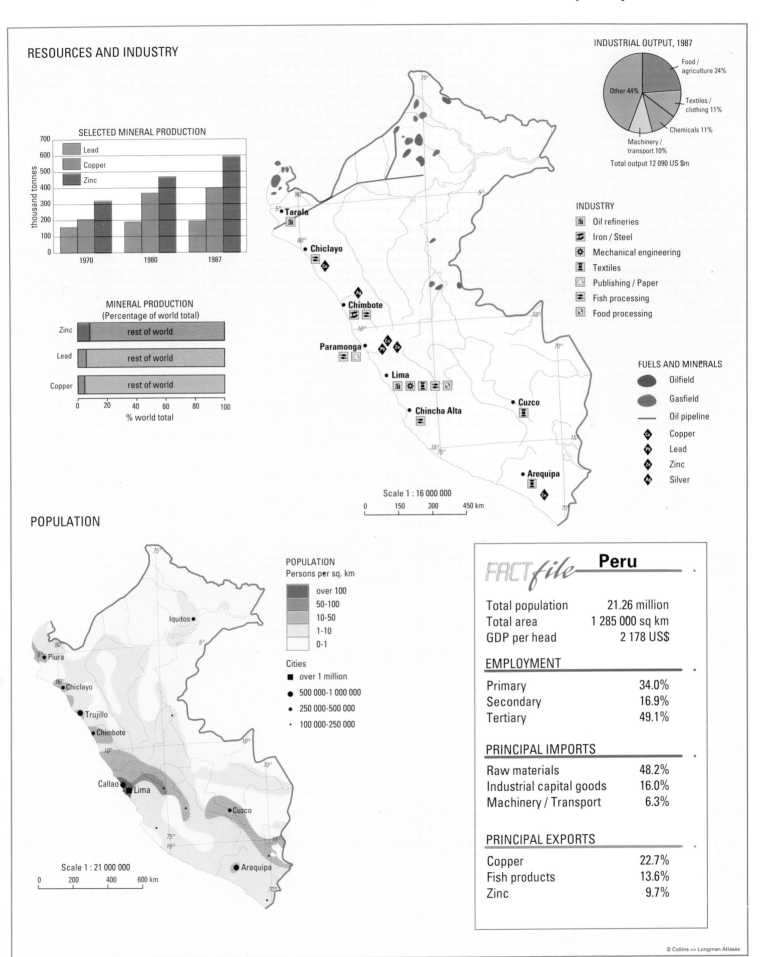

RESOURCES AND INDUSTRY

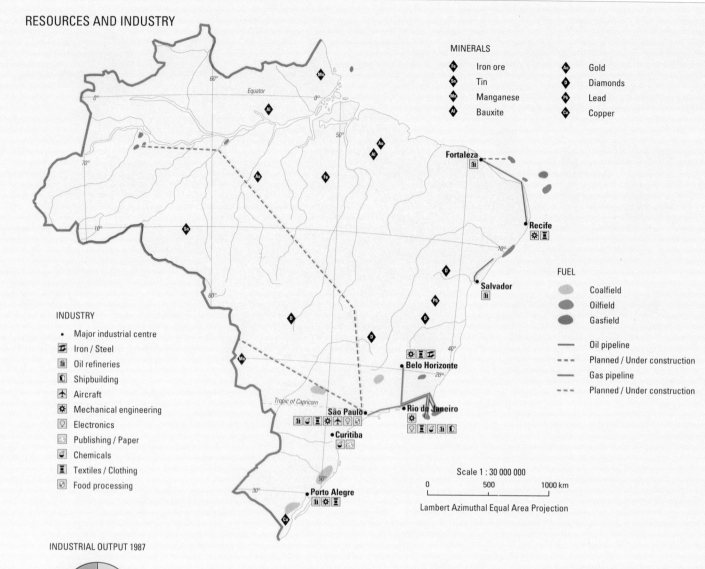

MINERALS

◇ Fe   Iron ore   ◇ Au   Gold
◇ Sn   Tin   ◇ D   Diamonds
◇ Mn   Manganese   ◇ Pb   Lead
◇ Al   Bauxite   ◇ Cu   Copper

INDUSTRY

- • Major industrial centre
- 🏭 Iron / Steel
- 🛢 Oil refineries
- ⚓ Shipbuilding
- ✈ Aircraft
- ❀ Mechanical engineering
- ▽ Electronics
- ▣ Publishing / Paper
- ◪ Chemicals
- ☰ Textiles / Clothing
- ▣ Food processing

FUEL

Coalfield
Oilfield
Gasfield

—— Oil pipeline
- - - Planned / Under construction
—— Gas pipeline
- - - Planned / Under construction

Scale 1 : 30 000 000

0   500   1000 km

Lambert Azimuthal Equal Area Projection

INDUSTRIAL OUTPUT 1987

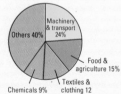

Machinery & transport 24%
Others 40%
Food & agriculture 15%
Chemicals 9%
Textiles & clothing 12

Total output: 116 130 US$m

GROWTH IN OIL PRODUCTION

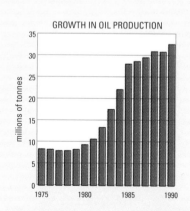

millions of tonnes

1975   1980   1985   1990

FACTfile — **Brazil**

Total population	144.43 million
Total area	8 512 000 sq km
GDP per head	2 451 US$

EMPLOYMENT

Primary	25.2%
Secondary	23.6%
Tertiary	51.2%

PRINCIPAL IMPORTS

Minerals & petroleum	33.2%
Machinery & electrical equipment	24.2%
Industrial chemicals	16.0%

PRINCIPAL EXPORTS

Metals and products	17.5%
Processed food	16.5%
Machinery	9.7%
Nonmetallic minerals	9.3%
Fresh vegetables	9.1%

NATURAL RESOURCES

Gold   Iron ore   Tin

Quartz crystal   Silver   Diamonds

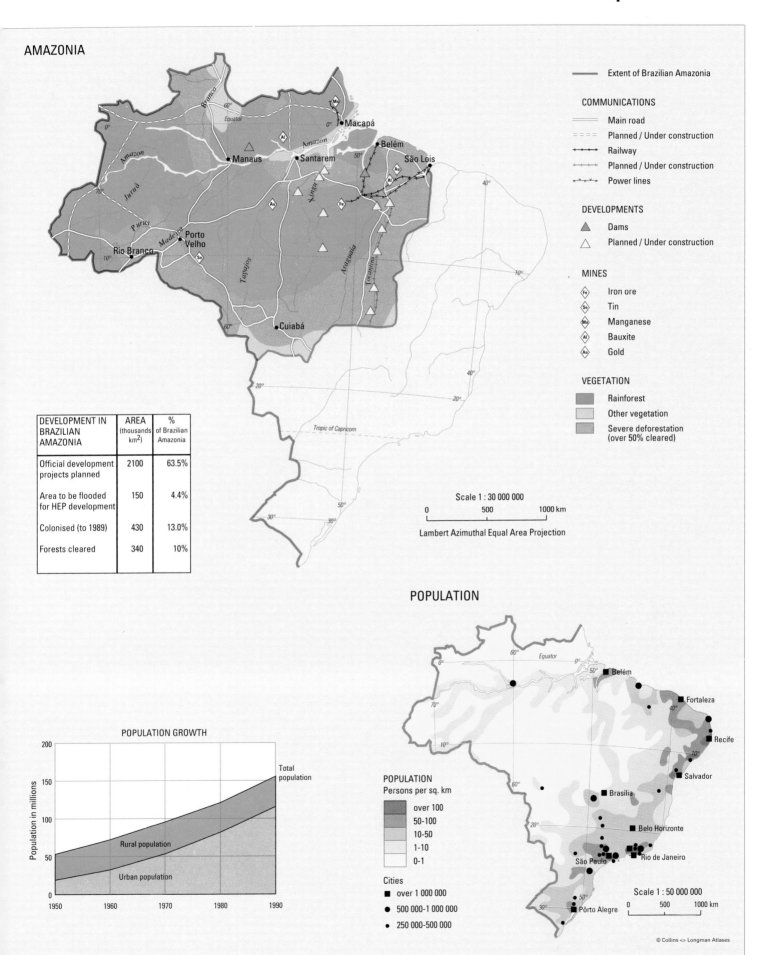

AMAZONIA

| Extent of Brazilian Amazonia |

COMMUNICATIONS

| Main road |
| Planned / Under construction |
| Railway |
| Planned / Under construction |
| Power lines |

DEVELOPMENTS

| Dams |
| Planned / Under construction |

MINES

Fe	Iron ore
Sn	Tin
Mn	Manganese
Al	Bauxite
Au	Gold

VEGETATION

| Rainforest |
| Other vegetation |
| Severe deforestation (over 50% cleared) |

DEVELOPMENT IN BRAZILIAN AMAZONIA	AREA (thousands km²)	% of Brazilian Amazonia
Official development projects planned	2100	63.5%
Area to be flooded for HEP development	150	4.4%
Colonised (to 1989)	430	13.0%
Forests cleared	340	10%

Scale 1 : 30 000 000

0   500   1000 km

Lambert Azimuthal Equal Area Projection

POPULATION GROWTH

Population in millions

Total population

Rural population

Urban population

1950 1960 1970 1980 1990

POPULATION

POPULATION
Persons per sq. km

| over 100 |
| 50-100 |
| 10-50 |
| 1-10 |
| 0-1 |

Cities
- ■ over 1 000 000
- ● 500 000-1 000 000
- • 250 000-500 000

Belém
Fortaleza
Recife
Salvador
Brasília
Belo Horizonte
Rio de Janeiro
São Paulo
Pôrto Alegre

Scale 1 : 50 000 000

0   500   1000 km

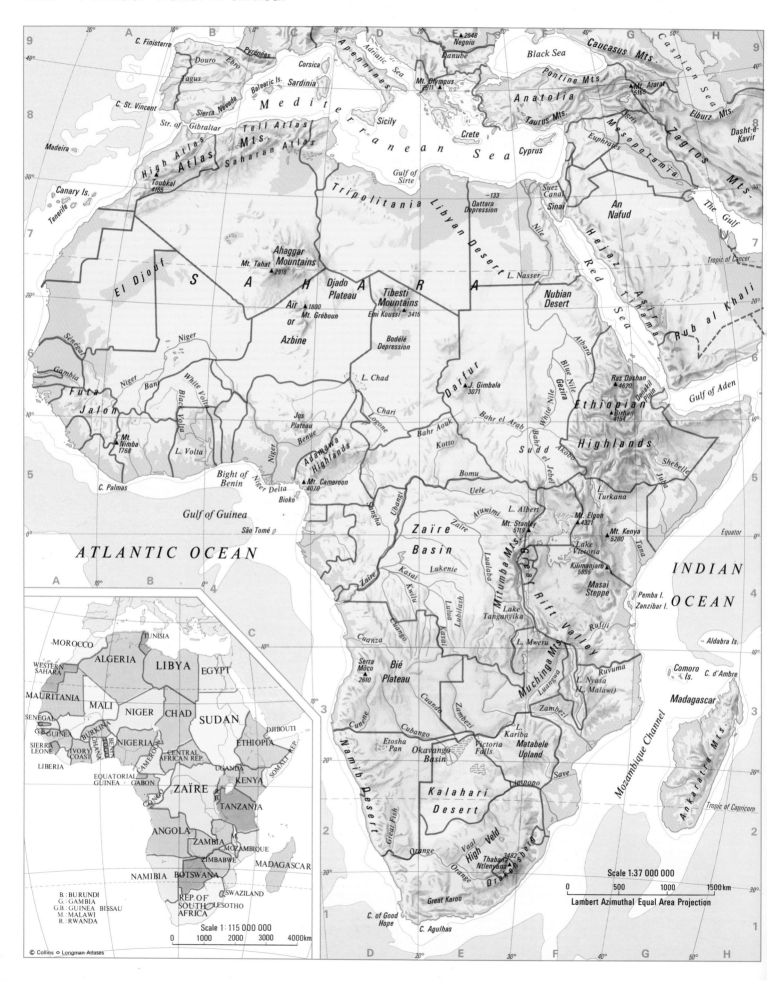

Scale 1:37 000 000

0   500   1000   1500km

Lambert Azimuthal Equal Area Projection

Scale 1:115 000 000

0   1000   2000   3000   4000km

B.: BURUNDI
G.: GAMBIA
G.B.: GUINEA BISSAU
M.: MALAWI
R.: RWANDA

© Collins ○ Longman Atlases

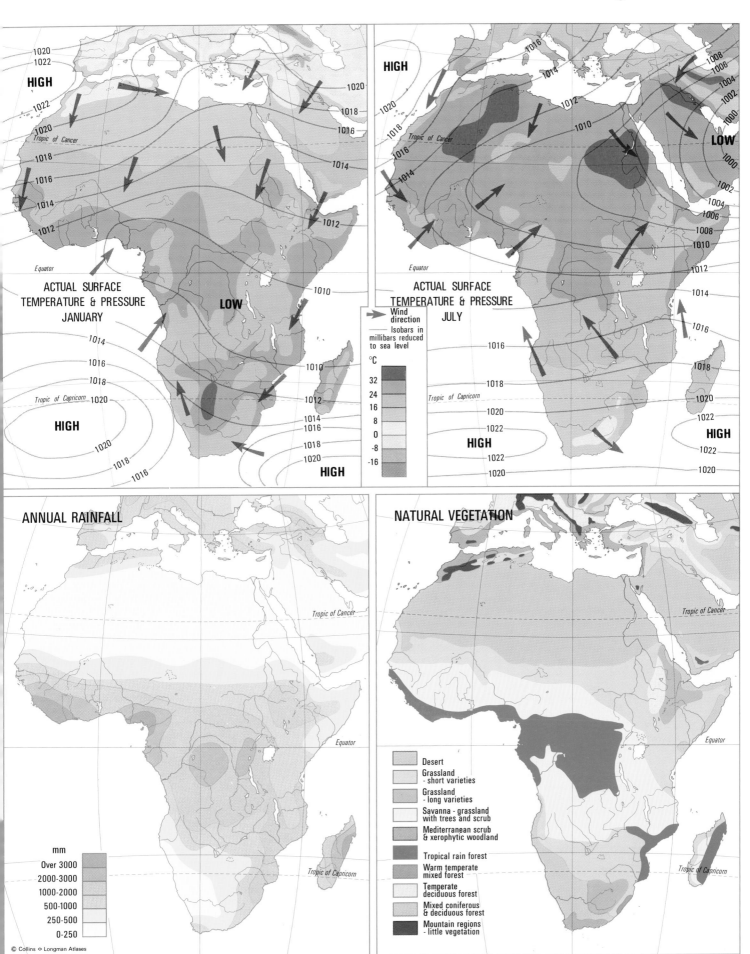

ACTUAL SURFACE TEMPERATURE & PRESSURE JANUARY

HIGH

1020
1022

1022

1020

Tropic of Cancer

1018

1016

1014

1012

Equator

LOW

1014

1016

1018

Tropic of Capricorn 1020

HIGH

1020

1018

1016

1014

1016

1010

1012

1014
1016

1018

1020

HIGH

1020

1018

1016

Wind direction
Isobars in millibars reduced to sea level

°C
32
24
16
8
0
-8
-16

ACTUAL SURFACE TEMPERATURE & PRESSURE JULY

HIGH

1016

1014

1012

1020

1018

1016

Tropic of Cancer

1010

1000

LOW

1002

1004

1006

1008

1010

1012

1014

1016

1018

Equator

1016

1018

Tropic of Capricorn

1020

1022

HIGH

1022

1020

HIGH

1020

1022

ANNUAL RAINFALL

Tropic of Cancer

Equator

Tropic of Capricorn

mm

Over 3000

2000-3000

1000-2000

500-1000

250-500

0-250

© Collins ◇ Longman Atlases

NATURAL VEGETATION

Tropic of Cancer

Equator

Tropic of Capricorn

Desert

Grassland - short varieties

Grassland - long varieties

Savanna - grassland with trees and scrub

Mediterranean scrub & xerophytic woodland

Tropical rain forest

Warm temperate mixed forest

Temperate deciduous forest

Mixed coniferous & deciduous forest

Mountain regions - little vegetation

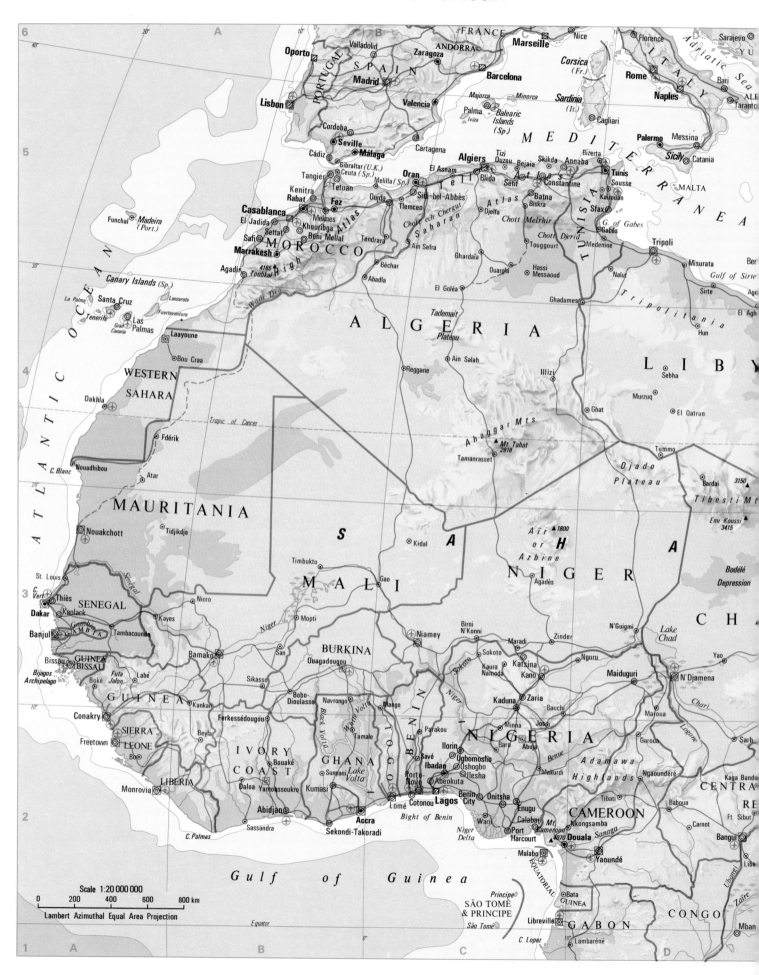

Scale 1:20 000 000

0   200   400   600   800 km

Lambert Azimuthal Equal Area Projection

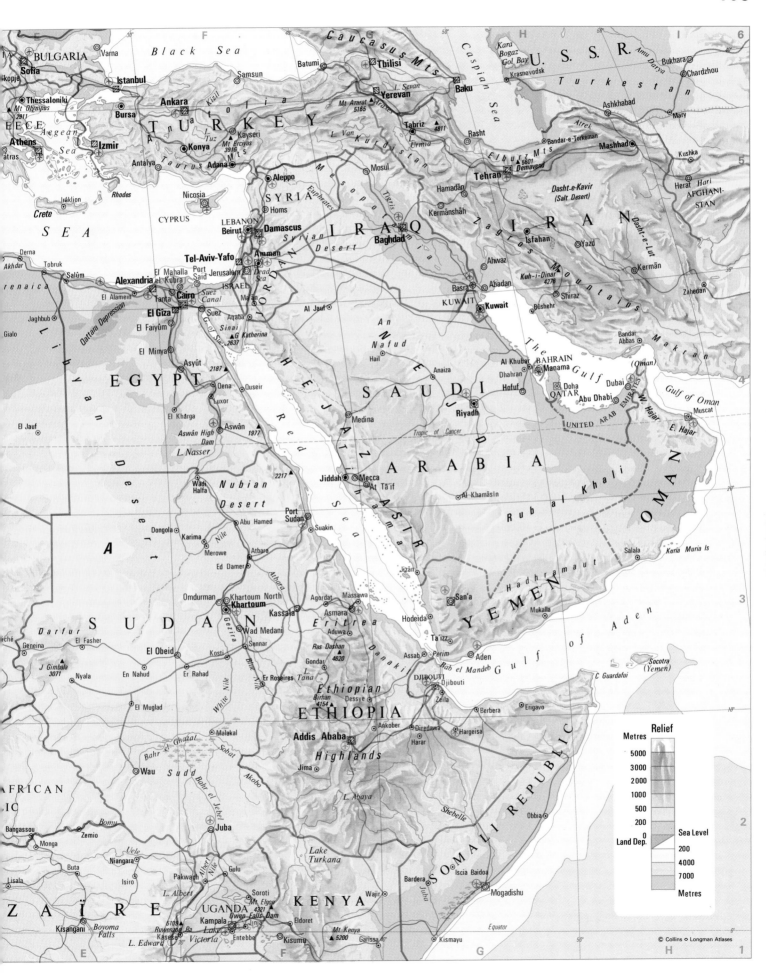

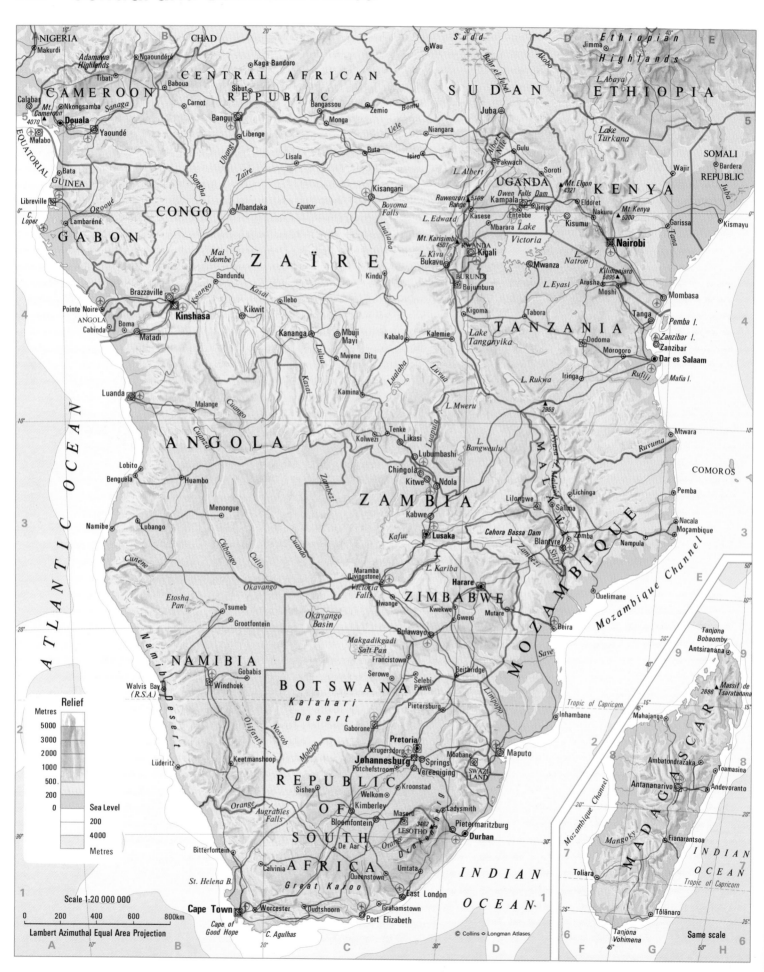

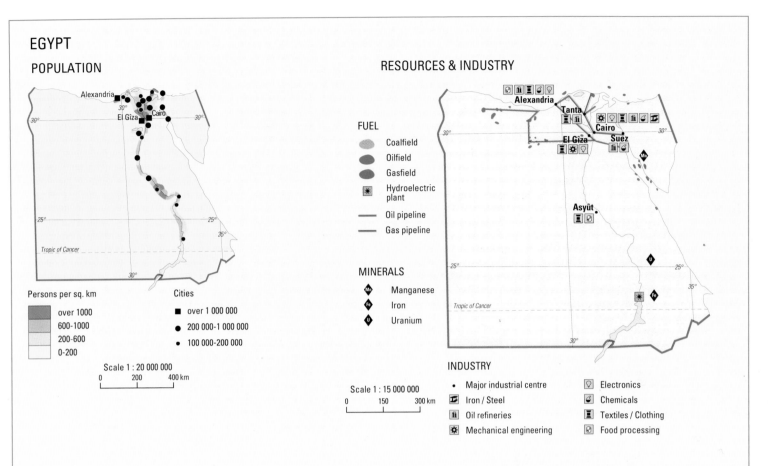

EGYPT
POPULATION

Persons per sq. km

over 1000
600-1000
200-600
0-200

Cities

■ over 1 000 000
● 200 000-1 000 000
• 100 000-200 000

Scale 1 : 20 000 000
0   200   400 km

RESOURCES & INDUSTRY

FUEL

Coalfield
Oilfield
Gasfield
Hydroelectric plant
Oil pipeline
Gas pipeline

MINERALS

Mn Manganese
Fe Iron
U   Uranium

Scale 1 : 15 000 000
0   150   300 km

INDUSTRY

• Major industrial centre
Iron / Steel
Oil refineries
Mechanical engineering
Electronics
Chemicals
Textiles / Clothing
Food processing

KENYA
RESOURCES AND INDUSTRY

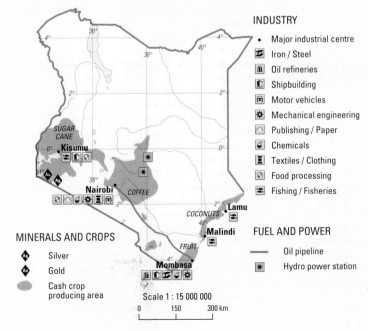

INDUSTRY

• Major industrial centre
Iron / Steel
Oil refineries
Shipbuilding
Motor vehicles
Mechanical engineering
Publishing / Paper
Chemicals
Textiles / Clothing
Food processing
Fishing / Fisheries

FUEL AND POWER

Oil pipeline
Hydro power station

MINERALS AND CROPS

Ag Silver
Au Gold
Cash crop producing area

Scale 1 : 15 000 000
0   150   300 km

POPULATION

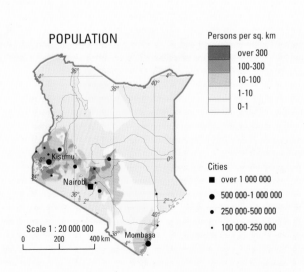

Persons per sq. km

over 300
100-300
10-100
1-10
0-1

Cities

■ over 1 000 000
● 500 000-1 000 000
• 250 000-500 000
· 100 000-250 000

Scale 1 : 20 000 000
0   200   400 km

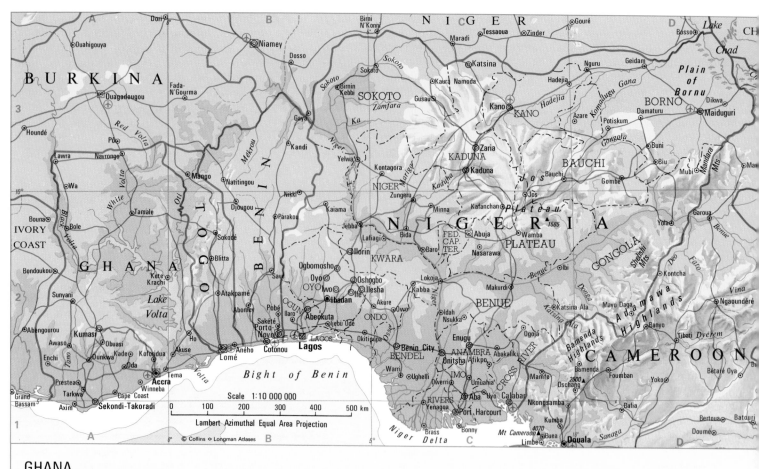

Scale 1:10 000 000

0   100   200   300   400   500 km

Lambert Azimuthal Equal Area Projection

© Collins ◇ Longman Atlases

GHANA

POPULATION

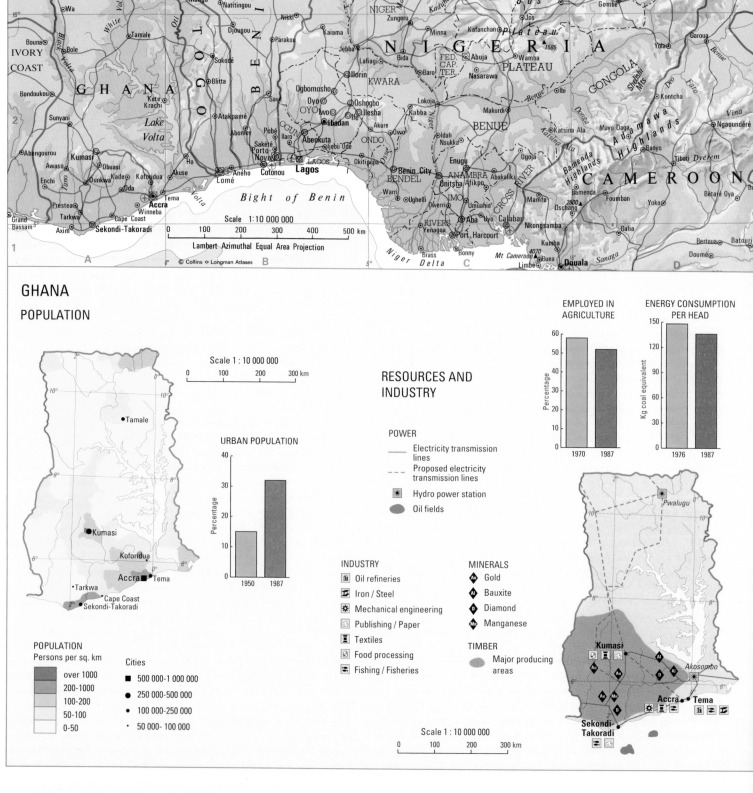

Scale 1 : 10 000 000

0   100   200   300 km

URBAN POPULATION

POPULATION
Persons per sq. km

- over 1000
- 200-1000
- 100-200
- 50-100
- 0-50

Cities
- ■ 500 000-1 000 000
- ● 250 000-500 000
- • 100 000-250 000
- · 50 000- 100 000

RESOURCES AND INDUSTRY

POWER

- —— Electricity transmission lines
- ---- Proposed electricity transmission lines
- ✳ Hydro power station
- ⬮ Oil fields

INDUSTRY

- Oil refineries
- Iron / Steel
- Mechanical engineering
- Publishing / Paper
- Textiles
- Food processing
- Fishing / Fisheries

MINERALS

- ◆ Au Gold
- ◆ Al Bauxite
- ◆ D Diamond
- ◆ Mn Manganese

TIMBER

- Major producing areas

EMPLOYED IN AGRICULTURE

ENERGY CONSUMPTION PER HEAD

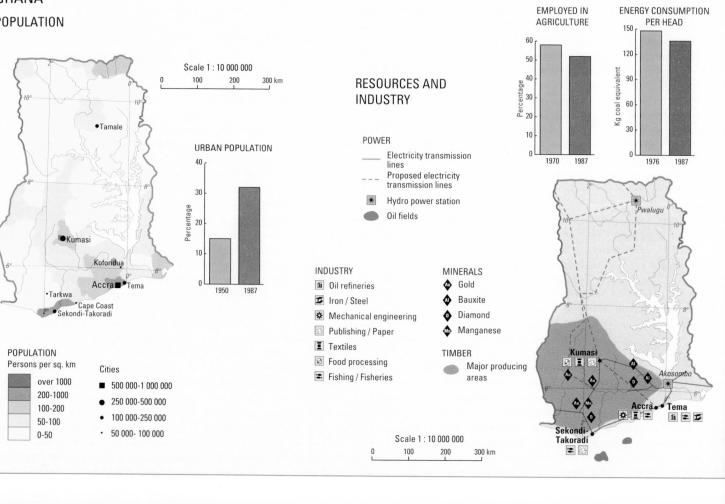

Scale 1 : 10 000 000

0   100   200   300 km

NIGERIA
POPULATION

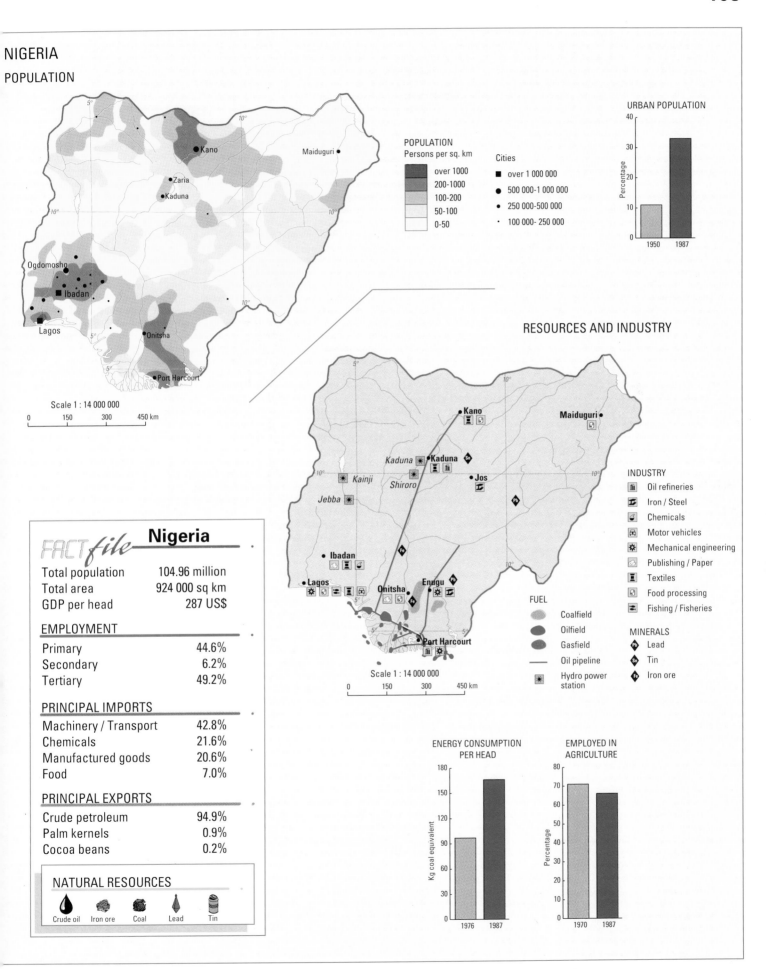

URBAN POPULATION

POPULATION
Persons per sq. km

	over 1000
	200-1000
	100-200
	50-100
	0-50

Cities

■ over 1 000 000
● 500 000-1 000 000
● 250 000-500 000
· 100 000- 250 000

Scale 1 : 14 000 000

0   150   300   450 km

RESOURCES AND INDUSTRY

INDUSTRY

🗊 Oil refineries
🡒 Iron / Steel
🗋 Chemicals
🏭 Motor vehicles
✿ Mechanical engineering
🗏 Publishing / Paper
▤ Textiles
🗐 Food processing
🡒 Fishing / Fisheries

FUEL

Coalfield
Oilfield
Gasfield
— Oil pipeline
✳ Hydro power station

MINERALS

Pb Lead
Sn Tin
Fe Iron ore

Scale 1 : 14 000 000

0   150   300   450 km

FACTfile Nigeria

Total population	104.96 million
Total area	924 000 sq km
GDP per head	287 US$

EMPLOYMENT

Primary	44.6%
Secondary	6.2%
Tertiary	49.2%

PRINCIPAL IMPORTS

Machinery / Transport	42.8%
Chemicals	21.6%
Manufactured goods	20.6%
Food	7.0%

PRINCIPAL EXPORTS

Crude petroleum	94.9%
Palm kernels	0.9%
Cocoa beans	0.2%

NATURAL RESOURCES

Crude oil   Iron ore   Coal   Lead   Tin

ENERGY CONSUMPTION PER HEAD

Kg coal equivalent

1976   1987

EMPLOYED IN AGRICULTURE

Percentage

1970   1987

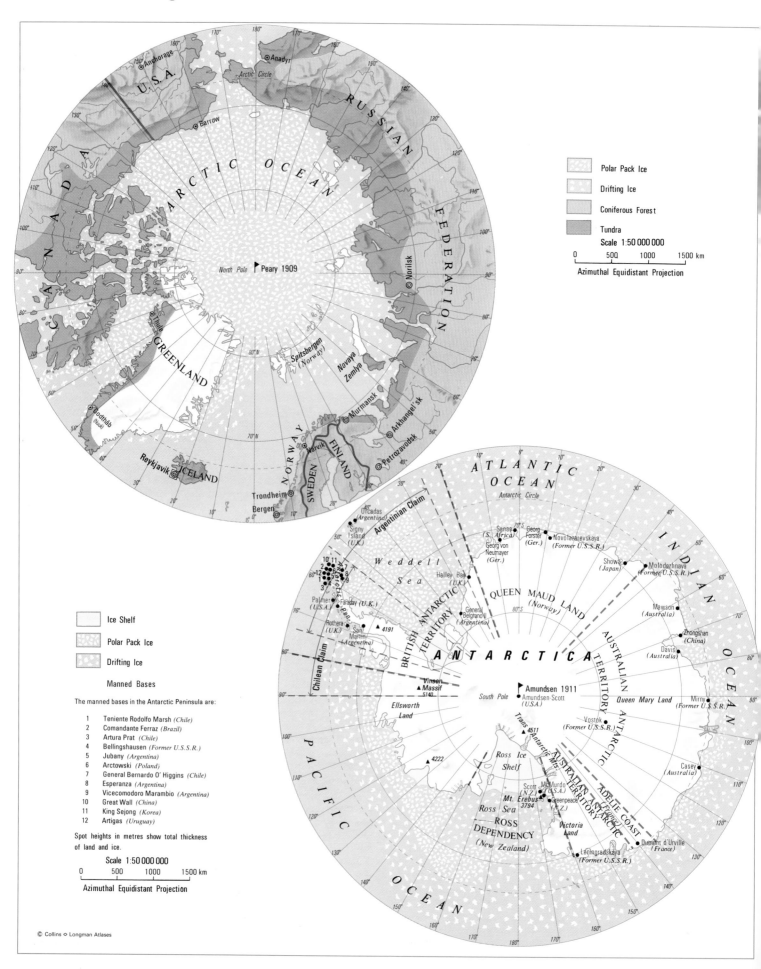

Polar Pack Ice
Drifting Ice
Coniferous Forest
Tundra
Scale 1:50 000 000
0   500   1000   1500 km
Azimuthal Equidistant Projection

Ice Shelf
Polar Pack Ice
Drifting Ice

Manned Bases

The manned bases in the Antarctic Peninsula are:

1   Teniente Rodolfo Marsh *(Chile)*
2   Comandante Ferraz *(Brazil)*
3   Artura Prat *(Chile)*
4   Bellingshausen *(Former U.S.S.R.)*
5   Jubany *(Argentina)*
6   Arctowski *(Poland)*
7   General Bernardo O' Higgins *(Chile)*
8   Esperanza *(Argentina)*
9   Vicecomodoro Marambio *(Argentina)*
10   Great Wall *(China)*
11   King Sejong *(Korea)*
12   Artigas *(Uruguay)*

Spot heights in metres show total thickness of land and ice.

Scale 1:50 000 000
0   500   1000   1500 km
Azimuthal Equidistant Projection

© Collins ◇ Longman Atlases

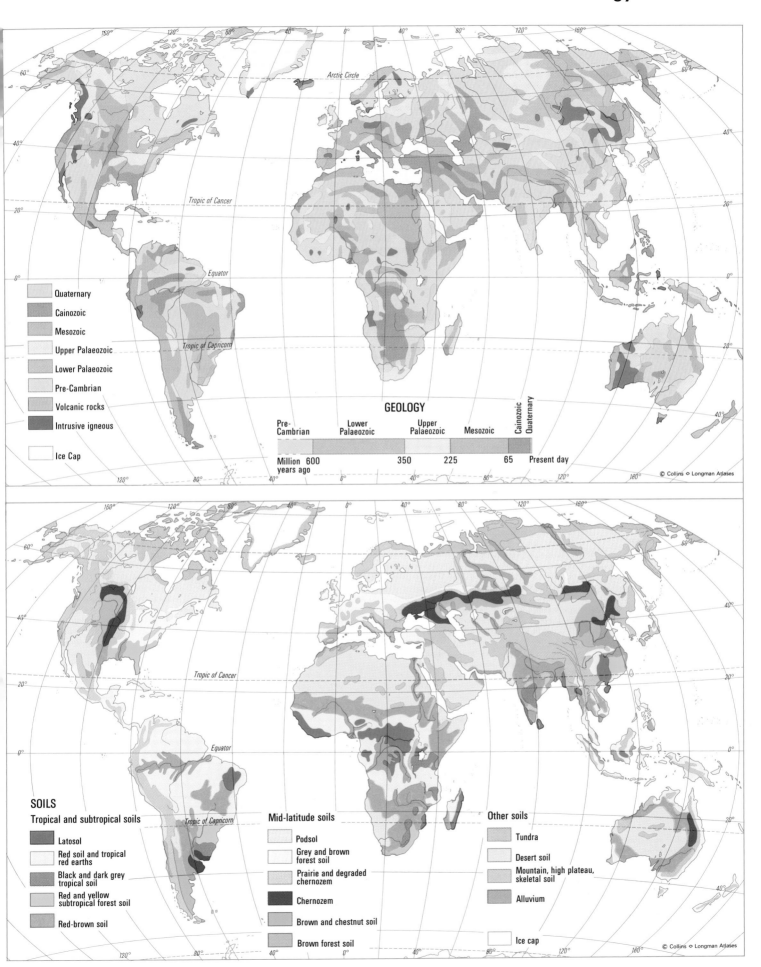

GEOLOGY

Quaternary
Cainozoic
Mesozoic
Upper Palaeozoic
Lower Palaeozoic
Pre-Cambrian
Volcanic rocks
Intrusive igneous
Ice Cap

Pre-Cambrian	Lower Palaeozoic	Upper Palaeozoic	Mesozoic	Cainozoic Quaternary

Million years ago 600   350   225   65   Present day

© Collins ○ Longman Atlases

SOILS

Tropical and subtropical soils

Latosol
Red soil and tropical red earths
Black and dark grey tropical soil
Red and yellow subtropical forest soil
Red-brown soil

Mid-latitude soils

Podsol
Grey and brown forest soil
Prairie and degraded chernozem
Chernozem
Brown and chestnut soil
Brown forest soil

Other soils

Tundra
Desert soil
Mountain, high plateau, skeletal soil
Alluvium
Ice cap

© Collins ○ Longman Atlases

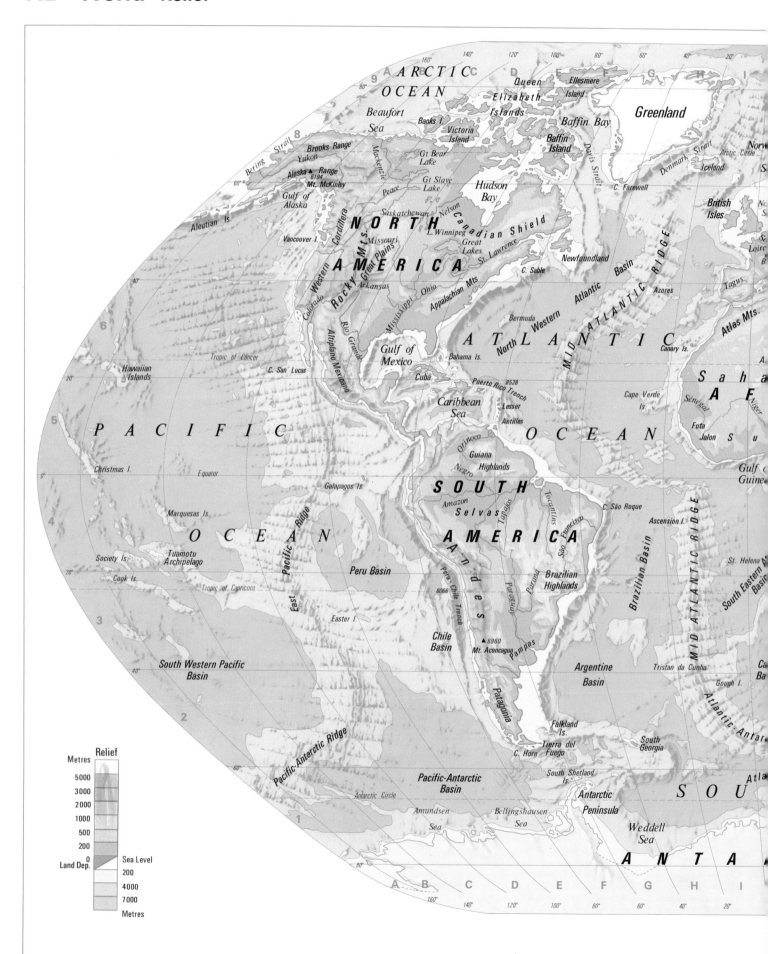

Relief

Metres

5000	
3000	
2000	
1000	
500	
200	
0	
Land Dep.	Sea Level
200	
4000	
7000	
Metres	

ARCTIC OCEAN

Queen Elizabeth Islands
Ellesmere Island
Greenland

Beaufort Sea
Banks I.
Victoria Island
Baffin Bay
Baffin Island

Bering Strait
Brooks Range
Yukon
Alaska Range ▲6194
Mt. McKinley
Gt Bear Lake
Mackenzie
Gt Slave Lake
Hudson Bay
Davis Strait
C. Farewell
Denmark Strait
Iceland
Arctic Circle
Norw

Gulf of Alaska
Aleutian Is.
Vancouver I.
Peace
Saskatchewan
Nelson
Canadian Shield
L. Winnipeg
Great Lakes
St. Lawrence
Newfoundland
C. Sable
British Isles
Loire

NORTH AMERICA
Western Cordillera
Rocky Mts.
Great Plains
Missouri
Arkansas
Mississippi
Ohio
Appalachian Mts
Bermuda
North Western Atlantic Basin
MID ATLANTIC RIDGE
Azores
Tagus
Atlas Mts.

Colorado
Rio Grande
Altiplano Mexicano
Gulf of Mexico
Bahama Is.
ATLANTIC
Canary Is.
Saha
AF

Tropic of Cancer
C. San Lucas
Cuba
Puerto Rico Trench 8528
Caribbean Sea
Lesser Antilles
OCEAN
Cape Verde Is.
Senegal
Futa Jalon
Su

Hawaiian Islands

PACIFIC
Christmas I.
Equator
Galapagos Is.
Orinoco
Negro
Guiana Highlands
SOUTH
Amazon Selvas
AMERICA
Gulf of Guine

Marquesas Is.
Society Is.
Tuamotu Archipelago
Cook Is.
East Pacific Ridge
OCEAN
Peru Basin
Andes
Peru Chile Trench
Tocantins
Tapajós
São Francisco
Paraguay
Paraná
Brazilian Highlands
Brazilian Basin
MID ATLANTIC RIDGE
Ascension I.
St. Helena I.
South Eastern Basin

Tropic of Capricorn
Easter I.
8066
Mt. Aconcagua ▲6960
Pampas
Argentine Basin
Tristan da Cunha
Ca Ba

South Western Pacific Basin
Chile Basin
Patagonia
Gough I.
Atlantic-Antar

Pacific-Antarctic Ridge
Falkland Is.
Tierra del Fuego
C. Horn
South Georgia
South Shetland Is.

Pacific-Antarctic Basin
Antarctic Circle
Amundsen Sea
Bellingshausen Sea
Antarctic Peninsula
Weddell Sea
Atla
SOU

ANTA
ANTA

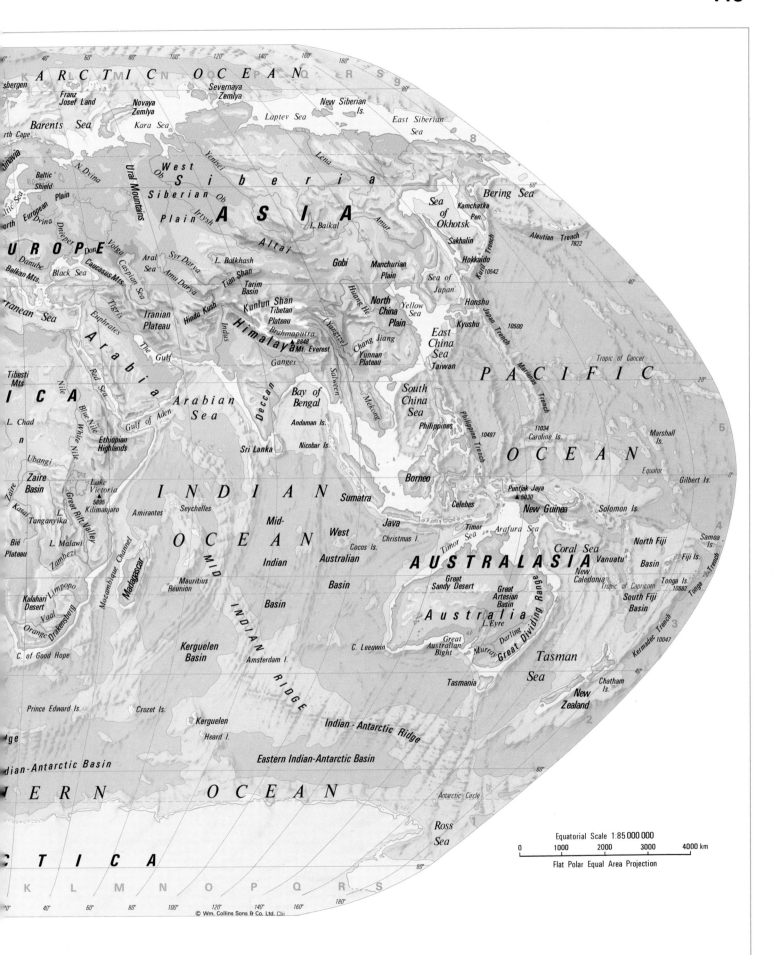

ARCTIC OCEAN

Spitsbergen
Franz Josef Land
Novaya Zemlya
Severnaya Zemlya
New Siberian Is.
East Siberian Sea

Barents Sea
Kara Sea
Laptev Sea

rth Cape
N. Dvina
Ural Mountains
West Siberian Plain
Yenisei
Ob
Lena
Sea of Okhotsk
Bering Sea
Kamchatka Pen.

Baltic Shield
Siberian Plain
Ob
Irtysh
ASIA
L. Baikal
Amur
Sakhalin
Aleutian Trench 7822

ltic Sea
European Plain
Dvina
Dnieper
Volga
Caspian Sea
Altai
Gobi
Manchurian Plain
Sea of Japan
Hokkaido
Kuril Trench 10542

EUROPE
Don
Volga
Caucasus Mts.
Aral Sea
Amu Darya
Syr Darya
L. Balkhash
Tian Shan
Tarim Basin
Kunlun Shan
Tibetan Plateau
Huang He
(Yangtze)
North China Plain
Yellow Sea
Honshu
Japan Trench 10500

Black Sea
Balkan Mts.
Danube
Tigris
Euphrates
Iranian Plateau
Hindu Kush
Himalaya
8848 Mt. Everest
Brahmaputra
Chang Jiang
Yunnan Plateau
East China Sea
Kyushu

ranean Sea
The Gulf
Indus
Ganges
Salween
Taiwan
PACIFIC
Tropic of Cancer

Tibesti Mts
Nile
Red Sea
Arabia
Deccan
Bay of Bengal
Mekong
South China Sea
Mariana Trench
OCEAN

ICA
Blue Nile
Gulf of Aden
Arabian Sea
Andaman Is.
Philippines
Philippine Trench 10497
11034 Caroline Is.
Marshall Is.

L. Chad
White Nile
Ethiopian Highlands
Sri Lanka
Nicobar Is.

Ubangi
Borneo
Puntjak Jaya 5030
Equator
Gilbert Is.

Zaire Basin
Lake Victoria
5895 Kilimanjaro
Amirantes
Seychelles
INDIAN
Sumatra
Celebes
New Guinea
Solomon Is.

Kasai
Tanganyika
Mid-Indian
West Australian
Java
Timor Sea
Arafura Sea

Bié Plateau
L. Malawi
Zambezi
OCEAN
Cocos Is.
Christmas I.
Timor Sea
AUSTRALASIA
Coral Sea
North Fiji
Samoa Is.

Kalahari Desert
Limpopo
Madagascar
Mauritius
Réunion
Basin
Basin
Great Sandy Desert
Great Artesian Basin
Vanuatu
New Caledonia
Basin
Fiji Is.

Vaal
Orange
Drakensberg
Mozambique Channel
Australia
L. Eyre
Great Dividing Range
Tropic of Capricorn
Tonga Is.
10882
South Fiji Basin
Tonga Trench

C. of Good Hope
Kerguelen Basin
Amsterdam I.
Basin
C. Leeuwin
Great Australian Bight
Murray
Darling
Tasman Sea
Kermadec Trench 10047

Prince Edward Is.
Crozet Is.
Kerguelen
MID INDIAN RIDGE
Tasmania
Chatham Is.
New Zealand

Heard I.
Indian - Antarctic Ridge

dian-Antarctic Basin
Eastern Indian-Antarctic Basin

ERN OCEAN
Antarctic Circle

CTICA
Ross Sea

Equatorial Scale 1:85 000 000

0   1000   2000   3000   4000 km

Flat Polar Equal Area Projection

© Wm. Collins Sons & Co. Ltd. Cbi

ARCTIC OCEAN

GREENLAND

Godthåb
Reykjavik ICELAND

U.S.A.
ALASKA

C A N A D A

Edmonton

UNITED DEN
KINGDOM
REP. OF Dublin Amst
IRELAND London Brussels B
Vancouver Winnipeg Paris FRANCE

Seattle Ottawa Montreal
Chicago Detroit Toronto PORTUGAL Madrid
San Francisco UNITED STATES Pittsburgh Boston Lisbon SPAIN M
New York Algiers
OF AMERICA St. Louis Philadelphia Rabat MOROCCO

Los Angeles Washington ATLANTIC

Canary Is. ALGERI
Dallas (Sp.)
Houston Bermuda OCEAN Laayoune
(U.K.) WESTERN
Tropic of Cancer SAHARA
Miami
Monterrey Nassau MAURITANIA MALI
Hawaiian Is. Havana BAHAMAS Nouakchott
(U.S.A.) CUBA
Guadalajara Mexico City JAMAICA HAITI DOMINICAN SENEGAL Bamako Niame
REP. PUERTO Dakar Ouagadoug
BELIZE RICO GAMBIA BURKINA NIG
Belmopan ANTIGUA Bissau GUINEA
GUAT. HONDURAS Kingston DOMINICA G.B. IVORY Abuj
Guatemala City Tegucigalpa ST. LUCIA Conakry GUINEA COAST La
EL SALVADOR NICARAGUA Freetown Yamoussoukro
P A C I F I C Managua Caracas TRINIDAD SIERRA LEONE Accra Porto-Novo
San José & TOBAGO Monrovia Lome EQUATO
COSTA VENEZUELA Georgetown LIBERIA GUIN
RICA PANAMA Paramaribo Libre
KIRIBATI Panama SURINAM Cayenne
Bogotá GUYANA (Fr.)
COLOMBIA

Quito
Galapagos Is. ECUADOR
(Ec.) Recife Ascension I.
Marquesas Is. (U.K.)
(Fr.) BRAZIL
O C E A N PERU
Lima ATLANTIC
Tuamotu Archipelago La Paz Brasília
Cook Is. BOLIVIA St. Helena
Samoa (N.Z.) Sucre Belo Horizonte (U.K.)
(U.S.A.) Society Is.
Tropic of Capricorn (Fr.) PARAGUAY Rio de Janeiro OCEAN
São Paulo
Easter I. Asunción
(Chile) URUGUAY
CHILE Tristan da Cunha (U.K.)
ARGENTINA
Montevideo Gough I. (U.K.)
Santiago Buenos
Aires

Falkland Is.
(U.K.)

South Georgia
(U.K.)

Argentinian Claim
Chilean Claim

Antarctic Circle

BRITISH ANTARCTIC TERRITORY NORWEGIA

Anta

A. : ANDORRA
ALB. : ALBANIA
AR. : ARMENIA
AUS. : AUSTRIA
AZ. : AZERBAIJAN
B. : BELGIUM
BANGLA. : BANGLADESH
BULG. : BULGARIA
CAM. : CAMBODIA
CZECH. : CZECHOSLOVAKIA
EST. : ESTONIA
G. : GEORGIA
G.B. : GUINEA BISSAU
GUAT. : GUATEMALA
HUNG. : HUNGARY
KIRG. : KIRGIZIA
L. : LUXEMBOURG
LAT. : LATVIA
LEB. : LEBANON
LITH. : LITHUANIA
M. : MONACO
MOL. : MOLDAVIA
NETH. : NETHERLANDS
S. : SWITZERLAND
S.M. : SAN MARINO
T. : TURKEY (in Europe)
TAJ. : TAJIKISTAN
U.A.E. : UNITED ARAB EMIRATES
UZBEK. : UZBEKISTAN
W.GER. : WEST GERMANY
YUGO. : YUGOSLAVIA

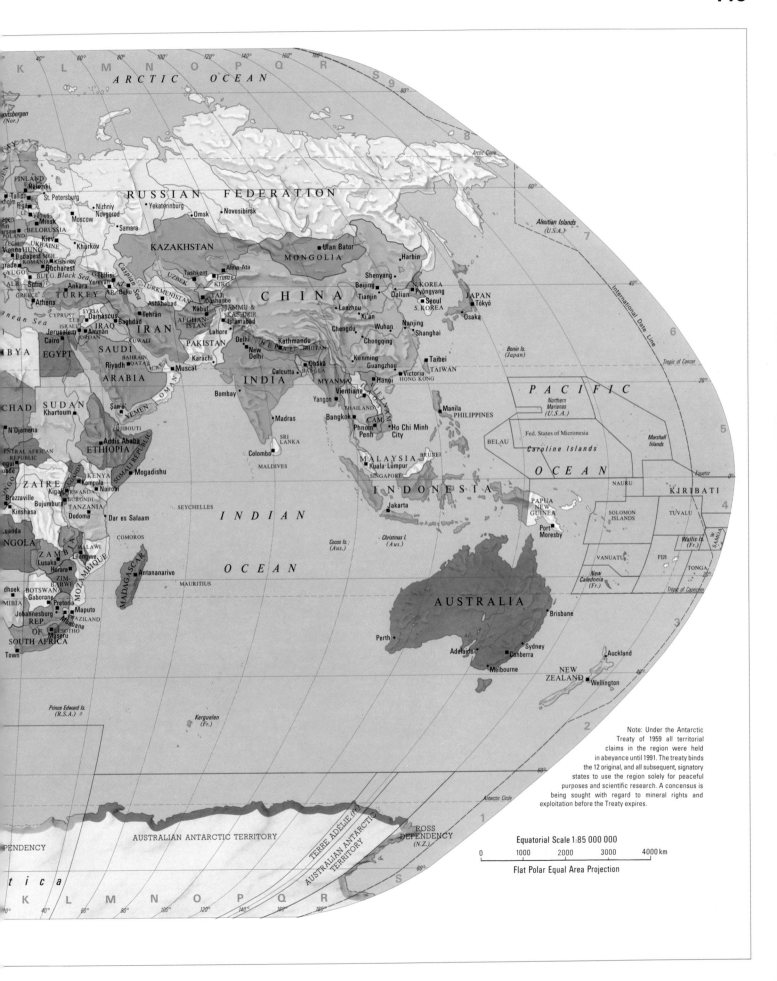

Note: Under the Antarctic Treaty of 1959 all territorial claims in the region were held in abeyance until 1991. The treaty binds the 12 original, and all subsequent, signatory states to use the region solely for peaceful purposes and scientific research. A concensus is being sought with regard to mineral rights and exploitation before the Treaty expires.

Equatorial Scale 1:85 000 000

0   1000   2000   3000   4000 km

Flat Polar Equal Area Projection

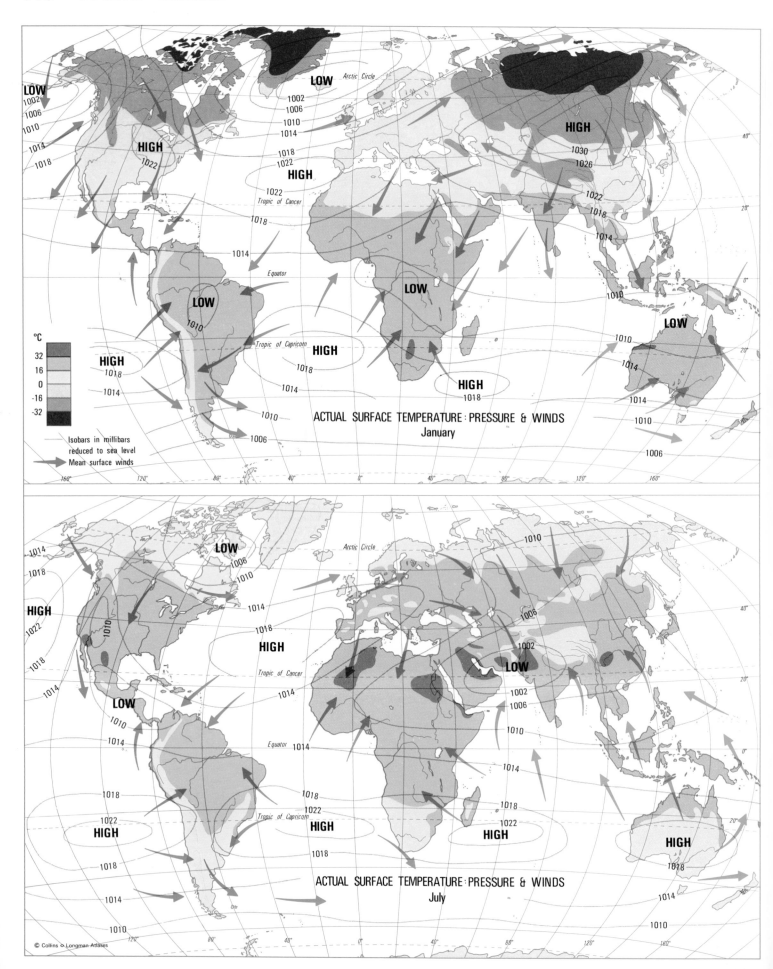

°C

32	
16	
0	
-16	
-32	

Isobars in millibars
reduced to sea level
Mean surface winds

ACTUAL SURFACE TEMPERATURE: PRESSURE & WINDS
January

ACTUAL SURFACE TEMPERATURE: PRESSURE & WINDS
July

© Collins ◇ Longman Atlases

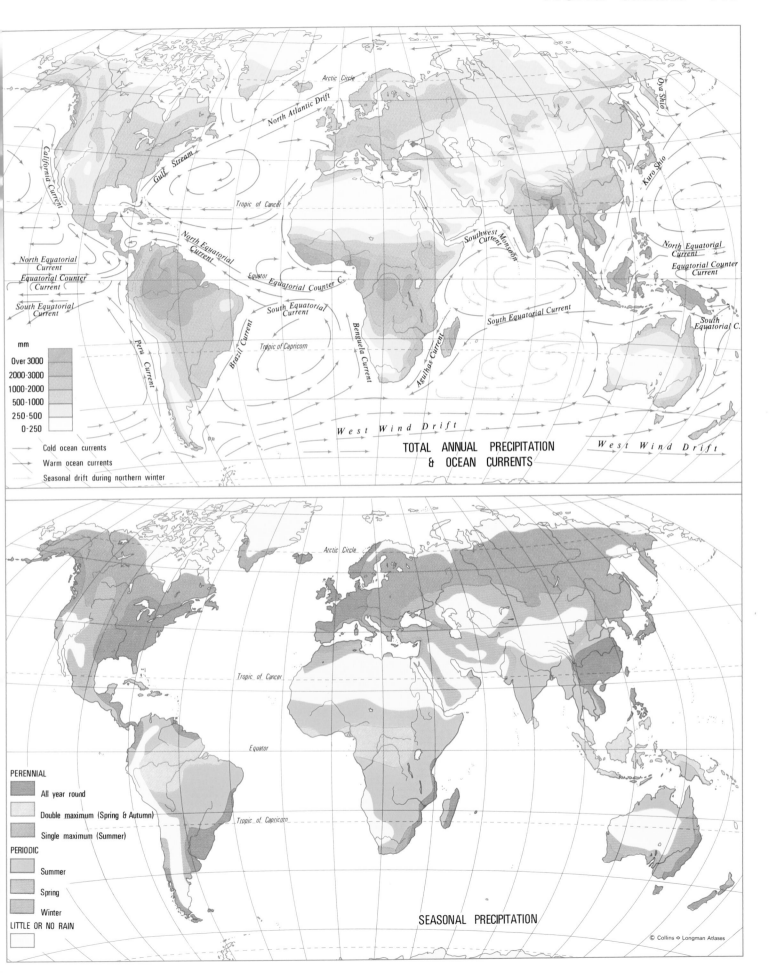

mm
- Over 3000
- 2000-3000
- 1000-2000
- 500-1000
- 250-500
- 0-250

→ Cold ocean currents
→ Warm ocean currents
→ Seasonal drift during northern winter

Arctic Circle
North Atlantic Drift
Gulf Stream
Tropic of Cancer
California Current
North Equatorial Current
Equatorial Counter Current
South Equatorial Current
Peru Current
Brazil Current
Tropic of Capricorn
Equator
Equatorial Counter C.
South Equatorial Current
Benguela Current
Agulhas Current
South Equatorial Current
Southwest Monsoon Current
North Equatorial Current
Equatorial Counter Current
South Equatorial C.
Oya Shio
Kuro Shio
West Wind Drift
West Wind Drift

TOTAL ANNUAL PRECIPITATION & OCEAN CURRENTS

PERENNIAL
- All year round
- Double maximum (Spring & Autumn)
- Single maximum (Summer)

PERIODIC
- Summer
- Spring
- Winter

LITTLE OR NO RAIN

Arctic Circle
Tropic of Cancer
Equator
Tropic of Capricorn

SEASONAL PRECIPITATION

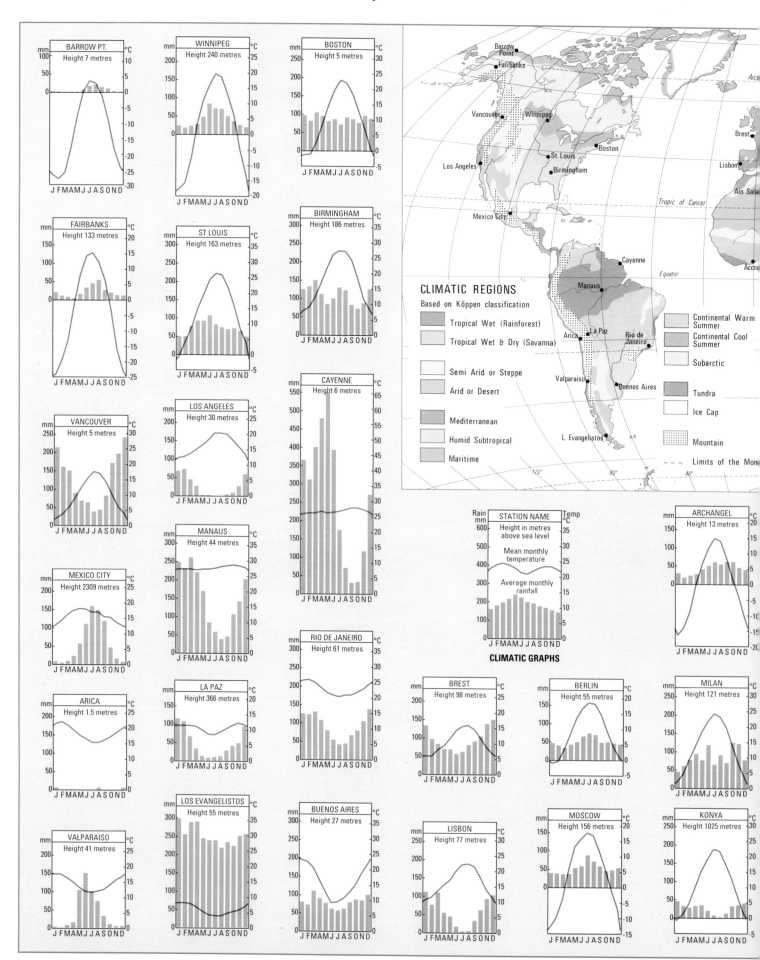

CLIMATIC REGIONS
Based on Köppen classification

Tropical Wet (Rainforest)

Tropical Wet & Dry (Savanna)

Semi Arid or Steppe

Arid or Desert

Mediterranean

Humid Subtropical

Maritime

Continental Warm Summer

Continental Cool Summer

Subarctic

Tundra

Ice Cap

Mountain

Limits of the Mon

CLIMATIC GRAPHS

STATION NAME
Height in metres above sea level
Mean monthly temperature
Average monthly rainfall

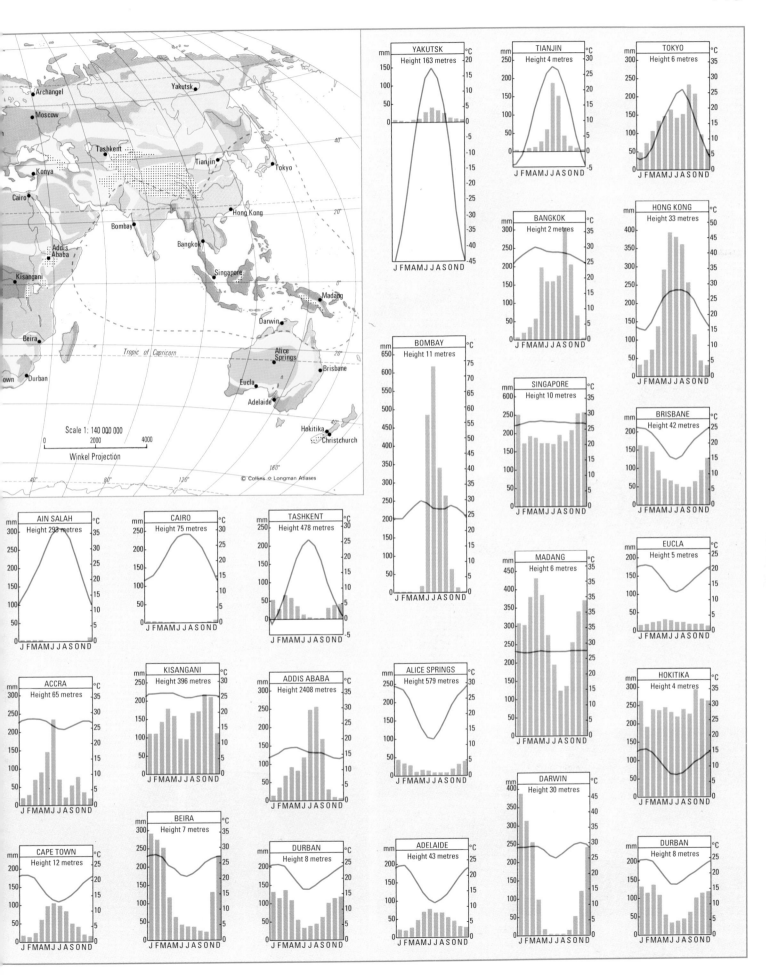

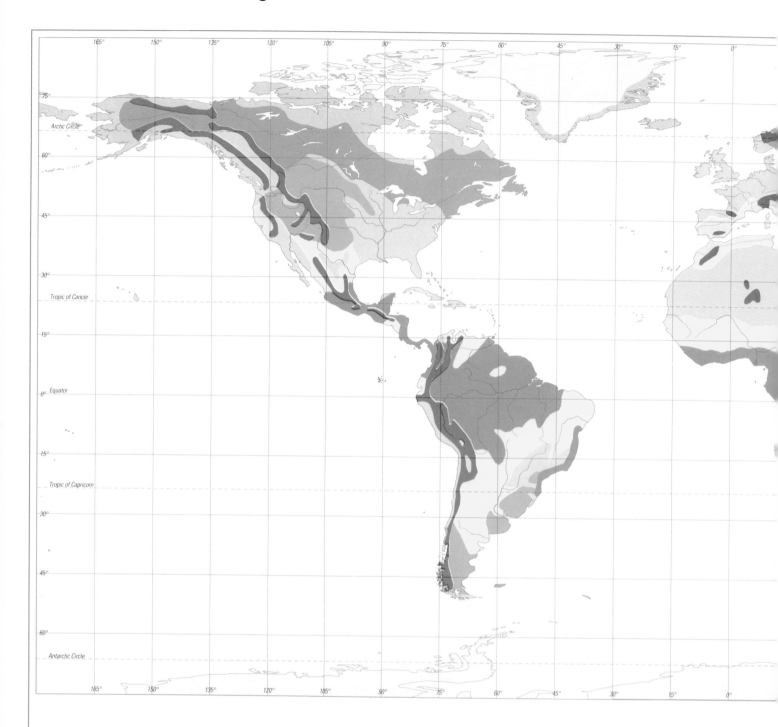

Ice cap, Antarctica

Tundra, Norway

Coniferous forest, Canada

Temperate deciduous forest, UK

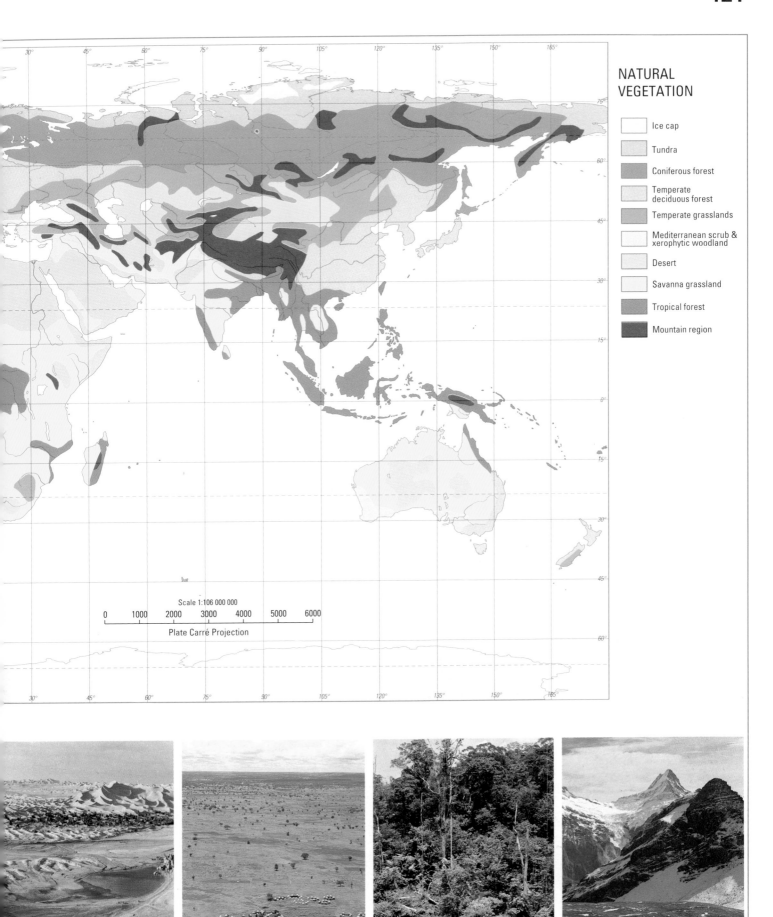

NATURAL VEGETATION

- Ice cap
- Tundra
- Coniferous forest
- Temperate deciduous forest
- Temperate grasslands
- Mediterranean scrub & xerophytic woodland
- Desert
- Savanna grassland
- Tropical forest
- Mountain region

Scale 1:106 000 000

0   1000   2000   3000   4000   5000   6000

Plate Carré Projection

...sert, Iran

Savanna grassland, Nigeria

Tropical forest, Malaysia

Mountain region, Nepal

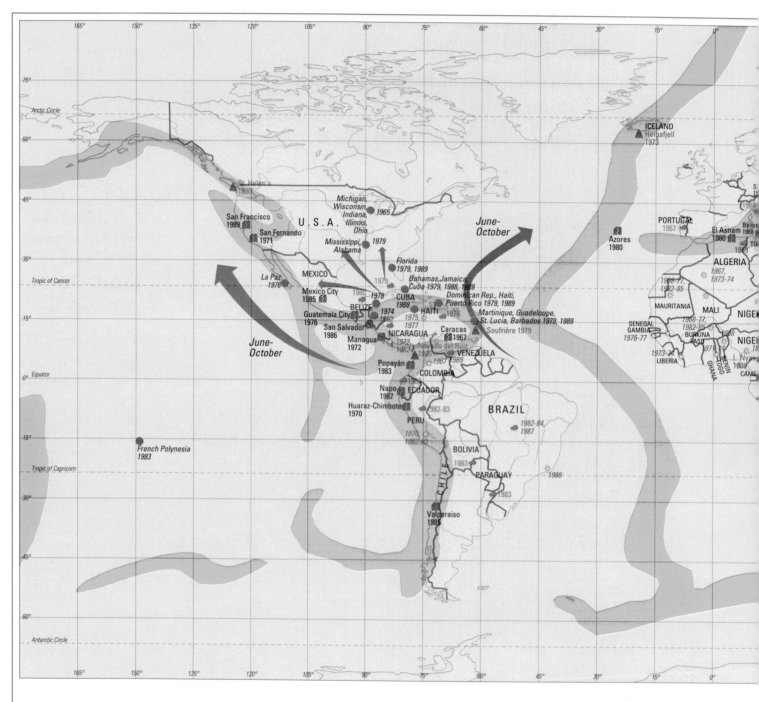

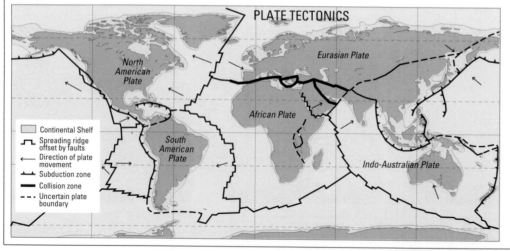

Volcanic eruption, Mt. St. Helens, USA

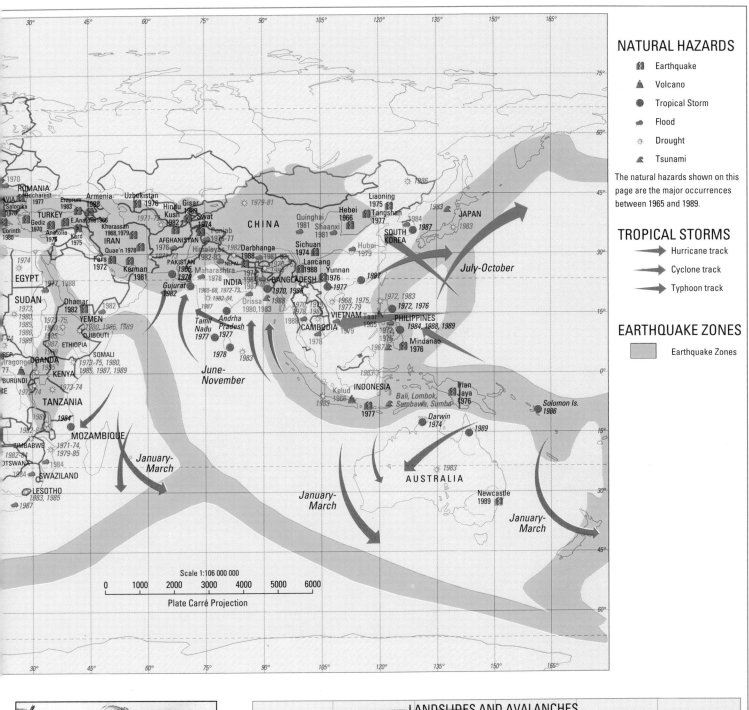

NATURAL HAZARDS

- 🏚 Earthquake
- ▲ Volcano
- ● Tropical Storm
- 🦐 Flood
- ☼ Drought
- 🌊 Tsunami

The natural hazards shown on this page are the major occurrences between 1965 and 1989.

TROPICAL STORMS

→ Hurricane track
→ Cyclone track
→ Typhoon track

EARTHQUAKE ZONES

Earthquake Zones

Scale 1:106 000 000

0 1000 2000 3000 4000 5000 6000

Plate Carré Projection

(Map labels include:) ROMANIA, Bucharest 1977, Erzurum 1983, Armenia 1988, Uzbekistan, Gisar 1989, Hindu Kush, Swat 1974, Liaoning 1975, Tangshan 1977, CHINA, Hebei 1966, Shaanxi 1981, Quinghai 1981, 1979-81, Sichuan 1974, Hubei 1979, JAPAN, 1986, 1983, 1984, 1987, SOUTH KOREA, July-October, TURKEY, Gediz 1970, E.Anatolia 1966, Corinth 1980, Anatolia 1975, Kurd 1975, IRAN, Fars 1972, Quae'n 1978, Kerman 1981, AFGHANISTAN 1975-77, 1976, Khorassan 1968,1979, Punjab 1982, PAKISTAN, 1966, Maharashtra 1970, Himalayas 1982-83, NEPAL, Darbhanga 1988, 1981, Lancang 1988, Yunnan 1976, 1977, 1987, Taal 1965, PHILIPPINES 1984, 1988, 1989, Mindanao 1976, 1967, EGYPT, SUDAN, 1977, 1988, Dhamar 1982, 1973, YEMEN, DJIBOUTI, 1980, 1985, 1986, 1989, ETHIOPIA, SOMALI, 1973-75, 1980, 1985, 1987, 1989, UGANDA, KENYA, 1973-74, BURUNDI, TANZANIA 1984, 1982-84, ZIMBABWE 1971-74, 1979-85, BOTSWANA 1984, SWAZILAND, LESOTHO 1983, 1985, 1987, MOZAMBIQUE, January-March, INDIA, Gujurat 1982, Tamil Nadu 1977, Andrha Pradesh 1977, 1978, 1983, Orissa 1980,1983, 1965-68, 1972-73, 1982-84, 1987, BANGLADESH 1970, 1988, VIETNAM, CAMBODIA 1978, June-November, 1968, 1975, 1977-79, 1978, 1985, 1970, 1976, 1972, 1983, 1972, 1976, INDONESIA, Kelud 1966, Bali, Lombok, Sumbawa, Sumba 1977, Irian Jaya 1976, Solomon Is. 1986, Darwin 1974, 1989, AUSTRALIA, 1983, Newcastle 1989, January-March

Earthquake damage, Armenia

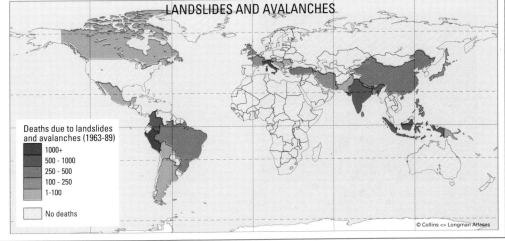

LANDSLIDES AND AVALANCHES

Deaths due to landslides and avalanches (1963-89)

- 1000+
- 500 - 1000
- 250 - 500
- 100 - 250
- 1-100
- No deaths

© Collins <> Longman Atlases

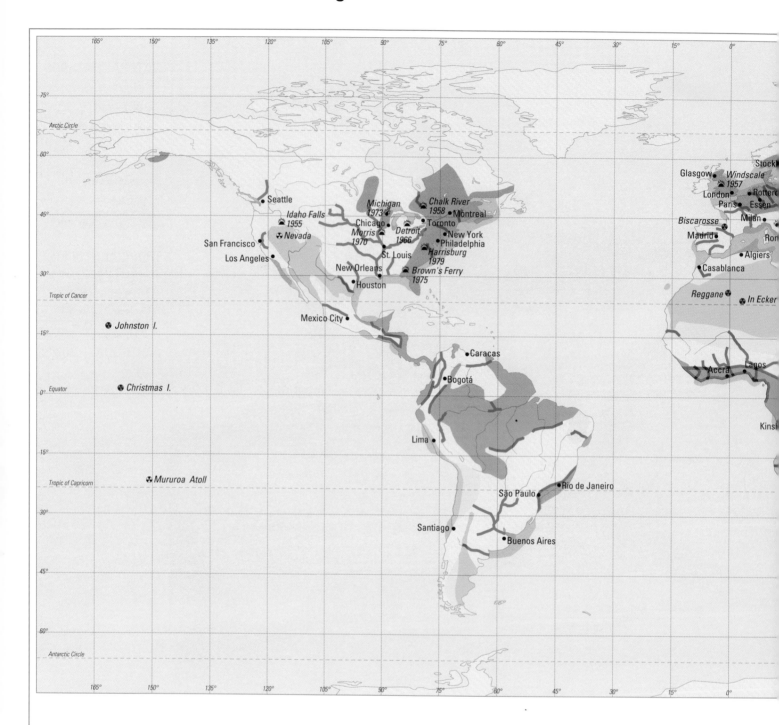

Deforestation in Amazonia, Brazil

Marine pollution in the North Sea

Industrial air pollution in Germany

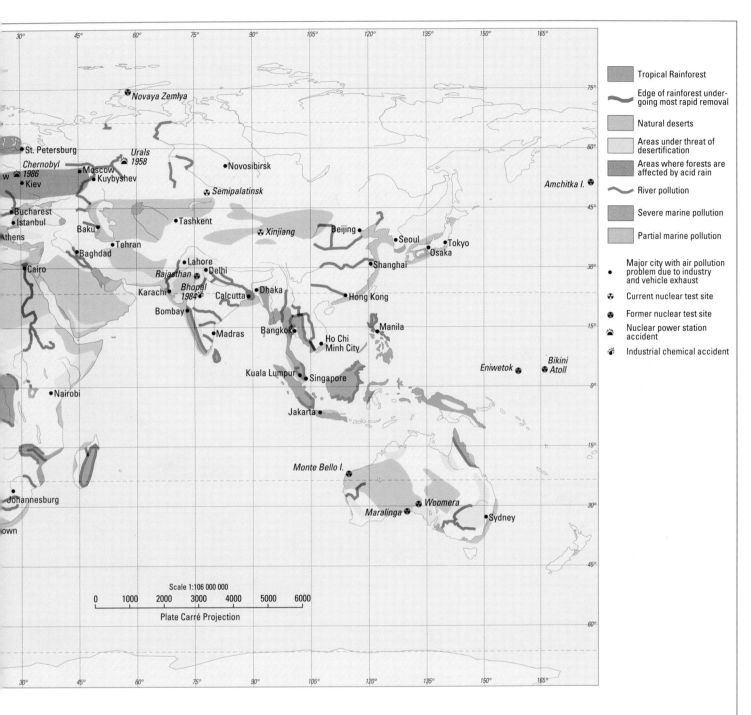

	Tropical Rainforest
	Edge of rainforest undergoing most rapid removal
	Natural deserts
	Areas under threat of desertification
	Areas where forests are affected by acid rain
	River pollution
	Severe marine pollution
	Partial marine pollution

● Major city with air pollution problem due to industry and vehicle exhaust

☢ Current nuclear test site

☢ Former nuclear test site

♨ Nuclear power station accident

☣ Industrial chemical accident

Scale 1:106 000 000

0 1000 2000 3000 4000 5000 6000

Plate Carré Projection

nd at risk from desertification, Sudan

Vehicle fumes in Guatemala

Effect of acid rain on the trees of Czechoslovakia

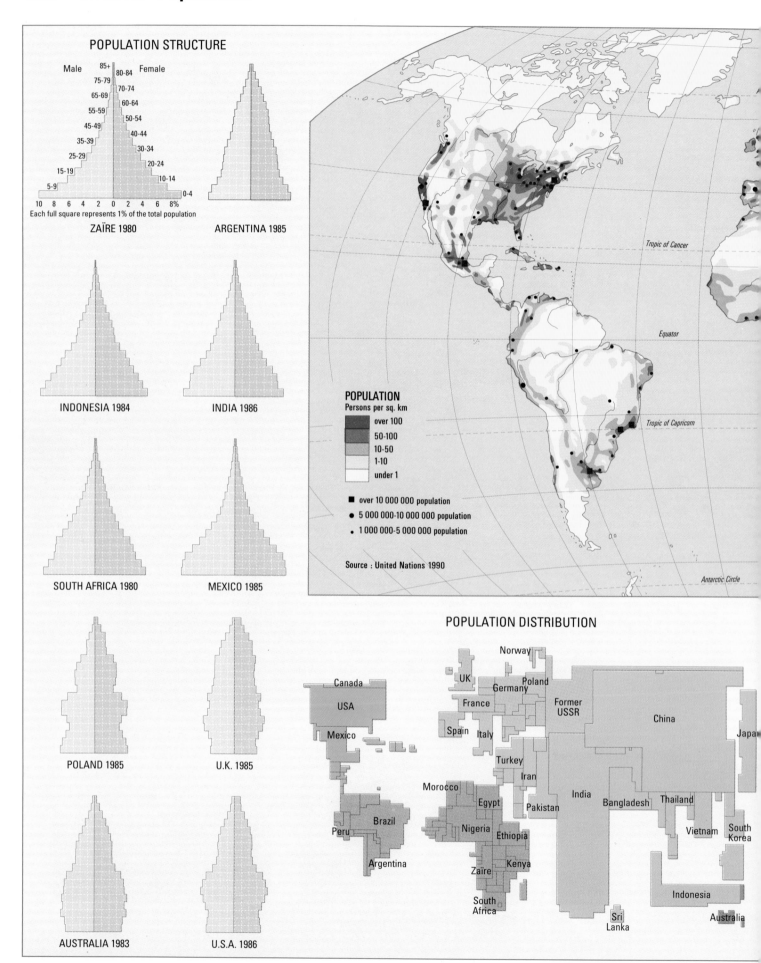

POPULATION STRUCTURE

Male   85+   Female
75-79   80-84
65-69   70-74
55-59   60-64
45-49   50-54
35-39   40-44
25-29   30-34
15-19   20-24
5-9   10-14
0-4

10 8 6 4 2 0 2 4 6 8%

Each full square represents 1% of the total population

ZAÏRE 1980

ARGENTINA 1985

INDONESIA 1984

INDIA 1986

SOUTH AFRICA 1980

MEXICO 1985

POLAND 1985

U.K. 1985

AUSTRALIA 1983

U.S.A. 1986

POPULATION
Persons per sq. km

over 100
50-100
10-50
1-10
under 1

■ over 10 000 000 population
● 5 000 000-10 000 000 population
• 1 000 000-5 000 000 population

Source : United Nations 1990

Tropic of Cancer
Equator
Tropic of Capricorn
Antarctic Circle

POPULATION DISTRIBUTION

Norway
Canada
UK
Germany
Poland
USA
France
Former USSR
China
Japan
Mexico
Spain
Italy
Turkey
Iran
India
Bangladesh
Thailand
Morocco
Pakistan
Egypt
Vietnam
South Korea
Peru
Brazil
Nigeria
Ethiopia
Argentina
Zaïre
Kenya
Indonesia
South Africa
Sri Lanka
Australia

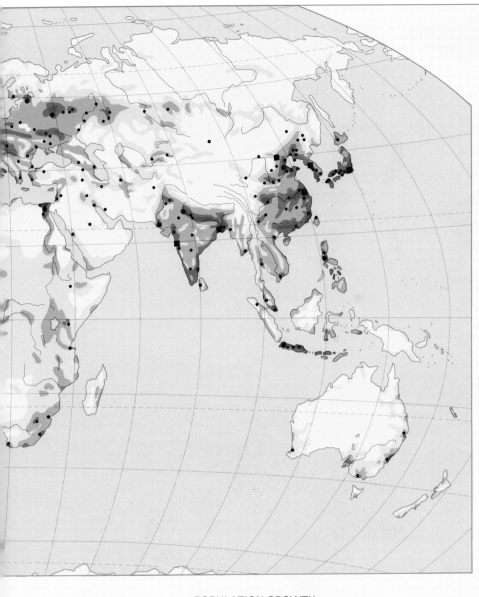

© Collins <> Longman Atlases

FACT*file* **Largest Cities**
Population figures in millions

AFRICA
Cairo	Egypt	9.0
Lagos	Nigeria	7.7
Alexandria	Egypt	3.7
Kinshasa	Zaïre	3.5
Casablanca	Morocco	3.2
Algiers	Algeria	3.0
Cape Town	South Africa	2.3
Abidjan	Côte d'Ivoire	2.2
Tripoli	Libya	2.1
Khartoum	Sudan	1.9

ASIA
Tokyo	Japan	18.1
Shanghai	China	13.4
Calcutta	India	11.8
Bombay	India	11.2
Seoul	South Korea	11.0
Beijing	China	10.8
Tianjin	China	9.4
Jakarta	Indonesia	9.3
Delhi	India	8.8
Manila	Philippines	8.5

EUROPE
Moscow	Russian Federation	8.8
Paris	France	8.5
London	United Kingdom	7.5
Milan	Italy	5.3
Madrid	Spain	5.2
St. Petersburg	Russian Federation	5.1
Naples	Italy	3.6
Barcelona	Spain	3.4
Athens	Greece	3.4
Katowice	Poland	3.4

NORTH AMERICA
Mexico City	Mexico	20.2
New York	USA	16.2
Los Angeles	USA	11.9
Chicago	USA	7.0
Philadelphia	USA	4.3
Detroit	USA	3.7
San Francisco	USA	3.7
Toronto	Canada	3.5
Dallas	USA	3.4
Guadalajara	Mexico	3.2

SOUTH AMERICA
São Paulo	Brazil	17.4
Buenos Aires	Argentina	11.5
Rio de Janeiro	Brazil	10.7
Lima	Peru	6.2
Santiago	Chile	4.7
Caracas	Venezuela	4.1
Belo Horizonte	Brazil	3.6
Porto Alegre	Brazil	3.1
Recife	Brazil	2.5
Salvador	Brazil	2.4

AUSTRALASIA
Sydney	Australia	3.4
Melbourne	Australia	2.8
Brisbane	Australia	1.2
Perth	Australia	1.1

Note: Figures refer to urban agglomerations as defined by the U. N.

POPULATION GROWTH

- Asia
- Australasia
- Africa
- Latin America
- U.S.A. & Canada
- Europe (incl. former U.S.S.R.)

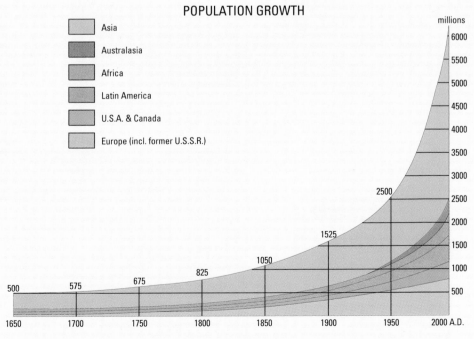

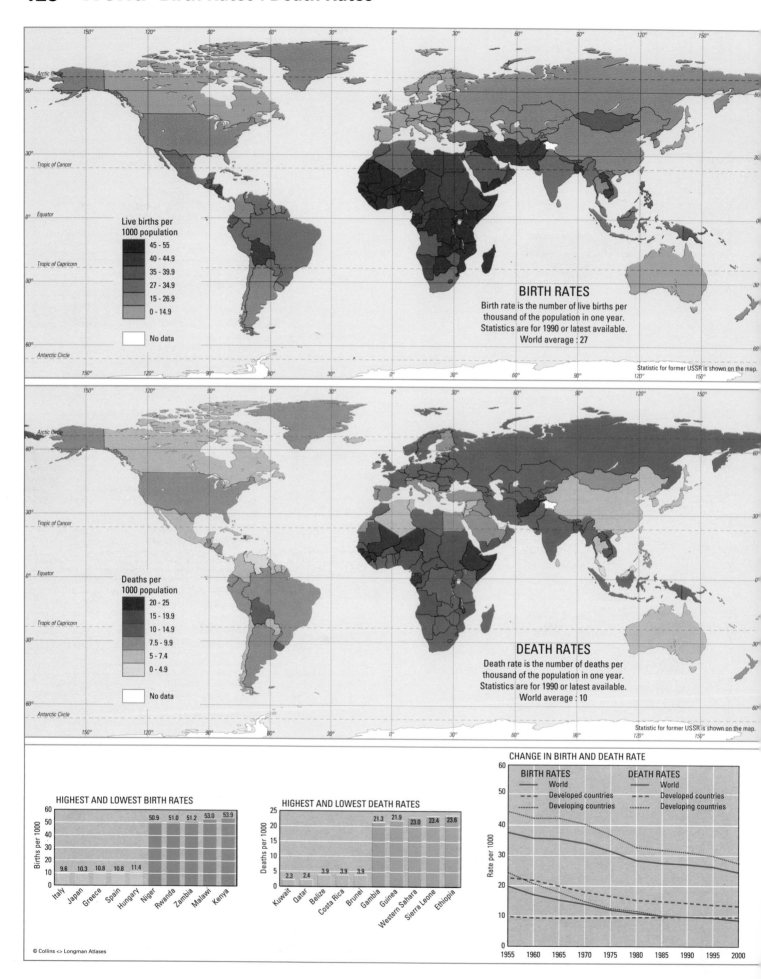

Live births per 1000 population
- 45 - 55
- 40 - 44.9
- 35 - 39.9
- 27 - 34.9
- 15 - 26.9
- 0 - 14.9
- No data

BIRTH RATES

Birth rate is the number of live births per thousand of the population in one year. Statistics are for 1990 or latest available.
World average : 27

Statistic for former USSR is shown on the map.

Deaths per 1000 population
- 20 - 25
- 15 - 19.9
- 10 - 14.9
- 7.5 - 9.9
- 5 - 7.4
- 0 - 4.9
- No data

DEATH RATES

Death rate is the number of deaths per thousand of the population in one year. Statistics are for 1990 or latest available.
World average : 10

Statistic for former USSR is shown on the map.

HIGHEST AND LOWEST BIRTH RATES

Births per 1000

Italy	Japan	Greece	Spain	Hungary	Niger	Rwanda	Zambia	Malawi	Kenya
9.6	10.3	10.8	10.8	11.4	50.9	51.0	51.2	53.0	53.9

HIGHEST AND LOWEST DEATH RATES

Deaths per 1000

Kuwait	Qatar	Belize	Costa Rica	Brunei	Gambia	Guinea	Western Sahara	Sierra Leone	Ethiopia
2.3	2.4	3.9	3.9	3.9	21.3	21.9	23.0	23.4	23.6

CHANGE IN BIRTH AND DEATH RATE

BIRTH RATES
- World
- Developed countries
- Developing countries

DEATH RATES
- World
- Developed countries
- Developing countries

Rate per 1000

1955 1960 1965 1970 1975 1980 1985 1990 1995 2000

© Collins <> Longman Atlases

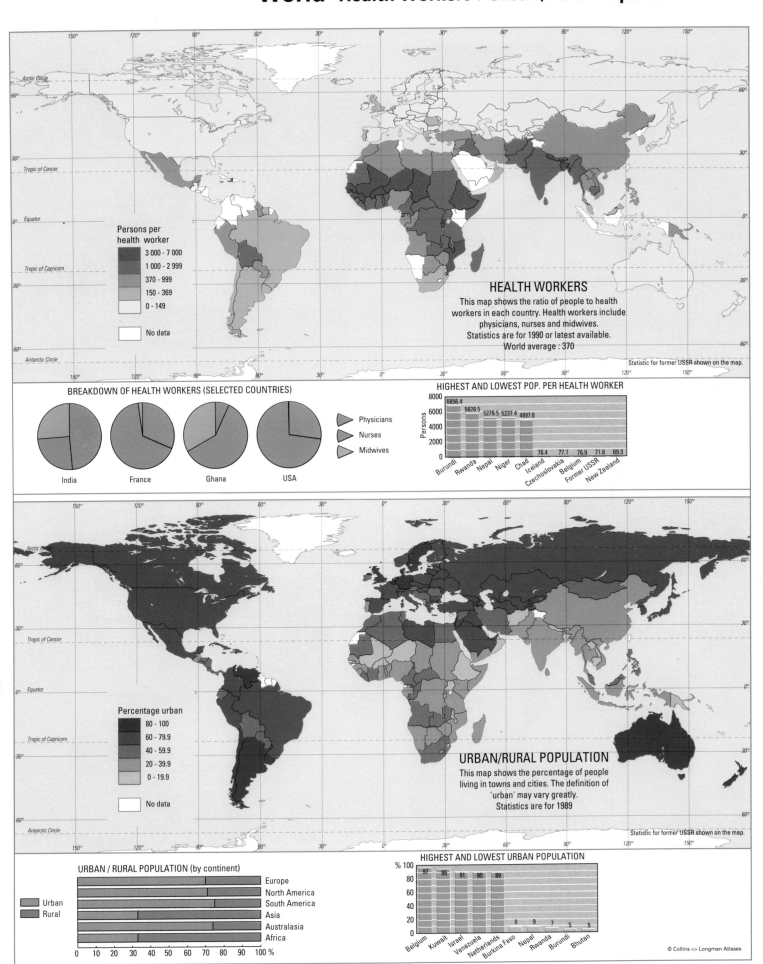

Persons per health worker

- 3 000 - 7 000
- 1 000 - 2 999
- 370 - 999
- 150 - 369
- 0 - 149
- No data

HEALTH WORKERS

This map shows the ratio of people to health workers in each country. Health workers include physicians, nurses and midwives. Statistics are for 1990 or latest available.
World average : 370

Statistic for former USSR shown on the map.

BREAKDOWN OF HEALTH WORKERS (SELECTED COUNTRIES)

India   France   Ghana   USA

- Physicians
- Nurses
- Midwives

HIGHEST AND LOWEST POP. PER HEALTH WORKER

Persons

Burundi	6856.4
Rwanda	5828.5
Nepal	5279.5
Niger	5237.4
Chad	4897.6
Iceland	78.4
Czechoslovakia	77.1
Belgium	76.9
Former USSR	71.6
New Zealand	69.3

Percentage urban

- 80 - 100
- 60 - 79.9
- 40 - 59.9
- 20 - 39.9
- 0 - 19.9
- No data

URBAN/RURAL POPULATION

This map shows the percentage of people living in towns and cities. The definition of 'urban' may vary greatly.
Statistics are for 1989

Statistic for former USSR shown on the map.

URBAN / RURAL POPULATION (by continent)

- Urban
- Rural

Europe
North America
South America
Asia
Australasia
Africa

0 10 20 30 40 50 60 70 80 90 100 %

HIGHEST AND LOWEST URBAN POPULATION

%

Belgium	97
Kuwait	95
Israel	91
Venezuela	90
Netherlands	89
Burkina Faso	9
Nepal	9
Rwanda	7
Burundi	5
Bhutan	5

© Collins <> Longman Atlases

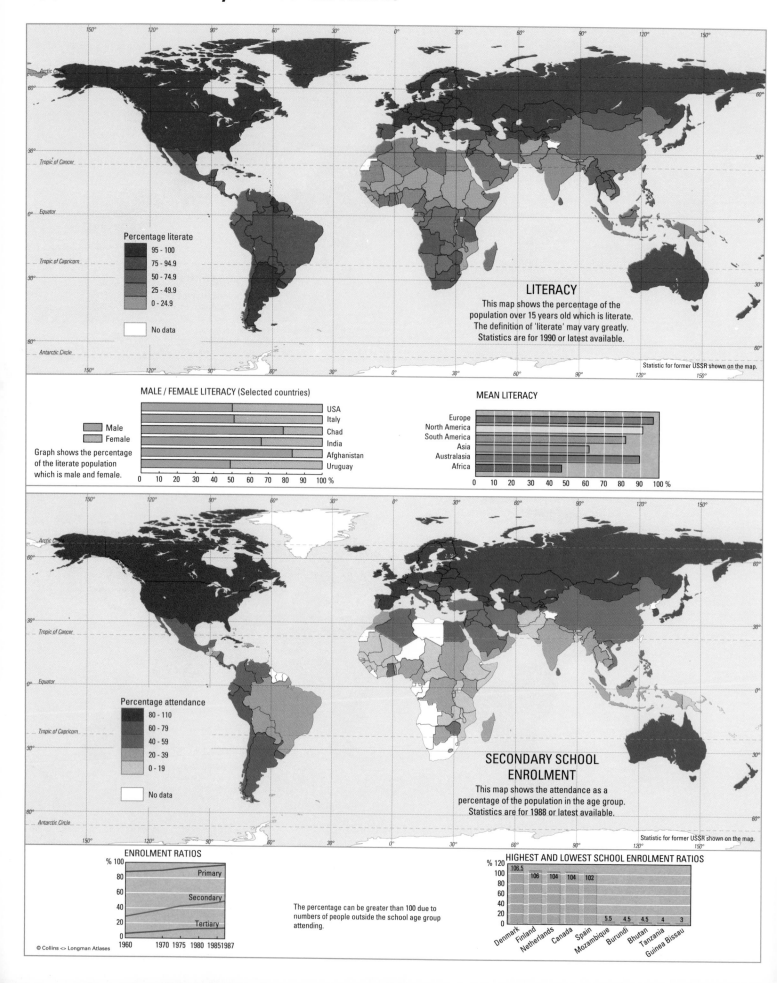

Percentage literate
- 95 - 100
- 75 - 94.9
- 50 - 74.9
- 25 - 49.9
- 0 - 24.9
- No data

LITERACY
This map shows the percentage of the population over 15 years old which is literate. The definition of 'literate' may vary greatly. Statistics are for 1990 or latest available.

Statistic for former USSR shown on the map.

MALE / FEMALE LITERACY (Selected countries)
- Male
- Female

Graph shows the percentage of the literate population which is male and female.

USA
Italy
Chad
India
Afghanistan
Uruguay

0 10 20 30 40 50 60 70 80 90 100 %

MEAN LITERACY
Europe
North America
South America
Asia
Australasia
Africa

0 10 20 30 40 50 60 70 80 90 100 %

Percentage attendance
- 80 - 110
- 60 - 79
- 40 - 59
- 20 - 39
- 0 - 19
- No data

SECONDARY SCHOOL ENROLMENT
This map shows the attendance as a percentage of the population in the age group. Statistics are for 1988 or latest available.

Statistic for former USSR shown on the map.

ENROLMENT RATIOS
% 100
80
60
40
20
0

Primary
Secondary
Tertiary

1960 1970 1975 1980 1985 1987

The percentage can be greater than 100 due to numbers of people outside the school age group attending.

HIGHEST AND LOWEST SCHOOL ENROLMENT RATIOS
% 120
100
80
60
40
20
0

106.5 106 104 104 102

Denmark Finland Netherlands Canada Spain

5.5 4.5 4.5 4 3

Mozambique Burundi Bhutan Tanzania Guinea Bissau

© Collins <> Longman Atlases

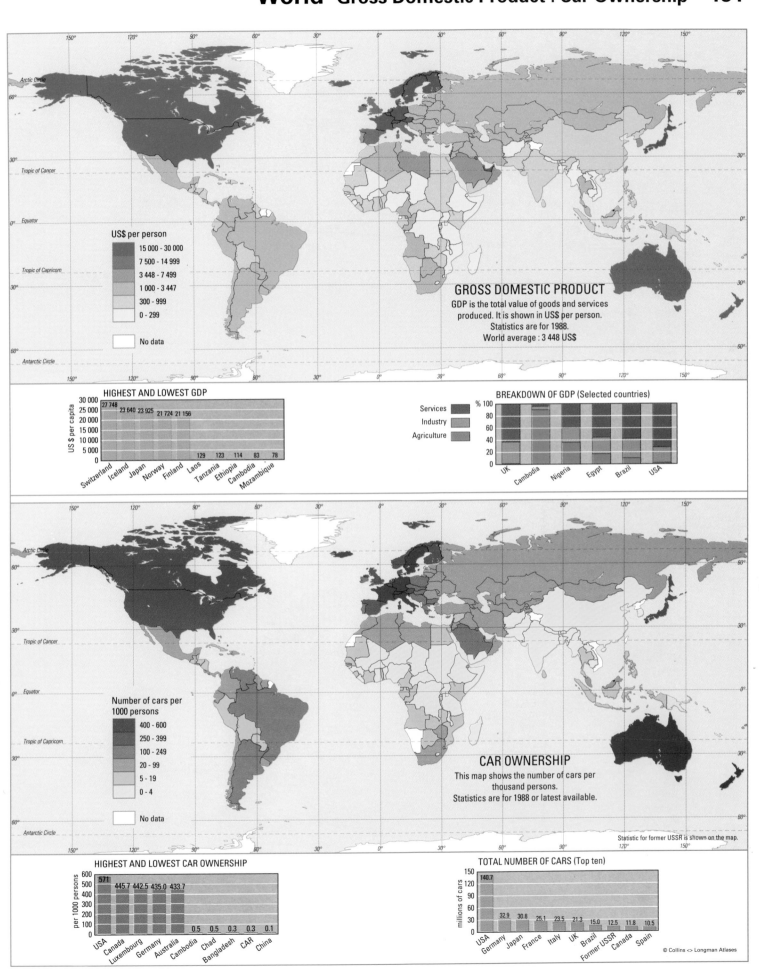

GROSS DOMESTIC PRODUCT

GDP is the total value of goods and services produced. It is shown in US$ per person. Statistics are for 1988. World average : 3 448 US$

US$ per person

- 15 000 - 30 000
- 7 500 - 14 999
- 3 448 - 7 499
- 1 000 - 3 447
- 300 - 999
- 0 - 299

No data

HIGHEST AND LOWEST GDP

US $ per capita

Country	US$
Switzerland	27 748
Iceland	23 640
Japan	23 925
Norway	21 724
Finland	21 156
Laos	129
Tanzania	123
Ethiopia	114
Cambodia	83
Mozambique	78

BREAKDOWN OF GDP (Selected countries)

- Services
- Industry
- Agriculture

% 100, 80, 60, 40, 20, 0

UK, Cambodia, Nigeria, Egypt, Brazil, USA

CAR OWNERSHIP

This map shows the number of cars per thousand persons. Statistics are for 1988 or latest available.

Number of cars per 1000 persons

- 400 - 600
- 250 - 399
- 100 - 249
- 20 - 99
- 5 - 19
- 0 - 4

No data

Statistic for former USSR is shown on the map.

HIGHEST AND LOWEST CAR OWNERSHIP

per 1000 persons

Country	per 1000
USA	571
Canada	445.7
Luxembourg	442.5
Germany	435.0
Australia	433.7
Cambodia	0.5
Chad	0.5
Bangladesh	0.3
CAR	0.3
China	0.1

TOTAL NUMBER OF CARS (Top ten)

millions of cars

Country	millions
USA	140.7
Germany	32.9
Japan	30.8
France	25.1
Italy	23.5
UK	21.3
Brazil	15.0
Former USSR	12.5
Canada	11.8
Spain	10.5

© Collins <> Longman Atlases

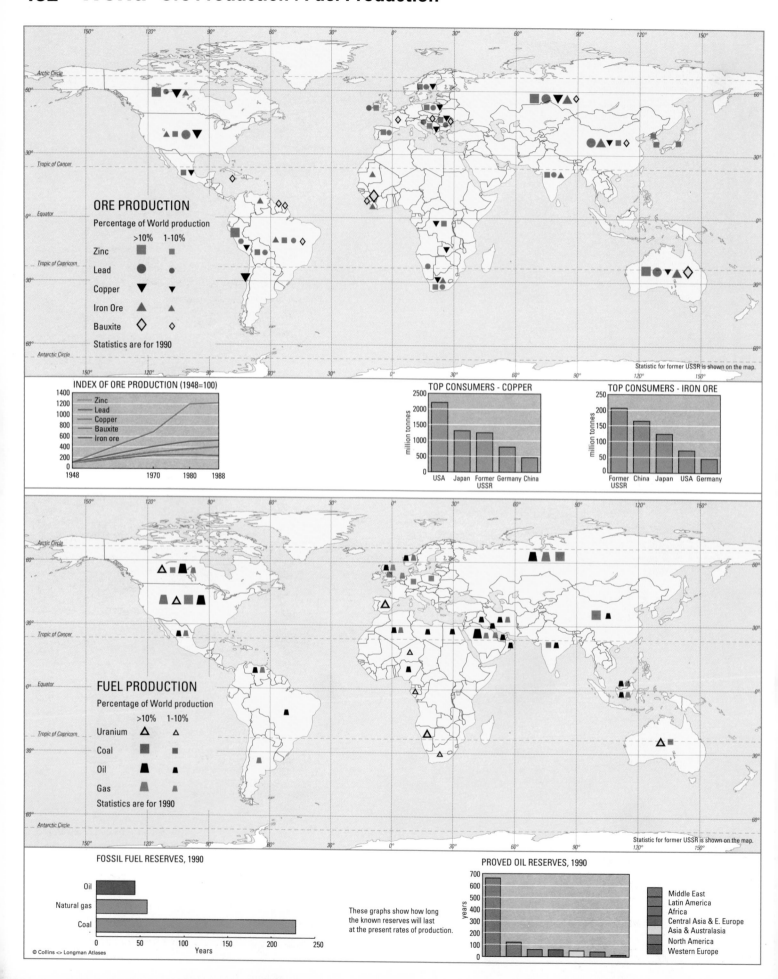

ORE PRODUCTION

Percentage of World production

	>10%	1-10%
Zinc	■	■
Lead	●	●
Copper	▼	▼
Iron Ore	▲	▲
Bauxite	◇	◇

Statistics are for 1990

Statistic for former USSR is shown on the map.

INDEX OF ORE PRODUCTION (1948=100)

- Zinc
- Lead
- Copper
- Bauxite
- Iron ore

TOP CONSUMERS - COPPER

million tonnes

USA Japan Former USSR Germany China

TOP CONSUMERS - IRON ORE

million tonnes

Former USSR China Japan USA Germany

FUEL PRODUCTION

Percentage of World production

	>10%	1-10%
Uranium	△	△
Coal	■	■
Oil	▲	▲
Gas	▲	▲

Statistics are for 1990

Statistic for former USSR is shown on the map.

FOSSIL FUEL RESERVES, 1990

Oil
Natural gas
Coal

0   50   100   150   200   250
Years

These graphs show how long the known reserves will last at the present rates of production.

PROVED OIL RESERVES, 1990

years

Middle East
Latin America
Africa
Central Asia & E. Europe
Asia & Australasia
North America
Western Europe

© Collins <> Longman Atlases

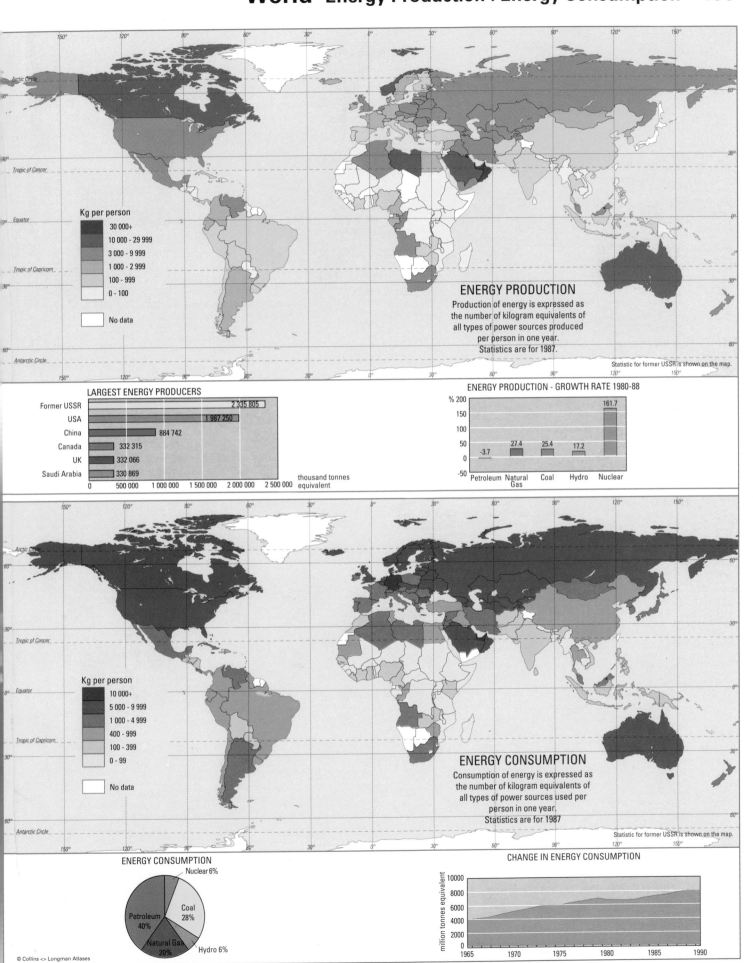

ENERGY PRODUCTION

Production of energy is expressed as the number of kilogram equivalents of all types of power sources produced per person in one year. Statistics are for 1987.

Statistic for former USSR is shown on the map.

Kg per person
- 30 000+
- 10 000 - 29 999
- 3 000 - 9 999
- 1 000 - 2 999
- 100 - 999
- 0 - 100
- No data

LARGEST ENERGY PRODUCERS

	thousand tonnes equivalent
Former USSR	2 335 805
USA	1 987 250
China	884 742
Canada	332 315
UK	332 066
Saudi Arabia	330 869

0   500 000   1 000 000   1 500 000   2 000 000   2 500 000

ENERGY PRODUCTION - GROWTH RATE 1980-88

	%
Petroleum	-3.7
Natural Gas	27.4
Coal	25.4
Hydro	17.2
Nuclear	161.7

ENERGY CONSUMPTION

Consumption of energy is expressed as the number of kilogram equivalents of all types of power sources used per person in one year. Statistics are for 1987

Statistic for former USSR is shown on the map.

Kg per person
- 10 000+
- 5 000 - 9 999
- 1 000 - 4 999
- 400 - 999
- 100 - 399
- 0 - 99
- No data

ENERGY CONSUMPTION

- Nuclear 6%
- Coal 28%
- Petroleum 40%
- Natural Gas 20%
- Hydro 6%

CHANGE IN ENERGY CONSUMPTION

million tonnes equivalent

10000 / 8000 / 6000 / 4000 / 2000 / 0

1965   1970   1975   1980   1985   1990

© Collins <> Longman Atlases

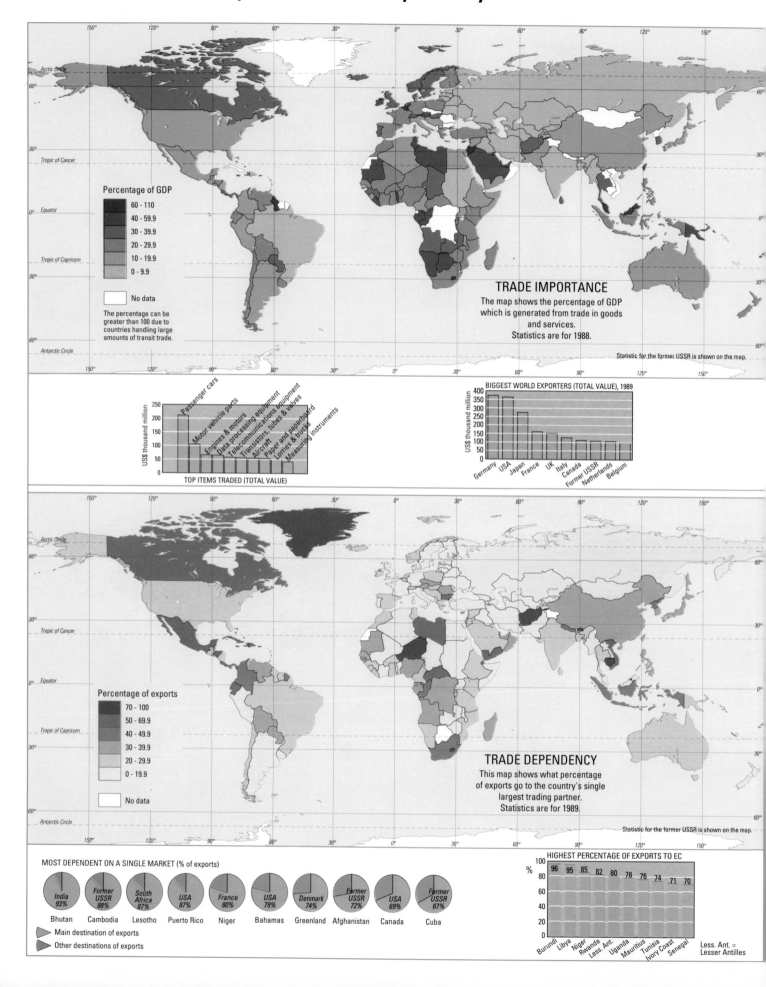

TRADE IMPORTANCE

The map shows the percentage of GDP which is generated from trade in goods and services.
Statistics are for 1988.

Statistic for the former USSR is shown on the map.

Percentage of GDP

	60 - 110
	40 - 59.9
	30 - 39.9
	20 - 29.9
	10 - 19.9
	0 - 9.9
	No data

The percentage can be greater than 100 due to countries handling large amounts of transit trade.

TOP ITEMS TRADED (TOTAL VALUE)

US$ thousand million

- Passenger cars
- Motor vehicle parts
- Engines & motors
- Data processing equipment
- Telecommunications equipment
- Transistors, tubes & valves
- Aircraft
- Paper and paperboard
- Lorries & trucks
- Measuring instruments

BIGGEST WORLD EXPORTERS (TOTAL VALUE), 1989

US$ thousand million

Germany, USA, Japan, France, UK, Italy, Canada, Former USSR, Netherlands, Belgium

TRADE DEPENDENCY

This map shows what percentage of exports go to the country's single largest trading partner.
Statistics are for 1989.

Statistic for the former USSR is shown on the map.

Percentage of exports

	70 - 100
	50 - 69.9
	40 - 49.9
	30 - 39.9
	20 - 29.9
	0 - 19.9
	No data

MOST DEPENDENT ON A SINGLE MARKET (% of exports)

Bhutan	Cambodia	Lesotho	Puerto Rico	Niger	Bahamas	Greenland	Afghanistan	Canada	Cuba
India 93%	Former USSR 88%	South Africa 87%	USA 87%	France 80%	USA 79%	Denmark 74%	Former USSR 72%	USA 69%	Former USSR 67%

▸ Main destination of exports
▸ Other destinations of exports

HIGHEST PERCENTAGE OF EXPORTS TO EC

Burundi	Libya	Niger	Rwanda	Less. Ant.	Uganda	Mauritius	Tunisia	Ivory Coast	Senegal
96	95	85	82	80	78	76	74	71	70

Less. Ant. = Lesser Antilles

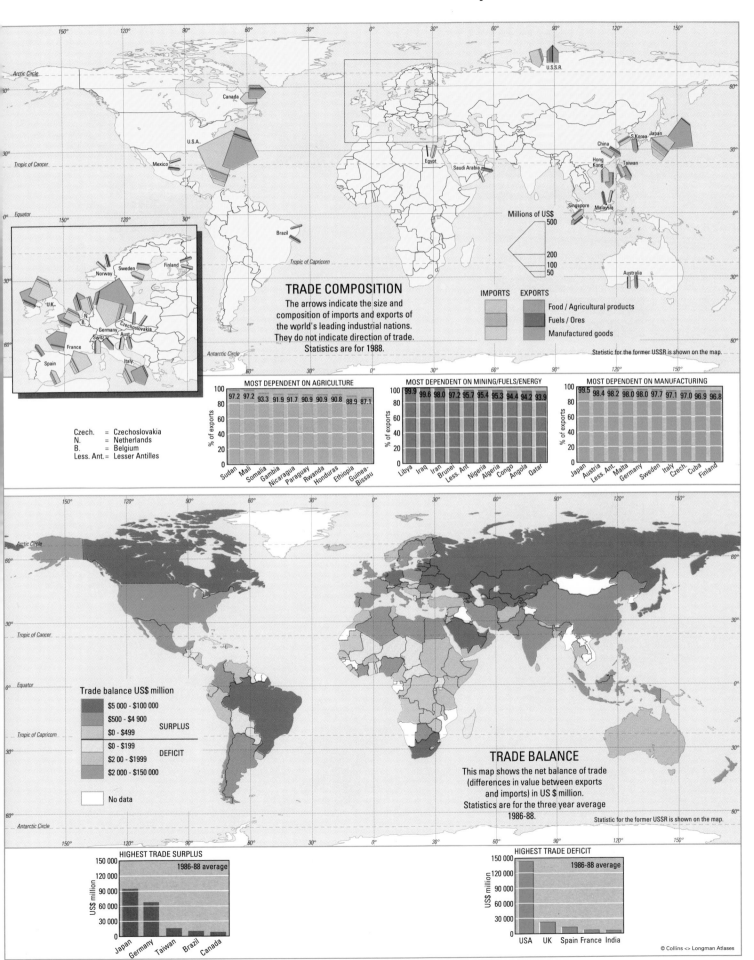

TRADE COMPOSITION

The arrows indicate the size and composition of imports and exports of the world's leading industrial nations. They do not indicate direction of trade. Statistics are for 1988.

Millions of US$
500
200
100
50

IMPORTS EXPORTS
Food / Agricultural products
Fuels / Ores
Manufactured goods

Statistic for the former USSR is shown on the map.

Czech. = Czechoslovakia
N. = Netherlands
B. = Belgium
Less. Ant. = Lesser Antilles

MOST DEPENDENT ON AGRICULTURE
% of exports

Sudan	97.2
Mali	97.2
Somalia	93.3
Gambia	91.9
Nicaragua	91.7
Paraguay	90.9
Rwanda	90.9
Honduras	90.8
Ethiopia	88.9
Guinea-Bissau	87.1

MOST DEPENDENT ON MINING/FUELS/ENERGY
% of exports

Libya	99.9
Iraq	99.6
Iran	98.0
Brunei	97.2
Less. Ant	95.7
Nigeria	95.4
Algeria	95.3
Congo	94.4
Angola	94.2
Qatar	93.9

MOST DEPENDENT ON MANUFACTURING
% of exports

Japan	99.5
Austria	98.4
Less. Ant.	98.2
Malta	98.0
Germany	98.0
Sweden	97.7
Italy	97.1
Czech.	97.0
Cuba	96.9
Finland	96.8

TRADE BALANCE

This map shows the net balance of trade (differences in value between exports and imports) in US $ million. Statistics are for the three year average 1986-88.

Statistic for the former USSR is shown on the map.

Trade balance US$ million

SURPLUS
$5 000 - $100 000
$500 - $4 900
$0 - $499

DEFICIT
$0 - $199
$2 00 - $1999
$2 000 - $150 000

No data

HIGHEST TRADE SURPLUS
US$ million
1986-88 average

Japan Germany Taiwan Brazil Canada

HIGHEST TRADE DEFICIT
US$ million
1986-88 average

USA UK Spain France India

© Collins <> Longman Atlases

SIZE OF SALES (TOP 20)

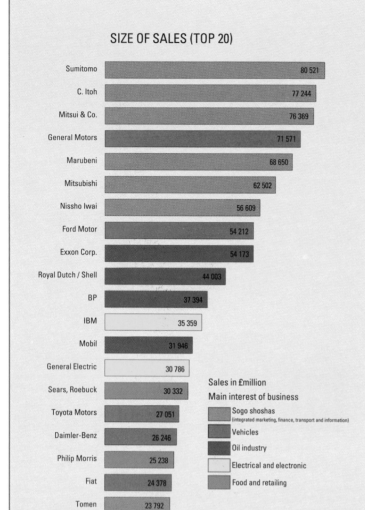

Company	Sales
Sumitomo	80 521
C. Itoh	77 244
Mitsui & Co.	76 369
General Motors	71 571
Marubeni	68 650
Mitsubishi	62 502
Nissho Iwai	56 609
Ford Motor	54 212
Exxon Corp.	54 173
Royal Dutch / Shell	44 003
BP	37 394
IBM	35 359
Mobil	31 946
General Electric	30 786
Sears, Roebuck	30 332
Toyota Motors	27 051
Daimler-Benz	26 246
Philip Morris	25 238
Fiat	24 378
Tomen	23 792

Sales in £million

Main interest of business

- Sogo shoshas (integrated marketing, finance, transport and information)
- Vehicles
- Oil industry
- Electrical and electronic
- Food and retailing

THE WORLD'S FIFTY LARGEST COMPANIES

UNITED KINGDOM
- Royal Dutch / Shell
- B.P.
- Unilever

FRANCE
- Renault
- Peugeot
- Elf Aquitaine
- Electricité de France
- C.G.E.

U.S.A.
- General Motors
- Ford Motor
- Exxon Group
- IBM
- Mobil
- General Electric
- Sears, Roebuck
- Philip Morris
- American T. & T.
- E.I. Du Pont De Nemours
- Chrysler
- Chevron
- Texaco
- K. Mart
- Wal Mart Stores

SIZE OF MULTINATIONALS

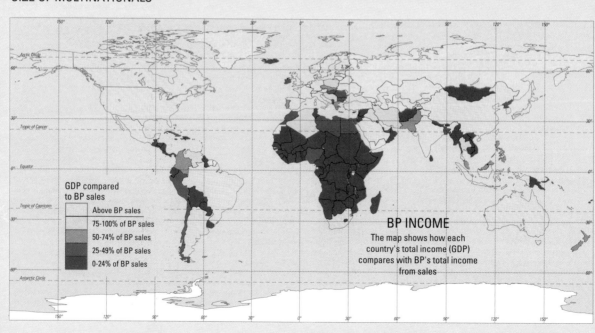

GDP compared to BP sales
- Above BP sales
- 75-100% of BP sales
- 50-74% of BP sales
- 25-49% of BP sales
- 0-24% of BP sales

BP INCOME
The map shows how each country's total income (GDP) compares with BP's total income from sales

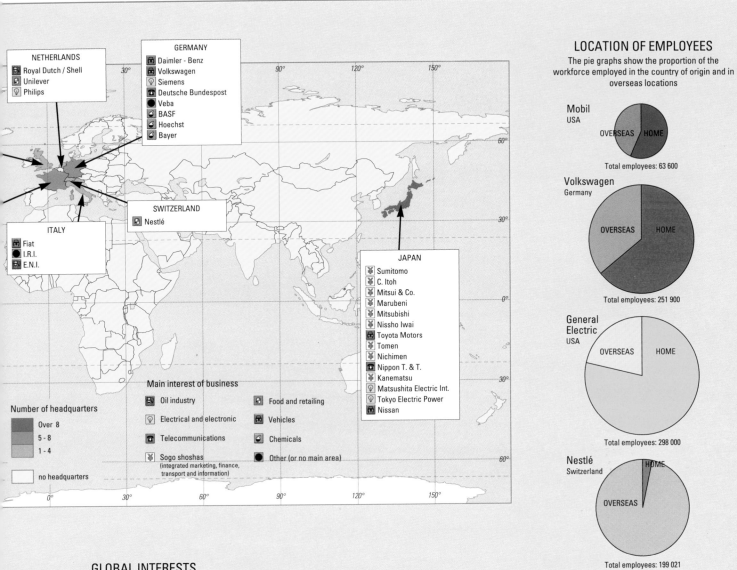

NETHERLANDS
- Royal Dutch / Shell
- Unilever
- Philips

GERMANY
- Daimler - Benz
- Volkswagen
- Siemens
- Deutsche Bundespost
- Veba
- BASF
- Hoechst
- Bayer

ITALY
- Fiat
- I.R.I.
- E.N.I.

SWITZERLAND
- Nestlé

JAPAN
- Sumitomo
- C. Itoh
- Mitsui & Co.
- Marubeni
- Mitsubishi
- Nissho Iwai
- Toyota Motors
- Tomen
- Nichimen
- Nippon T. & T.
- Kanematsu
- Matsushita Electric Int.
- Tokyo Electric Power
- Nissan

Main interest of business
- Oil industry
- Electrical and electronic
- Telecommunications
- Sogo shoshas (integrated marketing, finance, transport and information)
- Food and retailing
- Vehicles
- Chemicals
- Other (or no main area)

Number of headquarters
- Over 8
- 5 - 8
- 1 - 4
- no headquarters

LOCATION OF EMPLOYEES

The pie graphs show the proportion of the workforce employed in the country of origin and in overseas locations

Mobil
USA
OVERSEAS / HOME
Total employees: 63 600

Volkswagen
Germany
OVERSEAS / HOME
Total employees: 251 900

General Electric
USA
OVERSEAS / HOME
Total employees: 298 000

Nestlé
Switzerland
HOME / OVERSEAS
Total employees: 199 021

GLOBAL INTERESTS

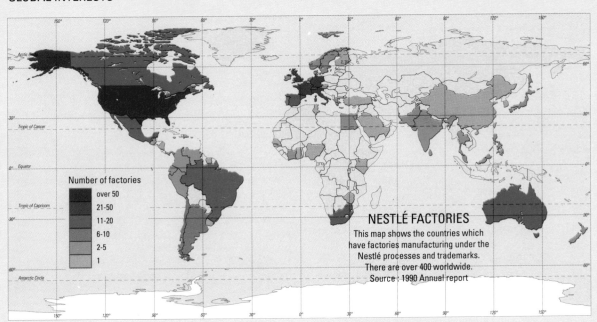

Number of factories
- over 50
- 21-50
- 11-20
- 6-10
- 2-5
- 1

NESTLÉ FACTORIES

This map shows the countries which have factories manufacturing under the Nestlé processes and trademarks. There are over 400 worldwide.
Source : 1990 Annual report

KEY STATISTICS

COUNTRY	CAPITAL CITY	POPULATION in millions, 1989	AREA in sq. km	MAIN LANGUAGES	MAIN RELIGIONS	CURRENCY
AFGHANISTAN	Kabul	15.7	647 497	Pushtu,Dari (Persian)	Muslim	afghani
ALBANIA	Tirane	3.2	28 748	Albanian	Non religious	lek
ALGERIA	Algiers	24.3	2 381 741	Arabic	Muslim	dinar
ANGOLA	Luanda	9.7	1 246 700	Portuguese	Christian	kwanza
ARGENTINA	Buenos Aires	31.9	2 766 889	Spanish	Roman Catholic	peso
ARMENIA	Yerevan	3.3	30 000	Armenian,Russian	Orthodox	rouble
AUSTRALIA	Canberra	16.7	7 686 848	English	Anglican, Roman Catholic	dollar
AUSTRIA	Vienna	7.6	83 849	German	Roman Catholic	schilling
AZERBAIJAN	Baku	7.1	87 000	Azerbaijani,Russian	Muslim	rouble
BAHAMAS	Nassau	0.2	13 935	English	Protestant	dollar
BAHRAIN	Manama	0.5	622	Arabic	Muslim	dinar
BANGLADESH	Dhaka	113.3	143 998	Bengali	Muslim	taka
BELGIUM	Brussels	9.8	30 513	French,Dutch,German	Roman Catholic	franc
BELIZE	Belmopan	0.2	22 965	English	Roman Catholic	dollar
BELORUSSIA	Minsk	10.3	208 000	Belorussian,Russian		rouble
BENIN	Porto-Novo	4.5	112 622	French	Traditional	CFA franc
BHUTAN	Thimbu	1.5	47 000	Dzongkha	Buddhist	Indian rupee,ngultrum
BOLIVIA	La Paz / Sucre	7.1	1 098 581	Spanish	Roman Catholic	boliviano
BOTSWANA	Gaborone	1.3	600 372	English,Tswana	Christian, Traditional	pula
BRAZIL	Brasilia	144.4	8 511 965	Portuguese	Roman Catholic	cruzeiro
BRUNEI	Bander Seri Begawan	0.3	5 765	Malay	Muslim	dollar
BULGARIA	Sofia	9	110 912	Bulgarian	Atheist	lev
BURKINA FASO	Ouagadougou	8.8	274 200	French	Traditional, Muslim	CFA franc
BURUNDI	Bujumbura	5.3	27 834	French,Kirundi	Roman Catholic	franc
CAMBODIA	Phnom Penh	8.1	181 035	Cambodian,Khmer	Buddhist	riel
CAMEROON	Yaounde	11.4	475 442	French,English	Roman Catholic	CFA franc
CANADA	Ottawa	26.3	9 976 139	English,French	Roman Catholic, Protestant	dollar
CENTRAL AFRICAN REP.	Bangui	3	622 984	French,Sango	Protestant	CFA franc
CHAD	N'Djamena	5.5	1 284 000	French,Arabic	Muslim	CFA franc
CHILE	Santiago	13	756 945	Spanish	Roman Catholic	peso
CHINA	Beijing	1104.0	9 561 000	Mandarin	Non religious	yuan
COLOMBIA	Bogota	32.3	1 138 914	Spanish	Roman Catholic	peso
CONGO	Brazzaville	2.2	342 000	French	Roman Catholic	CFA franc
COSTA RICA	San Jose	2.9	50 700	Spanish	Roman Catholic	colon
CUBA	Havana	10.5	110 861	Spanish	Non religious, Roman Catholic	peso
CYPRUS	Nicosia	0.7	9 251	Greek,Turkish	Greek Orthodox	pound
CZECHOSLOVAKIA	Prague	15.6	127 869	Czech, Slovak	Roman Catholic	koruna
DENMARK	Copenhagen	5.1	43 069	Danish	Evangelical Lutheran	krone
DJIBOUTI	Djibouti	0.4	22 000	French,Somali,Afar	Muslim	franc
DOMINICA	Roseau	0.1	751	English,French	Roman Catholic	East Caribbean dollar
DOMINICAN REPUBLIC	Santo Dominigo	7	48 734	Spanish	Roman Catholic	peso
ECUADOR	Quito	10.3	283 561	Spanish	Roman Catholic	sucre
EGYPT	Cairo	51.2	1 001 449	Arabic	Muslim	pound
EL SALVADOR	San Salvador	5.1	21 041	Spanish	Roman Catholic	colon
EQUATORIAL GUINEA	Malabo	0.3	28 051	Spanish	Roman Catholic	CFA franc
ESTONIA	Tallinn	1.6	45 000	Estonian,Russian		rouble
ETHIOPIA	Addis Ababa	47.9	1 221 900	Amharic	Ethiopian Orthodox	birr
FIJI	Suva	0.8	18 274	English,Filian,Hindustani	Christian, Hindu	dollar
FINLAND	Helsinki	5	337 032	Finnish,Swedish	Evangelical Lutheran	mark
FRANCE	Paris	56	547 026	French	Roman Catholic	franc
GABON	Libreville	1.1	267 667	French	Roman Catholic	CFA franc
GAMBIA	Banjul	0.8	11 295	English	Muslim	dalasi
GEORGIA	Tbilisi	5.5	70 000	Georgian,Russian		rouble
GERMANY	Berlin/Bonn	77.6	356 755	German	Protestant, Roman Catholic	mark
GHANA	Accra	14.6	238 537	English	Christian	cedi
GREECE	Athens	10	131 944	Greek	Greek Orthodox	drachma

HEALTH AND EDUCATION

CALORIES PER CAPITA	PEOPLE PER DOCTOR	POPULATION WITH ACCESS TO SAFE WATER	PRIMARY SCHOOL ENROLMENT
mean daily calorie intake as a % of the requirement, 1985	the ratio of people to doctors, 1988	% of population with access to clean water, 1987	% of children attending first level education, 1989
92	6 623	19	21
118	633		100
121	2 632	88	96
86	19 608	32	134
122	399	64	110
114	451	100	106
130	332	100	101
	1 111		
	927	94	110
78	6 993	41	70
139	321	100	100
		70	
94	18 868	18	63
	26 316	15	26
88	1 733	49	91
95	10 870	57	114
107	11 765	77	103
	2 070		
146	364	100	104
87	66 667	20	32
99	23 810	39	59
85	17 857	3	
89		26	109
130	531	100	105
92	29 412	16	66
79	58 824	26	51
102	1 316	94	102
111	1 192	85	132
111	1 285	70	114
108	9 009	21	
118	1 130	91	98
127	552		104
	551	73	106
143	280	100	96
129	390	100	99
110	1 934	62	101
88	924	47	117
127	5 464	76	90
91	3 067	40	79
94	90 909	6	37
	2 217		129
111	447	100	101
142	402	100	113
124	3 663	92	
			104
78	17 241	50	71
145	344	100	104

DEVELOPMENT

GROSS DOMESTIC PRODUCT	LIFE EXPECTANCY	ADULT LITERACY	UNDER 5 MORTALITY
total value of goods & services, US$ per person, 1989	years a new born child can expect to live given the mortality risk in the country, 1989	% of people over 15 years who can read and write, 1985	number of children of every 1000 live births who die before age 5, 1989
143	42	18.2	296
1 102	72	100.0	30
2 269	65	44.7	102
569	45	41.0	292
2 759	71	93.9	36
14 083	76	99.0	9
16 675	75	100.0	10
10 833	70	95.0	
7 583	71	69.8	19
170	51	29.2	184
15 394	75	100.0	12
	67	91.2	
389	47	16.5	150
197	49		193
858	54	63.2	165
1 488	59	41.0	87
2 451	65	77.8	85
15 417	74	77.8	
2 217	72	99.0	17
204	48	8.8	232
214	48	33.8	196
83	50	75	200
1 135	53	41.2	150
18 834	77	100.0	9
388	49	27.0	219
159	46	12.0	219
1 732	72	91.1	93
301	70	65.5	43
1 316	69	85.2	50
1 175	53	62.9	112
1 638	75	92.6	22
2 509	76	97.8	14
7 709	76	89.0	14
2 737	71	100.0	13
20 988	76	100.0	10
	48		167
	74	94.1	
671	66	68.6	68
691	66	80.2	85
568	60	38.2	94
1 090	64	67.3	90
	47	210.0	
114	45	62.4	226
1 431	64	79.0	32
21 156	75	100.0	7
17 004	76	100.0	9
2 733	52	12.0	167
	44	20.0	241
16 700	75	100.0	10
369	55	30.2	143
5 244	76	90.5	12

KEY STATISTICS

COUNTRY	CAPITAL CITY	POPULATION in millions, 1989	AREA in sq. km	MAIN LANGUAGES	MAIN RELIGIONS	CURRENCY
GREENLAND	Godthab (Nuuk)	0.1	2 175 600	Danish,Greenlandic	Evangelical Lutheran	kroner
GUATEMALA	Guatemala City	8.9	108 889	Spanish	Roman Catholic	quetzal
GUIANA	Cayenne	0.1	91 000	French	Roman Catholic	franc
GUINEA	Conakry	5.6	245 857	French	Muslim	franc
GUINEA BISSAU	Bissau	0.9	36 125	Portuguese	Traditional	peso
GUYANA	Georgetown	0.8	214 969	English	Hindu	dollar
HAITI	Port-au-Prince	6.4	27 750	French,Creole	Roman Catholic	gourde
HONDURAS	Tegucigalpa	5.0	112 088	Spanish	Roman Catholic	lempira
HONG KONG	Victoria	5.8	1 045	English,Cantonese	Buddhist and Taoist	dollar
HUNGARY	Budapest	10.6	93 030	Magyar	Roman Catholic	forint
ICELAND	Reykjavik	0.3	103 000	Icelandic	Evangelical Lutheran	krona
INDIA	New Delhi	796.6	3 287 590	Hindi,English	Hindu	rupee
INDONESIA	Jakarta	180.8	1 904 569	Bahasa Indonesia	Muslim	rupiah
IRAN	Tehran	53.4	1 648 000	Persian	Muslim	rial
IRAQ	Baghdad	18.3	434 924	Arabic	Muslim	dinar
IRELAND	Dublin	3.7	70 283	English,Irish	Roman Catholic	punt
ISRAEL	Jerusalem	4.5	20 770	Hebrew,Arabic	Jewish	shakel
ITALY	Rome	57.1	301 225	Italian	Roman Catholic	lira
IVORY COAST	Yamoussoukro	11.6	322 463	French	Traditional	CFA franc
JAMAICA	Kingston	2.4	10 991	English	Protestant	dollar
JAPAN	Tokyo	122.6	378 000	Japanese	Shintoist, Buddhist	yen
JORDAN	Amman	3.9	97 740	Arabic	Muslim	dinar
KAZAKHSTAN	Alma-Ata	16.7	2 717 000	Kazakh,Russian		rouble
KENYA	Nairobi	23.2	582 646	Swahili,English	Roman Catholic, Protestant	shilling
KIRGIZIA	Bishkek	4.4	199 000	Kirgiz,Russian		rouble
KUWAIT	Kuwait	2.0	17 818	Arabic	Muslim	dinar
LAOS	Vientiane	4.0	236 800	Lao	Buddhist	kip
LATVIA	Riga	2.7	64 000	Latvian,Russian		rouble
LEBANON	Beirut	2.7	10 400	Arabic	Muslim, Christian	pound
LESOTHO	Maseru	1.7	30 355	English,Sotho	Roman Catholic, Protestant	loti
LIBERIA	Monrovia	2.5	111 369	English	Christian	dollar
LIBYA	Tripoli	4.4	1 759 540	Arabic	Muslim	dinar
LITHUANIA	Vilnius	3.7	65 000	Lithuanian,Russian	Roman Catholic	rouble
LUXEMBOURG	Luxembourg	0.4	2 586	French,German	Roman Catholic	franc
MADAGASCAR	Antananarivo	11.6	587 041	Malagasy	Christian, Traditional	Malagasy franc
MALAWI	Lilongwe	8.4	118 484	English,Chichewa	Christian	kwacha
MALAYSIA	Kuala Lumpur	17.4	329 749	Malay	Muslim	ringgit
MALI	Bamako	8.9	1 240 000	French,Bambara	Muslim	franc
MAURITANIA	Nouakchott	2.0	1 030 700	French,Arabic	Muslim	ouguiya
MAURITIUS	Port-Louis	1.1	2 045	English,Creole	Hindu	rupee
MEXICO	Mexico City	86.7	1 972 547	Spanish	Roman Catholic	peso
MOLDAVIA	Kishinev	4.4	34 000	Romanian,Russian		rouble
MONGOLIA	Ulan Bator	2.1	1 565 000	Mongol	Atheist, Traditional	tugrik
MOROCCO	Rabat	24.4	446 550	Arabic	Muslim	dirham
MOZAMBIQUE	Maputo	15.2	801 590	Portuguese	Traditional, Roman Catholic	metical
MYANMA	Rangoon(Yangon)	40.8	676 552	Burmese	Buddhist	kyat
NAMIBIA	Windhoek	1.7	824 292	Afrikaans,English	Lutheran	
NEPAL	Kathmandu	18.7	140 797	Nepali	Hindu	rupee
NETHERLANDS	Amsterdam	14.9	40 844	Dutch	Roman Catholic, Dutch Reformed	guilder
NEW CALEDONIA	Noumea	0.2	19 058	French	Roman Catholic	franc
NEW ZEALAND	Wellington	3.4	268 676	English	Protestant, Roman Catholic	dollar
NICARAGUA	Managua	3.7	130 000	Spanish	Roman Catholic	cordoba
NIGER	Niamey	7.5	1 267 000	French	Muslim	CFA franc
NIGERIA	Abuja	105	923 768	English	Muslim	naira
NORTH KOREA	Pyongyang	21.4	120 538	Korean	Atheist	won
NORWAY	Oslo	4.2	324 219	Norwegian	Evangelical Lutheran	krone

HEALTH AND EDUCATION

CALORIES PER CAPITA	PEOPLE PER DOCTOR	POPULATION WITH ACCESS TO SAFE WATER	PRIMARY SCHOOL ENROLMENT
mean daily calorie intake as a % of the requirement, 1985	the ratio of people to doctors, 1988	% of population with access to clean water, 1987	% of children attending first level education, 1989
99	2 451	52	77
85	50 000	15	30
105		33	
111	8 065	73	90
79	6 803	35	95
95	1 715	69	106
	1 104		106
135	305	100	97
	382	100	99
94	2 681	56	98
109	10 526	36	118
118	3 106	75	114
118	1 828	89	98
140	684	100	100
119	414	93	95
143	234	100	95
102		19	70
112	2 198	86	105
106	677	100	102
117	1 332	93	104
87	11 111	28	96
	699	100	94
96	7 042	21	111
101	716	92	100
100		14	113
103		20	35
152	812	96	
	556	100	
111	12 500	18	118
95	29 412	51	66
110	3 425	69	102
69	26 316	12	23
97	13 514	43	52
118	2 188	95	106
126	2 618	75	118
117	474		102
108	4 878	27	71
68	47 619	13	68
117	4 000	29	99
88	37 037	34	82
128	397	100	115
131	572	100	107
105	1 715	56	99
97	41 667	34	29
92	9 259	33	77
126	485	60	
114	445	100	95

DEVELOPMENT

GROSS DOMESTIC PRODUCT	LIFE EXPECTANCY	ADULT LITERACY	UNDER 5 MORTALITY
total value of goods & services, US$ per person, 1989	years a new born child can expect to live given the mortality risk in the country, 1989	% of people over 15 years who can read and write, 1985	number of children of every 1000 live births who die before age 5, 1989
858	63	55.0	97
		82.8	
416	43	28.5	241
42	20	250	
356	64	91.6	73
440	55	34.8	133
917	65	59.5	103
9 613	77	8.0	
2 625	70	98.9	17
23 640	78	100.0	8
335	59	40.8	145
473	61	67.3	100
1 222	67	36.5	64
3 090	64	89.3	89
9 181	74	100.0	11
9 368	76	91.8	12
14 432	76	97.0	11
856	53	35.0	139
1 298	73	96.1	21
23 325	79	100.0	6
1 162	67	65.4	55
309	59	47.0	111
10 189	73	67.5	20
129	49	83.9	156
1 887	65	68.2	57
244	57	59.0	132
426	53	19.6	209
5 853	61	39.0	116
18 000	75	100.0	13
139	54	53.0	179
186	48	31.0	258
2 045	70	69.6	30
217	45	9.4	287
521	47	17.4	217
1 855	70		29
2 102	69	90.3	51
1 053	62	90.0	87
775	61	21.4	116
78	47	27.2	297
250	61	71.0	91
938	57		171
160	52	20.6	193
15 421	77	100.0	8
		91.3	
11 544	75	100.0	12
550	64	57.5	92
359	45	10.0	225
287	51	34.0	170
858	70		36
21 724	77	100.0	10

KEY STATISTICS

COUNTRY	CAPITAL CITY	POPULATION in millions, 1989	AREA in sq. km	MAIN LANGUAGES	MAIN RELIGIONS	CURRENCY
OMAN	Muscat	1.4	212 457	Arabic	Muslim	rial
PAKISTAN	Islamabad	105.4	796 095	Urdu,Punjabi,English	Muslim	rupee
PANAMA	Panama City	2.4	77 082	Spanish	Roman Catholic	balbao
PAPUA NEW GUINEA	Port Moresby	3.8	461 691	English,Pidgin,Motu	Protestant, Roman Catholic	kina
PARAGUAY	Asuncion	4.2	406 752	Spanish,Guarani	Roman Catholic	guarani
PERU	Lima	21.3	1 285 216	Spanish	Roman Catholic	sol
PHILIPPINES	Manila	60.9	300 000	Pilipino	Roman Catholic	peso
POLAND	Warsaw	38.2	312 677	Polish	Roman Catholic	zloty
PORTUGAL	Lisbon	10.3	92 082	Portuguese	Roman Catholic	escudo
PUERTO RICO	San Juan	3.3	8 897	Spanish,English	Roman Catholic	dollar
QATAR	Doha	0.4	11 000	Arabic	Muslim	riyal
ROMANIA	Bucharest	23.2	237 500	Romanian	Romanian Orthodox	leu
RUSSIAN FED.	Moscow	148	17 075 000	Russian		rouble
RWANDA	Kigali	7.0	26 338	Kinyarwanda,French	Roman Catholic	franc
SAUDI ARABIA	Riyadh	13.6	2 149 690	Arabic	Muslim	riyal
SENEGAL	Dakar	7.1	196 192	French	Muslim	CFA franc
SIERRA LEONE	Freetown	4.0	71 740	English	Traditional, Muslim	leone
SINGAPORE	Singapore	2.7	581	English,Chinese	Buddhist, Christian	dollar
SOLOMON ISLANDS	Honiara	0.3	28 446	English	Protestant	dollar
SOMALI REPUBLIC	Mogadishu	7.3	637 657	Arabic,Italian,English	Muslim	shilling
SOUTH AFRICA	Cape Town / Pretoria	34.5	1 221 037	Afrikaans, English	Christian	rand
SOUTH KOREA	Seoul	42.4	98 484	Korean	Buddhist, Confucian	won
SPAIN	Madrid	39.1	504 782	Spanish	Roman Catholic	peseta
SRI LANKA	Colombo	17.0	65 610	Sinhala,Tamil	Buddhist	rupee
SUDAN	Khartoum	24.5	2 505 813	Arabic	Muslim	pound
SURINAM	Paramaribo	0.4	163 265	Dutch,English	Hindu, Roman Catholic	guilder
SWAZILAND	Mbabane	0.8	17 363	English,Siswati	Christian	rand, lilangeni
SWEDEN	Stockholm	8.4	449 964	Swedish	Lutheran	krona
SWITZERLAND	Berne	6.6	41 288	German,French,Italian	Roman Catholic, Protestant	franc
SYRIA	Damascas	12.1	185 180	Arabic	Muslim	pound
TAIWAN	Taibei	20.0	35 961	Mandarin	Traditional, Buddhist	dollar
TAJIKISTAN	Dushanbe	5.3	143 000	Tajik,Russian		rouble
TANZANIA	Dodoma	26.3	945 087	Swahili	Christian, Muslim	shilling
THAILAND	Bangkok	54.9	514 000	Thai	Buddhist	baht
TOGO	Lome	3.4	56 785	French	Traditional	CFA franc
TONGA	Nuku'alofa	0.1	747		Free Wesleyan	dollar
TRINIDAD	Port of Spain	1.3	5 130	English	Roman Catholic, Hindu	dollar
TUNISIA	Tunis	8.0	163 610	Arabic	Muslim	dinar
TURKEY	Ankara	54.8	780 576	Turkish	Muslim	lira
TURKMENISTAN	Ashkhabad	3.6	488 000	Turkmen,Russian	Muslim	rouble
UGANDA	Kampala	18.1	236 036	English	Roman Catholic	shilling
UKRAINE	Kiev	51.8	604 000	Ukrainian,Russian	Orthodox,Roman Catholic	rouble
UNITED ARAB EMIRATES	Abu Dhabi Town	1.5	83 600	Arabic	Muslim	dirham
UNITED KINGDOM	London	57.1	244 046	English	Christian	pound
URUGUAY	Montevideo	3.1	176 215	Spanish	Roman Catholic	peso
USA	Washington	247.3	9 372 614	English	Protestant, Roman Catholic	dollar
UZBEKISTAN	Tashkent	20.3	447 000	Uzbek,Russian		rouble
VENEZUELA	Caracas	19.2	912 050	Spanish	Roman Catholic	bolivar
VIETNAM	Hanoi	65.3	329 556	Vietnamese	Buddhist	dong
WESTERN SAHARA	Laayoune	0.2	266 000	Arabic	Muslim	peseta
WESTERN SAMOA	Apia	0.2	2 842	Samoan,English	Congregational	tala
YEMEN REPUBLIC	Aden	11.3	527 968	Arabic	Muslim	dinar/riyal
YUGOSLAVIA	Belgrade	23.7	255 804	Serbo-Croat,Macedonian	Orthodox, Roman Catholic	dinar
ZAIRE	Kinshasa	34.5	2 345 409	French,Lingala	Roman Catholic	zaire
ZAMBIA	Lusaka	8.1	752 614	English	Christian	kwacha
ZIMBABWE	Harare	9.4	390 580	English	Christian, Traditional	dollar

HEALTH AND EDUCATION / DEVELOPMENT

CALORIES PER CAPITA	PEOPLE PER DOCTOR	POPULATION WITH ACCESS TO SAFE WATER	PRIMARY SCHOOL ENROLMENT	GROSS DOMESTIC PRODUCT	LIFE EXPECTANCY	ADULT LITERACY	UNDER 5 MORTALITY
mean daily calorie intake as a % of the requirement, 1985	the ratio of people to doctors, 1988	% of population with access to clean water, 1987	% of children attending first level education, 1989	total value of goods & services, US$ per person, 1989	years a new born child can expect to live given the mortality risk in the country, 1989	% of people over 15 years who can read and write, 1985	number of children of every 1000 live births who die before age 5, 1989
	1 112	14	97	5 500	65	38.0	53
93	3 021	53	40	350	57	26.2	162
98	1 071	82	106	1 918	72	88.2	87
79	13 158	16	70	733	55	32.1	83
127	1 647	26	102	1 545	67	87.5	61
84	1 168	55	122	2 178	62	81.9	119
101	7 246	66	106	662	64	83.3	72
126	517	100	101	1 719	72	98.8	18
124	395	100	124	4 017	74	84.0	16
			94	5 384		89.1	
	511	94	121	15 909	69	51.1	37
127	575	100	97	1 374	70	100.0	34
87	5 714	59	67	338	49	38.2	201
132	799	91	71	5 311	64	51.1	95
109	22 222	42	60	717	48	2.02	189
85	15 152	22	54	233	42	24.0	261
	2 439		115	9 019	74		12
					67		
91	21 739	36	15	241	46	54.8	218
118				2 958	61	80.0	91
117	1 176	60	104	4 081	70	87.6	31
130	282	100	113	8 668	77	92.9	10
114	8 696	36	104	423	71	86.8	36
93	11 364	21	49	467	50	31.4	175
					69	90.0	40
					56	55.2	170
114	365	100	100	21 155	77	100.0	7
126	624	100		27 748	77	100.0	9
129	1 319	75	110	1 314	66	40.0	62
				5 975			
99		50	66	123	54	46.3	173
102	6 757	66	95	1 063	66	88.0	35
97	14 286	35	101	422	54	31.4	150
					66	99.6	
126	1 022	99	100	3 379	71	94.9	18
119	2 262	75	116	1 287	66	50.7	66
125	1 350	78	117	1 382	65	74.2	90
109	27 778	16	70	204	52	52.0	167
	1 174	93	99	15 560	70	53.5	31
129	619	100	106	14 477	76	100.0	10
103	532	80	110	2 595	72	93.9	27
140	491	100	100	19 815	76	99.5	12
95	780		107	3 400	70	84.7	44
97	3 236	41	102	154	62	84.0	66
						97.8	
					51		192
134	557	100	95	2 279	72	89.6	27
96		9	76	193	53		132
85	8 547	47	97	347	54		125
84	7 752	52	128	518	59	74.0	90

All the names on the maps in this atlas, except some of those on the special topic maps, are included in the index.

The names are arranged in **alphabetical order**. Where the name has more than one word the separate words are considered as one to decide the position of the name in the index:

Thetford
The Wash
The Weald
Thiers

Where there is more than one place with the same name, the country name is used to decide the order:

London Canada
London U.K.

If both places are in the same country, the county or state name is also used:

Avon *r.* Dorset U.K.
Avon *r.* Glos U.K.

Each entry in the index starts with the name of the place or feature, followed by the name of the country or region in which it is located. This is followed by the number of the most appropriate page on which the name appears, usually the largest scale map. Next comes the alphanumeric reference followed by the latitude and longitude.

Names of physical features such as rivers, capes, mountains etc are followed by a description. The descriptions are usually shortened to one or two letters, these abbreviations are keyed below. Town names are followed by a description only when the name may be confused with that of a physical feature:

Black River *town*

To help to distinguish the different parts of each entry, different styles of type are used:

place name   country name   alphanumeric
              or   grid reference
              region name

       description   page   latitude/
       (if any)   number   longitude

Thames   *r.*   U.K.   **15**   **C2** 51.30N 0.05E

To use the **alphanumeric grid reference** to find a feature on the map, first find the correct page and then look at the letters printed in blue along the top and bottom of the map and the numbers printed in blue at the sides of the map. When you have found the correct letter and number follow the grid boxes up and along until you find the correct grid box in which the feature appears. You must then search the grid box until you find the name of the feature.

The **latitude and longitude reference** gives a more exact description of the position of the feature.

Page 6 of the atlas describes lines of latitude and lines of longitude, and explains how they are numbered and divided into degrees and minutes. Each name in the index has a different latitude and longitude reference, so the feature can be located accurately. The lines of latitude and lines of longitude shown on each map are numbered in degrees. These numbers are printed black along the top, bottom and sides of the map.

The drawing above shows part of the map on page 28 and the lines of latitude and lines of longitude.

The index entry for Wexford is given as follows

Wexford Rep. of Ire. **28** **E2** 52.20N 6.25W

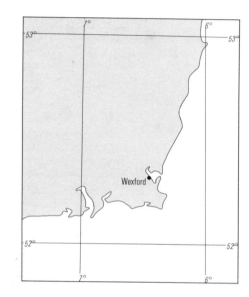

To locate Wexford, first find latitude 52N and estimate 20 minutes north from 52 degrees to find 52.20N, then find longitude 6W and estimate 25 minutes west from 6 degrees to find 6.25W. The symbol for the town of Wexford is where latitude 52.20N and longitude 6.25W meet.

On maps at a smaller scale than the map of Ireland, it is not possible to show every line of latitude and longitude. Only every 5 or 10 degrees of latitude and longitude may be shown. On these maps you must estimate the degrees and minutes to find the exact location of a feature.

Abbreviations

Afghan.	Afghanistan
Bangla.	Bangladesh
b., **B.**	bay, Bay
Beds.	Bedfordshire
Berks.	Berkshire
Bucks.	Buckinghamshire
Cambs.	Cambridgeshire
c., **C.**	cape, Cape
C.A.R.	Central African Republic
Czech.	Czechoslovakia
d.	internal division eg. county, state
Derbys.	Derbyshire
des.	desert
Dom. Rep.	Dominican Republic
D. and G.	Dumfries and Galloway
E. Sussex	East Sussex
Equat. Guinea	Equatorial Guinea
est.	estuary
f.	physical feature eg. valley, plain, geographic district
Glos.	Gloucestershire
G.L.	Greater London
G.M.	Greater Manchester
g., **G.**	Gulf
Hants.	Hampshire
H. and W.	Hereford and Worcester
Herts.	Hertfordshire
Humber.	Humberside

i., **I.**, *is.*, **Is.**	island, Island, islands, Islands
I.o.M.	Isle of Man
I.o.W.	Isle of Wight
l., **L.**	lake, Lake
Lancs.	Lancashire
Leics.	Leicestershire
Liech.	Liechtenstein
Lincs.	Lincolnshire
Lux.	Luxembourg
Mersey.	Merseyside
M.G.	Mid Glamorgan
Mt.	Mount
mtn., **Mtn.**	mountain, Mountain
mts., **Mts.**	mountains, Mountains
Neth.	Netherlands
N. Ireland	Northern Ireland
Northants.	Northamptonshire
Northum.	Northumberland
N. Korea	North Korea
N. Yorks.	North Yorkshire
Notts.	Nottinghamshire
Oxon.	Oxfordshire
P.N.G.	Papua New Guinea
pen., **Pen.**	peninsula, Peninsula
Phil.	Philippines
Pt.	Point
r., **R.**	river, River
Rep. of Ire.	Republic of Ireland
R.S.A.	Republic of South Africa

Resr.	Reservoir
Somali Rep.	Somali Republic
Sd.	Sound
S.G.	South Glamorgan
S. Korea	South Korea
S. Yorks.	South Yorkshire
Staffs.	Staffordshire
str., **Str.**	strait, Strait
Strath.	Strathclyde
Switz.	Switzerland
T. and W.	Tyne and Wear
U.A.E.	United Arab Emirates
U.K.	United Kingdom
U.S.A.	United States of America
Warwicks.	Warwickshire
W.G.	West Glamorgan
W. Isles	Western Isles
W. Midlands	West Midlands
W. Sahara	Western Sahara
W. Sussex	West Sussex
W. Yorks.	West Yorkshire
Wilts.	Wiltshire
Yugo.	Yugoslavia

A

Aachen Germany 47 E2 50.46N 6.06E
Äänekoski Finland 58 F3 62.36N 25.44E
Aarau Switz. 52 D2 47.24N 8.04E
Aardenburg Neth. 47 B3 51.16N 3.26E
Aare r. Switz. 52 D2 47.37N 8.13E
Aarschot Belgium 47 C2 50.59N 4.50E
Aba Nigeria 108 C2 5.06N 7.21E
Abadan Iran 69 H3 30.21N 48.15E
Abadan I. Iran 69 H3 30.10N 48.30E
Abadla Algeria 104 B5 31.01N 2.45W
Abakaliki Nigeria 108 C2 6.17N 8.04E
Abakan Russian Fed. 61 H3 53.43N 91.25E
Abariringa i. Kiribati 82 I7 2.50S171.40W
Abashiri wan b. Japan 76 F9 44.02N144.17E
Abaya, L. Ethiopia 82 F2 6.20N 38.00E
Abbeville France 48 D6 50.06N 1.51E
Abbey Town England 22 A1 54.50N 3.18W
Abbotsbury England 13 E2 50.40N 2.36W
Abéché Chad 105 E3 13.49N 20.49E
Åbenrå Denmark 46 C3 55.03N 9.26E
Abeokuta Nigeria 108 B2 7.10N 3.26E
Aberaeron Wales 18 B2 52.15N 4.16W
Abercarn Wales 18 C1 51.39N 3.09W
Aberdare Wales 18 C1 51.43N 3.27W
Aberdaron Wales 18 B2 52.48N 4.41W
Aberdeen Scotland 24 F4 57.08N 2.07W
Aberdeen S. Dak. U.S.A. 86 G6 45.28N 98.30W
Aberdeen Wash. U.S.A. 86 B6 46.58N123.49W
Aberdovey Wales 18 B2 52.33N 4.03W
Aberfan Wales 18 C1 51.42N 3.20W
Aberfeldy Scotland 24 E3 56.38N 3.52W
Aberffraw Wales 18 B3 53.11N 4.28W
Aberfoyle Scotland 26 D3 56.11N 4.23W
Abergavenny Wales 18 C1 51.49N 3.01W
Abergele Wales 18 C3 53.17N 3.34W
Abernethy Scotland 27 E3 56.20N 3.19W
Aberporth Wales 18 B2 52.08N 4.33W
Abersoch Wales 18 B2 52.50N 4.31W
Abersychan Wales 18 C1 51.44N 3.03W
Abertillery Wales 18 C1 51.44N 3.09W
Aberystwyth Wales 18 B2 52.25N 4.06W
Ab-i-Diz r. Iran 69 H3 31.38N 48.54E
Abidjan Côte d'Ivoire 104 B2 5.19N 4.01W
Abilene U.S.A. 86 G3 32.27N 99.45W
Abingdon England 14 A2 51.40N 1.17W
Abington Scotland 27 E2 55.29N 3.42W
Abitibi r. Canada 91 J3 51.20N 80.30W
Abomey Benin 108 B2 7.14N 2.00E
Aboyne Scotland 24 F4 57.05N 2.49W
Abqaiq Saudi Arabia 69 H2 25.55N 49.40E
Abrantes Portugal 50 A3 39.28N 8.12W
Abu Dhabi U.A.E. 69 I2 24.27N 54.23E
Abu Hamed Sudan 105 F3 19.32N 33.20E
Abuja Nigeria 108 C2 9.12N 7.11E
Abu Simbel Egypt 68 C1 22.18N 31.40E
Abu Tīg Egypt 68 C2 27.06N 31.17E
Abu Zenīma Egypt 68 D3 29.03N 33.06E
Acambaro Mexico 92 D4 20.01N101.42W
Acapulco Mexico 92 E3 16.51N 99.56W
Acarigua Venezuela 94 F2 9.35N 69.12W
Acatlán Mexico 92 E3 18.12N 98.02W
Accra Ghana 108 A2 5.33N 0.15W
Accrington England 20 C2 53.46N 2.22W
Achahoish Scotland 26 C2 55.57N 5.30W
Achill I. Rep. of Ire. 28 A3 53.57N 10.00W
Achinsk Russian Fed. 60 H3 56.10N 90.10E
Acklin's I. Bahamas 93 J4 22.30N 74.10W
Ackworth Moor Top town England 21 D2 53.39N 1.20W
Aconcagua mtn. Argentina 97 C4 32.37S 70.00W
Acqui Italy 54 B6 44.41N 8.28E
Adamawa Highlands Nigeria / Cameroon 108 D2 7.05N 12.00E
Adams, Mt. U.S.A. 86 B6 46.13N121.29W
Adana Turkey 68 D5 37.00N 35.19E
Adapazari Turkey 68 C6 40.45N 30.23E
Adda r. Italy 54 B6 45.08N 9.55E
Ad Dahana des. Saudi Arabia 69 G2 26.00N 47.00E
Adderbury England 14 A3 52.01N 1.19W
Addis Ababa Ethiopia 105 F2 9.03N 38.42E
Ad Diwaniya Iraq 69 G3 31.59N 44.57E
Adelaide Australia 80 C2 34.56S138.36E
Aden Yemen 105 G3 12.50N 45.00E
Aden, G. of Indian Oc. 105 G3 13.00N 50.00E
Adi i. Indonesia 79 I3 4.10S133.10E
Adige r. Italy 54 D6 45.10N 12.20E
Adiyaman Turkey 68 E5 37.46N 38.15E
Adlington England 20 C2 53.37N 2.36W
Admiralty Is. P.N.G. 79 L3 2.30S147.20E
Adour r. France 48 C2 43.28N 1.35W
Adrano Italy 54 E2 37.39N 14.49E
Adriatic Sea Med. Sea 56 B5 42.30N 16.00E
Aduwa Ethiopia 105 F3 14.12N 38.56E
Adwick le Street England 21 D2 53.35N 1.12W
Aegean Sea Med. Sea 56 G3 39.00N 25.00E
Aerö i. Denmark 46 D2 54.52N 10.25E
Aeron r. Wales 18 B2 52.14N 4.16W
Afghanistan Asia 70 B6 33.00N 65.30E
Afif Saudi Arabia 68 F1 23.53N 42.59E
Afikpo Nigeria 108 C2 5.53N 7.55E
Afobaka Surinam 95 H2 5.00N 55.05W
Africa 113
Afyon Turkey 68 C5 38.46N 30.32E
Agadès Niger 104 C3 17.00N 7.56E
Agadir Morocco 104 B5 30.26N 9.36W
Agana Guam 79 K6 13.28N144.45E
Agano r. Japan 76 D5 37.58N139.02E
Agartala India 71 G4 23.49N 91.15E
Agedabia Libya 104 E5 30.48N 20.15E
Agen France 48 D3 44.12N 0.38E
Agger r. Germany 47 F2 50.45N 7.06E
Aghada Rep. of Ire. 28 C1 51.50N 8.14W
Agnew's Hill N. Ireland 23 D1 54.51N 5.58W
Agordat Ethiopia 105 F3 15.35N 37.55E
Agra India 71 E5 27.09N 78.00E
Agra r. Spain 50 E5 42.12N 1.43W
Agreda Spain 50 E4 41.51N 1.55W
Agri r. Italy 54 F4 40.13N 16.45E
Agri Turkey 68 F5 39.44N 43.04E
Agrigento Italy 54 D2 37.19N 13.36E
Agrihan i. Mariana Is. 79 L7 18.44N145.39E
Aguascalientes Mexico 92 D4 21.51N102.18W
Aguascalientes d. Mexico 92 D4 22.00N102.00W
Águeda r. Spain 50 B4 41.00N 6.56W
Aguilas Spain 50 E2 37.25N 1.35W
Agulhas, C. R.S.A. 106 C1 34.50S 20.00E
Agulhas Negras mtn. Brazil 97 E5 22.20S 44.43W
Ahaggar Mts. Algeria 104 C4 24.00N 5.50E
Ahar Iran 69 G5 38.25N 47.07E
Ahaus Germany 47 F4 52.04N 7.01E
Ahlen Germany 52 C4 51.46N 7.53E
Ahmadabad India 71 D4 23.03N 72.40E
Ahmadnagar India 71 D3 19.08N 74.48E
Ahr r. Germany 47 F2 50.34N 7.16E
Ahwaz Iran 69 H3 31.17N 48.44E
Ailette r. France 47 B1 49.35N 3.09E
Ailsa Craig i. Scotland 26 C2 55.15N 5.07W
Ain r. France 48 F3 45.47N 5.12E
Ain Salah Algeria 104 C4 27.12N 2.29E
Aïn Sefra Algeria 104 B5 32.45N 0.35W
Aïr mts. Niger 104 C3 18.30N 8.30E
Airdrie Scotland 27 E2 55.52N 3.59W
Aire r. England 21 E2 53.42N 0.54W
Aire France 48 C2 43.39N 0.15W
Airedale f. England 20 D2 53.56N 1.54W
Aisne r. France 47 A1 49.27N 2.51E
Aitape P.N.G. 79 K3 3.10S142.17E
Aitutaki Atoll Cook Is. 83 K6 18.52S159.46W
Aix-en-Provence France 48 F2 43.31N 5.27E
Aíyina i. Greece 56 F2 37.43N 23.30E
Aizuwakamatsu Japan 76 D5 37.30N139.58E
Ajaccio France 49 H1 41.55N 8.43E
Ajama U.A.E. 69 I2 25.23N 55.26E
Ajmer India 71 D5 26.29N 74.40E
Akaishi san mts. Japan 76 D4 35.20N138.05E
Akashi Japan 76 C4 34.39N135.00E
Akhaltsikhe Georgia 68 F6 41.37N 42.59E
Akhdar, Jebel mts. Libya 105 E5 32.10N 22.00E
Akhdar, Jebel mts. Oman 69 J1 23.10N 57.25E
Akhdar, Wadi r. Saudi Arabia 68 E3 28.30N 36.48E
Akhelóös r. Greece 56 E3 38.20N 21.04E
Akhisar Turkey 68 B5 38.54N 27.49E
Akhtyrka Ukraine 59 C4 50.19N 34.54E
Akimiski I. Canada 91 J3 53.00N 81.20W
Akita Japan 76 D6 39.44N140.05E
Akkajaure l. Sweden 58 D4 67.40N 17.30E
Akobo r. Sudan / Ethiopia 105 F2 8.30N 33.15E
Akola India 71 D4 20.44N 77.00E
Akpatok I. Canada 91 L4 60.30N 68.30W
Akron U.S.A. 87 J5 41.04N 81.31W
Aksaray Turkey 68 D5 38.22N 34.02E
Akşehir Turkey 68 C5 38.22N 31.24E
Aksu China 74 C5 42.10N 80.00E
Aktogay Kazakhstan 74 C6 46.59N 79.42E
Aktyubinsk Kazakhstan 60 E2 50.16N 57.13E
Akure Nigeria 108 C2 7.14N 5.08E
Akureyri Iceland 58 J7 65.41N 18.04W
Akuse Ghana 108 B2 6.04N 0.12E
Akyab Myanma 71 G4 20.09N 92.55E
Alabama d. U.S.A. 87 I3 33.00N 87.00W
Alabama r. U.S.A. 87 I3 31.05N 87.55W
Alagez mtn. Armenia 69 G6 40.32N 44.11E
Al Ain, Wadi r. Oman 69 I1 22.18N 55.35E
Alakol, L. Kazakhstan 74 C6 46.00N 81.40E
Alakurtti Russian Fed. 58 G4 67.00N 30.23E
Alamagan i. Mariana Is. 79 L7 17.35N145.50E
Alamosa U.S.A. 86 E4 37.28N105.54W
Åland Is. Finland 58 E3 60.20N 20.00E
Alanya Turkey 68 D5 36.32N 32.02E
Alaşehir Turkey 68 C5 38.22N 28.29E
Alaska d. U.S.A. 90 C4 65.00N153.00W
Alaska, G. of U.S.A. 90 D3 58.45N145.00W
Alaska Pen. U.S.A. 90 B3 56.00N160.00W
Alaska Range mts. U.S.A. 90 C4 62.10N152.00W
Alazan r. Georgia 69 G6 41.06N 46.40E
Albacete Spain 50 E3 39.00N 1.52W
Ålbaek Denmark 46 D5 57.38N 10.26E
Alba-Iulia Romania 56 F7 46.04N 23.33E
Albania Europe 56 E4 41.00N 20.00E
Albany Australia 80 A2 34.57S117.54E
Albany r. Canada 91 J3 52.10N 82.00W
Albany Ga. U.S.A. 87 J3 31.37N 84.10W
Albany N.Y. U.S.A. 87 L5 42.40N 73.49W
Albany Oreg. U.S.A. 86 B5 44.38N123.07W
Albemarle Sd. U.S.A. 87 K4 36.10N 76.00W
Alberche r. Spain 50 C4 40.00N 4.45W
Albert France 48 E6 50.00N 2.40E
Alberta d. Canada 90 G3 55.00N115.00W
Albert Canal Belgium 47 D3 51.00N 5.15E
Albert, L. Africa 105 F2 1.45N 31.00E
Albert Nile r. Uganda 105 F2 3.30N 32.00E
Albi France 48 E2 43.56N 2.08E
Albina Surinam 95 I2 5.30N 54.03W
Alborán, Isla de i. Spain 50 D1 35.55N 3.10W
Ålborg Denmark 46 C5 57.03N 9.56E
Ålborg Bugt b. Denmark 46 D4 56.50N 10.30E
Albuquerque U.S.A. 86 E4 35.05N106.38W
Alburquerque Spain 50 B3 39.13N 6.59W
Alcácer do Sal Portugal 50 A3 38.22N 8.30W
Alcalá de Chisvert Spain 50 F4 40.19N 0.13E
Alcalá de Henares Spain 50 D4 40.28N 3.22W
Alcalá la Real Spain 50 D2 37.28N 3.55W
Alcamo Italy 54 D2 37.59N 12.58E
Alcañiz Spain 50 E4 41.03N 0.09W
Alcaudete Spain 50 C2 37.35N 4.05W
Alcázar de San Juan Spain 50 D3 39.24N 3.12W
Alcester England 16 C2 52.13N 1.52W
Alcira Spain 50 E3 39.10N 0.27W
Alcoy Spain 50 E3 38.42N 0.29W
Alcubierre, Sierra de mts. Spain 50 E4 41.40N 0.20W
Alcudia Spain 51 G3 39.51N 3.09E
Aldabra Is. Indian Oc. 102 G4 9.00S 47.00E
Aldan Russian Fed. 61 K3 58.44N125.22E
Aldan r. Russian Fed. 61 K3 63.30N130.00E
Aldbourne England 13 F3 51.28N 1.38W
Aldbrough England 21 E2 53.50N 0.07W
Aldeburgh England 15 D3 52.09N 1.35E
Alderney i. Channel Is. 48 B5 49.42N 2.11W
Aldershot England 15 B2 51.15N 0.47W
Aldridge England 16 C2 52.36N 1.55W
Aldsworth England 13 F3 51.48N 1.46W
Aleksandrovsk Sakhalinskiy Russian Fed. 61 L2 50.55N142.12E
Alençon France 48 D5 48.25N 0.05E
Aleppo Syria 68 E5 36.14N 37.10E
Aléria France 49 H2 42.05N 9.30E
Alès France 48 F3 44.08N 4.05E
Alessandria Italy 54 B6 44.54N 8.37E
Ålestrup Denmark 46 C4 56.41N 9.30E
Ålesund Norway 58 A3 62.28N 6.11E
Aleutian Basin Bering Sea 82 H13 57.00N179.00E
Aleutian Is. U.S.A. 84 C7 52.00N176.00W
Aleutian Range mts. U.S.A. 90 C3 58.00N156.00W
Aleutian Trench Pacific Oc. 82 J13 50.00N176.00W
Alexander Archipelago is. U.S.A. 90 E3 56.30N134.30W
Alexandria Egypt 68 C3 31.13N 29.55E
Alexandria Scotland 26 D2 55.59N 4.35W
Alexandria La. U.S.A. 87 H3 31.19N 92.29W
Alexandroúpolis Greece 56 G4 40.50N 25.53E
Alfaro Spain 50 E5 42.11N 1.45W
Alfiós r. Greece 56 E2 37.37N 21.27E
Alford Scotland 24 F4 57.14N 2.43W
Alfreton England 16 C3 53.06N 1.22W
Algeciras Spain 50 C2 36.08N 5.27W
Algeria Africa 104 C4 28.00N 2.00E
Al Ghadaf, Wadi r. Iraq 68 F4 32.54N 43.33E
Alghero Italy 54 B4 40.33N 8.20E
Algiers Algeria 104 C5 36.50N 3.00E
Al Hamra des. U.A.E. 69 I1 22.45N 55.10E
Aliákmon r. Greece 56 F4 40.30N 22.38E
Alicante Spain 50 E3 38.21N 0.29W
Alice U.S.A. 86 G2 27.45N 98.06W
Alice Springs town Australia 80 C3 23.42S133.52E
Aligarh India 71 E5 27.54N 78.04E
Aligudarz Iran 69 H4 33.25N 49.38E
Alingsås Sweden 58 C2 57.55N 12.30E
Al Jaub f. Saudi Arabia 69 H1 23.00N 50.00E
Al Jauf Saudi Arabia 68 E3 29.49N 39.52E
Al Jazi des. Iraq 68 F4 35.00N 41.00E
Al Khamāsīn Saudi Arabia 105 G4 20.29N 44.49E
Al Khubar Saudi Arabia 69 H2 26.18N 50.06E
Al Khurr r. Iraq 68 F3 32.00N 44.15E
Alkmaar Neth. 47 C4 52.37N 4.44E
Al Kut Iraq 69 G4 32.30N 45.51E
Allahabad India 71 E4 25.57N 81.50E
Allakaket U.S.A. 90 C4 66.30N152.45W
'Allaqi, Wadi r. Egypt 68 D1 22.55N 33.02E
Al Lawz, Jebel mtn. Saudi Arabia 68 D3 28.40N 35.20E
Allegheny Mts. U.S.A. 87 K5 40.00N 79.00W
Allen, Lough Rep. of Ire. 28 C4 54.07N 8.04W
Allentown U.S.A. 87 K5 40.37N 75.30W
Alleppey India 71 D2 9.30N 76.22E
Aller r. Germany 52 D5 52.57N 9.11E
Alliance Nebr. U.S.A. 86 F5 42.08N103.00W
Allier r. France 48 E4 46.58N 3.04E
Allingåbro Denmark 46 D4 56.29N 10.20E
Alloa Scotland 27 E3 56.07N 3.49W
Alma-Ata Kazakhstan 74 B5 43.19N 76.55E
Almadén Spain 50 C3 38.47N 4.50W
Al Maharadh des. Saudi Arabia 69 I1 22.00N 52.30E
Almansa Spain 50 E3 38.52N 1.06W
Almanzora r. Spain 50 E2 37.16N 1.49W
Almanzor, Pico de mtn. Spain 50 C4 40.20N 5.22W
Almazán Spain 50 D4 41.29N 2.31W
Almeirim Portugal 50 A3 39.12N 8.37W
Almelo Neth. 47 E4 52.21N 6.40E
Almería Spain 50 D2 36.50N 2.26W
Almetyevsk Russian Fed. 60 E3 54.50N 52.22E
Ålmhult Sweden 58 C2 56.32N 14.10E
Al Mira, Wadi r. Iraq 68 F4 32.27N 41.21E
Almond r. Scotland 27 E3 56.25N 3.28W
Almuñécar Spain 50 D2 36.44N 3.41W
Aln r. England 22 C2 55.23N 1.36W
Alnwick England 22 C2 55.25N 1.41W
Alofi Niue 82 J6 19.03S169.55W
Alor i. Indonesia 79 G2 8.20S124.30E
Alor Setar Malaysia 78 C5 6.06N100.23E
Alost Belgium 47 C2 50.57N 4.03E
Alpes Maritimes mts. France 48 G3 44.07N 7.08E
Alphen Neth. 47 C4 52.08N 4.40E
Alpine U.S.A. 86 F3 30.22N103.40W
Alps mts. Europe 48 G4 46.00N 7.30E
Al Qurna Iraq 69 G3 31.00N 47.26E
Als i. Denmark 46 C2 54.56N 9.55E
Alsager England 20 C2 53.07N 2.20W
Alsasua Spain 50 D5 42.54N 2.10W
Alston England 22 B1 54.48N 2.26W
Alta Norway 58 E5 69.57N 23.10E
Alta r. Norway 58 E5 70.00N 23.15E
Altagracia Venezuela 94 E3 10.44N 71.30W
Altagracia de Orituco Venezuela 95 F2 9.45N 66.24W
Altai mts. Mongolia 74 E6 46.30N 93.30E
Altaj Mongolia 74 F6 46.20N 97.00E
Altamaha r. U.S.A. 87 J3 31.15N 81.23W
Altamura Italy 54 F4 40.50N 16.32E
Altay China 74 D6 47.48N 88.07E
Altea Spain 50 E3 38.37N 0.03W
Altenburg Germany 52 F4 50.59N 12.27E
Altenkirchen Germany 47 F2 50.41N 7.40E
Al Tihama des. Saudi Arabia 68 D2 27.50N 35.30E
Altiplano Mexicano mts. N. America 84 J4 24.00N105.00W
Altnaharra Scotland 24 D5 58.16N 4.27W
Alton England 15 B2 51.08N 0.59W
Altoona U.S.A. 87 K5 40.32N 78.23W
Altrincham England 20 C2 53.25N 2.21W
Altun Shan mts. China 74 D5 38.10N 87.50E
Al Ula Saudi Arabia 68 E2 26.39N 37.58E
Alva Scotland 27 E3 56.09N 3.49W
Alva U.S.A. 86 G4 36.48N 98.40W
Alvarado Mexico 92 E3 18.49N 95.46W
Älvsbyn Sweden 58 E4 65.41N 21.00E
Al Wajh Saudi Arabia 68 E2 26.16N 36.28E
Al Wakrah Qatar 69 H2 25.09N 51.36E
Alwar India 71 D5 27.32N 76.35E
Alyaty Azerbaijan 69 H5 39.59N 49.20E
Alyth Scotland 27 E3 56.38N 3.14W
Alytus Lithuania 57 I7 54.24N 24.03E
Alzette r. Lux. 47 E1 49.52N 6.07E
Amagasaki Japan 76 C4 34.43N135.20E
Amager i. Denmark 46 F3 55.34N 12.30E
Amami i. Japan 75 K3 28.20N129.30E
Amara Iraq 69 G3 31.52N 47.50E
Amarillo U.S.A. 86 F4 35.14N101.50W
Amaro, Monte mtn. Italy 54 E5 42.06N 14.04E
Amasya Turkey 68 D6 40.37N 35.50E
Amazon r. Brazil 96 D7 2.00S 50.00W
Amazon Delta f. Brazil 96 E8 0.00 50.00W
Ambala India 71 D5 30.19N 76.49E
Ambarchik Russian Fed. 61 N4 69.39N162.27E
Ambatondrazaka Madagascar 106 G8 17.20S 48.30E
Amberg Germany 52 E3 49.27N 11.52E
Ambergris Cay i. Belize 94 B4 18.00N 87.58W
Amberley England 15 B1 50.54N 0.33W
Amble England 22 C2 55.20N 1.34W
Ambleside England 22 B1 54.26N 2.58W
Ambon Indonesia 79 H3 3.50S128.10E
Ambre, Cap d' c. Madagascar 106 G9 11.58S 49.14E
Ameland i. Neth. 47 D5 53.28N 5.48E
Amersfoort Neth. 47 D4 52.10N 5.23E
Amesbury England 13 F3 51.10N 1.46W
Amga Russian Fed. 61 K3 60.51N131.59E
Amga r. Russian Fed. 61 L3 62.40N135.20E
Amgun r. Russian Fed. 61 L3 53.10N139.47E
Amiata mtn. Italy 54 C5 42.53N 11.37E
Amiens France 48 E5 49.54N 2.18E
Amirantes is. Indian Oc. 113 L4 6.00S 52.00E
Amlwch Wales 18 B3 53.24N 4.21W
Amman Jordan 68 D3 31.57N 35.56E
Ammanford Wales 18 C1 51.48N 4.00W
Ammassalik Greenland 91 O4 65.40N 38.00W
Ampala Honduras 93 G2 13.16N 87.39W
Ampthill England 15 B3 52.03N 0.30W
Amraoti India 71 D4 20.58N 77.50E
Amritsar India 71 D5 31.35N 74.56E
Amrum i. Germany 46 B2 54.40N 8.20E
Amsterdam Neth. 47 C4 52.22N 4.54E
Amsterdam I. Indian Oc. 113 M3 37.00S 79.00E
Amu Darya r. Asia 60 E2 43.50N 59.00E
Amundsen G. Canada 90 F5 70.30N122.00W
Amundsen Sea Antarctica 112 D1 70.00S116.00W
Amuntai Indonesia 78 F3 2.24S115.14E
Amur r. Russian Fed. 61 L3 53.17N140.00E
Anabar r. Russian Fed. 61 J4 72.40N113.30E
Anaco Venezuela 95 G2 9.27N 64.28W
Anadyr Russian Fed. 61 O4 64.40N177.32E
Anadyr r. Russian Fed. 61 O4 65.00N176.00E
Anadyr, G. of Russian Fed. 61 P4 64.30N177.50W
Anaiza Saudi Arabia 69 F2 26.05N 43.57E
Anambas Is. Indonesia 78 D4 3.00N106.10E
Anan Japan 76 B3 33.55N134.39E
Anatahan i. Mariana Is. 79 L7 16.22N145.38E
Anatolia f. Turkey 68 D5 38.00N 35.00E
Anchorage U.S.A. 90 D4 61.10N150.00W
Ancona Italy 54 D5 43.37N 13.33E
Ancroft England 22 B2 55.42N 2.00W
Anda China 75 J6 46.25N125.20E
Andalsnes Norway 58 A3 62.33N 7.43E
Andalucia d. Spain 50 C2 38.00N 4.00W
Andaman Is. India 71 G2 12.00N 93.00E
Andaman Sea Indian Oc. 78 B6 11.00N 96.00E
Andernach Germany 47 F2 50.25N 7.24E
Anderson r. Canada 90 F4 69.45N129.00W
Andes mts. S. America 96 B6 15.00S 72.00W
Andevoranto Madagascar 106 G8 18.56S 49.07E
Andfjorden est. Norway 58 D5 69.10N 16.20E
Andhra Pradesh d. India 71 E3 17.00N 79.00E
Andikíthira i. Greece 56 F1 35.52N 23.18E
Andizhan Uzbekistan 74 B5 40.48N 72.23E
Andorra town Andorra 48 D2 42.30N 1.31E
Andorra Europe 48 D2 42.30N 1.32E
Andover England 14 A2 51.13N 1.29W
Andöy i. Norway 58 C5 69.00N 15.30E
Andreas I.o.M. 20 A3 54.22N 4.26W
Andreas, C. Cyprus 68 D4 35.40N 34.35E
Andropov Russian Fed. 59 D5 58.01N 38.52E
Ándros i. Greece 56 G2 37.50N 24.50E
Andros I. Bahamas 93 I4 24.30N 78.00W
Andújar Spain 50 C3 38.02N 4.03W
Anegada i. B.V.Is. 93 L3 18.46N 64.24W
Aného Togo 108 B2 6.17N 1.40E
Aneiza, Jebel mtn. Asia 68 E4 32.15N 39.19E
Aneto, Pico de mtn. Spain 50 F5 42.40N 0.19E
Angara r. Russian Fed. 61 I3 58.00N 93.00E
Angarsk Russian Fed. 61 I3 52.31N103.55E
Ånge Sweden 58 C3 62.31N 15.40E

Buckingham England **15 B2** 52.00N 0.59W
Buckinghamshire *d.* England **15 B2** 51.50N 0.48W
Buckley Wales **18 C3** 53.11N 3.04W
Budapest Hungary **57 F3** 47.30N 19.03E
Buddon Ness *c.* Scotland **27 F3** 56.29N 2.42W
Bude England **12 C2** 50.49N 4.33W
Bude B. England **12 C2** 50.50N 4.40W
Budleigh Salterton England **13 D2** 50.37N 3.19W
Buenaventura Colombia **94 D1** 3.54N 77.02W
Buenos Aires Argentina **97 D4** 34.40S 58.30W
Buffalo N.Y. U.S.A. **87 K5** 42.52N 78.55W
Buffalo Wyo. U.S.A. **86 E5** 44.21N106.40W
Bug *r.* Poland **57 G6** 52.29N 21.11E
Bug *r.* Ukraine **59 C3** 46.55N 31.59E
Buga Colombia **94 D1** 3.53N 76.17W
Buggs Island L. U.S.A. **87 K4** 36.35N 78.20W
Bugt China **75 J6** 48.45N121.58E
Bugulma Russian Fed. **59 G4** 54.32N 52.46E
Buie, Loch Scotland **26 C3** 56.20N 5.53W
Builth Wells Wales **18 C2** 52.09N 3.24W
Buitenpost Neth. **47 E5** 53.15N 6.09E
Bujumbura Burundi **106 C4** 3.22S 29.21E
Bukavu Zaïre **106 C4** 2.30S 28.49E
Bukhara Uzbekistan **60 F1** 39.47N 64.26E
Bukittinggi Indonesia **78 C3** 0.18S100.20E
Bula Indonesia **79 I3** 3.07S130.27E
Bulagan Mongolia **74 G6** 48.34N103.12E
Bulan Phil. **79 G6** 12.40N123.53E
Bulawayo Zimbabwe **106 C2** 20.10S 28.43E
Bulbjerg *mtn.* Denmark **46 C5** 57.09N 9.04E
Bulgaria Europe **56 G5** 42.30N 25.00E
Bulkington England **16 C2** 52.29N 1.25W
Bulolo P.N.G. **79 L2** 7.13S146.35E
Bulu, Gunung *mtn.* Indonesia **78 F4** 3.00N116.00E
Bulun Russian Fed. **61 K4** 70.50N127.20E
Bunbury Australia **80 A2** 33.20S115.34E
Buncrana Rep. of Ire. **28 D5** 55.08N 7.28W
Bundaberg Australia **80 E3** 24.50S152.21E
Bunde Germany **47 F5** 53.12N 7.16E
Bundoran Rep. of Ire. **28 C4** 54.28N 8.20W
Bunessan Scotland **26 B3** 56.18N 6.14W
Bungay England **15 D3** 52.27N 1.26E
Bungo suido *str.* Japan **76 B3** 32.52N132.30E
Bunguran *i.* Indonesia **78 D4** 4.00N108.20E
Bunguran Selatan *i.* Indonesia **78 D4** 3.00N108.50E
Buni Nigeria **108 D3** 11.20N 11.59E
Buntingford England **15 B2** 51.57N 0.01W
Buol Indonesia **79 G4** 1.12N121.28E
Buqbuq Egypt **68 B3** 31.30N 25.32E
Buraida Saudi Arabia **69 F2** 26.18N 43.58E
Buraimi U.A.E. **69 I2** 24.15N 55.45E
Burdur Turkey **68 C5** 37.44N 30.17E
Burdwan India **71 F4** 23.15N 87.52E
Bure *r.* England **15 D3** 52.36N 1.44E
Bures England **15 C2** 51.59N 0.46E
Burford England **14 A2** 51.48N 1.38W
Burg Germany **52 E5** 52.17N 11.51E
Burgan Kuwait **69 G3** 28.58N 47.58E
Burgas Bulgaria **59 B2** 42.30N 27.29E
Burgenland *d.* Austria **57 E3** 47.30N 16.20E
Burgess Hill *town* England **15 B1** 50.57N 0.07W
Burgh le Marsh England **17 E3** 53.10N 0.15E
Burgos Spain **50 D5** 42.21N 3.41W
Burgsteinfurt Germany **47 F4** 52.09N 7.21E
Burgsvik Sweden **58 D2** 57.03N 18.19E
Burhanpur India **71 D4** 21.18N 76.08E
Burias *i.* Phil. **79 G6** 12.50N123.10E
Burica, Punta Panama **94 C2** 8.05N 82.50W
Burkina Faso Africa **104 B3** 12.15N 1.30W
Burley U.S.A. **86 D5** 42.32N113.48W
Burlington Vt. U.S.A. **87 L5** 44.25N 73.14W
Burnham Market England **15 C3** 52.57N 0.43E
Burnham-on-Crouch England **15 C2** 51.37N 0.50E
Burnham-on-Sea England **13 D3** 51.15N 3.00W
Burnley England **20 C2** 53.47N 2.15W
Burntisland Scotland **27 E3** 56.03N 3.15W
Burntwood England **16 C2** 52.42N 1.54W
Burriana Spain **50 E3** 39.54N 0.05W
Burrow Head Scotland **26 D1** 54.41N 4.24W
Burry Port Wales **18 B1** 51.41N 4.17W
Bursa Turkey **68 C6** 40.11N 29.04E
Burscough England **20 C2** 53.37N 2.51W
Burton Agnes England **21 E3** 54.04N 0.18W
Burton Latimer England **16 D2** 52.23N 0.41W
Burton upon Trent England **16 C2** 52.58N 1.39W
Buru *i.* Indonesia **79 H3** 3.30S126.30E
Burujird Iran **69 H4** 33.54N 48.47E
Burullus, L. Egypt **68 C3** 31.30N 30.45E
Burundi Africa **106 C4** 3.30S 30.00E
Burwell Cambs. England **15 C3** 52.17N 0.20E
Burwell Lincs. England **17 E3** 53.19N 0.02E
Bury England **20 C2** 53.36N 2.19W
Bury St. Edmunds England **15 C3** 52.15N 0.42E
Bush *r.* N. Ireland **23 C2** 55.13N 6.33W
Būshehr Iran **69 H3** 28.57N 50.52E
Bushmills N. Ireland **23 C2** 55.12N 6.32W
Bussum Neth. **47 D4** 52.17N 5.10E
Büsum Germany **46 B2** 54.09N 8.52E
Buta Zaïre **105 E2** 2.49N 24.50E
Butaritari *i.* Kiribati **82 H8** 3.07N172.48E
Bute *i.* Scotland **26 C2** 55.51N 5.07W
Bute, Sd. of Scotland **26 C2** 55.44N 5.10W
Butser Hill England **15 B1** 50.58N 0.58W
Butte U.S.A. **86 D6** 46.00N112.31W
Butterworth Malaysia **78 C5** 5.24N100.22E
Buttevant Rep. of Ire. **28 C2** 52.13N 8.40W
Butt of Lewis *c.* Scotland **24 B5** 58.31N 6.15W
Butuan Phil. **79 H5** 8.56N125.31E
Butung *i.* Indonesia **79 G2** 5.00S122.50E
Bützow Germany **46 E1** 53.52N 11.59E
Buxton England **16 C3** 53.16N 1.54W
Buy Russian Fed. **59 E5** 58.23N 41.27E
Buzău Romania **56 H6** 45.10N 26.49E
Bydgoszcz Poland **57 E6** 53.16N 17.33E
Byfield England **16 C2** 52.10N 1.15W
Bylot I. Canada **91 K5** 73.00N 78.30W
Byrranga Mts. Russian Fed. **61 H4** 74.50N101.00E
Byske *r.* Sweden **58 E4** 64.58N 21.10E
Bytom Poland **57 F5** 50.22N 18.54E

C

Cabanatuan Phil. **79 G7** 15.30N120.58E
Cabimas Venezuela **94 E3** 10.26N 71.27W
Cabinda Angola **106 B4** 5.34S 12.12E
Cabot Str. Canada **91 M2** 47.00N 59.00W
Cabrera *i.* Spain **51 G3** 39.08N 2.56E
Cabrera, Sierra *mts.* Spain **50 B5** 42.10N 6.30W
Cabriel *r.* Spain **50 E3** 39.13N 1.07W
Cabruta Venezuela **95 F2** 7.40N 66.16W
Cáceres Spain **50 B3** 39.29N 6.23W
Cacín *r.* Spain **50 C2** 37.10N 4.01W
Cader Idris *mtn.* Wales **18 C2** 52.40N 3.55W
Cadillac U.S.A. **87 I5** 44.15N 85.23W
Cadí, Sierra del *mts.* Spain **50 F5** 42.12N 1.35E
Cadiz Phil. **79 G6** 10.57N123.18E
Cádiz Spain **50 B2** 36.32N 6.18W
Cádiz, G. of Spain **50 B2** 37.00N 7.10W
Caen France **48 C5** 49.11N 0.22W
Caerleon Wales **18 D1** 51.36N 2.57W
Caernarfon Wales **18 B3** 53.08N 4.17W
Caernarfon B. Wales **18 B3** 53.05N 4.25W
Caerphilly Wales **18 C1** 51.34N 3.13W
Cagayan de Oro Phil. **79 G5** 8.29N124.40E
Cagliari Italy **54 B3** 39.14N 9.07E
Cagliari, G. of Med. Sea **54 B3** 39.07N 9.15E
Caguas Puerto Rico **93 K3** 18.08N 66.00W
Caha Mts. Rep. of Ire. **28 B1** 51.44N 9.45W
Caherciveen Rep. of Ire. **28 A1** 51.51N 10.14W
Cahir Rep. of Ire. **28 D2** 52.21N 7.56W
Cahora Bassa Dam Mozambique **106 D3** 15.33S 32.42E
Cahore Pt. Rep. of Ire. **28 E2** 52.33N 6.11W
Cahors France **48 D3** 44.28N 0.26E
Caibarien Cuba **93 I4** 22.31N 79.28W
Caicos Is. Turks & Caicos Is. **93 J4** 21.30N 72.00W
Cairngorms *mts.* Scotland **24 E4** 57.04N 3.30W
Cairns Australia **80 D4** 16.51S145.43E
Cairnsmore of Carsphairn *mtn.* Scotland **26 D2** 55.15N 4.12W
Cairn Table *mtn.* Scotland **27 D2** 55.29N 4.02W
Cairo Egypt **68 C3** 30.03N 31.15E
Cairo U.S.A. **87 I4** 37.02N 89.02W
Caister-on-Sea England **15 D3** 52.38N 1.43E
Caistor England **17 D3** 53.29N 0.20W
Cajamarca Peru **96 B7** 7.09S 78.32W
Calabar Nigeria **108 C1** 4.56N 8.22E
Calabozo Venezuela **95 F2** 8.58N 67.28W
Calafat Romania **56 F5** 43.59N 22.57E
Calahorra Spain **50 D5** 42.18N 1.58W
Calais France **48 D6** 50.57N 1.50E
Calamar Colombia **94 E3** 10.16N 74.55W
Calamian Group *is.* Phil. **79 G6** 12.00N120.05E
Calamocha Spain **50 E4** 40.54N 1.18W
Calapan Phil. **79 G6** 13.23N121.10E
Calatayud Spain **50 E4** 41.21N 1.39W
Calbayog Phil. **79 G6** 12.04N124.58E
Calcutta India **71 F4** 22.35N 88.21E
Caldas Colombia **94 D2** 6.05N 75.36W
Caldas da Rainha Portugal **50 A3** 39.24N 9.08W
Caldbeck England **22 A1** 54.45N 3.03W
Caldy *i.* Wales **18 B1** 51.38N 4.43W
Caledon N. Ireland **23 C1** 54.21N 6.51W
Calgary Canada **90 G3** 51.05N114.05W
Cali Colombia **94 D1** 3.24N 76.30W
Calicut India **71 D2** 11.15N 75.45E
Caliente U.S.A. **86 D4** 37.36N114.31W
California *d.* U.S.A. **86 B4** 37.00N120.00W
California, G. of Mexico **92 B5** 28.30N112.30W
Callander Scotland **26 D3** 56.15N 4.13W
Callao Peru **96 B6** 12.05S 77.08W
Callington England **12 C2** 50.30N 4.19W
Calne England **13 F3** 51.26N 2.00W
Caloocan Phil. **79 G6** 14.38N120.58E
Caltagirone Italy **54 E2** 37.14N 14.30E
Caltanissetta Italy **54 E2** 37.30N 14.05E
Calvi France **49 H2** 42.34N 8.44E
Calvinia R.S.A. **106 B1** 31.25S 19.47E
Cam *r.* England **15 C3** 52.34N 0.21E
Camagüey Cuba **94 D5** 21.25N 77.55W
Camagüey, Archipelago de Cuba **94 D5** 22.30N 78.00W
Camarón, C. Honduras **93 H3** 15.59N 85.00W
Ca Mau, Pointe de *c.* Vietnam **78 C5** 8.30N104.35E
Cambay, G. of India **71 D4** 20.30N 72.00E
Camberley England **15 B2** 51.21N 0.45W
Cambodia Asia **78 C6** 12.00N105.00E
Camborne England **12 B2** 50.12N 5.19W
Cambrai France **48 E6** 50.10N 3.14E
Cambrian Mts. Wales **18 C2** 52.33N 3.33W
Cambridge England **15 C3** 52.13N 0.08E
Cambridge Bay *town* Canada **90 H4** 69.09N105.00W
Cambridgeshire *d.* England **15 C3** 52.15N 0.05E
Camelford England **12 C2** 50.37N 4.41W
Cameroon Africa **104 D2** 6.00N 12.30E
Cameroon, Mt. Cameroon **104 C2** 4.20N 9.05E
Campbell I. Pacific Oc. **82 G2** 52.30S169.02E
Campbeltown Scotland **26 C2** 55.25N 5.36W
Campeche Mexico **92 F3** 19.50N 90.30W
Campeche *d.* Mexico **92 F3** 19.00N 90.00W
Campeche B. Mexico **92 F3** 19.30N 94.00W
Campina Grande Brazil **96 F7** 7.15S 35.53W
Campinas Brazil **97 E5** 22.54S 47.06W
Campine *f.* Belgium **47 C3** 51.05N 5.00E
Campobasso Italy **54 E4** 41.34N 14.39E
Campo Grande Brazil **97 D5** 20.24S 54.35W
Campo Maior Portugal **50 B3** 39.01N 7.04W
Campos Brazil **97 E5** 21.46S 41.21W
Campsie Fells *hills* Scotland **26 D3** 56.02N 4.15W
Cam Ranh Vietnam **78 D6** 11.54N109.14E
Camrose Canada **90 G3** 53.01N112.48W
Canada N. America **90 H3** 60.00N105.00W
Canadian *r.* U.S.A. **87 G4** 35.20N 95.40W
Canadian Shield *f.* N. America **84 L7** 50.00N 80.00W
Çanakkale Turkey **68 B6** 40.09N 26.26E
Canal du Midi France **48 D2** 43.18N 2.00E
Canary Is. Atlantic Oc. **104 A4** 29.00N 15.00W
Canaveral, C. U.S.A. **87 J2** 28.28N 80.28W
Canberra Australia **80 D2** 35.18S149.08E
Candeleda Spain **50 C4** 40.10N 5.14W
Canea Greece **56 G1** 35.30N 24.02E
Çankiri Turkey **68 D6** 40.35N 33.37E
Canna *i.* Scotland **24 B4** 57.03N 6.30W
Cannes France **48 G2** 43.33N 7.00E
Cannich Scotland **24 D4** 57.21N 4.42W
Cannock England **16 B2** 52.42N 2.02W
Cannock Chase *f.* England **16 C2** 52.45N 2.00W
Canõas Brazil **97 D5** 29.55S 51.10W
Canonbie Scotland **27 F2** 55.05N 2.56W
Canon City U.S.A. **86 E4** 38.27N105.14W
Cantabria *d.* Spain **50 C5** 43.00N 4.00W
Cantabrian Mts. Spain **50 B5** 42.55N 5.10W
Cantabria, Sierra de *mts.* Spain **50 D5** 42.40N 2.30W
Cantaura Venezuela **95 G2** 9.22N 64.24W
Canterbury England **15 D2** 51.17N 1.05E
Can Tho Vietnam **78 D6** 10.03N105.46E
Canvey England **15 C2** 51.32N 0.35E
Cao Bang Vietnam **78 D8** 22.40N106.16E
Caoles Scotland **26 B3** 56.32N 6.44W
Caolisport, Loch Scotland **26 C2** 55.54N 5.38W
Cape Basin Atlantic Oc. **112 J3** 38.00S 10.00E
Cape Breton I. Canada **91 L2** 46.00N 61.00W
Cape Coast *town* Ghana **108 A2** 5.10N 1.13W
Cape Johnson Depth Pacific Oc. **79 H6** 10.20N127.20E
Capel England **15 B2** 51.08N 0.18W
Cape Town R.S.A. **106 B1** 33.56S 18.28E
Cape Verde Is. Atlantic Oc. **112 H5** 15.00N 24.00W
Cap Haïtien *town* Haiti **93 J3** 19.47N 72.17W
Cappoquin Rep. of Ire. **28 D2** 52.09N 7.52W
Capraia *i.* Italy **54 B5** 43.03N 9.50E
Caprera *i.* Italy **54 B4** 41.48N 9.27E
Capri *i.* Italy **54 E4** 40.33N 14.13E
Cara *i.* Scotland **26 C2** 55.58N 5.45W
Caracal Romania **56 G6** 44.08N 24.18E
Caracas Venezuela **95 F3** 10.35N 66.56W
Caratasca Lagoon Honduras **93 H3** 15.10N 84.00W
Caravaca Spain **50 E3** 38.06N 1.51W
Carbonara, C. Italy **54 B3** 39.06N 9.32E
Carcassonne France **48 E2** 43.13N 2.21E
Carcross Canada **90 E4** 60.11N134.41W
Cardenas Cuba **93 H4** 23.02N 81.12W
Cardenete Spain **50 E3** 39.46N 1.42W
Cardiff Wales **18 C1** 51.28N 3.11W
Cardigan Wales **18 B2** 52.06N 4.41W
Cardigan B. Wales **18 B2** 52.30N 4.30W
Carei Romania **57 H3** 47.42N 22.28E
Carentan France **48 C5** 49.18N 1.14W
Carhaix France **48 B5** 48.16N 3.35W
Caribbean Sea C. America **93 I3** 15.00N 75.00W
Caribou Mts. Canada **90 G3** 58.30N115.00W
Carignan France **47 D1** 49.38N 5.10E
Caripito Venezuela **95 G3** 10.07N 63.07W
Carlingford Rep. of Ire. **28 E4** 54.02N 6.12W
Carlingford Lough Rep. of Ire./N. Ireland **23 D1** 54.03N 6.09W
Carlisle England **22 B1** 54.54N 2.55W
Carlow Rep. of Ire. **28 E2** 52.50N 6.54W
Carlow *d.* Rep. of Ire. **28 E2** 52.43N 6.50W
Carlton England **16 C2** 52.58N 1.06W
Carluke Scotland **27 E2** 55.44N 3.51W
Carmacks Canada **90 E4** 62.04N136.21W
Carmarthen Wales **18 B1** 51.52N 4.20W
Carmarthen B. Wales **18 B1** 51.40N 4.30W
Carmel Head Wales **18 B3** 53.24N 4.35W
Carmen Colombia **94 D2** 9.46N 75.06W
Carmen Mexico **92 F3** 18.38N 91.50W
Carmen I. Baja Calif.Sur Mexico **92 B5** 25.55N111.10W
Carmen I. Campeche Mexico **92 F3** 18.35N 91.40W
Carmona Spain **50 C2** 37.28N 5.38W
Carmyllie Scotland **27 F3** 56.36N 2.41W
Carndonagh Rep. of Ire. **28 D5** 55.15N 7.17W
Carnedd y Filiast *mtn.* Wales **18 C2** 52.56N 3.40W
Carnew Rep. of Ire. **28 E2** 52.41N 6.31W
Carnforth England **20 C3** 54.08N 2.47W
Carnic Alps *mts.* Italy/Austria **57 C3** 46.40N 12.48E
Car Nicobar *i.* India **71 G2** 9.06N 92.57E
Carnot C.A.R. **104 D2** 4.59N 15.56E
Carnoustie Scotland **27 F3** 56.30N 2.44W
Carnsore Pt. Rep. of Ire. **28 E2** 52.10N 6.21W
Carnwath Scotland **27 E2** 55.43N 3.37W
Carolina Puerto Rico **95 F4** 18.23N 65.57W
Caroline I. Kiribati **83 K7** 10.00S150.30W
Caroline Is. Pacific Oc. **79 K5** 7.50N145.00E
Caroline-Solomon Ridge Pacific Oc. **82 F8** 8.00N150.00E
Caroní *r.* Venezuela **95 G2** 8.20N 62.45W
Carora Venezuela **94 E3** 10.12N 70.07W
Carpathians *mts.* Europe **59 A3** 48.45N 23.45E
Carpentaria, G. of Australia **80 C4** 14.00S140.00E
Carpentras France **48 F3** 44.03N 5.03E
Carpio Spain **50 C4** 41.13N 5.07W
Carradale Scotland **26 C2** 55.35N 5.28W
Carra, Lough Rep. of Ire. **28 B3** 53.40N 9.15W
Carrara Italy **54 C6** 44.04N 10.06E
Carrauntoohil *mtn.* Rep. of Ire. **28 B2** 52.00N 9.45W
Carriacou *i.* Grenada **95 G3** 12.30N 61.35W
Carrick *f.* Scotland **26 D2** 55.12N 4.38W
Carrickfergus N. Ireland **23 D1** 54.43N 5.49W
Carrick Forest *hills* Scotland **26 D2** 55.11N 4.29W
Carrickmacross Rep. of Ire. **28 E3** 53.59N 6.44W
Carrick-on-Shannon Rep. of Ire. **28 C3** 53.57N 8.06W
Carrick-on-Suir Rep. of Ire. **28 D2** 52.21N 7.26W
Carrowmore Lough Rep. of Ire. **28 B4** 54.11N 9.48W
Carşamba Turkey **68 E6** 41.13N 36.43E
Çarşamba *r.* Turkey **68 C5** 37.52N 31.48E
Carse of Gowrie *f.* Scotland **27 E3** 56.25N 3.15W
Carson City U.S.A. **86 C4** 39.10N119.46W
Carsphairn Scotland **26 D2** 55.13N 4.15W
Carstairs Scotland **27 E2** 55.42N 3.41W
Cartagena Colombia **94 D3** 10.24N 75.33W
Cartagena Spain **50 E2** 37.36N 0.59W
Cartago Colombia **94 D1** 4.45N 75.55W
Cartago Costa Rica **93 H1** 9.50N 83.52W
Caruaru Brazil **96 F7** 8.15S 35.55W
Carúpano Venezuela **95 G3** 10.39N 63.14W
Carvin France **47 A2** 50.30N 2.58E
Casablanca Morocco **104 B5** 33.39N 7.35W
Cascade Range *mts.* U.S.A. **86 B5** 44.00N121.30W
Caserta Italy **54 E4** 41.06N 14.21E
Cashel Rep. of Ire. **28 D2** 52.31N 7.54W
Caspe Spain **50 E4** 41.14N 0.03W
Casper U.S.A. **86 E5** 42.50N106.20W
Caspian Depression *f.* Russian Fed./Kazakhstan **60 E2** 47.00N 48.00E
Caspian Sea Asia **60 E2** 42.00N 51.00E
Castaños Mexico **92 D5** 26.48N101.26W
Casteljaloux France **48 D3** 44.19N 0.06W
Castellón de la Plana Spain **50 E3** 39.59N 0.03W
Castelo Branco Portugal **50 B3** 39.50N 7.30W
Castilla la Mancha *d.* Spain **50 C3** 39.00N 4.00W
Castilla y León *d.* Spain **50 C4** 42.00N 5.00W
Castilletes Colombia **94 E3** 11.55N 71.20W
Castlebar Rep. of Ire. **28 B3** 53.52N 9.19W
Castleblayney Rep. of Ire. **28 E4** 54.08N 6.46W
Castle Cary England **13 E3** 51.06N 2.31W
Castledawson N. Ireland **23 C1** 54.47N 6.35W
Castlederg N. Ireland **23 B1** 54.43N 7.37W
Castle Douglas Scotland **27 E1** 54.56N 3.56W
Castleford England **21 D2** 53.43N 1.21W
Castleisland *town* Rep. of Ire. **28 B2** 52.14N 9.29W
Castlerea Rep. of Ire. **28 C3** 53.45N 8.30W
Castlerock N. Ireland **23 C2** 55.10N 6.49W
Castletown I.o.M. **20 A3** 54.04N 4.38W
Castletownshend Rep. of Ire. **28 B1** 51.31N 9.11W
Castlewellan N. Ireland **23 D1** 54.15N 5.57W
Castres France **48 E2** 43.36N 2.14E
Castries St. Lucia **93 L2** 14.01N 60.59W
Cataluna *d.* Spain **50 F4** 42.00N 2.00E
Catamarca Argentina **97 C5** 28.28S 65.46W
Catanduanes *i.* Phil. **79 G6** 13.45N124.20E
Catania Italy **54 E2** 37.31N 15.05E
Catanzaro Italy **54 F3** 38.55N 16.35E
Catarman Phil. **79 G6** 12.28N124.50E
Catbalogan Phil. **79 G6** 11.46N124.55E
Caterham England **15 B2** 51.17N 0.04W
Cat I. Bahamas **93 I4** 24.30N 75.30W
Catoche, C. Mexico **93 G4** 21.38N 87.08W
Catterick England **20 D3** 54.23N 1.38W
Cauca *r.* Colombia **94 E2** 8.57N 74.30W
Caucasus Mts. Europe **59 E2** 43.00N 44.00E
Cauldcleuch Head *mtn.* Scotland **27 F2** 55.18N 2.50W
Cavan Rep. of Ire. **28 D3** 53.59N 7.22W
Cavan *d.* Rep. of Ire. **28 D3** 54.00N 7.15W
Cawood England **21 D2** 53.50N 1.07W
Caxias do Sul Brazil **97 D5** 29.14S 51.10W
Cayenne Guiana **95 I1** 4.55N 52.18W
Cayman Brac *i.* Cayman Is. **93 I3** 19.44N 79.48W
Cayman Is. C. America **93 H3** 19.00N 81.00W
Cebollera, Sierra de *mts.* Spain **50 D4** 41.58N 2.30W
Cebu Phil. **79 G6** 10.17N123.56E
Cebu *i.* Phil. **79 G6** 10.15N123.45E
Cecina Italy **54 C5** 43.18N 10.30E
Cedar City U.S.A. **86 D4** 37.40N113.04W
Cedar Rapids *town* U.S.A. **87 H5** 41.59N 91.31W
Cedros I. Mexico **92 A5** 28.15N115.15W
Cefalù Italy **54 E3** 38.01N 14.03E
Cegléd Hungary **57 F3** 47.10N 19.48E
Celaya Mexico **92 D4** 20.32N100.48W
Celebes *i.* Indonesia **79 G3** 2.00S120.30E
Celebes Sea Indonesia **79 G4** 3.00N122.00E
Celje Yugo. **56 B7** 46.15N 15.16E
Celle Germany **52 E5** 52.37N 10.05E
Celtic Sea U.K. **40 D5** 51.00N 9.00W
Cemaes Bay *town* Wales **18 B3** 53.24N 4.27W
Cemaes Head Wales **18 B2** 52.08N 4.42W
Central *d.* Scotland **26 D3** 56.10N 4.20W
Central African Republic Africa **104 D2** 6.30N 20.00E
Central, Cordillera *mts.* Colombia **94 D1** 5.00N 75.20W
Central Russian Uplands *f.* Russian Fed. **59 D4** 53.00N 37.00E
Central Siberian Plateau *f.* Russian Fed. **61 I4** 66.00N108.00E
Ceram *i.* Indonesia **79 H3** 3.10S129.30E
Ceram Sea Pacific Oc. **79 H3** 2.50S128.00E
Cereté Colombia **94 D2** 8.54N 75.51W
Cerignola Italy **54 E4** 41.17N 15.53E
Cerne Abbas England **13 E2** 50.49N 2.29W
Cerro de Pasco Peru **96 B6** 10.43S 76.15W
Cervera Spain **50 F4** 41.40N 1.16E
České Budějovice Czech. **57 D4** 49.00N 14.30E
Cetinje Yugo. **56 D5** 42.24N 18.55E
Ceuta Spain **50 C1** 35.53N 5.19W
Cévennes *mts.* France **48 E3** 44.25N 4.05E
Ceyhan *r.* Turkey **68 D5** 36.54N 34.58E

Chad Africa 104 D3 13.00N 19.00E
Chad, L. Africa 104 D3 13.30N 14.00E
Chagford England 13 D2 50.40N 3.50W
Chagos Archipelago is. Indian Oc. 65 J2 7.00S 72.00E
Chah Bahar Iran 69 K2 25.17N 60.41E
Chalfont St. Peter England 15 B2 51.37N 0.33W
Challans France 48 C4 46.51N 1.52W
Challenger Depth Pacific Oc. 79 K6 11.19N142.15E
Châlons-sur-Marne France 48 F5 48.58N 4.22E
Chalon-sur-Saône France 48 F4 46.47N 4.51E
Chamai Thailand 78 B5 8.10N 99.41E
Chambal r. India 74 C3 26.30N 79.20E
Chambéry France 48 F3 45.34N 5.55E
Chamonix France 48 G3 45.55N 6.52E
Champ Iran 69 K2 26.40N 60.31E
Champlain, L. U.S.A. 87 L5 44.45N 73.20W
Chanda India 71 E4 19.58N 79.21E
Chandeleur Is. U.S.A. 87 I2 29.50N 88.50W
Chandigarh India 71 D5 30.44N 76.54E
Changchun China 75 J5 43.50N125.20E
Changde China 75 H3 29.03N111.35E
Chang Jiang r. China 75 J3 31.40N121.15E
Changsha China 75 H3 28.10N113.00E
Changting China 75 I2 25.47N116.17E
Changzhi China 75 H4 36.09N113.12E
Changzhou China 75 I3 31.45N119.57E
Channel Is. U.K. 48 B5 49.28N 2.13W
Channel-Port-aux-Basques town Canada 91 M2 47.35N 59.10W
Chanthaburi Thailand 78 C6 12.38N102.12E
Chao'an China 75 I2 23.43N116.35E
Chaoyang Guangdong China 75 I2 23.17N116.33E
Chapala, Lago de l. Mexico 92 D4 20.00N103.00W
Chapayevsk Russian Fed. 59 F4 52.58N 49.44E
Chapel en le Frith England 16 C3 53.19N 1.54W
Chapel St. Leonards England 17 E3 53.14N 0.20E
Chard England 13 E2 50.52N 2.59W
Chardzhou Turkmenistan 60 F1 39.09N 63.34E
Chari r. Chad 104 D3 13.00N 14.30E
Charikar Afghan. 71 C6 35.02N 69.13E
Charing England 15 C2 51.12N 0.49E
Charleroi Belgium 47 C2 50.25N 4.27E
Charleston S.C. U.S.A. 87 K3 32.48N 79.58W
Charleston W.Va. U.S.A. 87 J4 38.23N 81.20W
Charlestown Rep. of Ire. 28 C3 53.57N 8.50W
Charleville-Mézières France 47 C1 49.46N 4.43E
Charlotte U.S.A. 87 J4 35.05N 80.50W
Charlottesville U.S.A. 87 K4 38.02N 78.29W
Charlottetown Canada 91 L2 46.14N 63.09W
Charolles France 48 F4 46.26N 4.17E
Chartres France 48 D5 48.27N 1.30E
Châteaubriant France 48 C4 47.43N 1.22W
Château-du-Loir France 48 D4 47.42N 0.25E
Châteaudun France 48 D5 48.04N 1.20E
Châteauroux France 48 D4 46.49N 1.41E
Château-Thierry France 48 E5 49.03N 3.24E
Châtelet Belgium 47 C2 50.24N 4.32E
Châtellerault France 48 D4 46.49N 0.33E
Chatham England 15 C2 51.23N 0.32E
Chatham Is. Pacific Oc. 82 I3 44.00S176.35W
Châtillon-s-Seine France 48 F4 47.52N 4.35E
Chattahoochee r. U.S.A. 87 I3 30.52N 84.57W
Chattanooga U.S.A. 87 I4 35.01N 85.18W
Chatteris England 15 C3 52.27N 0.03E
Chaumont France 48 F5 48.07N 5.08E
Chaves Portugal 50 B4 41.44N 7.28W
Cheadle England 20 C2 53.24N 2.13W
Cheb Czech. 57 C5 50.04N 12.20E
Cheboksary Russian Fed. 59 F5 56.08N 47.12E
Cheboygan U.S.A. 87 J6 45.40N 84.28W
Cheddar England 13 E3 51.16N 2.47W
Cheju S. Korea 75 K4 33.31N126.29E
Chełm Poland 57 H5 51.10N 23.28E
Chelmsford England 15 C2 51.44N 0.28E
Chełmża Poland 57 F6 53.12N 18.37E
Cheltenham England 13 E3 51.53N 2.07W
Chelyabinsk Russian Fed. 60 F3 55.10N 61.25E
Chelyuskin, C. Russian Fed. 61 I5 77.20N106.00E
Chenab r. Asia 71 C5 29.26N 71.09E
Chengde China 75 I5 40.48N118.06E
Chengdu China 74 G3 30.37N104.06E
Chen, Mt. Russian Fed. 61 L4 65.30N141.20E
Chepstow Wales 18 D1 51.38N 2.40W
Cher r. France 48 E4 47.12N 2.04E
Cherbourg France 48 C5 49.38N 1.37W
Cheremkhovo Russian Fed. 61 I3 53.08N103.01E
Cherepovets Russian Fed. 59 D5 59.05N 37.55E
Cherkassy Ukraine 59 C3 49.27N 32.04E
Cherkessk Russian Fed. 59 E2 44.14N 42.05E
Chernigov Ukraine 59 C4 51.30N 31.18E
Chernovtsy Ukraine 59 B3 48.19N 25.52E
Chernyakhovsk Russian Fed. 58 E1 54.36N 21.48E
Cherskogo Range mts. Russian Fed. 61 L4 65.50N143.00E
Chertsey England 15 B2 51.23N 0.27W
Chesapeake B. U.S.A. 87 K4 38.00N 76.00W
Chesham England 15 B2 51.43N 0.38W
Cheshire d. England 20 C2 53.14N 2.30W
Cheshunt England 15 B2 51.43N 0.02W
Chesil Beach f. England 13 E2 50.37N 2.33W
Chester England 20 C2 53.12N 2.53W
Chesterfield England 16 C3 53.14N 1.26W
Chesterfield Inlet town Canada 91 I4 63.00N 91.00W
Chesterfield Is. N. Cal. 82 F6 20.00S159.00E
Chester-le-Street England 22 C1 54.53N 1.34W
Chetumal Mexico 93 G3 18.30N 88.17W
Chetumal B. Mexico 93 G3 18.30N 88.00W
Cheviot Hills U.K. 24 F2 55.22N 2.24W
Chew r. England 13 E3 51.25N 2.30W
Chew Magna England 13 E3 51.21N 2.37W
Cheyenne U.S.A. 86 F5 41.08N104.50W
Chhindwara India 71 E4 22.04N 78.58E
Chiang Mai Thailand 78 B7 18.48N 98.59E
Chiapas d. Mexico 92 F3 16.30N 93.00W
Chiavari Italy 54 B6 44.19N 9.19E
Chiba Japan 76 D4 35.38N140.07E
Chibougamau Canada 91 K2 49.56N 74.24W
Chicago U.S.A. 87 I5 41.50N 87.45W
Chichagof I. U.S.A. 90 E3 57.55N135.45W
Chichester England 15 B1 50.50N 0.47W
Chiclayo Peru 96 B7 6.47S 79.47W
Chico U.S.A. 86 B4 39.46N121.50W
Chicoutimi-Jonquière Canada 91 K2 48.26N 71.06W
Chidley, C. Canada 91 L4 60.30N 65.00W
Chiemsee l. Germany 52 F3 47.55N 12.30E
Chieti Italy 54 E5 42.22N 14.12E
Chifeng China 75 I5 41.17N118.56E
Chigwell England 15 C2 51.38N 0.05E
Chihli, G. of China 75 I5 38.30N119.30E
Chihuahua Mexico 92 C5 28.40N106.06W
Chihuahua d. Mexico 92 C5 28.40N105.00W
Chil r. Iran 69 K2 25.12N 61.30E
Chilapa Mexico 92 E3 17.38N 99.11W
Chile S. America 97 B4 33.00S 71.00W
Chile Basin Pacific Oc. 112 E3 34.20S 80.00W
Chillán Chile 97 B4 36.37S 72.10W
Chiloé I. Chile 97 B3 43.00S 73.00W
Chilpancingo Mexico 92 E3 17.33N 99.30W
Chiltern Hills England 15 B2 51.40N 0.53W
Chimay Belgium 47 C2 50.03N 4.20E
Chimborazo mtn. Ecuador 96 B7 1.10S 78.50W
Chimbote Peru 96 B7 8.58S 78.34W
Chimkent Kazakhstan 74 A5 42.16N 69.05E
China Asia 74 G4 33.00N103.00E
Chinandega Nicaragua 93 G2 12.35N 87.10W
Chinati Peak U.S.A. 86 F3 30.05N104.30W
Chindwin r. Myanma 74 E2 21.30N 95.12E
Chingola Zambia 106 C3 12.31S 27.53E
Chin Hills Myanma 74 E2 22.40N 93.30E
Chippenham England 13 E3 51.27N 2.07W
Chipping Norton England 14 A2 51.56N 1.32W
Chipping Ongar England 15 C2 51.43N 0.15E
Chipping Sodbury England 13 E3 51.31N 2.23W
Chiquimula Guatemala 93 G2 14.52N 89.50W
Chiquinquirá Colombia 94 E2 5.37N 73.50W
Chir r. Russian Fed. 59 E3 48.34N 42.53E
Chirchik Uzbekistan 60 F2 41.28N 69.31E
Chiriqui mtn. Panama 93 H1 8.49N 82.38W
Chiriqui Lagoon Panama 93 H1 9.00N 82.00W
Chirnside Scotland 27 F2 55.48N 2.12W
Chirripo mtn. Costa Rica 93 H1 9.31N 83.30W
Chistopol Russian Fed. 59 G5 55.25N 50.38E
Chita Russian Fed. 75 H7 52.03N113.35E
Chitral Pakistan 71 C6 35.52N 71.58E
Chittagong Bangla. 71 G4 22.20N 91.48E
Chitterne England 13 E3 51.12N 2.01W
Chittoor India 71 E2 13.13N 79.06E
Chojnice Poland 57 E6 53.42N 17.32E
Chokai san mtn. Japan 76 D6 39.08N140.04E
Cholet France 48 C4 47.04N 0.53W
Cholon Vietnam 78 D6 10.45N106.39E
Choluteca Honduras 93 G2 13.16N 87.11W
Chomutov Czech. 57 C5 50.28N 13.25E
Chon Buri Thailand 78 C6 13.24N100.59E
Chongjin N. Korea 75 K5 41.55N129.50E
Chongju S. Korea 75 K4 36.39N127.31E
Chongqing China 74 G3 29.31N106.35E
Chonju S. Korea 75 K4 35.50N127.05E
Chorley England 20 C2 53.39N 2.39W
Chorzów Poland 57 F5 50.19N 18.56E
Chott Djerid f. Tunisia 104 C5 33.30N 8.30E
Chott ech Chergui f. Algeria 104 C5 34.00N 0.30E
Chott Melrhir f. Algeria 104 C5 34.15N 7.00E
Christchurch England 13 F2 50.44N 1.47W
Christchurch New Zealand 80 G1 43.32S172.37E
Christiansfeld Denmark 46 C3 55.23N 9.30E
Christianshåb Greenland 91 M4 68.50N 51.00W
Christmas I. Indian Oc. 78 D1 10.30S105.40E
Christmas I. Kiribati 83 K8 1.52N157.20W
Chu r. Asia 74 B5 42.30N 76.10E
Chuckchee Pen. Russian Fed. 61 P4 66.00N174.30W
Chudleigh England 13 D2 50.35N 3.36W
Chudovo Russian Fed. 59 C5 59.10N 31.41E
Chugoku d. Japan 76 B4 35.00N133.00E
Chugoku sanchi mts. Japan 76 B4 35.30N133.00E
Chukai Malaysia 78 C4 4.16N103.24E
Chulmleigh England 13 D2 50.55N 3.52W
Chumphon Thailand 78 B6 10.35N 99.14E
Chuna r. Russian Fed. 61 H3 58.00N 94.00E
Chunchon S. Korea 75 K4 37.53N127.45E
Chur Switz. 52 D2 46.52N 9.32E
Churchill Canada 91 I3 58.45N 94.00W
Churchill r. Man. Canada 91 I3 58.20N 94.15W
Churchill r. Nfld. Canada 91 L3 53.20N 60.00W
Churchill, C. Canada 91 I3 58.50N 93.00W
Churchill L. Canada 90 H3 56.00N108.00W
Churchill Peak mtn. Canada 90 F3 58.10N125.00W
Church Stoke Wales 18 C2 52.32N 3.04W
Church Stretton England 16 B2 52.32N 2.49W
Ciego de Avila Cuba 93 I4 21.51N 78.47W
Ciénaga Colombia 94 E3 11.11N 74.15W
Cienfuegos Cuba 93 H4 22.10N 80.27W
Cieza Spain 50 E3 38.14N 1.25W
Cifuentes Spain 50 D4 40.47N 2.37W
Cijara L. Spain 50 C3 39.20N 4.50W
Cilacap Indonesia 78 D2 7.44S109.00E
Cilo, Mt. Turkey 69 G5 37.29N 44.00E
Cimarron r. U.S.A. 87 G4 36.15N 96.55W
Cimone, Monte mtn. Italy 54 C6 44.12N 10.42E
Cinca r. Spain 50 F4 41.22N 0.20E
Cincinnati U.S.A. 87 J4 39.10N 84.30W
Cinderford England 13 E3 51.49N 2.30W
Ciney Belgium 47 D2 50.17N 5.06E
Cinto, Monte mtn. France 49 H2 42.23N 8.57E
Cirebon Indonesia 78 D2 6.46S108.33E
Cirencester England 13 F3 51.43N 1.59W
Ciudad Bolívar Venezuela 95 G2 8.06N 63.36W
Ciudad Camargo Mexico 92 C5 27.41N105.10W
Ciudadela Spain 51 G4 40.00N 3.50E
Ciudad Guayana Venezuela 96 C8 8.22N 62.40W
Ciudad Guerrero Mexico 92 C5 28.33N107.28W
Ciudad Ixtepec Mexico 92 E3 16.32N 95.10W
Ciudad Juárez Mexico 92 C6 31.42N106.29W
Ciudad Madero Mexico 92 E4 22.19N 97.50W
Ciudad Obregon Mexico 92 C5 27.28N109.55W
Ciudad Real Spain 50 D3 38.59N 3.55W
Ciudad Rodrigo Spain 50 B4 40.36N 6.33W
Ciudad Victoria Mexico 92 E4 23.43N 99.10W
Civitavecchia Italy 54 C5 42.06N 11.48E
Civray France 48 D4 46.09N 0.18E
Civril Turkey 68 C5 38.18N 29.43E
Cizre Turkey 68 F5 37.21N 42.11E
Clackmannan Scotland 27 E3 56.06N 3.46W
Clacton on Sea England 15 D2 51.47N 1.10E
Clara Rep. of Ire. 28 D3 53.21N 7.37W
Clare d. Rep. of Ire. 28 C2 52.52N 8.55W
Clare r. Rep. of Ire. 28 B3 53.20N 9.03W
Clare I. Rep. of Ire. 28 A3 53.50N 10.00W
Claremorris Rep. of Ire. 28 C3 53.44N 9.00W
Clatteringshaws Loch Scotland 26 D2 55.04N 4.25W
Claudy N. Ireland 23 B1 54.55N 7.09W
Clay Cross England 16 C3 53.11N 1.26W
Clay Head I.o.M. 20 A3 54.12N 4.23W
Clayton U.S.A. 86 F4 36.27N103.12W
Clear, C. Rep. of Ire. 28 B1 51.25N 9.31W
Clear I. Rep. of Ire. 28 B1 51.26N 9.30W
Clearwater L. Canada 91 K3 56.10N 74.30W
Cleator Moor town England 22 A1 54.30N 3.32W
Clee Hills England 16 B2 52.25N 2.37W
Cleethorpes England 21 E2 53.33N 0.02W
Cleobury Mortimer England 16 B2 52.23N 2.28W
Clermont-Ferrand France 48 E3 45.47N 3.05E
Clevedon England 13 E3 51.26N 2.52W
Cleveland d. England 22 C1 54.37N 1.08W
Cleveland f. England 22 D1 54.30N 0.55W
Cleveland U.S.A. 87 J5 41.30N 81.41W
Cleveland Hills England 21 D3 54.25N 1.10W
Cleveleys England 20 B2 53.52N 3.01W
Clew B. Rep. of Ire. 28 B3 53.50N 9.47W
Clifden Rep. of Ire. 28 A3 53.29N 10.02W
Clipperton i. Pacific Oc. 83 P9 10.17N109.13W
Clisham mtn. Scotland 24 B4 57.58N 6.50W
Clitheroe England 20 C2 53.52N 2.23W
Cloghan Rep. of Ire. 28 D3 53.12N 7.54W
Clogher N. Ireland 23 B1 54.25N 7.11W
Clogher Hd. Kerry Rep. of Ire. 28 A2 52.10N 10.28W
Clogh Mills N. Ireland 23 C1 55.00N 6.20W
Clonakilty Rep. of Ire. 28 C1 51.37N 8.55W
Clones Rep. of Ire. 28 D4 54.11N 7.15W
Clonmel Rep. of Ire. 28 D2 52.21N 7.44W
Clonroche Rep. of Ire. 28 E2 52.26N 6.45W
Cloppenburg Germany 47 G4 52.52N 8.02E
Cloud Peak mtn. U.S.A. 86 E5 44.23N107.11W
Cloughton England 21 E3 54.20N 0.27W
Clovelly England 12 C3 51.00N 4.25W
Clovis U.S.A. 86 F3 34.14N103.13W
Clowne England 16 C3 53.18N 1.16W
Clwyd d. Wales 18 C3 53.07N 3.20W
Clwyd r. Wales 18 C3 53.19N 3.30W
Clwydian Range mts. Wales 18 C3 53.08N 3.15W
Clyde r. Scotland 26 D2 55.58N 4.53W
Clydebank Scotland 26 D2 55.53N 4.23W
Clydesdale f. Scotland 27 E2 55.41N 3.48W
Coahuila d. Mexico 92 D5 27.00N103.00W
Coalisland N. Ireland 23 C1 54.33N 6.43W
Coalville England 16 C2 52.43N 1.21W
Coast Mts. Canada 90 F3 55.30N128.00W
Coast Range mts. U.S.A. 86 B5 40.00N123.00W
Coatbridge Scotland 27 D2 55.52N 4.02W
Coats I. Canada 91 J4 62.30N 83.00W
Coatzacoalcos Mexico 92 F3 18.10N 94.25W
Cobalt Canada 91 K2 47.24N 79.41W
Cobán Guatemala 92 F3 15.28N 90.20W
Cobh Rep. of Ire. 28 C1 51.50N 8.18W
Cobham Surrey England 15 B2 51.20N 0.25W
Cobija Bolivia 96 C6 11.01S 68.45W
Coburg Germany 52 E4 50.15N 10.58E
Cochabamba Bolivia 96 C6 17.26S 66.10W
Cochin India 71 D2 9.56N 76.15E
Cochrane Canada 91 J2 49.04N 81.02W
Cockburnspath Scotland 27 F2 55.56N 2.22W
Cockermouth England 22 A1 54.40N 3.22W
Coco r. Honduras 93 H2 14.58N 83.15W
Coco, Isla del i. Pacific Oc. 83 R8 5.32N 87.04W
Cocos Is. Indian Oc. 115 N4 13.00S 96.00E
Cod, C. U.S.A. 87 L5 42.08N 70.10W
Coesfeld Germany 47 F3 51.55N 7.13E
Coevorden Neth. 47 E4 52.39N 6.45E
Cofre de Perote mtn. Mexico 92 E3 19.30N 97.10W
Coggeshall England 15 C2 51.53N 0.41E
Coghinas r. Italy 54 B4 40.57N 8.50E
Cognac France 48 C3 45.42N 0.19W
Coiba I. Panama 93 H1 7.23N 81.45W
Coimbatore India 71 D2 11.00N 76.57E
Coimbra Portugal 50 A4 40.12N 8.25W
Coín Spain 50 C2 36.40N 4.45W
Colchester England 15 C2 51.54N 0.55E
Cold Fell mtn. England 22 B1 54.54N 2.37W
Coldingham Scotland 27 F2 55.53N 2.10W
Coldstream Scotland 27 F2 55.39N 2.15W
Coleford England 13 E3 51.46N 2.38W
Coleraine N. Ireland 23 C2 55.08N 6.41W
Colima Mexico 92 D3 19.14N103.41W
Colima d. Mexico 92 D3 19.05N104.00W
Colintraive Scotland 26 C2 55.56N 5.09W
Coll i. Scotland 26 B3 56.38N 6.34W
Collier Law mtn. England 22 C1 54.45N 1.58W
Collin Top mtn. N. Ireland 23 C1 54.58N 6.08W
Collon Rep. of Ire. 28 E3 53.47N 6.30W
Collooney Rep. of Ire. 28 C4 54.11N 8.29W
Colmar France 48 G5 48.05N 7.21E
Colmenar Viejo Spain 50 D4 40.39N 3.46W
Colne England 20 C2 53.51N 2.11W
Colne r. Essex England 15 C2 51.50N 0.59E
Colnett, C. Mexico 92 A6 31.00N116.20W
Cologne Germany 47 E2 50.56N 6.57E
Colombia S. America 96 B8 5.00N 75.00W
Colombo Sri Lanka 71 E1 6.55N 79.52E
Colon Panama 93 I1 9.21N 79.54W
Colonsay i. Scotland 26 B3 56.04N 6.13W
Colorado r. Argentina 97 C4 39.50S 62.02W
Colorado d. U.S.A. 86 E4 39.00N106.00W
Colorado r. Tex. U.S.A. 87 G2 28.30N 96.00W
Colorado Plateau f. U.S.A. 86 D4 35.45N112.00W
Colorado Springs town U.S.A. 86 F4 38.50N104.40W
Colsterworth England 16 D2 52.48N 0.37W
Coltishall England 15 D3 52.44N 1.22E
Columbia U.S.A. 87 J3 34.00N 81.00W
Columbia r. U.S.A. 86 B6 46.10N123.30W
Columbretes, Islas is. Spain 50 F3 39.50N 0.40E
Columbus Ga. U.S.A. 87 J3 32.28N 84.59W
Columbus Ohio U.S.A. 87 J4 39.59N 83.03W
Colville r. U.S.A. 90 C5 70.06N151.30W
Colwyn Bay town Wales 18 C3 53.18N 3.43W
Comayagua Honduras 93 G2 14.30N 87.39W
Combe Martin England 13 C3 51.12N 4.02W
Comber N. Ireland 23 D1 54.33N 5.45W
Comeragh Mts. Rep. of Ire. 28 D2 52.15N 7.35W
Comilla Bangla. 71 G4 23.28N 91.10E
Como Italy 54 B6 45.48N 9.04E
Comodoro Rivadavia Argentina 97 C3 45.50S 67.30W
Como, L. Italy 54 B7 46.05N 9.17E
Comorin, C. India 71 D2 8.04N 77.35E
Comoros Africa 106 E3 12.15S 44.00E
Comrie Scotland 27 E3 56.23N 4.00W
Conakry Guinea 104 A2 9.30N 13.43W
Concarneau France 48 B4 47.53N 3.55W
Concepción Chile 97 B4 36.50S 73.03W
Concepción Paraguay 97 D5 23.22S 57.26W
Conception, Pt. U.S.A. 86 B3 34.27N120.26W
Conchos r. Mexico 92 D5 29.34N104.30W
Concord U.S.A. 87 L5 43.13N 71.34W
Concordia Argentina 97 D4 31.25S 58.00W
Condom France 48 D3 43.58N 0.22E
Confolens France 48 D3 46.01N 0.40E
Congleton England 20 C2 53.10N 2.12W
Congo Africa 106 B4 1.00S 16.00E
Congresbury England 13 E3 51.20N 2.49W
Coningsby England 17 D3 53.07N 0.09W
Conisbrough England 21 D2 53.29N 1.12W
Coniston England 22 A1 54.22N 3.06W
Coniston Water l. England 22 A1 54.20N 3.05W
Connah's Quay town Wales 18 C3 53.13N 3.03W
Connecticut d. U.S.A. 87 L5 41.30N 73.00W
Connel Scotland 26 C3 56.27N 5.24W
Connemara f. Rep. of Ire. 28 B3 53.30N 9.50W
Conn, Lough Rep. of Ire. 28 B4 54.01N 9.15W
Conon r. Scotland 24 D4 57.33N 4.28W
Consett England 22 C1 54.52N 1.50W
Con Son Is. Vietnam 78 D5 8.30N106.30E
Constance, L. Europe 52 D2 47.40N 9.30E
Constanța Romania 59 B2 44.10N 28.31E
Constantina Spain 50 C2 37.54N 5.36W
Constantine Algeria 104 C5 36.22N 6.38E
Conwy Wales 18 C3 53.17N 3.50W
Conwy r. Wales 18 C3 53.17N 3.49W
Conwy B. Wales 18 C3 53.19N 3.55W
Cook Is. Pacific Oc. 82 J6 15.00S160.00W
Cook, Mt. New Zealand 80 G1 43.36S170.09E
Cookstown N. Ireland 23 C1 54.39N 6.46W
Cook Str. New Zealand 80 G1 41.15S174.30E
Cooktown Australia 80 D4 15.29S145.15E
Cootehill Rep. of Ire. 28 D4 54.05N 7.05W
Copán ruins Honduras 93 G2 14.52N 89.10W
Copeland I. N. Ireland 23 D1 54.40N 5.32W
Copenhagen Denmark 46 F3 55.43N 12.34E
Copenhagen d. Denmark 46 F3 55.40N 12.10E
Copiapo Chile 97 B5 27.20S 70.23W
Coppermine r. Canada 90 G4 67.54N115.10W
Coppermine town Canada 90 G4 67.49N115.12W
Coquet I. England 22 C2 55.20N 1.30W
Coquimbo Chile 97 B5 30.00S 71.25W
Corabia Romania 56 G5 43.45N 24.29E
Coral Sea Pacific Oc. 80 E4 13.00S148.00E
Corbeil France 48 E5 48.37N 2.29E
Corbridge England 22 B1 54.58N 2.01W
Corby England 16 D2 52.29N 0.41W
Córdoba Argentina 97 C4 31.25S 64.11W
Cordoba Mexico 92 E3 18.55N 96.55W
Córdoba Spain 50 C2 37.53N 4.46W
Corentyne r. Guyana 95 H2 5.50N 57.08W
Corfu Greece 56 D3 39.37N 19.50E
Corfu i. Greece 56 D3 39.35N 19.50E
Corigliano Italy 54 F3 39.36N 16.31E
Corinth Greece 56 F2 37.56N 22.55E
Corinth, G. of Greece 56 F3 38.15N 22.30E
Corinto Nicaragua 93 G2 12.29N 87.14W
Cork Rep. of Ire. 28 C1 51.54N 8.28W
Cork d. Rep. of Ire. 28 C1 52.00N 8.40W
Cork Harbour est. Rep. of Ire. 28 C1 51.50N 8.17W
Corner Brook town Canada 91 M2 48.58N 57.58W
Corno, Monte mtn. Italy 54 D5 42.29N 13.33E
Cornwall d. England 12 C2 50.26N 4.40W
Cornwallis I. Canada 91 I5 75.00N 95.00W
Coro Venezuela 94 F3 11.27N 69.41W
Coronation G. Canada 90 G4 68.00N112.00W
Corozal Belize 93 G3 18.23N 88.23W

Eskişehir Turkey 68 C5 39.46N 30.30E
Esla r. Spain 50 B4 41.29N 6.03W
Eslāmābād Iran 69 G4 34.08N 46.35E
Eslöv Sweden 46 G3 55.50N 13.19E
Espinal Colombia 94 D1 4.08N 75.00W
Espíritu Santo I. Vanuatu 82 G6 15.50S166.50E
Esquel Argentina 97 B3 42.55S 71.20W
Essen Germany 47 E3 51.27N 6.57E
Essequibo r. Guyana 95 H2 6.48N 58.23W
Essex d. England 15 C2 51.46N 0.30E
Estepona Spain 50 C2 36.26N 5.09W
Estevan Canada 90 H2 49.09N103.00W
Eston England 22 C1 54.34N 1.07W
Estonia Europe 58 F2 58.45N 25.30E
Estrela, Serra da mts. Portugal 50 B4 40.20N 7.40W
Estremoz Portugal 50 B3 38.50N 7.35W
Étaples France 48 D6 50.31N 1.39E
Ethiopia Africa 105 F3 10.00N 39.00E
Ethiopian Highlands Ethiopia 105 F3 10.00N 37.00E
Etive, Loch Scotland 26 C3 56.27N 5.15W
Etna, Mt. Italy 54 E2 37.43N 14.59E
Eton England 15 B2 51.31N 0.37W
Etosha Pan f. Namibia 106 B3 18.50S 16.30E
Ettelbrück Lux. 47 E1 49.51N 6.06E
Ettrick Forest f. Scotland 27 E2 55.30N 3.00W
Ettrick Pen mtn. Scotland 27 E2 55.21N 3.16W
Et Tubeiq, Jebel mts. Saudi Arabia 68 E3 29.30N 37.15E
Euboea i. Greece 56 G3 38.30N 23.50E
Eufaula Resr. U.S.A. 87 G4 35.15N 95.35W
Eugene U.S.A. 86 B5 44.03N123.07W
Eugenia, Punta c. Mexico 92 A5 27.50N115.50W
Eupen Belgium 47 E2 50.38N 6.04E
Euphrates r. Asia 69 G3 31.00N 47.27E
Eureka U.S.A. 86 B5 40.49N124.10W
Europa, Picos de mts. Spain 50 C5 43.10N 4.40W
Europe 113
Europoort Neth. 47 C3 51.56N 4.08E
Euskirchen Germany 47 E2 50.40N 6.47E
Eutin Germany 46 D2 54.08N 10.38E
Evansville U.S.A. 87 I4 38.02N 87.24W
Evercreech England 13 E3 51.08N 2.30W
Everest, Mt. Asia 71 F5 27.59N 86.56E
Evesham England 16 C2 52.06N 1.57W
Evje Norway 58 A2 58.36N 7.51E
Évora Portugal 50 B3 38.34N 7.54W
Évreux France 48 D5 49.03N 1.11E
Ewe, L. Scotland 24 C4 57.52N 5.40W
Exe r. England 13 D2 50.40N 3.28W
Exeter England 13 D2 50.43N 3.31W
Exmoor Forest hills England 13 D3 51.08N 3.45W
Exmouth England 13 D2 50.37N 3.24W
Extremadura d. Spain 50 B3 39.00N 6.00W
Exuma Is. Bahamas 93 I4 24.00N 76.00W
Eyasi, L. Tanzania 106 D4 3.40S 35.00E
Eye England 15 D3 52.19N 1.09E
Eyemouth Scotland 27 F2 55.52N 2.05W
Eygurande France 48 E3 45.40N 2.26E
Eyre, L. Australia 80 C3 28.30S137.25E

F

Fåborg Denmark 46 D3 55.06N 10.15E
Facatativá Colombia 94 E1 4.48N 74.32W
Faenza Italy 54 C6 44.17N 11.52E
Fagernes Norway 58 B3 60.59N 9.17E
Fagersta Sweden 58 C3 59.59N 15.49E
Fairbanks U.S.A. 90 D4 64.50N147.50W
Fairbourne Wales 18 B2 52.42N 4.03W
Fair Head N. Ireland 23 C2 55.14N 6.10W
Fair Isle Scotland 24 G6 59.32N 1.38W
Fairweather, Mt. U.S.A. 90 E3 59.00N137.30W
Faisalabad Pakistan 71 D5 31.25N 73.09E
Faizabad India 71 E5 26.46N 82.08E
Fajr, Wadi r. Saudi Arabia 68 E3 30.00N 38.25E
Fakaofu Pacific Oc. 82 I7 9.30S171.15W
Fakenham England 15 C3 52.50N 0.51E
Fakfak Indonesia 79 I3 2.55S132.17E
Fakse Bugt b. Denmark 46 F3 55.10N 12.20E
Falaise France 48 C5 48.54N 0.11W
Falcarragh Rep. of Ire. 28 C5 55.09N 8.09W
Falcone, C. Italy 54 B4 40.57N 8.12E
Falkenberg Sweden 58 C2 56.55N 12.30E
Falkirk Scotland 27 E2 56.00N 3.48W
Falkland Scotland 27 E3 56.15N 3.13W
Falkland Is. S. America 97 C2 52.00S 60.00W
Falmouth England 12 B2 50.09N 5.05W
Falmouth B. England 12 B2 50.06N 5.05W
Falster i. Denmark 46 F2 54.30N 12.00E
Falun Sweden 58 C3 60.37N 15.40E
Famagusta Cyprus 68 D4 35.07N 33.57E
Fannich, L. Scotland 24 D4 57.38N 4.58W
Fanö i. Denmark 46 B3 55.25N 8.25E
Fao Iraq 69 H3 29.57N 48.30E
Faradofay Madagascar 106 G6 25.01S 47.00E
Farafra Oasis Egypt 68 C2 27.00N 28.20E
Farah Afghan. 70 B6 32.23N 62.07E
Farah r. Afghan. 70 B5 31.25N 61.30E
Farallon de Medinilla i. Mariana Is. 79 L7 16.01N146.04E
Farallon de Pajaros i. Mariana Is. 79 K8 20.33N144.59E
Faraulep is. Mariana Is. 79 K5 8.36N144.33E
Farcet Fen England 15 B3 52.32N 0.11W
Fareham England 14 A1 50.52N 1.11W
Farewell, C. Greenland 91 N3 60.00N 44.20W
Fargo U.S.A. 87 G6 46.52N 96.59W
Faringdon England 14 A2 51.39N 1.34W
Farnborough Hants. England 15 B2 51.17N 0.46W
Farndon England 20 C2 53.06N 2.53W
Farne Is. England 22 C2 55.38N 1.36W
Farnham England 15 B2 51.13N 0.49W
Farnworth England 20 C2 53.33N 2.33W
Faro Portugal 50 B2 37.01N 7.56W
Faroe Is. Europe 58 L8 62.00N 7.00W
Fårösund Sweden 58 D2 57.51N 19.05E
Farrukhabad India 71 E5 27.23N 79.35E
Fársala Greece 56 F3 39.17N 22.22E
Farsö Denmark 46 C4 56.47N 9.20E
Farsund Norway 58 A2 58.05N 6.49E
Farum Denmark 46 F3 55.49N 12.20E
Fasa Iran 69 I3 28.55N 53.38E
Fastov Ukraine 59 B4 50.08N 29.59E
Fauldhouse Scotland 27 E2 55.49N 3.41W
Fauske Norway 58 C4 67.17N 15.25E
Faversham England 15 C2 51.18N 0.54E
Favignana i. Italy 54 D2 37.57N 12.19E
Fawley England 14 A1 50.49N 1.20W
Faxaflói b. Iceland 58 I7 64.30N 22.50W
Faxe r. Sweden 58 D3 63.15N 17.15E
Fayetteville U.S.A. 87 K4 35.03N 78.53W
Fdérik Mauritania 104 A4 22.30N 12.30W
Feale r. Rep. of Ire. 28 B2 52.28N 9.38W
Fear, C. U.S.A. 87 K3 33.51N 77.59W
Fécamp France 48 D5 49.45N 0.23E
Feeagh, Lough Rep. of Ire. 28 B3 53.55N 9.35W
Fehmarn i. Germany 52 E6 54.30N 11.05E
Feira de Santana Brazil 96 F6 12.17S 38.53W
Felanitx Spain 51 G3 39.27N 3.08E
Feldkirch Austria 57 A3 47.15N 9.38E
Felixstowe England 15 D2 51.58N 1.20E
Felton England 22 C2 55.18N 1.42W
Femer Baelt str. Denmark / Germany 46 E2 54.35N 11.20E
Femunden l. Norway 58 B3 62.05N 11.55E
Fengfeng China 75 I4 36.34N114.19E
Fengjie China 75 H3 31.00N109.30E
Fenyang China 75 H4 37.14N111.43E
Feodosiya Ukraine 59 D3 45.03N 35.23E
Fergana Uzbekistan 60 F2 40.23N 71.19E
Fergus Falls town U.S.A. 87 G6 46.18N 96.00W
Ferkéssédougou Côte d'Ivoire 104 B2 9.30N 5.10W
Fermanagh d. N. Ireland 23 B1 54.15N 7.45W
Fermoselle Spain 50 B4 41.19N 6.24W
Fermoy Rep. of Ire. 28 C2 52.08N 8.17W
Ferndown England 13 F2 50.48N 1.55W
Ferozepore India 71 D5 30.55N 74.38E
Ferrara Italy 54 C6 44.49N 11.38E
Ferret, Cap c. France 48 C3 44.42N 1.16W
Ferryhill England 22 C1 54.41N 1.33W
Fethiye Turkey 68 C5 36.37N 29.06E
Fetlar i. Scotland 24 H7 60.37N 0.52W
Fevzipaşa Turkey 68 E5 37.07N 36.38E
Fez Morocco 104 B5 34.05N 5.00W
Ffestiniog Wales 18 C2 52.58N 3.56W
Ffostrasol Wales 18 B2 52.06N 4.23W
Fianarantsoa Madagascar 106 G7 21.27S 47.05E
Fife d. Scotland 27 E3 56.10N 3.10W
Fife Ness c. Scotland 27 F3 56.17N 2.36W
Figeac France 48 E3 44.32N 2.01E
Figueira da Foz Portugal 50 A4 40.09N 8.51W
Figueras Spain 51 G5 42.16N 2.57E
Fiji Pacific Oc. 82 H6 18.00S178.00E
Filey England 21 E3 54.13N 0.18W
Findhorn r. Scotland 24 E4 57.37N 3.40W
Finisterre, C. Spain 50 A5 42.54N 9.16W
Finland Europe 58 F3 64.30N 27.00E
Finland, G. of Finland / Estonia 58 F2 60.00N 26.50E
Finlay r. Canada 90 F3 56.30N124.40W
Finn r. Rep. of Ire. 28 D4 54.50N 7.30W
Finschhafen P.N.G. 79 L2 6.35S147.51E
Fintona N. Ireland 23 B1 54.29N 7.19W
Fionnphort Scotland 26 B3 56.19N 6.23W
Firozabad India 71 E5 27.09N 78.24E
Firth of Clyde est. Scotland 26 D2 55.35N 4.53W
Firth of Forth est. Scotland 27 F3 56.05N 3.00W
Firth of Lorn est. Scotland 26 C3 56.20N 5.40W
Firth of Tay est. Scotland 27 E3 56.24N 3.08W
Firuzabad Iran 69 I3 28.50N 52.35E
Fisher Str. Canada 91 J4 63.00N 84.00W
Fishguard Wales 18 B1 51.59N 4.59W
Fishguard B. Wales 18 B2 52.06N 4.54W
Flagstaff U.S.A. 86 D4 35.12N111.38W
Flåm Norway 58 A3 60.51N 7.08E
Flamborough England 21 E3 54.07N 0.07W
Flamborough Head England 21 E3 54.06N 0.05W
Flaming Gorge Resr. U.S.A. 86 E5 41.10N109.30W
Flanders f. Belgium 47 B2 50.52N 3.00E
Flanders East d. Belgium 47 B3 51.00N 3.45E
Flanders West d. Belgium 47 A2 51.00N 3.00E
Flannan Is. Scotland 24 A5 58.16N 7.40W
Flathead L. U.S.A. 86 D6 47.50N114.05W
Flat Holm i. England 18 C1 51.23N 3.08W
Flattery, C. U.S.A. 86 B6 48.23N124.43W
Fleet England 15 B2 51.16N 0.50W
Fleetwood England 20 B2 53.55N 3.01W
Flekkefjord town Norway 58 A2 58.17N 6.40E
Flen Sweden 58 D2 59.04N 16.39E
Flensburg Germany 52 D6 54.47N 9.27E
Flensburg Fjord b. Denmark / Germany 46 C2 54.50N 9.50E
Flers France 48 C5 48.45N 0.34W
Flimby England 22 A1 54.42N 3.31W
Flinders r. Australia 80 D4 15.12S141.40E
Flinders I. Australia 80 D2 40.00S148.00E
Flinders Range mts. Australia 80 C2 31.00S138.30E
Flin Flon Canada 91 H3 54.47N101.51W
Flint U.S.A. 87 J5 43.03N 83.40W
Flint r. U.S.A. 87 J3 30.52N 84.35W
Flint Wales 18 C3 53.15N 3.07W
Flint I. Kiribati 83 K6 11.26S151.48W
Flitwick England 15 B3 51.59N 0.30W
Florence Italy 54 C5 43.46N 11.15E
Florence U.S.A. 87 K3 34.12N 79.44W
Florencia Colombia 94 D1 1.37N 75.37W
Florenville Belgium 47 D1 49.42N 5.19E
Flores i. Indonesia 79 G2 8.40S121.20E
Flores Sea Indonesia 79 G2 7.00S121.00E
Florianópolis Brazil 97 E5 27.35S 48.31W
Florida d. U.S.A. 87 J2 29.00N 82.00W
Florida, Straits of U.S.A. 94 C5 24.00N 81.00W
Flórina Greece 56 E4 40.48N 21.25E
Florö Norway 58 A3 61.45N 4.55E
Flushing Neth. 47 B3 51.27N 3.35E
Fly r. P.N.G. 79 K2 8.22S142.23E
Focşani Romania 59 B3 45.40N 27.12E
Foggia Italy 54 E4 41.28N 15.33E
Föhr i. Germany 46 B2 54.44N 8.30E
Foix France 48 D2 42.57N 1.35E
Folda est. N. Trönd. Norway 58 B4 64.45N 11.20E
Foligno Italy 54 D5 42.56N 12.43E
Folkestone England 15 D2 51.05N 1.11E
Folkingham England 17 D2 52.54N 0.24W
Fond du Lac Canada 90 H3 59.20N107.09W
Fonseca, G. of Honduras 93 G2 13.10N 87.30W
Fontainebleau France 48 E5 48.24N 2.42E
Fontenay France 48 C4 46.28N 0.48W
Ford Scotland 26 C3 56.10N 5.26W
Fordingbridge England 14 A1 50.56N 1.48W
Foreland c. England 14 A1 50.42N 1.06W
Foreland Pt. England 13 D3 51.15N 3.47W
Forel, Mt. Greenland 91 O4 67.00N 37.00W
Forest of Atholl f. Scotland 24 E3 56.53N 3.55W
Forest of Bowland hills England 20 C2 53.57N 2.30W
Forest of Dean f. England 13 E3 51.48N 2.32W
Forest of Rossendale f. England 20 C2 53.43N 2.15W
Forest Row England 15 C2 51.06N 0.03E
Forfar Scotland 27 F3 56.38N 2.54W
Forlì Italy 54 D6 44.13N 12.02E
Formby England 20 B2 53.34N 3.04W
Formby Pt. England 20 B2 53.34N 3.07W
Formentera i. Spain 50 F3 38.41N 1.30E
Fornaes c. Denmark 46 D4 56.28N 10.58E
Forres Scotland 24 E4 57.37N 3.38W
Forssa Finland 58 E3 60.49N 23.40E
Forst Germany 52 G4 51.46N 14.39E
Fort Albany Canada 91 J3 52.15N 81.35W
Fortaleza Brazil 96 F7 3.45S 38.45W
Fort Augustus Scotland 24 D4 57.09N 4.41W
Fort Chimo Canada 91 L3 58.10N 68.15W
Fort Chipewyan Canada 90 G3 58.46N111.09W
Fort Collins U.S.A. 86 E5 40.35N105.05W
Fort-de-France Martinique 93 L2 14.36N 61.05W
Fort Frances Canada 91 I2 48.37N 93.23W
Fort George Canada 91 K3 53.50N 79.01W
Fort Good Hope Canada 90 F4 66.16N128.37W
Forth Scotland 27 E2 55.46N 3.42W
Forth r. Scotland 27 E3 56.06N 3.48W
Fort Lauderdale U.S.A. 87 J2 26.08N 80.08W
Fort Liard Canada 90 F4 60.14N123.28W
Fort McMurray Canada 90 G3 56.45N111.27W
Fort McPherson Canada 90 E4 67.29N134.50W
Fort Myers U.S.A. 87 J2 26.39N 81.51W
Fort Nelson Canada 90 F3 58.48N122.44W
Fort Norman Canada 90 F4 64.55N125.29W
Fort Peck Dam U.S.A. 86 E6 47.55N106.15W
Fort Peck Resr. U.S.A. 86 E6 47.55N107.00W
Fort Randall U.S.A. 90 B3 55.10N162.47W
Fort Reliance Canada 90 H4 62.45N109.08W
Fort Resolution Canada 90 G4 61.10N113.39W
Fortrose Scotland 24 D4 57.34N 4.07W
Fort Rupert Canada 91 K3 51.30N 79.45W
Fort Scott U.S.A. 87 H4 37.52N 94.43W
Fort Severn Canada 91 J3 56.00N 87.40W
Fort Shevchenko Kazakhstan 60 E2 44.31N 50.15E
Fort Sibut C.A.R. 104 D2 5.46N 19.06E
Fort Simpson Canada 90 F4 61.46N121.15W
Fort Smith Canada 90 G4 60.00N111.51W
Fort Smith d. Canada 90 G4 63.30N118.00W
Fort Smith U.S.A. 87 H4 35.22N 94.27W
Fort St. John Canada 90 F3 56.14N120.55W
Fortuneswell England 13 E2 50.33N 2.27W
Fort Vermilion Canada 90 G3 58.22N115.59W
Fort Wayne U.S.A. 87 I5 41.05N 85.08W
Fort William Scotland 24 C3 56.49N 5.07W
Fort Worth U.S.A. 87 G3 32.45N 97.20W
Fort Yukon U.S.A. 90 D4 66.35N145.20W
Foshan China 75 H2 23.03N113.08E
Fougères France 48 C5 48.21N 1.12W
Foula i. Scotland 24 F7 60.08N 2.05W
Foulness I. England 15 C2 51.35N 0.55E
Foulness Pt. England 15 C2 51.37N 1.00E
Fowey England 12 C2 50.20N 4.39W
Foxe Basin b. Canada 91 K4 67.30N 79.00W
Foxe Channel Canada 91 J4 65.00N 80.00W
Foyle r. N. Ireland 23 B1 55.00N 7.20W
Foyle, Lough Rep. of Ire. / N. Ireland 23 B2 55.07N 7.06W
Framlingham England 15 D3 52.14N 1.20E
France Europe 48 C4 47.00N 2.00E
Francistown Botswana 106 C2 21.11S 27.32E
Frankfort U.S.A. 87 J4 38.11N 84.53W
Frankfurt Brandenburg Germany 52 G5 52.20N 14.32E
Frankfurt Hessen Germany 52 D4 50.06N 8.41E
Franklin D. Roosevelt L. U.S.A. 86 C6 47.55N118.20W
Franz Josef Land is. Russian Fed. 60 E5 81.00N 54.00E
Fraser r. Canada 90 F2 49.05N123.00W
Fraserburgh Scotland 24 G4 57.42N 2.00W
Fredericia Denmark 46 C3 55.34N 9.47E
Fredericksburg U.S.A. 87 K4 38.18N 77.30W
Fredericton Canada 91 L2 45.57N 66.40W
Frederiksborg d. Denmark 46 F3 55.50N 12.10E
Frederikshåb Greenland 91 N4 62.05N 49.30W
Frederikshavn Denmark 46 D5 57.28N 10.33E
Frederikssund Denmark 46 F3 55.51N 12.04E
Fredrikstad Norway 58 B2 59.15N 10.55E
Freeport Bahamas 93 I5 26.40N 78.30W
Freetown Sierra Leone 104 A2 8.30N 13.17W
Freiberg Germany 52 F4 50.54N 13.20E
Freiburg Germany 52 C2 48.00N 7.52E
Freilingen Germany 47 F2 50.33N 7.50E
Freising Germany 52 E3 48.24N 11.45E
Fréjus France 48 G2 43.26N 6.44E
Freshford Rep. of Ire. 28 D2 52.43N 7.25W
Fresno U.S.A. 86 C4 36.41N119.57W
Fribourg Switz. 52 C2 46.50N 7.10E
Friedrichshafen Germany 52 D2 47.39N 9.29E
Friedrichstadt Germany 46 C2 54.23N 9.07E
Friesland d. Neth. 47 D5 53.05N 5.45E
Friesoythe Germany 47 F5 53.02N 7.52E
Frinton England 15 D2 51.50N 1.16E
Frio, Cabo c. Brazil 97 E5 22.50S 42.10W
Frisa, Loch Scotland 26 B3 56.33N 6.05W
Frisian Is. Europe 40 G5 53.30N 6.00E
Frobisher B. Canada 91 L4 63.00N 66.45W
Frobisher Bay town Canada 91 L4 63.45N 68.30W
Frodsham England 20 C2 53.17N 2.45W
Frohavet est. Norway 58 B3 63.55N 9.05E
Frome England 13 E3 51.16N 2.17W
Frome, L. Australia 80 C2 30.45S139.45E
Frosinone Italy 54 D4 41.36N 13.21E
Fröya i. Norway 58 B3 63.45N 8.30E
Frýdek-Místek Czech. 57 F4 49.41N 18.22E
Fuerte r. Mexico 92 C5 25.42N109.20W
Fuerteventura i. Canary Is. 104 A4 28.20N 14.10W
Fujairah U.A.E. 69 J2 25.10N 56.20E
Fujian d. China 75 I3 26.30N118.00E
Fujin China 75 K6 47.15N131.59E
Fujiyama mtn. Japan 76 D4 35.23N138.42E
Fukui Japan 76 C5 36.04N136.12E
Fukuoka Japan 76 A3 33.39N130.21E
Fukushima Japan 76 D5 37.44N140.28E
Fukuyama Japan 76 B4 34.29N133.21E
Fulda Germany 52 D4 50.35N 9.45E
Fumay France 47 C1 49.59N 4.42E
Funabashi Japan 76 D4 35.42N139.59E
Funafuti Tuvalu 82 H7 8.31S179.13E
Funchal Madeira Is. 104 A5 32.38N 16.54W
Fundy, B. of N. America 87 M5 44.30N 66.30W
Fünen i. Denmark 46 D3 56.15N 10.30E
Furakawa Japan 76 D6 38.30N140.50E
Furg Iran 69 I3 28.19N 55.10E
Furnas Dam Brazil 97 E5 20.40S 46.22W
Furneaux Group is. Australia 82 E3 40.10S148.05E
Furnes Belgium 47 A3 51.04N 2.40E
Fürstenau Germany 47 F4 52.32N 7.41E
Fürstenwalde Germany 52 F5 52.22N 14.04E
Fürth Germany 52 E3 49.28N 11.00E
Fusagasugá Colombia 94 E1 4.22N 74.21W
Fushun China 75 J5 41.51N123.53E
Futa Jalon f. Guinea 104 A3 11.30N 12.30W
Fuxin China 75 J5 42.08N121.39E
Fuyu China 75 J6 45.12N124.49E
Fuzhou Fujian China 75 I3 26.01N119.20E
Fuzhou Jiangxi China 75 I3 28.03N116.15E
Fyne, Loch Scotland 26 C2 55.55N 5.23W
Fyns d. Denmark 46 D3 55.10N 10.30E

G

Gabès Tunisia 104 D5 33.52N 10.06E
Gabès, G. of Tunisia 104 D5 34.00N 11.00E
Gabon Africa 106 B4 0.00 12.00E
Gaborone Botswana 106 C2 24.45S 25.55E
Gach Saran Iran 69 H3 30.13N 50.49E
Gadsden U.S.A. 87 I3 34.00N 86.00W
Gaeta Italy 54 D4 41.13N 13.35E
Gaeta, G. of Med. Sea 54 D4 41.05N 13.30E
Gaferut i. Caroline Is. 79 L5 9.14N145.23E
Gagnon Canada 91 L3 51.56N 68.16W
Gaillac France 48 D2 43.54N 1.53E
Gainesville U.S.A. 87 J2 29.37N 82.31W
Gainford England 22 C1 54.34N 1.44W
Gainsborough England 16 D3 53.23N 0.46W
Gairdner, L. Australia 80 C2 31.30S136.00E
Gairloch town Scotland 24 C4 57.43N 5.41W
Galapagos Is. Pacific Oc. 83 Q7 0.30S 90.30W
Galashiels Scotland 27 F2 55.37N 2.49W
Galati Romania 59 B3 45.27N 27.59E
Galena U.S.A. 90 C4 64.43N157.00W
Galicia d. Spain 50 A5 43.00N 8.00W
Galle Sri Lanka 71 E1 6.01N 80.13E
Gállego r. Spain 50 E4 41.40N 0.55W
Galley Head Rep. of Ire. 28 C1 51.31N 8.57W
Gallinas, C. Colombia 94 E3 12.20N 71.30W
Gallipoli Italy 54 G4 40.02N 18.01E
Gallipoli Turkey 68 B6 40.25N 26.31E
Gällivare Sweden 58 E4 67.10N 20.40E
Galloway f. Scotland 26 D2 55.00N 4.28W
Gallup U.S.A. 86 E4 35.32N108.46W
Galston Scotland 26 D2 55.36N 4.23W
Galtby Finland 58 E3 60.08N 21.33E
Galty Mts. Rep. of Ire. 28 C2 52.20N 8.10W
Galveston U.S.A. 87 H2 29.17N 94.48W
Galveston B. U.S.A. 87 H2 29.40N 94.40W
Galway Rep. of Ire. 28 B3 53.17N 9.04W
Galway d. Rep. of Ire. 28 B3 53.25N 9.00W
Galway B. Rep. of Ire. 28 B3 53.12N 9.07W
Gambia Africa 104 A3 13.30N 15.00W
Gambia r. Gambia 104 A3 13.28N 15.55W
Gambier, Îles is. Pacific Oc. 83 M5 23.10S135.00W
Gander Canada 91 M2 48.58N 54.34W
Gandía Spain 50 E3 38.59N 0.11W
Ganges r. India 71 G4 23.30N 90.25E

Guatemala Trench Pacific Oc. **83 Q9** 15.00N 93.00W
Guatire Venezuela **95 F3** 10.28N 66.32W
Guaviare *r.* Colombia **95 F1** 4.00N 67.35W
Guayaquil Ecuador **96 B7** 2.13S 79.54W
Guayaquil, G. of Ecuador **96 A7** 2.30S 80.00W
Guaymas Mexico **92 B5** 27.59N110.54W
Gubin Poland **57 D5** 51.59N 14.42E
Guecho Spain **50 D5** 43.21N 3.01W
Guéret France **48 D4** 46.10N 1.52E
Guernsey *i.* Channel Is. **48 B5** 49.27N 2.35W
Guerrero *d.* Mexico **92 D3** 18.00N100.00W
Guguan *i.* Mariana Is. **79 L7** 17.20N145.51E
Guiana S. America **95 I1** 3.40N 53.00W
Guiana Highlands S. America **95 H1** 4.00N 59.00W
Guildford England **15 B2** 51.14N 0.35W
Guildtown Scotland **27 E3** 56.28N 3.25W
Guilin China **75 H2** 25.21N110.11E
Guinea Africa **104 A3** 10.30N 10.30W
Guinea Bissau Africa **104 A3** 12.00N 15.30W
Guinea, G. of Africa **104 B2** 3.00N 3.00E
Güines Cuba **93 H4** 22.50N 82.02W
Guingamp France **48 B5** 48.34N 3.09W
Guiping China **75 H2** 23.20N110.04E
Güiria Venezuela **96 C9** 10.37N 62.21W
Guisborough England **22 C1** 54.32N 1.02W
Guise France **47 B1** 49.54N 3.39E
Guiseley England **20 D2** 53.53N 1.42W
Guiuan Phil. **79 H6** 11.02N125.44E
Guiyang China **74 G3** 26.35N106.40E
Guizhou *d.* China **74 G3** 27.00N106.30E
Gujarat *d.* India **71 C4** 22.45N 71.30E
Gujranwala Pakistan **71 D6** 32.06N 74.11E
Gujrāt Pakistan **71 D6** 32.35N 74.06E
Gulbarga India **71 D3** 17.22N 76.47E
Gullane Scotland **27 F3** 56.02N 2.49W
Gulpaigan Iran **69 H4** 33.23N 50.18E
Gulu Uganda **106 D5** 2.46N 32.21E
Gümüshane Turkey **68 E6** 40.26N 39.26E
Gunnislake England **12 C2** 50.31N 4.12W
Guntersville L. U.S.A. **87 I3** 34.35N 86.00W
Guntur India **71 E3** 16.20N 80.27E
Gurnard's Head *c.* England **12 B2** 50.12N 5.35W
Gürün Turkey **68 E5** 38.44N 37.15E
Guryev Kazakhstan **60 E2** 47.08N 51.59E
Gusau Nigeria **108 C3** 12.12N 6.40E
Güstrow Germany **52 F5** 53.48N 12.11E
Gütersloh Germany **52 D4** 51.54N 8.22E
Guyana S. America **95 H2** 5.00N 59.00W
Guyhirn England **15 C3** 52.37N 0.05E
Gwadar Pakistan **70 B4** 25.09N 62.21E
Gwalior India **71 E5** 26.12N 78.09E
Gwatar Iran **69 K2** 25.10N 61.31E
Gweebarra B. Rep. of Ire. **28 C4** 54.52N 8.30W
Gwent *d.* Wales **18 D1** 51.44N 3.00W
Gweru Zimbabwe **106 C3** 19.25S 29.50E
Gwynedd *d.* Wales **18 B3** 53.00N 4.00W
Gyandzha Azerbaijan **69 G6** 40.39N 46.20E
Gyangzê China **74 D3** 29.00N 89.40E
Gydanskiy Pen. Russian Fed. **60 G4** 70.00N 78.30E
Gyöngyös Hungary **57 F3** 47.47N 19.56E
Györ Hungary **57 E3** 47.41N 17.40E
Gyuzovska Ukraine **59 D3** 48.00N 37.50E

H

Ha'apai Group *is.* Tonga **82 I5** 19.50S174.30W
Haapajärvi Finland **58 F3** 63.45N 25.20E
Haapamäki Finland **58 F3** 62.15N 24.25E
Haapsalu Estonia **58 E2** 58.58N 23.32E
Haarlem Neth. **47 C4** 52.22N 4.38E
Hachinohe Japan **76 E7** 40.30N141.30E
Haddington Scotland **27 F2** 55.57N 2.47W
Hadejia Nigeria **108 D3** 12.30N 10.03E
Hadejia *r.* Nigeria **108 D3** 12.47N 10.44E
Haderslev Denmark **46 C3** 55.15N 9.30E
Hadfield England **16 C3** 53.28N 1.59W
Hadhramaut *f.* Yemen **105 G3** 16.30N 49.30E
Hadleigh England **15 C3** 52.03N 0.58E
Hadsten Denmark **46 D4** 56.19N 10.04E
Hadsund Denmark **46 D4** 56.43N 10.09E
Haeju N. Korea **75 J5** 38.04N125.40E
Hafar Saudi Arabia **69 G3** 28.28N 46.00E
Hafnarfjördhur *town* Iceland **58 I7** 64.04N 21.58W
Haft Kel Iran **69 H3** 31.28N 49.35E
Hagen Germany **47 F3** 51.22N 7.27E
Hagested Denmark **46 E3** 55.46N 11.37E
Hagi Japan **76 A4** 34.25N131.22E
Ha Giang Vietnam **78 D8** 22.50N105.01E
Hags Head Rep. of Ire. **28 B2** 52.56N 9.29W
Hai Duong Vietnam **78 D8** 20.56N106.21E
Haifa Israel **68 D4** 32.49N 34.59E
Haikou China **75 H2** 20.05N110.25E
Hail Saudi Arabia **68 F2** 27.31N 41.45E
Hailar China **75 I6** 49.15N119.41E
Hailsham England **15 C1** 50.52N 0.17E
Hailun China **75 K6** 47.29N126.58E
Hailuoto *i.* Finland **58 F4** 65.00N 24.50E
Hainan *i.* China **75 H1** 18.30N109.40E
Hainaut *d.* Belgium **47 B2** 50.30N 3.45E
Haines U.S.A. **90 E3** 59.11N135.23W
Haiphong Vietnam **78 D8** 20.58N106.41E
Haiti C. America **93 J3** 19.00N 73.00W
Hajiki saki *c.* Japan **76 D6** 38.25N138.32E
Hakari Turkey **69 F5** 37.36N 43.45E
Hakodate Japan **76 D7** 41.46N140.44E
Halberstadt Germany **52 E4** 51.54N 11.04E
Halden Norway **58 B2** 59.08N 11.13E
Halesowen England **16 B2** 52.27N 2.02W
Halesworth England **15 D3** 52.21N 1.30E
Halifax Canada **91 L2** 44.38N 63.35W
Halifax England **20 D2** 53.43N 1.51W
Halkett, C. U.S.A. **90 C5** 71.00N152.00W
Halkirk Scotland **24 E5** 58.30N 3.30W
Halladale *r.* Scotland **24 E5** 58.32N 3.53W
Halle Belgium **47 C2** 50.45N 4.14E
Halle Germany **52 E4** 51.28N 11.58E
Hall Is. Pacific Oc. **82 F8** 8.37N152.00E
Hallow England **16 B2** 52.14N 2.15W
Hallsberg Sweden **58 C2** 59.05N 15.07E
Hallstavik Sweden **58 D3** 60.06N 18.42E
Halmahera *i.* Indonesia **79 H4** 0.45N128.00E
Halmstad Sweden **58 C2** 56.41N 12.55E
Hälsingborg Sweden **58 C2** 56.05N 12.45E
Halstead England **15 C2** 51.57N 0.39E
Haltern Germany **47 F3** 51.45N 7.10E
Haltia Tunturi *mtn.* Finland **58 E5** 69.20N 21.10E
Haltwhistle England **22 B1** 54.58N 2.27W
Hama Syria **68 E4** 35.09N 36.44E
Hamadān Iran **69 H4** 34.47N 48.33E
Hamamatsu Japan **76 C4** 34.42N137.42E
Hamar Norway **58 B3** 60.47N 10.55E
Hamata, Gebel *mtn.* Egypt **68 D2** 24.11N 35.01E
Hamble England **14 A1** 50.52N 1.19W
Hambleton England **21 D2** 53.46N 1.11W
Hambleton Hills England **21 D3** 54.15N 1.11W
Hamborn Germany **47 E3** 51.29N 6.46E
Hamburg Germany **52 E5** 53.33N 10.00E
Hamdh, Wadi *r.* Saudi Arabia **68 E2** 25.49N 36.37E
Hämeenlinna Finland **58 F3** 61.00N 24.25E
Hameln Germany **52 D5** 52.06N 9.21E
Hamersley Range *mts.* Australia **80 A3** 22.00S118.00E
Hamhung N. Korea **75 K5** 39.54N127.35E
Hami China **74 E5** 42.40N 93.30E
Hamilton Canada **91 K2** 43.15N 79.50W
Hamilton New Zealand **80 G2** 37.47S175.17E
Hamilton Scotland **27 D2** 55.46N 4.02W
Hamina Finland **58 F3** 60.33N 27.15E
Hamm Germany **47 F3** 51.40N 7.49E
Hammel Denmark **46 C4** 56.15N 9.51E
Hammerfest Norway **58 E5** 70.40N 23.44E
Hamoir Belgium **47 D2** 50.25N 5.32E
Hampreston England **13 F2** 50.47N 1.56W
Hampshire *d.* England **14 A2** 51.03N 1.20W
Hampshire Downs *hills* England **14 A2** 51.18N 1.25W
Hamrin, Jabal *mts.* Iraq **69 G4** 34.40N 44.10E
Hamstreet England **15 C2** 51.03N 0.52E
Hanakiya Saudi Arabia **68 F2** 24.53N 40.30E
Hanamaki Japan **76 E6** 39.23N141.07E
Hanggin Houqi China **74 G5** 40.52N107.04E
Hangö Finland **58 E2** 59.50N 23.00E
Hangzhou China **75 J3** 30.10N120.07E
Hannibal U.S.A. **87 H4** 39.41N 91.25W
Hannover Germany **52 D5** 52.23N 9.44E
Hannut Belgium **47 D2** 50.40N 5.05E
Hanoi Vietnam **78 D8** 21.01N105.52E
Han Shui *r.* China **75 I3** 30.45N114.24E
Hanstholm Denmark **46 B5** 57.08N 8.38E
Hantengri Feng *mtn.* China **74 C5** 42.09N 80.12E
Haparanda Sweden **58 E4** 65.50N 24.10E
Haradh Saudi Arabia **69 H2** 24.12N 49.08E
Harar Ethiopia **105 G2** 9.20N 42.10E
Harare Zimbabwe **106 D3** 17.43S 31.05E
Harbin China **75 K6** 45.45N126.41E
Harburg Germany **52 D5** 53.27N 9.58E
Hårby Denmark **46 D3** 55.13N 10.07E
Hardangerfjorden *est.* Norway **58 A3** 60.15N 6.25E
Hardanger Vidda *f.* Norway **58 A3** 60.20N 8.00E
Harderwijk Neth. **47 D4** 52.21N 5.37E
Haren Germany **47 F4** 52.48N 7.15E
Hargeisa Somali Rep. **105 G2** 9.31N 44.02E
Har Hu *l.* China **74 F5** 38.20N 97.40E
Hari *r.* Afghan. **70 B6** 35.42N 61.12E
Hari *r.* Indonesia **78 C3** 1.00S104.15E
Harima nada *str.* Japan **76 B4** 34.30N134.30E
Harlech Wales **18 B2** 52.52N 4.08W
Harleston England **15 D3** 52.25N 1.18E
Harlingen Neth. **47 D5** 53.10N 5.25E
Harlow England **15 C2** 51.47N 0.08E
Harmerhill England **16 B2** 52.48N 2.45W
Harney Basin *f.* U.S.A. **86 C5** 43.20N119.00W
Härnösand Sweden **58 D3** 62.37N 17.55E
Harpenden England **15 B2** 51.49N 0.22W
Harre Denmark **46 B4** 56.43N 8.55E
Harris *i.* Scotland **24 B4** 57.50N 6.55W
Harrisburg U.S.A. **87 K5** 40.35N 76.59W
Harrison, C. Canada **91 M3** 55.00N 58.00W
Harris, Sd. of Scotland **24 A4** 57.43N 7.05W
Harrogate England **21 D2** 53.59N 1.32W
Harrow England **15 B2** 51.35N 0.21W
Harstad Norway **58 D5** 68.48N 16.30E
Hartford U.S.A. **87 L5** 41.40N 72.51W
Hartington England **16 C3** 53.08N 1.49W
Hartland England **12 C2** 50.59N 4.29W
Hartland Pt. England **12 C3** 51.01N 4.32W
Hartlepool England **22 C1** 54.42N 1.11W
Harwich England **15 D2** 51.56N 1.18E
Haryana *d.* India **71 D5** 29.15N 76.00E
Harz Mts. Europe **40 H5** 51.43N 10.40E
Hasa Oasis Saudi Arabia **69 H2** 25.37N 49.40E
Hase *r.* Germany **47 F4** 52.42N 7.17E
Hashtrud Iran **69 G5** 37.29N 47.05E
Haslemere England **15 B2** 51.05N 0.41W
Haslev Denmark **46 E3** 55.19N 11.59E
Haslingden England **20 C2** 53.43N 2.20W
Hasselt Belgium **47 D2** 50.56N 5.20E
Hassi Messaoud Algeria **104 C5** 31.43N 6.03E
Hässleholm Sweden **58 C2** 56.09N 13.45E
Hastings England **15 C1** 50.51N 0.36E
Hatfield England **15 B2** 51.46N 0.13W
Hatherleigh England **13 C2** 50.49N 4.04W
Hathersage England **16 C3** 53.20N 1.39W
Ha Tinh Vietnam **78 D7** 18.21N105.55E
Hatteras, C. U.S.A. **87 K4** 35.14N 75.31W
Hattiesburg U.S.A. **87 I3** 31.25N 89.19W
Hatton England **16 C2** 52.52N 1.40W
Haugesund Norway **58 A2** 59.25N 5.16E
Haukivesi *l.* Finland **58 G3** 62.10N 28.30E
Hauran, Wadi *r.* Iraq **68 F4** 33.57N 42.35E
Havana Cuba **93 H4** 23.07N 82.25W
Havant England **15 B1** 50.51N 0.59W
Havel *r.* Germany **52 F5** 52.51N 11.57E
Haverfordwest Wales **18 B1** 51.48N 4.59W
Haverhill England **15 C3** 52.06N 0.27E
Havering England **15 C2** 51.34N 0.14E
Havlíčkuv Brod Czech. **57 D4** 49.38N 15.35E
Havre U.S.A. **86 E6** 48.34N109.45W
Hawaii *d.* U.S.A. **86 O9** 21.00N156.00W
Hawaii *i.* Hawaii U.S.A. **86 O8** 19.30N155.30W
Hawaiian Is. U.S.A. **86 O9** 21.00N157.00W
Hawes England **20 C3** 54.18N 2.12W
Hawes Water *l.* England **22 B1** 54.30N 2.45W
Hawick Scotland **27 F2** 55.25N 2.47W
Hawkhurst England **15 C2** 51.02N 0.31E
Hawthorne U.S.A. **86 C4** 38.13N118.37W
Haydon Bridge England **22 B1** 54.58N 2.14W
Hayes *r.* Canada **91 I3** 57.00N 92.30W
Hayle England **12 B2** 50.12N 5.25W
Hay-on-Wye Wales **18 C2** 52.04N 3.09W
Hay River *town* Canada **90 G4** 60.51N115.42W
Haywards Heath *town* England **15 B1** 51.00N 0.05W
Hazelton Canada **90 F3** 55.16N127.18W
Heacham England **15 C3** 52.55N 0.30E
Headcorn England **15 C2** 51.11N 0.37E
Heads of Ayr *c.* Scotland **26 D2** 55.26N 4.42W
Heanor England **16 C3** 53.01N 1.20W
Heard I. Indian Oc. **113 M2** 53.00S 74.00E
Hearst Canada **91 J2** 49.42N 83.40W
Heath End England **14 A2** 51.21N 1.08W
Heathfield England **15 C1** 50.58N 0.18E
Hebden Bridge *town* England **20 C2** 53.45N 2.00W
Hebei *d.* China **75 I5** 39.20N117.15E
Hebi China **75 I4** 35.57N114.08E
Hebrides *is.* U.K. **40 D6** 58.00N 7.00W
Hebron Jordan **68 D3** 31.32N 35.06E
Hecate Str. Canada **90 E3** 53.00N131.00W
Hechtel Belgium **47 D3** 51.07N 5.22E
Heckington England **17 D2** 52.59N 0.18W
Hedon England **21 E2** 53.44N 0.11W
Heemstede Neth. **47 C4** 52.21N 4.38E
Heerde Neth. **47 E4** 52.23N 6.02E
Heerenveen Neth. **47 D4** 52.57N 5.55E
Heerlen Neth. **47 D2** 50.53N 5.59E
Hefei China **75 I3** 31.55N117.18E
Hegang China **75 K6** 47.36N130.30E
Heide Germany **46 C2** 54.11N 9.09E
Heidelberg Germany **52 D3** 49.25N 8.42E
Heilbronn Germany **52 D3** 49.08N 9.14E
Heiligenhafen Germany **46 D2** 54.22N 10.59E
Heilongjiang *d.* China **75 K6** 47.00N126.00E
Heinola Finland **58 F3** 61.13N 26.05E
Heinsberg Germany **47 E3** 51.04N 6.06E
Hejaz *f.* Saudi Arabia **68 E2** 26.00N 37.30E
Hekla, Mt. Iceland **58 J6** 64.00N 19.45W
Hekura jima *i.* Japan **76 C5** 37.52N136.56E
Helena U.S.A. **86 D6** 46.35N112.00W
Helen Reef *i.* Caroline Is. **79 I4** 2.43N131.46E
Helensburgh Scotland **26 D3** 56.01N 4.44W
Heligoland B. Germany **52 D6** 54.00N 8.15E
Heliopolis Egypt **68 C3** 30.06N 31.20E
Hellendoorn Neth. **47 E4** 52.24N 6.29E
Hellevoetsluis Neth. **47 C3** 51.49N 4.08E
Hellifield England **20 C3** 54.00N 2.13W
Hellín Spain **50 E3** 38.31N 1.43W
Helmand *r.* Asia **70 B5** 31.10N 61.20E
Helmond Neth. **47 D3** 51.28N 5.40E
Helmsdale Scotland **24 E5** 58.08N 3.40W
Helmsdale *r.* Scotland **24 E5** 58.06N 3.40W
Helmsley England **21 D3** 54.15N 1.20W
Helsinge Denmark **46 E3** 55.31N 11.11E
Helsingör Denmark **46 F4** 56.03N 12.38E
Helsinki Finland **58 F3** 60.08N 25.00E
Helston England **12 B2** 50.07N 5.17W
Helvellyn *mtn.* England **22 A1** 54.31N 3.00W
Helwân Egypt **68 C3** 29.51N 31.20E
Hemel Hempstead England **15 B2** 51.46N 0.28W
Hemsworth England **21 D2** 53.37N 1.21W
Henan *d.* China **75 H4** 33.45N113.00E
Henares *r.* Spain **50 D4** 40.26N 3.35W
Hendaye France **48 C2** 43.22N 1.46W
Henderson I. Pacific Oc. **83 N5** 24.20S128.20W
Henfield England **15 B1** 50.56N 0.17W
Hengelo Neth. **47 E4** 52.16N 6.46E
Hengyang China **75 H3** 26.58N112.31E
Henley-on-Thames England **15 B2** 51.32N 0.53W
Henrietta Maria, C. Canada **91 J3** 55.00N 82.15W
Henzada Myanma **71 G3** 17.38N 95.35E
Herat Afghan. **70 B6** 34.21N 62.10E
Herauabad Iran **69 H5** 37.36N 48.36E
Hérault *r.* France **48 E2** 43.17N 3.28E
Hereford England **16 B2** 52.04N 2.43W
Hereford and Worcester *d.* England **16 B2** 52.08N 2.30W
Herford Germany **52 D5** 52.07N 8.40E
Hermon, Mt. Lebanon **68 D4** 33.24N 35.52E
Hermosillo Mexico **92 B5** 29.15N110.59W
Herne Germany **47 F3** 51.32N 7.12E
Herne Bay *town* England **15 D2** 51.23N 1.10E
Herning Denmark **46 B4** 56.08N 9.00E
Herstal Belgium **47 D2** 50.14N 5.38E
Hertford England **15 B2** 51.48N 0.05W
Hertfordshire *d.* England **15 B2** 51.51N 0.05W
Hesbaye *f.* Belgium **47 D2** 50.32N 5.07E
Hessen *d.* Germany **52 D4** 50.30N 9.15E
Hessle England **21 E2** 53.44N 0.28W
Heswall England **20 B2** 53.20N 3.06W
Hetton-le-Hole England **22 C1** 54.49N 1.26W
Hexham England **22 B1** 54.58N 2.06W
Heysham England **20 C3** 54.03N 2.53W
Heywood England **20 C2** 53.36N 2.13W
Hidaka Sammyaku *mts.* Japan **76 E8** 42.50N143.00E
Hidalgo *d.* Mexico **92 E4** 20.50N 98.30W
Hieradhsvotn *r.* Iceland **58 J7** 65.45N 18.50W
Higashiosaka Japan **76 C4** 34.34N135.45E
Higham Ferrers England **17 D2** 52.18N 0.36W
High Atlas *mts.* Morocco **104 B5** 32.00N 5.50W
High Bentham England **20 C3** 54.08N 2.31W
Highland *d.* Scotland **24 C4** 57.42N 5.00W
High Peak *mtn.* England **16 C3** 53.22N 1.48W
High Veld *f.* R.S.A. **102 E2** 27.00S 26.00E
High Willhays *mtn.* England **13 C2** 50.41N 4.00W
Highworth England **13 F3** 51.38N 1.42W
High Wycombe England **15 B2** 51.38N 0.46W
Hiiumaa *i.* Estonia **58 E2** 58.50N 22.30E
Hildesheim Germany **52 D5** 52.09N 9.58E
Hilla Iraq **69 G4** 32.28N 44.29E
Hilleröd Denmark **46 F3** 55.56N 12.18E
Hillingdon England **15 B2** 51.32N 0.27W
Hilo Hawaii U.S.A. **86 O8** 19.42N155.04W
Hilpsford Pt. England **22 A1** 54.02N 3.10W
Hilversum Neth. **47 D4** 52.14N 5.12E
Himachal Pradesh *d.* India **71 D5** 31.45N 77.30E
Himalaya *mts.* Asia **71 E5** 29.00N 84.00E
Himeji Japan **76 B4** 34.50N134.40E
Himi Japan **76 C5** 36.51N136.59E
Hinckley England **16 C2** 52.33N 1.21W
Hindhead England **15 B2** 51.06N 0.42W
Hindu Kush *mts.* Asia **71 C6** 36.40N 70.00E
Hindustan *f.* India **64 J5** 25.00N 75.00E
Hingol *r.* Pakistan **70 B4** 25.25N 65.32E
Hinnöy *i.* Norway **58 C5** 68.30N 16.00E
Hīrākud Resr. India **71 E4** 21.32N 83.55E
Hiratsuka Japan **76 D4** 35.20N139.19E
Hirgis Nur *l.* Mongolia **74 E6** 49.20N 93.40E
Hirosaki Japan **76 D7** 40.34N140.28E
Hiroshima Japan **76 B4** 34.30N132.27E
Hirson France **47 C1** 49.56N 4.05E
Hirstshals Denmark **46 C5** 57.36N 9.58E
Hirwaun Wales **18 C1** 51.43N 3.30W
Hispaniola *i.* C. America **93 J3** 19.00N 71.00W
Histon England **15 C3** 52.15N 0.05E
Hit Iraq **68 F4** 33.38N 42.50E
Hitachi Japan **76 D5** 36.35N140.40E
Hitchin England **15 B2** 51.57N 0.16W
Hitra *i.* Norway **58 B3** 63.30N 8.50E
Hiva Oa *i.* Marquesas Is. **83 M7** 9.45S139.00W
Hjälmaren *l.* Sweden **58 C2** 59.10N 15.45E
Hjörring Denmark **46 C5** 57.28N 9.59E
Ho Ghana **108 B2** 6.38N 0.38E
Hobart Australia **80 D1** 42.54S147.18E
Hobro Denmark **46 C4** 56.39N 9.49E
Ho Chi Minh City Vietnam **78 D6** 10.46N106.43E
Hockley Heath England **16 C2** 52.21N 1.46W
Hodder *r.* England **20 C2** 53.50N 2.26W
Hoddesdon England **15 B2** 51.46N 0.01W
Hodeida Yemen **105 G3** 14.50N 42.58E
Hódmezövásárhely Hungary **56 E7** 46.26N 20.21E
Hodnet England **16 B2** 52.51N 2.35W
Hof Germany **52 E4** 50.19N 11.56E
Höfn Iceland **58 K7** 64.16N 15.10W
Hofors Sweden **58 D3** 60.34N 16.17E
Hofsjökull *mtn.* Iceland **58 J7** 64.50N 19.00W
Hofuf Saudi Arabia **69 H2** 25.20N 49.34E
Höganäs Sweden **46 F4** 56.13N 12.31E
Hog's Back *hill* England **15 B2** 51.14N 0.39W
Hohhot China **75 H5** 40.49N111.37E
Hoi An Vietnam **78 D7** 15.54N108.19E
Hokkaido *d.* Japan **76 E8** 43.00N143.00E
Hokkaido *i.* Japan **76 E8** 43.00N144.00E
Hokuriko *d.* Japan **76 C5** 37.00N138.00E
Holbaek Denmark **46 E3** 55.42N 11.41E
Holbeach England **17 E2** 52.48N 0.01E
Holbrook U.S.A. **86 E3** 34.58N110.00W
Holderness *f.* England **21 E2** 53.45N 0.05W
Holguín Cuba **93 I4** 20.54N 76.15W
Hollabrunn Austria **57 E4** 48.34N 16.05E
Holland Fen *f.* England **17 D3** 53.02N 0.12W
Hollesley B. England **15 D3** 52.02N 1.33E
Holmes Chapel England **20 C2** 53.13N 2.21W
Holme upon Spalding Moor England **21 E2** 53.50N 0.47W
Holmfirth England **20 D2** 53.34N 1.48W
Holmsland Klit *f.* Denmark **46 B4** 56.00N 8.05E
Holstebro Denmark **46 B4** 56.22N 8.38E
Holsworthy England **12 C2** 50.48N 4.21W
Holt England **15 D3** 52.55N 1.04E
Holten Neth. **47 E4** 52.18N 6.26E
Holtenau Germany **46 D2** 54.23N 10.04E
Holwerd Neth. **47 D5** 53.22N 5.54E
Holyhead Wales **18 B3** 53.18N 4.38W
Holyhead B. Wales **18 B3** 53.22N 4.40W
Holy I. England **22 C2** 55.41N 1.47W
Holy I. Scotland **26 C2** 55.32N 5.04W
Holy I. Wales **18 B3** 53.15N 4.38W
Holywell Wales **18 C3** 53.17N 3.13W
Holywood N. Ireland **23 D1** 54.38N 5.50W
Home B. Canada **91 L4** 69.00N 66.00W
Homer Alas. U.S.A. **90 C3** 59.40N151.37W
Homs Syria **68 E4** 34.44N 36.43E
Honda Colombia **94 E2** 5.15N 74.50W
Hondo *r.* Mexico **93 G3** 18.33N 88.22W
Honduras C. America **93 G2** 14.30N 87.00W
Honduras, G. of Carib. Sea **93 G3** 16.20N 87.30W
Hönefoss Norway **58 B3** 60.10N 10.16E
Honfleur France **48 D5** 49.25N 0.14E
Hong Kong Asia **75 I2** 22.30N114.10E
Hongshui He *r.* China **75 H2** 23.20N110.04E
Honiara Solomon Is. **80 E5** 9.27S159.57E
Honiton England **13 D2** 50.48N 3.13W
Honolulu Hawaii U.S.A. **86 O9** 21.19N157.50W
Honshu *i.* Japan **76 D5** 36.00N138.00E

Jerez de la Frontera Spain 50 B2 36.41N 6.08W
Jericho Jordan 68 D3 31.51N 35.27E
Jersey i. Channel Is. 48 B5 49.13N 2.08W
Jersey City U.S.A. 87 L5 40.40N 74.04W
Jerusalem Israel / Jordan 68 D3 31.47N 35.13E
Jessore Bangla. 71 F4 23.10N 89.12E
Jever Germany 47 F5 53.34N 7.54E
Jeypore India 71 E3 18.51N 82.41E
Jhansi India 71 E4 25.27N 78.34E
Jhelum r. Pakistan 71 D5 31.04N 72.10E
Jiamusi China 75 K6 46.50N130.21E
Ji'an China 75 I3 27.08N115.00E
Jiangling China 75 H3 30.20N112.20E
Jiangsu d. China 75 I4 34.00N119.00E
Jiangxi d. China 75 I3 27.25N115.20E
Jianyang Fujian China 75 I3 27.20N117.50E
Jiaxing China 75 J3 30.40N120.50E
Jiayi Taiwan 75 J2 23.38N120.27E
Jiddah Saudi Arabia 105 F4 21.30N 39.10E
Jihlava Czech. 57 D4 49.24N 15.35E
Jilin China 75 K5 43.53N126.35E
Jilin d. China 75 K5 43.00N127.30E
Jilong Taiwan 75 J2 25.10N121.43E
Jiménez Mexico 92 D5 27.08N104.55W
Jimma Ethiopia 105 F2 7.39N 36.47E
Jinan China 75 I4 36.50N117.00E
Jingdezhen China 75 I3 29.16N117.11E
Jinggu China 74 F2 23.29N100.19E
Jinhua China 75 I3 29.06N119.40E
Jining Nei Monggol China 75 H5 40.56N113.00E
Jining Shantung China 75 I4 35.25N116.40E
Jinja Uganda 106 D5 0.27N 33.14E
Jinotepe Nicaragua 93 G2 11.50N 86.10W
Jinxi China 75 J5 40.54N120.36E
Jin Xian Liaoning China 75 J5 39.04N121.45E
Jinzhou China 75 J5 41.07N121.06E
Jiu r. Romania 56 F5 43.44N 23.52E
Jiujiang China 75 I3 29.41N116.03E
Jixi China 75 K6 45.17N131.00E
Jizān Saudi Arabia 105 G3 16.56N 42.33E
Jizl, Wadi r. Saudi Arabia 68 E2 25.37N 38.20E
João Pessoa Brazil 96 F7 7.06S 34.53W
Jódar Spain 50 D2 37.50N 3.21W
Jodhpur India 71 D5 26.18N 73.08E
Joensuu Finland 58 G3 62.35N 29.46E
Joetsu Japan 76 D5 37.06N138.15E
Johannesburg R.S.A. 106 C2 26.10S 28.02E
John O' Groats Scotland 24 E5 58.39N 3.04W
Johnstone Scotland 26 D2 55.50N 4.30W
Johnston I. Pacific Oc. 82 J9 16.45N169.32W
Johnston's Pt. Scotland 26 C2 55.22N 5.31W
Johor Bahru Malaysia 78 C4 1.29N103.40E
Jokkmokk Sweden 58 D4 66.37N 19.50E
Jökulsá á Brú r. Iceland 58 K7 65.33N 14.23W
Jökulsá á Fjöllum r. Iceland 58 J7 66.05N 16.32W
Jolo i. Phil. 79 G5 5.55N121.20E
Jombang Indonesia 78 E2 7.30S112.21E
Jönköping Sweden 58 C2 57.45N 14.10E
Joplin U.S.A. 87 H4 37.04N 94.31W
Jordan Asia 68 E3 31.00N 36.00E
Jordan r. Asia 68 D3 31.47N 35.31E
Jos Nigeria 108 C2 9.54N 8.53E
Jos Plateau f. Nigeria 108 C2 10.00N 9.00E
Jotunheimen mts. Norway 58 B3 61.30N 9.00E
Juan Fernandez Is. Chile 97 A4 34.20S 80.00W
Juba r. Somali Rep 102 G4 0.20S 42.53E
Juba Sudan 105 F2 4.50N 31.35E
Jubail Saudi Arabia 69 H2 26.59N 49.40E
Júcar r. Spain 50 E3 39.10N 0.15W
Juchitán Mexico 92 F3 16.27N 95.05W
Judenburg Austria 57 D3 47.10N 14.40E
Juelsminde Denmark 46 C3 55.42N 10.00E
Juist i. Germany 47 E5 53.43N 7.00E
Juiz de Fora Brazil 97 E5 21.47S 43.23W
Juliana Canal Neth. 47 D2 51.00N 5.48E
Julianehåb Greenland 91 N4 60.45N 46.00W
Jülich Germany 47 E2 50.55N 6.21E
Jullundur India 71 D5 31.18N 75.40E
Jumet Belgium 47 C2 50.27N 4.27E
Jumla Nepal 71 E5 29.17N 82.10E
Jumna r. see Yamuna r. India 71
Junagadh India 71 C4 21.32N 70.32E
Junction City Kans. U.S.A. 87 G4 39.02N 96.51W
Jundiaí Brazil 97 E5 22.59S 47.00W
Juneau U.S.A. 90 E3 58.20N134.20W
Jungfrau mtn. Switz. 52 C2 46.30N 8.00E
Junggar Pendi f. Asia 74 D6 44.20N 86.30E
Jura i. Scotland 26 C2 55.58N 5.55W
Jura Mts. Europe 52 C2 46.55N 6.45E
Jura, Sd. of Scotland 26 C2 56.00N 5.45W
Jurby Head I.o.M. 20 A3 54.22N 4.33W
Juruá r. Brazil 96 C7 2.30S 65.40W
Juticalpa Honduras 93 G2 14.45N 86.12W
Jutland f. Denmark 40 G6 56.00N 9.00E
Jyväskylä Finland 58 F3 62.16N 25.50E

K

Ka r. Nigeria 108 B3 11.35N 4.10E
Kabaena i. Indonesia 79 G2 5.25S122.00E
Kabalo Zaïre 106 C4 6.02S 26.55E
Kabba Nigeria 108 C2 7.50N 6.07E
Kabia i. Indonesia 79 G2 6.07S120.28E
Kabir Kuh mts. Iran 69 G4 33.00N 47.00E
Kabul Afghan. 71 C6 34.30N 69.10E
Kabwe Zambia 106 C3 14.29S 28.25E
Kacha Kuh mts. Iran 69 K3 29.30N 61.20E
Kade Ghana 108 A2 6.08N 0.51W
Kadiyevka Ukraine 59 D3 48.34N 38.40E
Kaduna Nigeria 108 C3 10.28N 7.25E
Kaduna r. Nigeria 108 C2 8.45N 5.45E
Kaesong N. Korea 75 K4 37.59N126.30E
Kafanchan Nigeria 108 C2 9.38N 8.20E
Kafirévs, C. Greece 56 G3 38.11N 24.30E
Kafue r. Zambia 106 C3 15.43S 28.55E
Kaga Bandoro C.A.R. 104 D2 7.00N 19.10E
Kagizman Turkey 68 F6 40.08N 43.07E
Kagoshima Japan 76 A2 31.37N130.32E
Kagoshima wan b. Japan 76 A2 31.00N131.00E
Kagul Moldavia 59 B3 45.58N 28.10E
Kahraman Maraş Turkey 68 E5 37.34N 36.54E
Kaiama Nigeria 108 B2 9.37N 4.03E
Kaifeng China 75 I4 34.47N114.20E
Kai Is. Indonesia 79 I2 5.45S132.55E
Kaimana Indonesia 79 I3 3.39S133.44E
Kainantu P.N.G. 79 L2 6.16S145.50E
Kairouan Tunisia 104 D5 35.40N 10.04E
Kaiserslautern Germany 47 F1 49.27N 7.47E
Kaitum r. Sweden 58 E4 67.30N 21.00E
Kajaani Finland 58 F4 64.14N 27.37E
Kakinada India 71 E3 16.59N 82.20E
Kalahari Desert Botswana 106 C2 23.55S 23.00E
Kalámai Greece 56 F2 37.02N 22.05E
Kalat Pakistan 70 C5 29.01N 66.38E
Kalecik Turkey 68 D6 40.06N 33.22E
Kalemie Zaïre 106 C4 5.57S 29.10E
Kalgoorlie Australia 80 B2 30.49S121.29E
Kalimantan d. Indonesia 78 E3 1.00S113.00E
Kaliningrad Russian Fed. 58 E1 54.40N 20.30E
Kalispell U.S.A. 86 D6 48.12N114.19W
Kalisz Poland 57 F5 51.46N 18.02E
Kalix r. Sweden 58 E4 65.50N 23.10E
Kallavesi l. Finland 58 G3 62.45N 28.00E
Kallsjön l. Sweden 58 C3 63.30N 13.00E
Kalmar Sweden 58 D2 56.39N 16.20E
Kaluga Russian Fed. 59 D4 54.31N 36.16E
Kalundborg Denmark 46 E3 55.42N 11.06E
Kama r. Russian Fed. 60 E3 55.30N 52.00E
Kamaishi Japan 76 E6 39.16N141.53E
Kamchatka Pen. Russian Fed. 61 N3 56.00N160.00E
Kamen mtn. Russian Fed. 61 H4 68.40N 94.20E
Kamenets Podolskiy Ukraine 59 B3 48.40N 26.36E
Kamenskoye Russian Fed. 61 N3 62.31N165.15E
Kamensk-Shakhtinskiy Russian Fed. 59 E3 48.20N 40.16E
Kamensk-Ural'skiy Russian Fed. 60 F3 56.29N 61.49E
Kames Scotland 26 C2 55.54N 5.15W
Kamina Zaïre 106 C4 8.46S 25.00E
Kamloops Canada 90 F3 50.39N120.24W
Kampala Uganda 106 D5 0.19N 32.35E
Kampar r. Indonesia 78 C4 0.20N102.55E
Kampen Neth. 47 D4 52.33N 5.55E
Kampot Cambodia 78 C6 10.37N104.11E
Kamyshin Russian Fed. 59 F4 50.05N 45.24E
Kananga Zaïre 106 C4 5.53S 22.26E
Kanazawa Japan 76 C5 36.35N136.40E
Kanchenjunga mtn. Asia 71 F5 27.44N 88.11E
Kanchipuram India 71 E2 12.50N 79.44E
Kandahar Afghan. 70 B5 31.36N 65.47E
Kandalaksha Russian Fed. 58 H4 67.09N 32.31E
Kandalakskaya G. Russian Fed. 58 H4 66.30N 34.00E
Kandangan Indonesia 78 F3 2.50S115.15E
Kandi Benin 108 B2 11.05N 2.59E
Kandira Turkey 68 C6 41.05N 30.08E
Kandy Sri Lanka 71 E1 7.18N 80.43E
Kangan Iran 69 I2 27.50N 52.07E
Kangar Malaysia 78 C5 6.28N100.10E
Kangaroo I. Australia 80 C2 35.45S137.30E
Kangding China 74 G3 30.05N102.04E
Kangean Is. Indonesia 78 F2 7.00S115.45E
Kangnŭng S. Korea 75 K4 37.30N129.02E
Kanin, C. Russian Fed. 60 D4 68.38N 43.20E
Kanin Pen. Russian Fed. 60 D4 68.00N 45.00E
Kankakee U.S.A. 87 I5 41.08N 87.52W
Kankan Guinea 104 B3 10.22N 9.11W
Kanker India 71 E4 20.17N 81.30E
Kano Nigeria 108 C3 12.00N 8.31E
Kanoya Japan 76 A2 31.22N130.50E
Kanpur India 71 E5 26.27N 80.14E
Kansas d. U.S.A. 86 G4 38.00N 99.00W
Kansas City U.S.A. 87 H4 39.02N 94.33W
Kansk Russian Fed. 61 H3 56.11N 95.20E
Kanto d. Japan 76 D5 37.00N140.00E
Kaolack Senegal 104 A3 14.09N 16.04W
Kapfenberg Austria 57 D3 47.27N 15.18E
Kaposvár Hungary 56 C7 46.22N 17.47E
Kappeln Germany 46 C2 54.40N 9.55E
Kapsukas Lithuania 57 H7 54.31N 23.20E
Kapuas r. Indonesia 78 D3 0.13S109.12E
Kara Russian Fed. 60 F4 69.12N 65.00E
Kara Bogaz Gol B. Turkmenistan 60 E2 41.20N 53.40E
Karabuk Turkey 68 D6 41.12N 32.36E
Karachi Pakistan 70 C4 24.51N 67.02E
Karaganda Kazakhstan 60 G2 49.53N 73.07E
Karak Jordan 68 D3 31.11N 35.42E
Karakelong i. Indonesia 79 H4 4.20N126.50E
Karakoram Pass Asia 71 D6 35.53N 77.51E
Karakoram Range mts. Jammu & Kashmir 71 D6 35.30N 76.30E
Kara Kum des. Turkmenistan 60 E2 38.45N 58.00E
Karaman Turkey 68 D5 37.11N 33.13E
Karamay China 74 D6 45.48N 84.30E
Karamürsel Turkey 68 C6 40.42N 29.37E
Karand Iran 69 G4 34.16N 46.15E
Kara Nur l. Mongolia 74 E6 48.10N 93.30E
Kara Sea Russian Fed. 60 F4 73.00N 65.00E
Karasjok Norway 58 F5 69.27N 25.30E
Kara Usa Nor l. Mongolia 74 E6 48.10N 92.10E
Karbala Iraq 69 G4 32.37N 44.03E
Karcag Hungary 57 G3 47.19N 20.56E
Kardhítsa Greece 56 E3 39.22N 21.59E
Karhula Finland 58 F3 60.31N 26.50E
Kariba, L. Zimbabwe / Zambia 106 C3 16.50S 28.00E
Karikal India 71 E2 10.58N 79.50E
Karima Sudan 105 F3 18.32N 31.48E
Karis Finland 58 E3 60.05N 23.40E
Karisimbi, Mt. Zaïre / Rwanda 106 C4 1.31S 29.25E
Karkheh r. Iran 69 G3 31.45N 47.52E
Karkinit B. Ukraine 59 C3 45.50N 32.45E
Karkkila Finland 58 F3 60.32N 24.10E
Karl-Marx-Stadt Germany 52 F4 50.50N 12.55E
Karlovac Yugo. 56 B6 45.30N 15.34E
Karlovy Vary Czech. 57 C5 50.14N 12.53E
Karlsborg Sweden 58 C2 58.32N 14.32E
Karlshamn Sweden 58 C2 56.10N 14.50E
Karlskoga Sweden 58 C2 59.19N 14.33E
Karlskrona Sweden 58 C2 56.10N 15.35E
Karlsruhe Germany 52 D3 49.00N 8.24E
Karlstad Sweden 58 C2 59.24N 13.32E
Karmöy i. Norway 58 A2 59.15N 5.05E
Karnafuli Resr. Bangla. 71 G4 22.40N 92.05E
Karnataka d. India 71 D3 14.45N 76.00E
Karnin Germany 46 F2 54.19N 12.49E
Kärnten d. Austria 57 C3 46.50N 13.50E
Kárpathos i. Greece 68 B4 35.35N 27.08E
Kars Turkey 68 F6 40.35N 43.05E
Karsakpay Kazakhstan 60 F2 47.47N 66.43E
Karun r. Iran 69 H3 30.25N 48.12E
Karup Denmark 46 C4 56.18N 9.11E
Kasai r. Zaïre 106 B4 3.10S 16.13E
Kasese Uganda 106 D5 0.14N 30.08E
Kashi China 74 B5 39.29N 76.02E
Kassala Sudan 105 F3 15.24N 36.30E
Kassel Germany 52 D4 51.18N 9.30E
Kastamonu Turkey 68 D6 41.22N 33.47E
Kastoría Greece 56 E4 40.32N 21.15E
Kasur Pakistan 71 D5 31.07N 74.30E
Katha Myanma 71 H4 24.11N 96.20E
Katherina, Gebel mtn. Egypt 68 D3 28.30N 33.57E
Kathmandu Nepal 71 F5 27.42N 85.19E
Katowice Poland 57 F5 50.15N 18.59E
Katrineholm Sweden 58 D2 58.59N 16.15E
Katrine, Loch Scotland 26 D3 56.15N 4.30W
Katsina Nigeria 108 C3 13.00N 7.32E
Katsina Ala Nigeria 108 C2 7.10N 9.30E
Katsina Ala r. Nigeria 108 C2 7.50N 8.58E
Kattegat str. Denmark 46 E5 57.00N 11.20E
Katwijk aan Zee Neth. 47 C4 52.13N 4.27E
Kauai i. Hawaii U.S.A. 86 O9 22.05N159.30W
Kaufbeuren Germany 52 E2 47.53N 10.37E
Kauhajoki Finland 58 E3 62.26N 22.10E
Kauhava Finland 58 E3 63.06N 23.05E
Kaunas Lithuania 58 E1 54.52N 23.55E
Kaura Namoda Nigeria 108 C3 12.39N 6.38E
Kavála Greece 56 G4 40.56N 24.24E
Kawagoe Japan 76 D4 35.58N139.30E
Kawaguchi Japan 76 D4 35.55N139.50E
Kawasaki Japan 76 D4 35.30N139.45E
Kayan r. Indonesia 78 F4 2.47N117.46E
Kayes Mali 104 A3 14.26N 11.28W
Kayseri Turkey 68 D5 38.42N 35.28E
Kazachye Russian Fed. 61 L4 70.46N136.15E
Kazakh Hills Kazakhstan 64 J7 49.00N 75.00E
Kazakhstan Asia 60 F2 48.00N 52.30E
Kazan Russian Fed. 59 F5 55.45N 49.10E
Kazanlŭk Bulgaria 56 G5 42.38N 25.26E
Kazarun Iran 69 H3 29.35N 51.39E
Kazbek mtn. Georgia 59 E2 42.42N 44.30E
Kazincbarcika Hungary 57 G4 48.16N 20.37E
Kéa i. Greece 56 G2 37.36N 24.20E
Keady N. Ireland 23 C1 54.15N 6.43W
Keal, Loch na Scotland 26 B3 56.28N 6.04W
Kearney U.S.A. 86 G5 40.42N 99.04W
Kebnekaise mtn. Sweden 58 D4 67.55N 18.30E
Kecskemét Hungary 57 F3 46.54N 19.42E
Kediri Indonesia 78 E2 7.55S112.01E
Keele Peak mtn. Canada 90 E4 63.15N130.20W
Keetmanshoop Namibia 106 B2 26.36S 18.08E
Keewatin d. Canada 91 I4 65.00N 90.00W
Kefallinía i. Greece 56 E3 38.15N 20.33E
Keflavík Iceland 58 I7 64.01N 22.35W
Keighley England 20 D2 53.52N 1.54W
Keitele l. Finland 58 F3 62.59N 26.00E
Keith Scotland 24 F4 57.32N 2.57W
Kelang Malaysia 78 C4 2.57N101.24E
Kelberg Germany 47 E2 50.17N 6.56E
Kelkit r. Turkey 68 E6 40.46N 36.32E
Kelloselkä Finland 58 G4 66.55N 28.50E
Kells Meath Rep. of Ire. 28 E3 53.44N 6.53W
Kelowna Canada 90 G2 49.50N119.29W
Kelsall England 20 C2 53.14N 2.44W
Kelso Scotland 27 F2 55.36N 2.26W
Keluang Malaysia 78 C4 2.01N103.18E
Kelvedon England 15 C2 51.50N 0.43E
Kemaliye Turkey 68 E5 39.16N 38.29E
Kemerovo Russian Fed. 60 H3 55.25N 86.10E
Kemi Finland 58 F4 65.45N 24.12E
Kemi r. Finland 58 F4 65.47N 24.28E
Kemijärvi Finland 58 F4 66.40N 27.21E
Kempston England 15 B3 52.07N 0.30W
Kempten Germany 52 E2 47.44N 10.19E
Kendal England 22 B1 54.19N 2.44W
Kendari Indonesia 79 G3 3.57S122.36E
Kengtung Myanma 74 F2 21.16N 99.39E
Kenilworth England 16 C2 52.22N 1.35W
Kenitra Morocco 104 B5 34.20N 6.34W
Ken, Loch Scotland 27 D2 55.02N 4.04W
Kenmare Rep. of Ire. 28 B1 51.53N 9.36W
Kennet r. England 15 B2 51.28N 0.57W
Kennington England 15 C2 51.10N 0.54E
Keno Hill town Canada 90 E4 63.58N135.22W
Kenora Canada 91 I2 49.47N 94.26W
Kent d. England 15 C2 51.12N 0.40E
Kentford England 15 C3 52.16N 0.30E
Kentucky d. U.S.A. 87 I4 38.00N 85.00W
Kentucky L. U.S.A. 87 I4 36.15N 88.00W
Kenya Africa 106 D5 0.00 38.00E
Kenya, Mt. Kenya 106 D4 0.10S 37.19E
Kerala d. India 71 D2 10.30N 76.30E
Kerch Ukraine 59 D3 45.22N 36.27E
Kerch Str. Ukraine / Russian Fed. 59 D3 45.15N 36.35E
Kerema P.N.G. 79 L2 7.59S145.46E
Kerguelen i. Indian Oc. 115 M2 49.30S 69.30E
Kerguelen Basin f. Indian Oc. 113 M3 35.00S 67.00E
Kerinci, Gunung mtn. Indonesia 78 C3 1.45S101.20E
Kerkrade Neth. 47 E2 50.52N 6.02E
Kermadec Is. Pacific Oc. 82 I5 30.00S178.30W
Kermadec Trench Pacific Oc. 82 I4 33.30S176.00W
Kermān Iran 105 H5 30.18N 57.05E
Kermānshāh Iran 69 G4 34.19N 47.04E
Kerme, G. of Turkey 68 B5 36.52N 27.53E
Kerpen Germany 47 E2 50.52N 6.42E
Kerrera i. Scotland 26 C3 56.24N 5.33W
Kerry d. Rep. of Ire. 28 B2 52.07N 9.35W
Kerry Head Rep. of Ire. 28 B2 52.24N 9.56W
Kerteminde Denmark 46 D3 55.27N 10.39E
Kerulen r. Mongolia 75 I6 48.45N117.00E
Kesh N. Ireland 23 B1 54.31N 7.44W
Kessingland England 15 D3 52.25N 1.41E
Keswick England 22 A1 54.35N 3.09W
Ketapang Kalimantan Indonesia 78 E3 1.50S110.02E
Ketchikan U.S.A. 90 E3 55.25N131.40W
Kete Krachi Ghana 108 A2 7.50N 0.03W
Kettering England 16 D2 52.24N 0.44W
Keweenaw B. U.S.A. 87 I6 47.00N 88.00W
Keyingham England 21 E2 53.42N 0.07W
Key, Lough Rep. of Ire. 28 C4 54.00N 8.15W
Keynsham England 13 E3 51.25N 2.30W
Keyworth England 16 C2 52.52N 1.08W
Khabarovsk Russian Fed. 75 L6 48.32N135.08E
Khabur r. Syria 68 F4 35.07N 40.30E
Khaburah Oman 69 J1 23.58N 57.10E
Khairpur Sind Pakistan 70 C5 27.30N 68.50E
Khalkís Greece 56 F3 38.27N 23.36E
Khanaqin Iraq 69 G4 34.22N 45.22E
Khandwa India 71 D4 21.49N 76.23E
Khangai Mts. Mongolia 64 L7 49.00N 95.00E
Khanka, L. Russian Fed. 75 L6 45.00N132.30E
Khanty-Mansiysk Russian Fed. 60 F3 61.00N 69.00E
Khanu Iran 69 J2 27.55N 57.45E
Kharagpur India 71 F4 22.23N 87.22E
Kharan r. Iran 69 J2 27.37N 58.48E
Kharga Oasis Egypt 68 C2 25.00N 30.40E
Kharkov Ukraine 59 D4 50.00N 36.15E
Kharovsk Russian Fed. 59 E5 59.67N 40.07E
Khartoum Sudan 105 F3 15.33N 32.35E
Khartoum North Sudan 105 F3 15.39N 32.34E
Khaskovo Bulgaria 56 G4 41.57N 25.33E
Khatanga Russian Fed. 61 I4 71.50N102.31E
Khatangskiy G. Russian Fed. 61 J4 75.00N112.10E
Kherson Ukraine 59 C3 46.39N 32.38E
Khimki Russian Fed. 60 D3 55.53N 37.26E
Khíos i. Greece 68 B5 38.23N 26.04E
Khirsan r. Iran 69 H3 31.29N 48.53E
Khmelnitskiy Ukraine 59 B3 49.25N 27.02E
Khöbsögöl Dalai l. Mongolia 74 F7 51.00N100.30E
Khodzhent Tajikistan 74 A5 40.14N 69.40E
Khoi Iran 69 G5 38.32N 45.02E
Khoper r. Russian Fed. 59 E3 49.35N 42.17E
Khor Qatar 69 H2 25.39N 51.32E
Khorramabad Iran 69 H4 33.29N 48.21E
Khorramshahr Iran 69 H3 30.26N 48.09E
Khotin Ukraine 59 B3 48.30N 26.31E
Khouribga Morocco 104 B5 32.54N 6.57W
Khulna Bangla. 71 F4 22.49N 89.34E
Khunsar Iran 69 H4 33.10N 50.19E
Khurmuj Iran 69 H3 28.40N 51.20E
Khwash Iran 69 K3 28.14N 61.15E
Khyber Pass Asia 71 C6 34.06N 71.05E
Kicking Horse Pass Canada 90 G3 51.28N116.23W
Kidal Mali 104 C3 18.27N 1.25E
Kidan des. Saudi Arabia 69 I1 22.20N 54.20E
Kidderminster England 16 B2 52.24N 2.13W
Kidsgrove England 16 B3 53.06N 2.15W
Kidwelly Wales 18 B1 51.44N 4.20W
Kiel Germany 52 E6 54.20N 10.08E
Kiel B. Germany 52 E6 54.30N 10.30E
Kiel Canal Germany 52 D6 53.54N 9.12E
Kielce Poland 57 G5 50.52N 20.37E
Kielder Forest hills England 22 B2 55.15N 2.30W
Kielder Resr. England 22 B2 55.14N 2.30W
Kieta P.N.G. 80 E5 6.13S155.38E
Kiev Ukraine 59 C4 50.28N 30.29E
Kigali Rwanda 106 D4 1.59S 30.05E
Kigoma Tanzania 106 C4 4.52S 29.36E
Kii sanchi mts. Japan 76 C3 34.00N135.20E
Kii suido str. Japan 76 C3 34.00N135.00E
Kikinda Yugo. 56 E6 45.51N 20.30E
Kikori P.N.G. 79 K2 7.25S144.13E
Kikwit Zaïre 106 B4 5.02S 18.51E
Kil Sweden 58 C2 59.30N 13.20E
Kila Kila P.N.G. 79 L2 9.31S147.10E
Kilberry Head Scotland 26 C2 55.47N 5.38W
Kilbirnie Scotland 26 D2 55.45N 4.41W
Kilbrannan Sd. Scotland 26 C2 55.37N 5.25W
Kilchrenan Scotland 26 C3 56.21N 5.11W
Kilcreggan Scotland 26 D2 55.59N 4.50W
Kilcullen Rep. of Ire. 28 E3 53.08N 6.47W
Kildare Rep. of Ire. 28 E3 53.10N 6.55W
Kildare d. Rep. of Ire. 28 E3 53.10N 6.50W
Kilfinan Scotland 26 C2 55.58N 5.18W
Kilimanjaro mtn. Tanzania 106 D4 3.02S 37.20E
Kilis Turkey 68 E5 36.43N 37.07E

Lagos Nigeria **108 B2** 6.27N 3.28E
Lagos Portugal **50 A2** 37.05N 8.40W
La Grande *r.* Canada **91 K3** 53.50N 79.00W
La Guaira Venezuela **95 F3** 10.38N 66.55W
Laguna Dam U.S.A. **86 D3** 32.55N114.25W
Lagunillas Venezuela **94 E3** 10.07N 71.16W
La Habana *see* Havana Cuba **93**
Lahad Datu Malaysia **78 F5** 5.05N118.20E
La Hague, Cap de France **48 C5** 49.44N 1.56W
Lahat Indonesia **78 C3** 3.46S103.32E
Lahijan Iran **69 H5** 37.12N 50.00E
Lahn *r.* Germany **47 F2** 50.18N 7.36E
Lahnstein Germany **47 F2** 50.17N 7.38E
Lahore Pakistan **71 D5** 31.34N 74.22E
Lahti Finland **58 F3** 61.00N 25.40E
Laiagam P.N.G. **79 K2** 5.31S143.39E
Lainio *r.* Sweden **58 E4** 67.26N 22.37E
Lairg Scotland **24 D5** 58.01N 4.25W
La Junta U.S.A. **86 F4** 37.59N103.34W
Lake Charles *town* U.S.A. **87 H3** 30.13N 93.13W
Lake City U.S.A. **87 J3** 30.05N 82.40W
Lake District *f.* England **22 A1** 54.30N 3.10W
Lakeland *town* U.S.A. **87 J2** 28.02N 81.59W
Lakeview U.S.A. **86 B5** 42.13N120.21W
Lakonia, G. of Med. Sea **56 F2** 36.35N 22.42E
Laksefjorden *est.* Norway **58 F5** 70.40N 26.50E
Lakselv Norway **58 F5** 70.03N 25.06E
Lakshadweep Is. Indian Oc. **71 D2** 11.00N 72.00E
La Libertad El Salvador **93 G2** 13.28N 89.20W
La Línea Spain **50 C2** 36.10N 5.21W
La Louvière Belgium **47 C2** 50.29N 4.11E
Lamar U.S.A. **86 F4** 38.04N102.37W
Lambaréné Gabon **106 B4** 0.41S 10.13E
Lambay I. Rep. of Ire. **28 E3** 53.30N 6.01W
Lambourn England **14 A2** 51.31N 1.31W
Lamego Portugal **50 B4** 41.05N 7.49W
Lamía Greece **56 F3** 38.53N 22.25E
Lamlash Scotland **26 C2** 55.32N 5.08W
Lammermuir *f.* Scotland **27 F2** 55.50N 2.25W
Lammermuir Hills Scotland **27 F2** 55.51N 2.40W
Lamotrek *i.* Caroline Is. **79 L5** 7.28N146.23E
Lampedusa *i.* Italy **54 D1** 35.30N 12.35E
Lampeter Wales **18 B2** 52.06N 4.06W
Lampione *i.* Italy **54 D1** 35.33N 12.18E
La Nao, Cabo de *c.* Spain **50 F3** 38.42N 0.15E
Lanark Scotland **27 E2** 55.41N 3.47W
Lancang Jiang *r. see* Mekong *r.* China **74**
Lancashire *d.* England **20 C2** 53.53N 2.30W
Lancaster England **20 C3** 54.03N 2.48W
Lancaster Sd. Canada **91 J5** 74.00N 85.00W
Lancing England **15 B1** 50.50N 0.19W
Land's End *c.* England **12 B2** 50.03N 5.45W
Landshut Germany **52 F3** 48.31N 12.10E
Landskrona Sweden **58 C1** 55.53N 12.50E
Langå Denmark **46 C4** 56.24N 9.55E
Langanes *c.* Iceland **58 K7** 66.30N 14.30W
Langeland *i* Denmark **46 D2** 54.50N 10.50E
Langeoog *i.* Germany **47 F5** 53.46N 7.30E
Langeskov Denmark **46 D3** 55.21N 10.32E
Langholm Scotland **27 E2** 55.09N 3.00W
Langkawi *i.* Malaysia **78 B5** 6.20N 99.30E
Langness *c.* I.o.M. **20 A3** 54.03N 4.37W
Langon France **48 C3** 44.33N 0.14W
Langöy *i.* Norway **58 C5** 68.50N 15.00E
Langport England **13 E3** 51.02N 2.51W
Langres France **48 F4** 47.53N 5.20E
Langsa Indonesia **78 B4** 4.28N 97.59E
Långseleån *r.* Sweden **58 D3** 63.30N 16.53E
Lang Son Vietnam **78 D8** 21.50N106.55E
Langstrothdale Chase *hills* England **20 C3** 54.13N 2.15W
Lannion France **48 B5** 48.44N 3.27W
Lansing U.S.A. **87 J5** 42.44N 84.34W
Lanzarote *i.* Canary Is. **104 A4** 29.00N 13.55W
Lanzhou China **74 G4** 36.01N103.45E
Laoag Phil. **79 G7** 18.14N120.36E
Laois *d.* Rep. of Ire. **28 D2** 53.00N 7.20W
Laokay Vietnam **78 C8** 22.30N104.00E
Laon France **47 B1** 49.34N 3.37E
La Oroya Peru **96 B6** 11.36S 75.54W
Laos Asia **78 C7** 19.00N104.00E
La Palma *i.* Canary Is. **104 A4** 28.50N 18.00W
La Palma Spain **50 B2** 37.23N 6.33W
La Paragua Venezuela **95 G2** 6.53N 63.22W
La Paz Bolivia **96 C6** 16.30S 68.10W
La Paz Mexico **92 B4** 24.10N110.17W
La Peña, Sierra de *mts.* Spain **50 E5** 42.30N 0.50W
La Perouse Str. Russian Fed. **61 L2** 45.50N142.30E
Lapford England **13 D2** 50.52N 3.49W
Lapland *f.* Sweden / Finland **58 E5** 68.10N 24.00E
La Plata Argentina **97 D4** 34.52S 57.55W
La Plata, Rio de *est.* S. America **97 D4** 35.15S 56.45W
Lappajärvi *l.* Finland **58 E3** 63.05N 23.30E
Lappeenranta Finland **58 G3** 61.04N 28.05E
Laptev Sea Russian Fed. **61 K4** 74.30N125.00E
L'Aquila Italy **54 D5** 42.22N 13.25E
Lar Iran **69 I2** 27.37N 54.16E
Laramie U.S.A. **86 E5** 41.20N105.38W
Laramie Mts. U.S.A. **86 E5** 42.00N105.40W
Larbert Scotland **27 E3** 56.02N 3.51W
Larch *r.* Canada **91 L3** 57.40N 69.30W
Laredo U.S.A. **86 G2** 27.32N 99.22W
Largo Ward Scotland **27 F3** 56.15N 2.52W
Largs Scotland **26 D2** 55.48N 4.52W
La Rioja Argentina **97 C5** 29.26S 66.50W
La Rioja *d.* Spain **50 D5** 42.15N 2.30W
Lárisa Greece **56 F3** 39.36N 22.24E
Lark *r.* England **15 C3** 52.26N 0.20E
Larkana Pakistan **70 C5** 27.32N 68.18E
Larkhall Scotland **27 E2** 55.45N 3.59W
Larnaca Cyprus **68 D4** 34.54N 33.39E
Larne N. Ireland **23 D1** 54.51N 5.50W
Larne Lough N. Ireland **23 D1** 54.50N 5.47W
La Roche Belgium **47 D2** 50.11N 5.35E
La Rochelle France **48 C4** 46.10N 1.10W
La Roche-sur-Yon France **48 C4** 46.40N 1.25W
La Roda Spain **50 D3** 39.13N 2.10W
La Romana Dom. Rep. **93 K3** 18.27N 68.57W
La Ronge Canada **90 H3** 55.07N105.18W
Larvik Norway **58 B2** 59.04N 10.02E
La Sagra *mtn.* Spain **50 D2** 37.58N 2.35W
Las Cruces U.S.A. **86 E3** 32.18N106.47W
La Seine, Baie de France **48 C5** 49.40N 0.30W
Lashio Myanma **71 H4** 22.58N 97.48E
Las Palmas Canary Is. **104 A4** 28.08N 15.27W
Las Perlas, Archipelago de Panama **93 I1** 8.45N 79.30W
La Spezia Italy **54 B6** 44.07N 9.49E
Lastovo *i.* Yugo. **56 C5** 42.45N 16.52E
Las Vegas U.S.A. **86 C4** 36.10N115.10W
Latakia Syria **68 D4** 35.31N 35.47E
Latvia Europe **58 C3** 57.00N 25.00E
Lauchhammer Germany **52 F4** 51.30N 13.48E
Lauder Scotland **27 F2** 55.43N 2.45W
Lauderdale *f.* Scotland **27 F2** 55.43N 2.42W
Laugharne Wales **18 B1** 51.45N 4.28W
Lau Group *is.* Fiji **82 I6** 19.00S178.30W
Launceston Australia **80 D1** 41.25S147.07E
Launceston England **12 C2** 50.38N 4.21W
Laurencekirk Scotland **24 F3** 56.50N 2.30W
Lauritsala Finland **58 G3** 61.05N 28.20E
Lausanne Switz. **52 C2** 46.32N 6.39E
Laut *i.* Indonesia **78 F3** 3.45S116.20E
Lauterecken Germany **47 F1** 49.39N 7.36E
Lavagh More *mtn.* Rep. of Ire. **28 C4** 54.45N 8.07W
Laval France **48 C5** 48.04N 0.45W
La Vega Dom. Rep. **93 J3** 19.15N 70.33W
Lavernock Pt. Wales **18 C1** 51.25N 3.10W
Lawra Ghana **108 A3** 10.40N 2.49W
Laxey I.o.M. **20 A3** 54.14N 4.24W
Laysan *i.* Hawaiian Is. **82 I10** 25.46N171.44W
Leadburn Scotland **27 E2** 55.47N 3.14W
Leadhills Scotland **27 E2** 55.25N 3.46W
Leaf *r.* Canada **91 K3** 58.47N 70.06W
Leatherhead England **15 B2** 51.18N 0.20W
Lebanon Asia **68 D4** 34.00N 36.00E
Łebork Poland **57 E7** 54.33N 17.44E
Lebrija Spain **50 B2** 36.55N 6.10W
Le Cateau France **47 B2** 50.07N 3.33E
Lecce Italy **54 G4** 40.21N 18.11E
Lech *r.* Germany **52 E3** 48.45N 10.51E
Le Chesne France **47 C1** 49.31N 4.46E
Lechlade England **13 F3** 51.42N 1.40W
Le Creusot France **48 F4** 46.48N 4.27E
Lectoure France **48 D2** 43.56N 0.38E
Ledbury England **16 B2** 52.03N 2.25W
Ledesma Spain **50 C4** 41.05N 6.00W
Lee *r.* Rep. of Ire. **28 C1** 51.53N 8.25W
Leech L. U.S.A. **87 H6** 47.10N 94.30W
Leeds England **21 D2** 53.48N 1.34W
Leek England **16 B3** 53.07N 2.02W
Leer Germany **47 F5** 53.14N 7.27E
Leeuwarden Neth. **47 D5** 53.12N 5.48E
Leeuwin, C. Australia **80 A2** 34.00S115.00E
Leeward Is. C. America **93 L3** 18.00N 61.00W
Legazpi Phil. **79 G6** 13.10N123.45E
Leghorn Italy **54 C5** 43.33N 10.18E
Legionowo Poland **57 G6** 52.25N 20.56E
Legnica Poland **57 E5** 51.12N 16.10E
Leh Jammu & Kashmir **71 D6** 34.09N 77.35E
Le Havre France **48 D5** 49.30N 0.06E
Leicester England **16 C2** 52.39N 1.09W
Leicestershire *d.* England **16 C2** 52.29N 1.10W
Leiden Neth. **47 C4** 52.10N 4.30E
Leie *r.* Belgium **47 B3** 51.03N 3.44E
Leigh G.M. England **20 C2** 53.30N 2.33W
Leighton Buzzard England **15 B2** 51.55N 0.39W
Leipzig Germany **52 F4** 51.20N 12.20E
Leiston England **15 D3** 52.13N 1.35E
Leith Scotland **27 E2** 55.59N 2.09W
Leith Hill England **15 B2** 51.11N 0.21W
Leitrim *d.* Rep. of Ire. **28 C4** 54.08N 8.00W
Leizhou Pen. China **75 H2** 20.40N109.30E
Lek *r.* Neth. **47 C3** 51.55N 4.29E
Lelystad Neth. **47 D4** 52.32N 5.29E
Le Mans France **48 D5** 48.01N 0.10E
Lemmer Neth. **47 D4** 52.50N 5.43E
Lemmon U.S.A. **86 F6** 45.56N102.00W
Lemvig Denmark **46 B4** 56.33N 8.19E
Lena *r.* Russian Fed. **61 K4** 72.00N127.10E
Lena Mts. Russian Fed. **64 N9** 61.00N115.00E
Lengerich Germany **47 F4** 52.12N 7.52E
Lenina Canal Russian Fed. **59 F2** 43.46N 45.00E
Lenina, Peak *mtn.* Tajikistan **74 B5** 39.20N 72.55E
Leninogorsk Kazakhstan **60 G2** 50.23N 83.32E
Leninsk Kuznetskiy Russian Fed. **60 H3** 54.44N 86.13E
Lenkoran Azerbaijan **69 H5** 38.45N 48.50E
Lenne *r.* Germany **47 F3** 51.24N 7.30E
Lennoxtown Scotland **26 D2** 55.59N 4.12W
Lens France **47 A2** 50.26N 2.50E
Leominster England **16 B2** 52.15N 2.43W
León Mexico **92 D4** 21.10N101.42W
León Nicaragua **93 G2** 12.24N 86.52W
Léon Spain **50 C5** 42.35N 5.34W
Le Puy France **48 E3** 45.03N 3.54E
Le Quesnoy France **47 B2** 50.15N 3.39E
Lerma Spain **50 D5** 42.02N 3.46W
Lerwick Scotland **24 G7** 60.09N 1.09W
Les Cayes Haiti **93 J3** 18.15N 73.46W
Les Ecrins *mtn.* France **48 G3** 44.50N 6.20E
Leshan China **74 G3** 29.34N103.42E
Leskovac Yugo. **56 E5** 43.00N 21.56E
Leslie Scotland **27 E3** 56.13N 3.13W
Lesmahagow Scotland **27 E2** 55.38N 3.54W
Lesotho Africa **106 C2** 29.30S 28.00E
Les Sables d'Olonne France **48 C4** 46.30N 1.47W
Lesser Antilles *is.* C. America **93 K2** 13.00N 65.00W
Lesser Slave L. Canada **90 G3** 55.30N115.00W
Lesser Sunda Is. Indonesia **78 F2** 8.30S118.00E
Lessines Belgium **47 B2** 50.43N 3.50E
Lésvos *i.* Greece **68 B5** 39.10N 26.16E
Leszno Poland **57 E5** 51.51N 16.35E
Letchworth England **15 B2** 51.58N 0.13W
Lethbridge Canada **90 G2** 49.43N112.48W
Lethem Guyana **95 H1** 3.23N 59.48W
Letícia Colombia **96 C7** 4.09S 69.57W
Leti Is. Indonesia **79 H2** 8.20S128.00E
Le Tréport France **48 D6** 50.04N 1.22E
Letterkenny Rep. of Ire. **28 D4** 54.56N 7.45W
Leuser *mtn.* Indonesia **78 B4** 3.50N 97.10E
Leuze Hainaut Belgium **47 B2** 50.36N 3.37E
Leven England **21 E2** 53.54N 0.18W
Leven Scotland **27 F3** 56.12N 3.00W
Leven, Loch Scotland **27 E3** 56.13N 3.23W
Le Verdon France **48 C3** 45.33N 1.04W
Leverkusen Germany **47 E3** 51.02N 6.59E
Levis Canada **91 K2** 46.47N 71.12W
Levkás *i.* Greece **56 E3** 38.44N 20.37E
Lewes England **15 C1** 50.53N 0.02E
Lewis *i.* Scotland **24 B5** 58.10N 6.40W
Lexington U.S.A. **87 J4** 38.02N 84.30W
Leyburn England **20 D3** 54.19N 1.50W
Leyland England **20 C2** 53.41N 2.42W
Leysdown-on-Sea England **15 C2** 51.23N 0.57E
Leyte *i.* Phil. **79 G6** 10.40N124.50E
Lezignan France **48 E2** 43.12N 2.46E
Lhasa China **74 E3** 29.41N 91.10E
Lhokseumawe Indonesia **78 B5** 5.09N 97.09E
Lianyungang China **75 I4** 34.37N119.10E
Liaocheng China **75 I4** 36.29N115.55E
Liaodong B. China **75 J5** 40.20N121.00E
Liaodong Pen. China **75 J5** 40.00N122.50E
Liaoning *d.* China **75 J5** 41.30N123.00E
Liaoyang China **75 J5** 41.16N123.12E
Liaoyuan China **75 J5** 42.53N125.10E
Liard *r.* Canada **90 F4** 61.56N120.35W
Libenge Zaïre **106 B5** 3.39N 18.39E
Liberal U.S.A. **86 F4** 37.03N100.56W
Liberec Czech. **57 D5** 50.48N 15.05E
Liberia Africa **104 B2** 6.30N 9.30W
Liberia Costa Rica **93 G2** 10.39N 85.28W
Libourne France **48 C3** 44.55N 0.14W
Libreville Gabon **106 A5** 0.30N 9.25E
Libya Africa **104 D4** 26.30N 17.00E
Libyan Desert Africa **105 E4** 25.00N 26.10E
Libyan Plateau *f.* Africa **68 B3** 30.45N 26.00E
Licata Italy **54 D2** 37.07N 13.58E
Lichfield England **16 C2** 52.40N 1.50W
Lichinga Mozambique **106 D3** 13.19S 35.13E
Liddesdale *f.* Scotland **27 F2** 55.10N 2.50W
Lidköping Sweden **58 C2** 58.30N 13.10E
Liechtenstein Europe **52 D2** 47.08N 9.35E
Liège Belgium **47 D2** 50.38N 5.35E
Liège *d.* Belgium **47 D2** 50.32N 5.35E
Lieksa Finland **58 G3** 63.13N 30.01E
Lienz Austria **57 C3** 46.50N 12.47E
Liepāja Latvia **58 E2** 56.30N 21.00E
Lier Belgium **47 C3** 51.08N 4.35E
Liévin France **47 A2** 50.27N 2.49E
Liffey *r.* Rep. of Ire. **28 E3** 53.21N 6.14W
Ligurian Sea Med. Sea **54 B5** 43.30N 9.00E
Lihue Hawaii U.S.A. **86 O9** 21.59N159.23W
Likasi Zaïre **106 C3** 10.58S 26.47E
Lille France **47 B2** 50.39N 3.05E
Lille Baelt *str.* Denmark **46 C3** 55.10N 9.50E
Lillehammer Norway **58 B3** 61.06N 10.27E
Lillers France **47 A2** 50.34N 2.29E
Lilleström Norway **58 B2** 59.58N 11.05E
Lilongwe Malaŵi **106 D3** 13.58S 33.49E
Lim *r.* Yugo. **56 D5** 43.45N 19.13E
Lima Peru **96 B6** 12.06S 77.03W
Lima *r.* Portugal **50 A4** 41.40N 8.50W
Limassol Cyprus **68 D4** 34.40N 33.03E
Limavady N. Ireland **23 C2** 55.03N 6.57W
Limbang Malaysia **78 F4** 4.50N115.00E
Limbourg Belgium **47 D2** 50.36N 5.57E
Limbourg *d.* Belgium **47 D3** 51.00N 5.30E
Limburg *d.* Neth. **47 D3** 51.15N 5.45E
Limerick Rep. of Ire. **28 C2** 52.40N 8.37W
Limerick *d.* Rep. of Ire. **28 C2** 52.40N 8.37W
Limfjorden *str.* Denmark **46 C4** 56.55N 9.10E
Límnos *i.* Greece **56 G3** 39.55N 25.14E
Limoges France **48 D3** 45.50N 1.15E
Límon Costa Rica **93 H2** 10.00N 83.01W
Limpopo *r.* Mozambique **106 D2** 25.14S 33.33E
Lina Saudi Arabia **69 F3** 28.48N 43.45E
Linares Mexico **92 E4** 24.54N 99.38W
Linares Spain **50 D3** 38.05N 3.38W
Lincang China **74 F2** 24.00N100.10E
Lincoln England **17 D3** 53.14N 0.32W
Lincoln Nebr. U.S.A. **87 G5** 40.49N 96.41W
Lincoln Edge *hills* England **17 D3** 53.13N 0.31W
Lincolnshire *d.* England **17 D3** 53.14N 0.32W
Lincoln Wolds *hills* England **17 D3** 53.22N 0.08W
Lindesnes *c.* Norway **58 A2** 58.00N 7.05E
Line Is. Pacific Oc. **83 K7** 3.00S155.00W
Lingayen Phil. **79 G7** 16.02N120.14E
Lingen Germany **47 F4** 52.32N 7.19E
Lingfield England **15 B2** 51.11N 0.01W
Lingga *i.* Indonesia **78 C3** 0.20S104.30E
Linköping Sweden **58 C2** 58.25N 15.35E
Linlithgow Scotland **27 E2** 55.58N 3.36W
Linney Head Wales **18 A1** 51.37N 5.05W
Linnhe, Loch Scotland **26 C3** 56.35N 5.25W
Linosa *i.* Italy **54 D1** 35.52N 12.50E
Linslade England **15 B2** 51.55N 0.40W
Lintan China **74 G4** 34.39N103.40E
Linton England **15 C3** 52.06N 0.19E
Linxe France **48 C2** 43.56N 1.10W
Linxia China **74 G4** 35.31N103.08E
Linz Austria **57 D4** 48.19N 14.18E
Lions, G. of France **48 F2** 43.12N 4.15E
Lipari Is. Italy **54 E3** 38.35N 14.45E
Lipetsk Russian Fed. **59 D4** 52.37N 39.36E
Liphook England **15 B2** 51.05N 0.49W
Lippe *r.* Germany **47 E3** 51.38N 6.37E
Lippstadt Germany **52 D4** 51.41N 8.20E
Lisala Zaïre **106 C5** 2.08N 21.37E
Lisboa *see* Lisbon Portugal **50**
Lisbon Portugal **50 A3** 38.44N 9.08W
Lisburn N. Ireland **23 C1** 54.31N 6.03W
Lisburne, C. U.S.A. **90 B4** 69.00N165.50W
Liscannor B. Rep. of Ire. **28 B2** 52.55N 9.25W
Lishui China **75 I3** 28.30N119.59E
Lisianski *i.* Hawaiian Is. **82 I10** 26.04N173.58W
Lisichansk Ukraine **60 D2** 48.53N 38.25E
Liskeard England **12 C2** 50.27N 4.29W
Liski Russian Fed. **59 D4** 51.00N 39.30E
Lismore Australia **80 E3** 28.48S153.17E
Lismore Rep. of Ire. **28 D2** 52.08N 7.59W
Lismore *i.* Scotland **26 C3** 56.31N 5.30W
Lisnaskea N. Ireland **23 B1** 54.15N 7.28W
Liss England **15 B2** 51.03N 0.53W
Listowel Rep. of Ire. **28 B2** 52.27N 9.30W
Lithuania Europe **58 E1** 55.00N 24.00E
Little Andaman *i.* India **71 G2** 10.50N 92.38E
Little Cayman *i.* Cayman Is. **93 H3** 19.40N 80.00W
Little Coco *i.* Myanma **78 A6** 13.50N 93.10E
Little Fen *f.* England **15 C3** 52.18N 0.30E
Littlehampton England **15 B1** 50.48N 0.32W
Little Inagua *i.* Bahamas **93 J4** 21.30N 73.00W
Little Ouse *r.* England **15 C3** 52.34N 0.20E
Littleport England **15 C3** 52.27N 0.18E
Little Rock *town* U.S.A. **87 H3** 34.42N 92.17W
Little St. Bernard Pass France / Italy **54 A6** 45.40N 6.53E
Little Zab *r.* Iraq **69 F4** 35.15N 43.27E
Liuzhou China **75 H2** 24.17N109.15E
Livermore, Mt. U.S.A. **86 F3** 30.39N104.11W
Liverpool Canada **91 L2** 44.03N 64.43W
Liverpool England **20 C2** 53.25N 3.00W
Liverpool B. England **20 B2** 53.30N 3.10W
Livingston Scotland **27 E2** 55.54N 3.31W
Livingstone *see* Maramba Zambia **106**
Lizard England **12 B1** 49.58N 5.12W
Lizard Pt. England **12 B1** 49.57N 5.15W
Ljubljana Yugo. **56 B7** 46.04N 14.28E
Ljungan *r.* Sweden **58 D3** 62.20N 17.19E
Ljungby Sweden **58 C2** 56.49N 13.55E
Ljusdal Sweden **58 D3** 61.49N 16.09E
Ljusnan *r.* Sweden **58 D3** 61.15N 17.08E
Ljusnarsberg Sweden **58 C2** 59.48N 14.57E
Llanbedr Wales **18 B2** 52.40N 4.07W
Llanberis Wales **18 B3** 53.07N 4.07W
Llanbister Wales **18 C2** 52.22N 3.19W
Llandeilo Wales **18 B1** 51.54N 4.00W
Llandovery Wales **18 C1** 51.59N 3.49W
Llandrillo Wales **18 C2** 52.55N 3.25W
Llandrindod Wells Wales **18 C2** 52.15N 3.23W
Llandudno Wales **18 C3** 53.19N 3.49W
Llandyssul Wales **18 B2** 52.03N 4.20W
Llanelli Wales **18 B1** 51.41N 4.11W
Llanerchymedd Wales **18 B3** 53.20N 4.22W
Llanes Spain **50 C5** 43.25N 4.45W
Llanfair-ar-y-bryn Wales **18 C2** 52.04N 3.43W
Llanfair Caereinion Wales **18 C2** 52.39N 3.20W
Llanfairfechan Wales **18 C3** 53.15N 3.58W
Llanfihangel-Ystrad Wales **18 B2** 52.11N 4.11W
Llanfyllin Wales **18 C2** 52.47N 3.17W
Llangadfan Wales **18 C2** 52.41N 3.28W
Llangadog Wales **18 C1** 51.56N 3.53W
Llangefni Wales **18 B3** 53.15N 4.20W
Llangollen Wales **18 C2** 52.58N 3.10W
Llangynog Wales **18 C2** 52.50N 3.24W
Llanidloes Wales **18 C2** 52.28N 3.31W
Llanos *f.* Colombia / Venezuela **96 B8** 5.30N 72.00W
Llanrhystyd Wales **18 B2** 52.19N 4.09W
Llanrwst Wales **18 C3** 53.08N 3.48W
Llantrisant Wales **18 C1** 51.33N 3.23W
Llantwit Major Wales **18 C1** 51.24N 3.29W
Llanuwchllyn Wales **18 C2** 52.52N 3.41W
Llanwrtyd Wells Wales **18 C2** 52.06N 3.39W
Llanybyther Wales **18 B2** 52.04N 4.10W
Lleida Spain **50 F4** 41.37N 0.38E
Llerena Spain **50 B3** 38.14N 6.00W
Lleyn Pen. Wales **18 B2** 52.50N 4.35W
Lloydminster Canada **90 H3** 53.18N110.00W
Loanhead Scotland **27 E2** 55.53N 3.09W
Lobito Angola **106 B3** 12.20S 13.34E
Locarno Switz. **52 D2** 46.10N 8.48E
Lochboisdale *town* Scotland **24 A4** 57.09N 7.19W
Lochbuie Scotland **26 C3** 56.22N 5.52W
Lochdonhead Scotland **26 C3** 56.26N 5.41W
Lochearnhead Scotland **26 D3** 56.23N 4.17W
Lochem Neth. **47 E4** 52.10N 6.25E
Loches France **48 D4** 47.08N 1.00E
Lochgelly Scotland **27 E3** 56.08N 3.19W
Lochgilphead Scotland **26 C3** 56.02N 5.26W
Lochgoilhead Scotland **26 D3** 56.10N 4.54W
Lochinver Scotland **24 C5** 58.09N 5.13W
Lochmaben Scotland **27 E2** 55.08N 3.27W
Lochmaddy *town* Scotland **24 A4** 57.36N 7.10W
Lochnagar *mtn.* Scotland **24 E3** 56.57N 3.15W
Lochranza Scotland **26 C2** 55.42N 5.18W
Lochwinnoch Scotland **26 D2** 55.48N 4.38W
Lochy, L. Scotland **24 D3** 56.58N 4.57W
Lockerbie Scotland **27 E2** 55.07N 3.21W
Loc Ninh Vietnam **78 D6** 11.55N106.35E
Lodeynoye Pole Russian Fed. **59 C6** 60.43N 33.30E
Łódź Poland **57 F5** 51.49N 19.28E
Lofoten *is.* Norway **58 C5** 68.15N 13.50E
Loftus England **22 D1** 54.33N 0.52W

Montargis France **48 E4** 48.00N 2.44E
Montauban France **48 D3** 44.01N 1.20E
Montbéliard France **48 G4** 47.31N 6.48E
Montbrison France **48 F3** 45.37N 4.04E
Mont Cenis Pass France **48 G3** 45.15N 6.55E
Montcornet France **47 C1** 49.41N 4.01E
Mont de Marsan *town* France **48 C2** 43.54N 0.30W
Monte Carlo Monaco **48 G2** 43.44N 7.25E
Montecristo *i.* Italy **54 C5** 42.20N 10.19E
Montego Bay *town* Jamaica **93 I3** 18.27N 77.56W
Montélimar France **48 F3** 44.33N 4.45E
Monterey U.S.A. **86 B4** 36.35N121.55W
Monterey B. U.S.A. **86 B4** 36.45N122.00W
Montería Colombia **94 D2** 8.45N 75.54W
Monterrey Mexico **92 D5** 25.40N100.20W
Monte Santu, C. Italy **54 B4** 40.05N 9.44E
Montes Claros Brazil **96 E6** 16.45S 43.52W
Montevideo Uruguay **97 D4** 34.55S 56.10W
Montfort-sur-Meu France **48 C5** 48.08N 1.57W
Montgomery Ala. U.S.A. **87 I3** 32.22N 86.20W
Montgomery Wales **18 C2** 52.34N 3.09W
Montijo Portugal **50 A3** 38.42N 8.59W
Montijo Dam Spain **50 B3** 38.52N 6.20W
Montluçon France **48 E4** 46.20N 2.36E
Montmédy France **47 D1** 49.31N 5.21E
Montmorillon France **48 D4** 46.26N 0.52E
Montoro Spain **50 C2** 38.02N 4.23W
Montpelier U.S.A. **87 L5** 44.16N 72.34W
Montpellier France **48 E2** 43.36N 3.53E
Montreal Canada **91 K2** 45.30N 73.36W
Montrejeau France **48 D2** 43.05N 0.33E
Montreuil France **48 D6** 50.28N 1.46E
Montrose Scotland **27 F3** 56.43N 2.29W
Montrose U.S.A. **86 E4** 38.29N107.53W
Montserrat *i.* Leeward Is. **93 L3** 16.45N 62.14W
Montserrat, Sierra de *mts.* Spain **50 F4** 41.20N 1.00E
Monywa Myanma **71 G4** 22.07N 95.11E
Monza Italy **54 B6** 45.35N 9.16E
Monzón Spain **50 F4** 41.52N 0.10E
Moorfoot Hills Scotland **27 E2** 55.43N 3.03W
Moorhead U.S.A. **87 G6** 46.51N 96.44W
Moose Jaw Canada **90 H3** 50.23N105.35W
Moosonee Canada **91 J3** 51.18N 80.40W
Mopti Mali **104 B3** 14.29N 4.10W
Mora Sweden **58 C3** 61.00N 14.30E
Moradabad India **71 E5** 28.50N 78.45E
Morar, Loch Scotland **24 C3** 56.56N 4.00W
Morava *r.* Czech. **57 E4** 48.10N 16.59E
Morava *r.* Yugo. **56 E6** 44.43N 21.02E
Moray Firth *est.* Scotland **24 E4** 57.35N 3.50W
Morcenx France **48 C3** 44.02N 0.55W
Morden Canada **91 I2** 49.15N 98.10W
Morecambe England **20 C3** 54.03N 2.52W
Morecambe B. England **20 C3** 54.05N 3.00W
Morelia Mexico **92 D3** 19.40N101.11W
Morella Spain **50 E4** 40.37N 0.06W
Morelos *d.* Mexico **92 E3** 18.40N 99.00W
Morena, Sierra *mts.* Spain **50 C3** 38.10N 5.00W
Moretonhampstead England **13 D2** 50.39N 3.45W
Morez France **48 G4** 46.31N 6.02E
Morgan City U.S.A. **87 H2** 29.41N 91.13W
Morioka Japan **76 E6** 39.43N141.10E
Morlaix France **48 B5** 48.35N 3.50W
Morley England **21 D2** 53.45N 1.36W
Morocco Africa **104 B5** 31.00N 5.00W
Moro G. Phil. **79 G5** 6.30N123.20E
Morogoro Tanzania **106 D4** 6.49S 37.40E
Morón Cuba **93 I4** 22.08N 78.39W
Mörön Mongolia **74 F6** 49.36N100.08E
Morotai *i.* Indonesia **79 H4** 2.10N128.30E
Morpeth England **22 C2** 55.10N 1.40W
Mors *i.* Denmark **46 B4** 56.50N 8.45E
Morsbach Germany **47 F2** 50.52N 7.44E
Mortagne France **48 D5** 48.32N 0.33E
Morte Pt. England **12 C3** 51.12N 4.13W
Mortimer Common England **14 A2** 51.22N 1.05W
Morvern *f.* Scotland **24 C3** 56.37N 5.45W
Morwell Australia **80 D2** 38.14S146.25E
Moscow Russian Fed. **59 D5** 55.45N 37.42E
Mosel *r.* Germany **47 F2** 50.23N 7.37E
Moselle *r.* see Mosel *r.* France/Lux. **47**
Moshi Tanzania **106 D4** 3.20S 37.21E
Mosjöen Norway **58 C4** 65.50N 13.10E
Moskog Norway **58 A3** 61.30N 5.59E
Moskva *r.* Russian Fed. **59 D5** 55.08N 38.50E
Mosquitia Plain Honduras **93 H3** 15.00N 84.00W
Mosquito Coast *f.* Nicaragua **93 H2** 13.00N 84.00W
Mosquitos, G. of Panama **93 H1** 9.00N 81.00W
Moss Norway **58 B2** 59.26N 10.41E
Mosso *l.* Denmark **46 C4** 56.02N 9.47E
Mossoró Brazil **96 F7** 5.10S 37.20W
Most Czech. **57 C5** 50.31N 13.39E
Mostar Yugo. **56 C5** 43.20N 17.50E
Mosul Iraq **68 F5** 36.21N 43.08E
Motagua *r.* Guatemala **93 G3** 15.56N 87.45W
Motala Sweden **58 C2** 58.34N 15.05E
Motherwell Scotland **27 E2** 55.48N 4.00W
Moulins France **48 E4** 46.34N 3.20E
Moulmein Myanma **78 B7** 16.20N 97.50E
Mountain Ash Wales **18 C1** 51.42N 3.22W
Mount Bellew *town* Rep. of Ire. **28 C3** 53.29N 8.30W
Mount Gambier *town* Australia **80 D2** 37.51S140.50E
Mount Hagen *town* P.N.G. **79 K2** 5.54S144.13E
Mount Isa *town* Australia **80 C3** 20.50S139.29E
Mount Magnet *town* Australia **80 A3** 28.06S117.50E
Mountmellick Rep. of Ire. **28 D3** 53.08N 7.21W
Mount Newman *town* Australia **80 A3** 23.20S119.39E
Mount's B. England **12 B2** 50.05N 5.25W
Mourne *r.* N. Ireland **23 B1** 54.50N 7.29W
Mourne Mts. N. Ireland **23 C1** 54.10N 6.02W
Moy N. Ireland **23 C1** 54.27N 6.43W
Moy *r.* Rep. of Ire. **28 B4** 54.10N 9.09W
Mozambique Africa **106 D3** 18.00S 35.00E
Mozambique Channel Indian Oc. **106 E3** 16.00S 42.30E
Mozdok Russian Fed. **59 E2** 43.45N 44.43E
Mozyr Belorussia **59 B4** 52.02N 29.10E
Msta *r.* Russian Fed. **59 C5** 58.28N 31.20E
Mtsensk Russian Fed. **59 D4** 53.18N 36.35E
Mtwara Tanzania **106 E3** 10.17S 40.11E
Muang Chiang Rai Thailand **78 B7** 19.56N 99.51E
Muang Khon Kaen Thailand **78 C7** 16.25N102.50E
Muang Lampang Thailand **78 B7** 18.16N 99.30E
Muang Nakhon Phanom Thailand **78 C7** 17.22N104.45E
Muang Nakhon Sawan Thailand **78 C7** 15.35N100.10E
Muang Nan Thailand **78 C7** 18.45N100.42E
Muang Phitsanulok Thailand **78 C7** 16.50N100.15E
Muang Phrae Thailand **78 C7** 18.07N100.09E
Muar Malaysia **78 C4** 2.01N102.35E
Muara Brunei **78 F5** 5.01N115.01E
Muara Indonesia **78 C3** 0.32S101.20E
Mubi Nigeria **108 D3** 10.16N 13.17E
Muchinga Mts. Zambia **102 F3** 12.00S 31.00E
Much Wenlock England **16 B2** 52.36N 2.34W
Muck *i.* Scotland **24 B3** 56.50N 6.14W
Muckamore N. Ireland **23 C1** 54.42N 6.11W
Mudanjiang China **75 K6** 44.36N129.42E
Mudhnib Saudi Arabia **69 G2** 25.52N 44.15E
Mugía Spain **50 A5** 43.06N 9.14W
Muğla Turkey **68 C5** 37.12N 28.22E
Muharraq Bahrain **69 H2** 26.16N 50.38E
Mühlhausen Germany **52 E4** 51.12N 10.27E
Muine Bheag Rep. of Ire. **28 E2** 52.41N 6.59W
Muirkirk Scotland **27 D2** 55.31N 4.04W
Mukachevo Ukraine **57 H4** 48.26N 22.45E
Mukah Malaysia **78 E4** 2.56N112.02E
Mukalla Yemen **105 G3** 14.34N 49.09E
Mukawa *r.* Japan **76 E8** 42.30N142.20E
Mulgrave I. Australia **79 K1** 10.05S142.00E
Mulhacén *mtn.* Spain **50 D2** 37.04N 3.22W
Mülheim N.-Westfalen Germany **47 F2** 50.58N 7.00E
Mülheim N.-Westfalen Germany **47 E3** 51.25N 6.50E
Mulhouse France **48 G4** 47.45N 7.21E
Mull *i.* Scotland **26 C3** 56.28N 5.56W
Mullaghanattin *mtn.* Rep. of Ire. **28 B1** 51.55N 9.52W
Mullaghareirk Mts. Rep. of Ire. **28 B2** 52.20N 9.10W
Mullaghcarn *mtn.* N. Ireland **23 B1** 54.40N 7.14W
Mullaghmore *mtn.* N. Ireland **23 C1** 54.51N 6.51W
Mullet Pen. Rep. of Ire. **28 A4** 54.10N 10.05W
Mullingar Rep. of Ire. **28 D3** 53.31N 7.21W
Mullion England **12 B2** 50.01N 5.15W
Mull of Galloway *c.* Scotland **26 D1** 54.39N 4.52W
Mull of Kintyre *c.* Scotland **26 C2** 55.17N 5.45W
Mull of Oa *c.* Scotland **26 B2** 55.36N 6.20W
Mull, Sd. of *str.* Scotland **26 C3** 56.32N 5.55W
Multan Pakistan **71 C5** 30.10N 71.36E
Multyfarnham Rep. of Ire. **28 D3** 53.37N 7.24W
Muna *i.* Indonesia **79 G2** 5.00S122.30E
Mundesley England **15 D3** 52.53N 1.24E
Mundo *r.* Spain **50 E3** 38.20N 1.50W
Munich Germany **52 E3** 48.08N 11.35E
Münster Germany **47 F3** 51.58N 7.37E
Muonio Finland **58 E4** 67.52N 23.45E
Muonio *r.* Sweden/Finland **58 E4** 67.13N 23.30E
Murallón *mtn.* Argentina/Chile **97 B3** 49.48S 73.26W
Murashi Russian Fed. **59 F5** 59.20N 48.59E
Murat *r.* Turkey **41 M2** 38.40N 39.30E
Murchison *r.* Australia **80 A3** 27.30S114.10E
Murcia Spain **50 E2** 37.59N 1.08W
Murcia *d.* Spain **50 E3** 38.00N 1.30W
Mureş *r.* Romania **57 G3** 46.16N 20.10E
Muret France **48 D2** 43.28N 1.19E
Murghab *r.* Afghan. **70 B6** 36.50N 63.00E
Müritz, L. Germany **52 F5** 53.25N 12.45E
Murmansk Russian Fed. **58 H5** 68.59N 33.08E
Murom Russian Fed. **59 E5** 55.04N 42.04E
Muroran Japan **76 D8** 42.21N140.59E
Murray *r.* S.A. Australia **80 C2** 35.23S139.20E
Murrumbidgee *r.* Australia **80 D2** 34.38S143.10E
Murud *mtn.* Malaysia **78 F4** 3.45N115.30E
Murwara India **71 E4** 23.49N 80.28E
Muryo *mtn.* Indonesia **78 E2** 6.30S110.55E
Murzuq Libya **104 D4** 25.56N 13.57E
Muş Turkey **68 F5** 38.45N 41.30E
Musala *mtn.* Bulgaria **56 F5** 42.11N 23.35E
Muscat Oman **69 J1** 23.36N 58.37E
Musgrave Ranges *mts.* Australia **80 C3** 26.30S131.10E
Musi *r.* Indonesia **78 C3** 2.20S104.57E
Muskegon U.S.A. **87 I5** 43.13N 86.10W
Muskogee U.S.A. **87 G4** 35.45N 95.21W
Musselburgh Scotland **27 E2** 55.57N 3.04W
Mustang Nepal **71 E5** 29.10N 83.55E
Mustjala Estonia **58 E2** 58.30N 22.10E
Mut Turkey **68 D5** 36.38N 33.27E
Mutare Zimbabwe **106 D3** 18.58S 32.38E
Mutsu wan *b.* Japan **76 E7** 41.10N141.05E
Muwai Hakran Saudi Arabia **68 F1** 22.41N 41.37E
Muzaffarnagar India **71 D5** 29.28N 77.42E
Muzaffarpur India **71 F5** 26.07N 85.23E
Mwanza Tanzania **106 D4** 2.30S 32.54E
Mwene Ditu Zaïre **106 C4** 7.01S 23.27E
Mweru, L. Zambia/Zaïre **106 C4** 9.00S 28.40E
Myanaung Myanma **71 G3** 18.25N 95.10E
Myanma Asia **71 G4** 21.00N 95.00E
Myingyan Myanma **71 G4** 21.25N 95.20E
Myitkyina Myanma **71 H4** 25.24N 97.25E
Mymensingh Bangla. **71 G4** 24.45N 90.23E
Mynydd Bach *mts.* Wales **18 B2** 52.18N 4.03W
Mynydd Eppynt *mts.* Wales **18 C2** 52.06N 3.30W
Mynydd Prescelly *mts.* Wales **18 B1** 51.58N 4.47W
Myrdal Norway **58 A3** 60.44N 7.08E
Mysore India **71 D2** 12.18N 76.37E
My Tho Vietnam **78 D6** 10.21N106.21E
Mytishchi Russian Fed. **59 D5** 55.54N 37.47E

N

Naas Rep. of Ire. **28 E3** 53.13N 6.41W
Naberezhnye Chelny Russian Fed. **59 G5** 55.42N 52.20E
Nacala Mozambique **106 E3** 14.30S 40.37E
Nadiad India **71 D4** 22.42N 72.55E
Naestved Denmark **46 E3** 55.14N 11.47E
Naft Safid Iran **69 H3** 31.38N 49.20E
Naga Phil. **79 G6** 13.36N123.12E
Nagaland *d.* India **71 G5** 26.10N 94.30E
Nagano Japan **76 D5** 36.39N138.10E
Nagaoka Japan **76 D5** 37.30N138.50E
Nagappattinam India **71 E2** 10.45N 79.50E
Nagasaki Japan **76 A3** 32.45N129.52E
Nagercoil India **71 D2** 8.11N 77.30E
Nag' Hammadi Egypt **68 D2** 26.04N 32.13E
Nagles Mts. Rep. of Ire. **28 C2** 52.05N 8.31W
Nagoya Japan **76 C4** 35.08N136.53E
Nagpur India **71 E4** 21.10N 79.12E
Nagykanizsa Hungary **57 E3** 46.27N 17.01E
Naha Japan **75 K3** 26.10N127.40E
Nahavand Iran **69 H4** 34.13N 48.23E
Nahe *r.* Germany **47 F1** 49.58N 7.54E
Nailsworth England **13 E3** 51.41N 2.12W
Nain Canada **91 L3** 56.30N 61.45W
Nairn Scotland **24 E4** 57.35N 3.52W
Nairobi Kenya **106 D4** 1.17S 36.50E
Nakaminato Japan **76 D5** 36.21N140.36E
Nakatsu Japan **76 A3** 33.37N131.11E
Nakhichevan Azerbaijan **69 G5** 39.12N 45.24E
Nakhodka Russian Fed. **75 L5** 42.53N132.54E
Nakhon Pathom Thailand **78 C6** 13.50N100.01E
Nakhon Ratchasima Thailand **78 C7** 15.02N102.12E
Nakhon Si Thammarat Thailand **78 B5** 8.29N 99.55E
Naknek U.S.A. **90 C3** 58.45N157.00W
Nakskov Denmark **46 E2** 54.50N 11.10E
Nakuru Kenya **106 D4** 0.16S 36.04E
Nalchik Russian Fed. **59 E2** 43.31N 43.38E
Nalón *r.* Spain **50 B5** 43.35N 6.06W
Nalut Libya **104 D5** 31.53N 10.59E
Namangan Uzbekistan **74 A5** 40.59N 71.41E
Nam Co *l.* China **74 E3** 30.40N 90.30E
Nam Dinh Vietnam **78 D8** 20.25N106.12E
Namib Desert Namibia **106 B2** 22.50S 14.40E
Namibe Angola **106 B3** 15.10S 12.10E
Namibia Africa **106 B2** 22.00S 17.00E
Namlea Indonesia **79 H3** 3.15S127.07E
Namonuito *i.* Pacific Oc. **82 F8** 8.46N150.02E
Nampo N. Korea **75 J5** 38.40N125.30E
Nampula Mozambique **106 D3** 15.09S 39.14E
Namsos Norway **58 B4** 64.28N 11.30E
Namur Belgium **47 C2** 50.28N 4.52E
Namur *d.* Belgium **47 C2** 50.20N 4.45E
Nanaimo Canada **90 F2** 49.08N123.58W
Nanao Japan **76 C5** 37.03N136.58E
Nanchang China **75 I3** 28.38N115.56E
Nanchong China **74 G3** 30.54N106.06E
Nancy France **48 G5** 48.42N 6.12E
Nanda Devi *mtn.* India **71 E5** 30.21N 79.50E
Nander India **71 D3** 19.11N 77.21E
Nanga Parbat *mtn.* Jammu & Kashmir **71 D6** 35.10N 74.35E
Nanjing China **75 I4** 32.00N118.40E
Nan Ling *mts.* China **75 H2** 25.20N110.30E
Nanning China **75 H2** 22.50N108.19E
Nanping Fujian China **75 I3** 26.40N118.07E
Nanshan Is. S. China Sea **78 F6** 10.30N116.00E
Nantaise *r.* France **48 C4** 47.12N 1.35W
Nantes France **48 C4** 47.14N 1.35W
Nantong China **75 J4** 32.05N120.59E
Nantucket I. U.S.A. **87 M5** 41.16N 70.00W
Nantwich England **20 C2** 53.05N 2.31W
Nanumea *i.* Tuvalu **82 H7** 5.40S176.10E
Nanyang China **75 H4** 33.06N112.31E
Napier New Zealand **80 G2** 39.30S176.54E
Naples Italy **54 E4** 40.50N 14.14E
Naples, G. of Med. Sea **54 E4** 40.42N 14.15E
Narayanganj Bangla. **71 G4** 23.36N 90.28E
Narbada *r.* see Narmada *r.* India **71**
Narberth Wales **18 B1** 51.48N 4.45W
Narbonne France **48 E2** 43.11N 3.00E
Nare Head England **12 C2** 50.12N 4.55W
Nares Str. Canada **91 K5** 78.30N 75.00W
Narmada *r.* India **71 D4** 21.40N 73.00E
Narodnaya *mtn.* Russian Fed. **60 F4** 65.00N 61.00E
Narsimhapur India **71 E4** 22.58N 79.15E
Narva Estonia **58 G2** 59.22N 28.17E
Narva *r.* Estonia **58 F2** 59.30N 28.00E
Narvik Norway **58 D5** 68.26N 17.25E
Naryan Mar Russian Fed. **60 E4** 67.37N 53.02E
Nasarawa Nigeria **108 C2** 8.35N 7.44E
Nash Pt. Wales **18 C1** 51.25N 3.35W
Nashville U.S.A. **87 I4** 36.10N 86.50W
Näsijärvi *l.* Finland **58 E3** 61.30N 23.50E
Nasik India **71 D4** 20.00N 73.52E
Nasratabad Iran **69 J3** 29.54N 59.58E
Nassau Bahamas **94 D6** 25.03N 77.20W
Nassau I. Cook Is. **82 J6** 11.33S165.25W
Nasser, L. Egypt **68 D1** 22.40N 32.00E
Nässjö Sweden **58 C2** 57.39N 14.40E
Natal Brazil **96 F7** 5.46S 35.15W
Natal Indonesia **78 B4** 0.35N 99.07E
Natchez U.S.A. **87 H3** 31.22N 91.24W
Natitingou Benin **108 B3** 10.17N 1.19E
Natron, L. Tanzania **106 D4** 2.18S 36.05E
Naumburg Germany **52 E4** 51.09N 11.48E
Nauru Pacific Oc. **82 G7** 0.32S166.55E
Navalmoral de la Mata Spain **50 C3** 39.54N 5.33W
Navan Rep. of Ire. **28 E3** 53.39N 6.42W
Navarra *d.* Spain **50 E5** 42.40N 1.40W
Nave *i.* Scotland **26 B2** 55.55N 6.20W
Navenby England **17 D3** 53.07N 0.32W
Naver *r.* Scotland **24 D5** 58.29N 4.12W
Navojoa Mexico **92 C5** 27.06N109.26W
Návpaktos Greece **56 E3** 38.24N 21.49E
Návplion Greece **56 F2** 37.33N 22.47E
Navrongo Ghana **108 A2** 10.51N 1.03W
Nawabshah Pakistan **70 C5** 26.15N 68.26E
Náxos *i.* Greece **56 G2** 37.03N 25.30E
Nayarit *d.* Mexico **92 D4** 21.30N104.00W
Nayland England **15 C2** 51.59N 0.52E
Nazareth Israel **68 F4** 32.41N 35.16E
Nazas *r.* Mexico **92 D5** 25.34N103.25W
Nazilli Turkey **68 C5** 37.55N 28.20E
N'Djamena Chad **104 D3** 12.10N 14.59E
Ndola Zambia **106 C3** 13.00S 28.39E
Neagh, Lough N. Ireland **23 C1** 54.36N 6.26W
Neath Wales **18 C1** 51.39N 3.49W
Neath *r.* Wales **18 C1** 51.39N 3.50W
Nebraska *d.* U.S.A. **86 F5** 41.30N100.00W
Nebrodi Mts. Italy **54 E2** 37.53N 14.32E
Neches *r.* U.S.A. **87 H2** 29.55N 93.50W
Neckar *r.* Germany **52 D3** 49.32N 8.26E
Needham Market England **15 D3** 52.09N 1.02E
Needles U.S.A. **86 D3** 34.51N114.36W
Neerpelt Belgium **47 D3** 51.13N 5.28E
Nefyn Wales **18 B2** 52.55N 4.31W
Negev *des.* Israel **68 D3** 30.42N 34.55E
Negoiu *mtn.* Romania **56 G6** 45.36N 24.32E
Negotin Yugo. **56 F6** 44.14N 22.33E
Negra, C. Peru **96 A7** 6.06S 81.09W
Negrais, C. Myanma **71 G3** 16.00N 94.30E
Negro *r.* Argentina **97 C3** 41.00S 62.48W
Negro *r.* Brazil **96 C7** 3.30S 60.00W
Negros *i.* Phil. **79 G5** 10.00N123.00E
Neijiang China **74 G3** 29.32N105.03E
Nei Monggol *d.* see Inner Mongolia *d.* China **75**
Neisse *r.* Poland/Germany **52 G5** 52.05N 14.42E
Neiva Colombia **94 D1** 2.58N 75.15W
Nejd *d.* Saudi Arabia **68 F2** 25.00N 43.00E
Neksö Denmark **58 C1** 55.04N 15.09E
Nellore India **71 E3** 14.29N 80.00E
Nelson Canada **90 G2** 49.29N117.17W
Nelson *r.* Canada **91 I3** 57.00N 93.20W
Nelson England **20 C2** 53.50N 2.14W
Nelson New Zealand **80 G1** 41.16S173.15E
Nelson U.S.A. **86 D4** 35.30N113.16W
Neman *r.* Lithuania **58 E1** 55.23N 21.15E
Nemours France **48 E5** 48.16N 2.41E
Nemuro Japan **76 F8** 43.22N145.36E
Nemuro kaikyo *str.* Japan **76 F8** 44.00N145.50E
Nenagh Rep. of Ire. **28 C2** 52.52N 8.13W
Nenana U.S.A. **90 D4** 64.35N149.20W
Nene *r.* England **15 C3** 52.49N 0.12E
Nenjiang China **75 J6** 49.10N125.15E
Nepal Asia **71 E5** 28.00N 84.00E
Nephin Beg Range *mts.* Rep. of Ire. **28 B4** 54.00N 9.40W
Nera *r.* Italy **54 D5** 42.33N 12.43E
Neretva *r.* Yugo. **56 C5** 43.02N 17.28E
Nero Deep Pacific Oc. **79 L6** 12.40N145.50E
Nes Neth. **47 D5** 53.27N 5.46E
Ness, Loch Scotland **24 D4** 57.16N 4.30W
Nesterov Ukraine **59 A4** 50.04N 24.00E
Neston England **20 B2** 53.17N 3.03W
Netherlands Europe **47 D4** 52.00N 5.30E
Netherlands Antilles S. America **93 K2** 12.30N 69.00W
Nether Stowey England **13 D3** 51.10N 3.10W
Neto *r.* Italy **54 F3** 39.12N 17.08E
Neubrandenburg Germany **52 F5** 53.33N 13.16E
Neuchâtel Switz. **52 C2** 47.00N 6.56E
Neuchâtel, Lac de *l.* Switz. **52 C2** 46.55N 6.55E
Neuenhaus Germany **47 E4** 52.30N 6.58E
Neufchâteau Belgium **47 D1** 49.51N 5.26E
Neufchâtel France **48 D5** 49.44N 1.26E
Neukalen Germany **46 F1** 53.50N 12.47E
Neumünster Germany **52 D6** 54.05N 10.01E
Neuquén Argentina **97 C4** 38.55S 68.55W
Neuse *r.* U.S.A. **87 K4** 35.04N 77.04W
Neusiedler, L. Austria **57 E3** 47.52N 16.45E
Neuss Germany **47 E3** 51.12N 6.42E
Neustadt Germany **46 D2** 54.07N 10.49E
Neustrelitz Germany **52 F5** 53.22N 13.05E
Neuwied Germany **47 F2** 50.26N 7.28E
Nevada *d.* U.S.A. **86 C4** 39.00N117.00W
Nevada de Santa Marta, Sierra *mts.* Colombia **94 E3** 11.00N 73.30W
Nevada, Sierra *mts.* Spain **50 D2** 37.04N 3.20W
Nevada, Sierra *mts.* U.S.A. **86 C4** 37.30N119.00W
Nevel Russian Fed. **59 B5** 56.00N 29.59E
Nevers France **48 E4** 47.00N 3.09E
Nevinnomyssk Russian Fed. **59 E2** 44.38N 41.59E
Nevşehir Turkey **68 D5** 38.38N 34.43E
New Alresford England **14 A2** 51.06N 1.10W
New Amsterdam Guyana **95 H2** 6.14N 57.30W
Newark N.J. U.S.A. **87 L5** 40.44N 74.11W
Newark-on-Trent England **16 D3** 53.06N 0.48W
New Bedford U.S.A. **87 L5** 41.38N 70.55W
New Bern U.S.A. **87 K4** 35.05N 77.04W
Newbiggin-by-the-Sea England **22 C2** 55.11N 1.30W
Newbridge on Wye Wales **18 C2** 52.13N 3.27W
New Britain *i.* P.N.G. **80 D5** 6.00S143.00E
New Brunswick *d.* Canada **91 L2** 47.00N 66.00W
Newburgh Fife Scotland **27 E3** 56.21N 3.15W
Newbury England **14 A2** 51.24N 1.19W
New Caledonia *i.* Pacific Oc. **80 F3** 22.00S165.00E

Newcastle Australia **80 E2** 32.55S151.46E
Newcastle N. Ireland **23 D1** 54.13N 5.54W
Newcastle Wyo. U.S.A. **86 F5** 43.52N104.14W
Newcastle Emlyn Wales **18 B2** 52.02N 4.29W
Newcastleton Scotland **27 F2** 55.21N 2.49W
Newcastle-under-Lyme England **16 B3** 53.02N 2.15W
Newcastle upon Tyne England **22 C1** 54.58N 1.36W
Newcastle West Rep. of Ire. **28 B2** 52.27N 9.04W
New Cumnock Scotland **26 D2** 55.24N 4.11W
New Delhi India **71 D5** 28.37N 77.13E
Newent England **13 E3** 51.56N 2.24W
New Forest *f.* England **14 A1** 50.50N 1.35W
Newfoundland *d.* Canada **91 L3** 55.00N 60.00W
Newfoundland *i.* Canada **91 M2** 48.30N 56.00W
New Galloway Scotland **26 D2** 55.05N 4.09W
New Guinea *i.* Austa. **79 K2** 5.00S140.00E
New Hampshire *d.* U.S.A. **87 L5** 44.00N 71.30W
Newhaven England **15 C1** 50.47N 0.04E
New Haven U.S.A. **87 L5** 41.14N 72.50W
New Holland England **21 E2** 53.42N 0.22W
New Ireland *i.* P.N.G. **80 E5** 2.30S151.30E
New Jersey *d.* U.S.A. **87 L5** 40.00N 74.30W
Newmarket England **15 C3** 52.15N 0.23E
Newmarket Rep. of Ire. **28 B2** 52.13N 9.01W
Newmarket on Fergus Rep. of Ire. **28 C2** 52.46N 8.55W
New Mexico *d.* U.S.A **86 E3** 34.00N106.00W
New Mills England **16 C3** 53.23N 2.00W
Newmilns Scotland **26 D2** 55.37N 4.20W
Newnham England **13 E3** 51.48N 2.27W
New Orleans U.S.A. **87 H2** 30.00N 90.03W
New Plymouth New Zealand **80 G2** 39.04S174.04E
Newport Essex England **15 C2** 51.58N 0.13E
Newport Hants. England **14 A1** 50.43N 1.18W
Newport Shrops. England **16 B2** 52.47N 2.22W
Newport Mayo Rep. of Ire. **28 B3** 53.53N 9.35W
Newport Tipperary Rep. of Ire. **28 C2** 52.42N 8.26W
Newport Dyfed Wales **18 B2** 52.01N 4.51W
Newport Gwent Wales **18 D1** 51.34N 2.59W
Newport News U.S.A. **87 K4** 36.59N 76.26W
Newport-on-Tay Scotland **27 F3** 56.27N 2.56W
Newport Pagnell England **15 B3** 52.05N 0.42W
New Providence *i.* Bahamas **93 I5** 25.03N 77.25W
Newquay England **12 B2** 50.24N 5.06W
New Quay Wales **18 B2** 52.13N 4.22W
New Radnor Wales **18 C2** 52.15N 3.10W
New Romney England **15 C1** 50.59N 0.58E
New Ross Rep. of Ire. **28 E2** 52.23N 6.59W
Newry N. Ireland **23 C1** 54.11N 6.20W
New Scone Scotland **27 E3** 56.25N 3.25W
New Siberian Is. Russian Fed. **61 L4** 76.00N144.00E
New South Wales *d.* Australia **80 D2** 33.45S147.00E
Newton Abbot England **13 D2** 50.32N 3.37W
Newton Aycliffe England **22 C1** 54.36N 1.34W
Newton-le-Willows England **20 C2** 53.28N 2.38W
Newton Mearns Scotland **26 D2** 55.46N 4.18W
Newtonmore Scotland **24 D4** 57.03N 4.10W
Newton Stewart Scotland **26 D1** 54.57N 4.29W
Newtown Wales **18 C2** 52.31N 3.19W
Newtownabbey N. Ireland **23 D1** 54.40N 5.57W
Newtownards N. Ireland **23 D1** 54.35N 5.42W
Newtown Butler N. Ireland **23 B1** 54.11N 7.22W
Newtown Hamilton N. Ireland **23 C1** 54.11N 6.35W
Newtown St. Boswells Scotland **27 F2** 55.35N 2.40W
Newtownstewart N. Ireland **23 B1** 54.43N 7.25W
New York U.S.A. **87 L5** 40.40N 73.50W
New York *d.* U.S.A. **87 K5** 43.00N 75.00W
New Zealand Austa. **80 G1** 41.00S175.00E
Neyland Wales **18 B1** 51.43N 4.58W
Nezhin Ukraine **59 C4** 51.03N 31.54E
Ngaoundéré Cameroon **104 D2** 7.20N 13.35E
Nguigmi Niger **104 D3** 14.00N 13.11E
Nguru Nigeria **108 D3** 12.53N 10.30E
Nha Trang Vietnam **78 D6** 12.15N109.10E
Niagara Falls *town* U.S.A. **87 K5** 43.06N 79.04W
Niamey Niger **104 C3** 13.32N 2.05E
Niangara Zaïre **105 E2** 3.45N 27.54E
Niapa, Gunung *mtn.* Indonesia **78 F4** 1.45N117.30E
Nias *i.* Indonesia **78 B4** 1.05N 97.30E
Nibe Denmark **46 C4** 56.59N 9.39E
Nicaragua C. America **94 B3** 13.00N 85.00W
Nicaragua, L. Nicaragua **94 B3** 11.30N 85.30W
Nicastro Italy **54 F3** 38.58N 16.16E
Nice France **48 G2** 43.42N 7.16E
Nicobar Is. India **71 G2** 8.00N 94.00E
Nicosia Cyprus **68 D4** 35.11N 33.23E
Nicoya, G. of Costa Rica **94 C2** 9.30N 85.00W
Nicoya Pen. Costa Rica **94 B3** 10.30N 85.30W
Nid *r.* Norway **58 B2** 58.26N 8.44E
Nidd *r.* England **21 D3** 54.01N 1.12W
Nidderdale *f.* England **20 D3** 54.07N 1.50W
Nidzica Poland **57 G6** 53.22N 20.26E
Niebüll Germany **46 B2** 54.47N 8.51E
Niederösterreich *d.* Austria **57 D4** 48.20N 15.50E
Niedersachsen *d.* Germany **52 D5** 53.00N 10.00E
Niers *r.* Neth. **47 D3** 51.43N 5.56E
Nieuw Nickerie Surinam **95 H2** 5.57N 56.59W
Nieuwpoort Belgium **47 A3** 51.08N 2.45E
Niğde Turkey **68 D5** 37.58N 34.42E
Niger Africa **104 C3** 17.00N 10.00E
Niger *r.* Nigeria **108 C1** 4.15N 6.05E
Niger Delta Nigeria **108 C1** 4.00N 6.10E
Nigeria Africa **108 C2** 9.00N 9.00E
Nihoa *i.* Hawaiian Is. **82 J10** 23.03N161.55W
Niigata Japan **76 D5** 37.58N139.02E
Niihama Japan **76 B3** 33.57N133.15E
Niiza Japan **76 D4** 35.48N139.34E
Nijmegen Neth. **47 D3** 51.50N 5.52E
Nikel Russian Fed. **58 G5** 69.20N 29.44E
Nikiniki Indonesia **79 G2** 9.49S124.29E
Nikki Benin **108 B2** 9.55N 3.18E
Nikolayev Ukraine **59 C3** 46.57N 32.00E
Nikolayevsk-na-Amur Russian Fed. **61 L3** 53.20N140.44E
Nikopol Ukraine **59 C3** 47.34N 34.25E
Niksar Turkey **68 E6** 40.35N 36.59E
Nikšić Yugo. **56 D5** 42.48N 18.56E
Nikumaroro *i.* Kiribati **82 I7** 4.40S174.32W
Nila *i.* Indonesia **79 H2** 6.45S129.30E
Nile *r.* Egypt **68 C3** 31.30N 30.25E
Nile Delta Egypt **68 C3** 31.00N 31.00E
Nilgiri Hills India **71 D2** 11.30N 77.30E
Nimba, Mt. Guinea **102 B5** 7.35N 8.28W
Nîmes France **48 F2** 43.50N 4.21E
Nineveh *ruins* Iraq **68 F5** 36.24N 43.08E
Ningbo China **75 J3** 29.54N121.33E
Ningwu China **75 H5** 39.00N112.19E
Ningxia-Huizu *d.* China **74 G4** 37.00N106.00E
Ninh Binh Vietnam **78 D8** 20.14N106.00E
Ninove Belgium **47 C2** 50.50N 4.02E
Niobrara *r.* U.S.A. **86 G5** 42.45N 98.10W
Nioro Mali **104 B3** 15.12N 9.35W
Niort France **48 C4** 46.19N 0.27W
Nipigon Canada **91 J2** 49.02N 88.26W
Nipigon, L. Canada **91 J2** 49.50N 88.30W
Niriz Iran **69 I3** 29.12N 54.17E
Niš Yugo. **56 E5** 43.20N 21.54E
Nissum Bredning *b.* Denmark **46 B4** 56.40N 8.20E
Nissum Fjord *b.* Denmark **46 B4** 56.21N 8.11E
Niterói Brazil **97 E5** 22.45S 43.06W
Nith *r.* Scotland **27 E2** 55.00N 3.35W
Nithsdale *f.* Scotland **27 E2** 55.15N 3.48W
Nitra Czech. **57 F4** 48.20N 18.05E
Niue *i.* Cook Is. **82 J6** 19.02S169.52W
Niut, Gunung *mtn.* Indonesia **78 D4** 1.00N110.00E
Nivelles Belgium **47 C2** 50.36N 4.20E
Nizamabad India **71 E3** 18.40N 78.05E
Nizhneudinsk Russian Fed. **61 I3** 54.55N 99.00E
Nizhnevartovsk Russian Fed. **60 G3** 60.57N 76.40E
Nizhniy Novgorod Russian Fed. **59 E5** 56.20N 44.00E
Nizhniy Tagil Russian Fed. **60 F3** 58.00N 60.00E
Nkongsamba Cameroon **104 D2** 4.59N 9.53E
Nobeoka Japan **76 A3** 32.36N131.40E
Nogales Mexico **92 B6** 31.20N111.00W
Nogent-le-Rotrou France **48 D5** 48.19N 0.50E
Noguera Ribagorzana *r.* Spain **50 F4** 41.27N 0.25E
Noirmoutier, Île de *i.* France **48 B4** 47.00N 2.15W
Nokia Finland **58 E3** 61.29N 23.31E
Nome U.S.A. **90 B4** 64.30N165.30W
Nong Khai Thailand **78 C7** 17.50N102.46E
Nonthaburi Thailand **78 C6** 13.48N100.31E
Noord Brabant *d.* Neth. **47 D3** 51.37N 5.00E
Noorvik U.S.A. **90 B4** 66.50N161.14W
Nordborg Denmark **46 C3** 55.04N 9.47E
Norddeich Germany **47 F5** 53.35N 7.10E
Norden Germany **47 F5** 53.34N 7.13E
Nordenham Germany **52 D5** 53.30N 8.29E
Norderney *i.* Germany **47 F5** 53.45N 7.15E
Nordfjord *est.* Norway **58 A3** 61.50N 6.00E
Nordhausen Germany **52 E4** 51.31N 10.48E
Nordhorn Germany **47 F4** 52.27N 7.05E
Nord-Jyllands *d.* Denmark **46 C5** 57.20N 10.00E
Nordrhein-Westfalen *d.* Germany **52 D4** 51.30N 8.00E
Nordstrand *i.* Germany **46 B2** 54.30N 8.52E
Nordvik Russian Fed. **61 J4** 73.40N110.50E
Nore *r.* Rep. of Ire. **28 E2** 52.25N 6.58W
Norfolk *d.* England **15 D3** 52.39N 1.00E
Norfolk U.S.A. **87 K4** 36.54N 76.18W
Norfolk Broads *f.* England **15 D3** 52.43N 1.35E
Norfolk I. Pacific Oc. **80 F3** 28.58S168.03E
Norham England **22 B2** 55.43N 2.10W
Norilsk Russian Fed. **61 H4** 69.21N 88.02E
Normandie, Collines de *hills* France **48 C5** 48.50N 0.40W
Normanton England **21 D2** 53.41N 1.26W
Norman Wells Canada **90 F4** 65.19N126.46W
Nörresundby Denmark **46 C5** 57.05N 9.52E
Norris L. U.S.A. **87 J4** 36.20N 83.55W
Norrköping Sweden **58 D2** 58.35N 16.10E
Norrtälje Sweden **58 D2** 59.46N 18.43E
Northallerton England **21 D3** 54.20N 1.26W
Northam England **12 C3** 51.02N 4.13W
North America 112
Northampton England **16 D2** 52.14N 0.54W
Northamptonshire *d.* England **16 D2** 52.18N 0.55W
North Battleford Canada **90 H3** 52.47N108.19W
North Bay *town* Canada **91 K2** 46.20N 79.28W
North Bend U.S.A. **86 B5** 43.26N124.14W
North Berwick Scotland **27 F3** 56.04N 2.43W
North Beveland *f.* Neth. **47 B3** 51.35N 3.45E
North C. Norway **58 F5** 71.10N 25.45E
North Canadian *r.* U.S.A. **87 G4** 35.30N 95.45W
North Carolina *d.* U.S.A. **87 K4** 35.30N 79.00W
North Channel U.K. **26 C2** 55.15N 5.52W
North China Plain *f.* China **75 I4** 34.30N117.00E
North Dakota *d.* U.S.A. **86 F6** 47.00N100.00W
North Dorset Downs *hills* England **13 E2** 50.46N 2.25W
North Downs *hills* England **15 C2** 51.18N 0.40E
North Dvina *r.* Russian Fed. **60 D4** 64.40N 40.50E
Northeast China Plain *f.* China **75 J6** 46.00N125.00E
North East Polder *f.* Neth. **47 D4** 52.45N 5.45E
Northern Ireland *d.* U.K. **23 C1** 54.40N 6.45W
Northern Territory *d.* Australia **80 C4** 20.00S133.00E
North Esk *r.* Scotland **24 F3** 56.45N 2.25W
North European Plain *f.* Europe **40 K6** 56.00N 27.00E
North Fiji Basin Pacific Oc. **113 R4** 17.00S173.00E
North Foreland *c.* England **15 D2** 51.23N 1.26E
North Frisian Is. Germany **52 C6** 54.30N 8.00E
North Holland *d.* Neth. **47 C4** 52.37N 4.50E
North I. New Zealand **80 G2** 39.00S175.00E
Northiam England **15 C1** 50.59N 0.39E
North Korea Asia **75 K5** 40.00N128.00E
North Kyme England **17 D3** 53.04N 0.17W
Northleach England **13 F3** 51.49N 1.50W
North Platte U.S.A. **86 F5** 41.09N100.45W
North Platte *r.* U.S.A. **86 F5** 41.09N100.55W
North Ronaldsay *i.* Scotland **24 F6** 59.23N 2.26W
North Sea Europe **40 F6** 56.00N 4.00E
North Somercotes England **17 E3** 53.28N 0.08E
North Sporades *is.* Greece **56 F3** 39.00N 24.00E
North Tawton England **13 D2** 50.48N 3.55W
North Tidworth England **13 F3** 51.14N 1.40W
North Truchas Peak *mtn.* U.S.A. **86 E4** 35.58N105.48W
North Tyne *r.* England **22 B1** 54.59N 2.08W
North Uist *i.* Scotland **24 A4** 57.35N 7.20W
Northumberland *d.* England **22 B2** 55.12N 2.00W
North Walsham England **15 D3** 52.49N 1.22E
Northway U.S.A. **90 D4** 62.58N142.00W
North Western Atlantic Basin Atlantic Oc. **112 G6** 33.00N 55.00W
North West Highlands Scotland **24 C4** 57.30N 5.15W
North West River *town* Canada **91 L3** 53.30N 60.10W
Northwest Territories *d.* Canada **91 I4** 66.00N 95.00W
Northwich England **20 C2** 53.16N 2.30W
North York Moors *hills* England **21 E3** 54.21N 0.50W
North Yorkshire *d.* England **21 D3** 54.14N 1.14W
Norton England **21 E3** 54.08N 0.47W
Norton Sound *b.* U.S.A. **90 B4** 63.50N164.00W
Norway Europe **58 B3** 65.00N 13.00E
Norway House *town* Canada **91 I3** 53.59N 97.50W
Norwegian Sea Europe **40 F8** 66.00N 2.00E
Norwich England **15 D3** 52.38N 1.17E
Noss Head Scotland **24 E5** 58.29N 3.02W
Nossob *r.* R.S.A./Botswana **106 C2** 26.54S 20.39E
Noteć *r.* Poland **57 D6** 52.44N 15.26E
Nottingham England **16 C2** 52.57N 1.10W
Nottinghamshire *d.* England **16 D3** 53.10N 1.00W
Nouadhibou Mauritania **104 A4** 20.54N 17.01W
Nouakchott Mauritania **104 A3** 18.09N 15.58W
Nouméa New Caledonia **82 G5** 22.16S166.27E
Nouvelle Calédonie *is.* Pacific Oc. **82 G5** 21.30S165.30E
Novara Italy **54 B6** 45.27N 8.37E
Nova Scotia *d.* Canada **91 L2** 45.00N 64.00W
Novaya Ladoga Russian Fed. **59 C6** 60.09N 32.15E
Novaya Siberia *i.* Russian Fed. **61 M4** 75.20N148.00E
Novaya Zemlya *i.* Russian Fed. **60 E4** 74.00N 56.00E
Novelda Spain **50 E3** 38.24N 0.45W
Nové Zámky Czech. **57 F3** 47.59N 18.11E
Novgorod Russian Fed. **59 C5** 58.30N 31.20E
Novi Pazar Yugo. **56 E5** 43.08N 20.28E
Novi Sad Yugo. **56 D6** 45.16N 19.52E
Novocherkassk Russian Fed. **59 E3** 47.25N 40.05E
Novograd Volynskiy Ukraine **59 B4** 50.34N 27.32E
Novogrudok Belorussia **59 B4** 53.35N 25.50E
Novokazalinsk Kazakhstan **60 F2** 45.48N 62.06E
Novokuybyshevsk Russian Fed. **60 E3** 53.05N 49.59E
Novokuznetsk Russian Fed. **60 H3** 53.45N 87.12E
Novomoskovsk Russian Fed. **59 D4** 54.06N 38.15E
Novomoskovsk Ukraine **59 D3** 48.38N 35.15E
Novorossiysk Russian Fed. **59 D2** 44.44N 37.46E
Novoshakhtinsk Russian Fed. **59 D3** 47.46N 39.55E
Novosibirsk Russian Fed. **60 G3** 55.04N 82.55E
Novouzensk Russian Fed. **59 F4** 50.29N 48.08E
Novy Port Russian Fed. **60 G4** 67.38N 72.33E
Nowa Sól Poland **57 D5** 51.49N 15.41E
Nowgong India **71 G5** 26.20N 92.41E
Nowy Korczyn Poland **57 G5** 50.19N 20.48E
Nowy Sącz Poland **57 G4** 49.39N 20.40E
Noyon France **47 A1** 49.35N 3.00E
Nsukka Nigeria **108 C2** 6.51N 7.29E
Nubian Desert Sudan **105 F4** 21.00N 34.00E
Nueces *r.* U.S.A. **87 G2** 27.55N 97.30W
Nueva Gerona Cuba **94 C5** 21.53N 82.49W
Nuevitas Cuba **94 D5** 21.34N 77.18W
Nuevo Laredo Mexico **92 E5** 27.30N 99.30W
Nuevo León *d.* Mexico **92 E5** 26.00N 99.00W
Nui *i.* Tuvalu **82 H7** 7.12S177.10E
Nu Jiang *r. see* Salween *r.* China **74**
Nukha Azerbaijan **69 G6** 41.12N 47.10E
Nuku'alofa Tonga **82 I5** 21.07S175.12W
Nuku Hiva *i.* Marquesas Is. **83 L7** 8.56S140.00W
Nukunono Pacific Oc. **82 I7** 9.10S171.55W
Nukus Uzbekistan **60 E2** 42.28N 59.07E
Nullarbor Plain *f.* Australia **80 B2** 31.30S128.00E
Numazu Japan **76 D4** 35.08N138.50E
Nuneaton England **16 C2** 52.32N 1.29W
Nunivak I. U.S.A. **90 B3** 60.00N166.30W
Nuqra Saudi Arabia **68 F2** 25.35N 41.28E
Nurmes Finland **58 G3** 63.32N 29.10E
Nürnberg Germany **52 E3** 49.27N 11.05E
Nusaybin Turkey **68 F5** 37.05N 41.11E
Nuuk *see* Godthåb Greenland **91**
Nyala Sudan **105 E3** 12.01N 24.50E
Nyasa, L. Africa **106 D3** 12.00S 34.30E
Nyborg Denmark **46 D3** 55.19N 10.49E
Nybro Sweden **58 C2** 56.44N 15.55E
Nyíregyháza Hungary **57 G3** 47.59N 21.43E
Nyköbing Falstar Denmark **46 E2** 54.47N 11.53E
Nyköbing Thisted Denmark **46 B4** 56.49N 8.50E
Nyköbing Zealand Denmark **46 E3** 55.55N 11.40E
Nyköping Sweden **58 D2** 58.45N 17.03E
Nynäshamn Sweden **58 D2** 58.54N 17.55E
Nyons France **48 F3** 44.22N 5.08E
Nysa Poland **57 E5** 50.29N 17.20E

O

Oadby England **16 C2** 52.37N 1.07W
Oahe Resr. U.S.A. **86 F6** 45.45N100.20W
Oahu *i.* Hawaiian Is. **83 K10** 21.30N158.00W
Oakengates England **16 B2** 52.42N 2.29W
Oakham England **16 D2** 52.40N 0.43W
Oakland U.S.A. **86 B4** 37.50N122.15W
Oaxaca Mexico **92 E3** 17.05N 96.41W
Oaxaca *d.* Mexico **92 E3** 17.30N 97.00W
Ob *r.* Russian Fed. **60 F4** 66.50N 69.00E
Oban Scotland **26 C3** 56.26N 5.28W
Obbia Somali Rep. **105 G2** 5.20N 48.30E
Oberhausen Germany **47 E3** 51.28N 6.51E
Oberösterreich *d.* Austria **57 C4** 48.15N 14.00E
Ob, G. of Russian Fed. **60 G4** 68.30N 74.00E
Obi *i.* Indonesia **79 H3** 1.45S127.30E
Obihiro Japan **76 E8** 42.55N143.00E
Obuasi Ghana **108 A2** 6.15N 1.36W
Ocaña Colombia **94 E2** 8.16N 73.21W
Ocaña Spain **50 D3** 39.57N 3.30W
Occidental, Cordillera Colombia **94 D1** 5.00N 76.15W
Ocean I. *see* Banaba *i.* Kiribati **82**
Ochil Hills Scotland **27 E3** 56.16N 3.25W
Ocotlán Mexico **92 D4** 20.21N102.42W
October Revolution *i.* Russian Fed. **61 I5** 79.30N 96.00E
Oda Ghana **108 A2** 5.55N 0.56W
Odádhahraun *mts.* Iceland **58 J7** 65.00N 17.30W
Odate Japan **76 D7** 40.16N140.34E
Odawara Japan **76 D4** 35.20N139.08E
Odda Norway **58 A3** 60.03N 6.45E
Odder Denmark **46 D3** 55.59N 10.11E
Ödemiş Turkey **59 B1** 38.12N 28.00E
Odense Denmark **46 D3** 55.24N 10.25E
Oder *r.* Poland/Germany **57 D6** 53.30N 14.36E
Odessa Ukraine **59 C3** 46.30N 30.46E
Odessa U.S.A. **86 F3** 31.50N102.23W
Odorhei Romania **56 G7** 46.18N 25.18E
Oeno I. Pacific Oc. **83 M5** 23.55S130.45W
Ofanto *r.* Italy **54 F4** 41.22N 16.12E
Offaly *d.* Rep. of Ire. **28 D3** 53.15N 7.30W
Offenbach Germany **52 D4** 50.06N 8.46E
Offenburg Germany **52 C3** 48.29N 7.57E
Ogaki Japan **76 C4** 35.25N136.36E
Ogbomosho Nigeria **108 B2** 8.05N 4.11E
Ogden U.S.A. **86 D5** 41.14N111.59W
Ogeechee *r.* U.S.A. **87 J3** 32.54N 81.05W
Ognon *r.* France **48 F4** 47.20N 5.37E
Ogoja Nigeria **108 C2** 6.40N 8.45E
Ogooué *r.* Gabon **106 A4** 1.00S 9.05E
Ogosta *r.* Bulgaria **56 F5** 43.44N 23.51E
Ogulin Yugo. **56 B6** 45.17N 15.14E
Ohio U.S.A. **87 J5** 40.00N 83.00W
Ohio *r.* U.S.A. **87 I4** 37.07N 89.10W
Ohře *r.* Czech. **57 D5** 50.32N 14.08E
Ohrid Yugo. **56 E4** 41.06N 20.48E
Ohridsko, L. Albania/Yugo. **56 E4** 41.00N 20.43E
Oil City U.S.A. **87 K5** 41.26N 79.30W
Oise *r.* France **48 E5** 49.00N 2.10E
Oita Japan **76 A3** 33.15N131.40E
Ojocaliente Mexico **92 D4** 22.35N102.18W
Oka *r.* Russian Fed. **59 E5** 56.09N 43.00E
Okaba Indonesia **79 J2** 8.06S139.46E
Okanogan *r.* U.S.A. **86 B6** 47.45N120.05W
Okavango *r.* Botswana **106 C3** 18.30S 22.04E
Okavango Basin *f.* Botswana **106 C3** 19.30S 23.00E
Okayama Japan **76 B4** 34.40N133.54E
Okazaki Japan **76 C4** 34.58N137.10E
Okeechobee, L. U.S.A. **87 J2** 27.00N 80.45W
Okefenokee Swamp *f.* U.S.A. **87 J3** 30.40N 82.40W
Okehampton England **13 C2** 50.44N 4.01W
Okement *r.* England **13 C2** 50.50N 4.04W
Okha India **70 C4** 22.25N 69.00E
Okha Russian Fed. **61 L3** 53.35N142.50E
Okhotsk Russian Fed. **61 L3** 59.20N143.15E
Okhotsk, Sea of Russian Fed. **61 M3** 55.00N150.00E
Oki gunto *is.* Japan **76 B5** 36.10N133.10E
Okinawa *i.* Japan **75 K3** 26.30N128.00E
Okino Torishima *i.* Pacific Oc. **79 J8** 20.24N136.02E
Okitipupa Nigeria **108 B2** 6.31N 4.50E
Oklahoma *d.* U.S.A. **87 G4** 35.00N 97.00W
Oklahoma City U.S.A. **87 G4** 35.28N 97.33W
Oksby Denmark **46 B3** 55.33N 8.11E
Okushiri shima *i.* Japan **76 D7** 42.00N139.50E
Öland *i.* Sweden **58 D2** 56.50N 16.50E
Olbia Italy **54 B4** 40.55N 9.29E
Old Crow Canada **90 E4** 67.34N139.43W
Oldenburg Nschn. Germany **47 G5** 53.08N 8.13E
Oldenburg Sch.-Hol. Germany **52 E6** 54.17N 10.52E
Oldenzaal Neth. **47 E4** 52.19N 6.55E
Old Fletton England **15 B3** 52.34N 0.14W
Oldham England **20 C2** 53.33N 2.08W
Old Head of Kinsale *c.* Rep. of Ire. **28 C1** 51.37N 8.33W
Old Rhine *r.* Neth. **47 C4** 52.14N 4.26E
Olean U.S.A. **87 K5** 42.05N 78.26W
Olekma *r.* Russian Fed. **61 K3** 60.20N120.30E
Olekminsk Russian Fed. **61 K3** 60.25N120.00E
Olenëk Russian Fed. **61 J4** 68.38N112.15E
Olenëk *r.* Russian Fed. **61 K4** 73.00N120.00E
Olenekskiy G. Russian Fed. **61 J4** 74.00N120.00E
Oléron, Île d' *i.* France **48 C3** 45.55N 1.16W
Oleśnica Poland **57 E5** 51.13N 17.23E
Olga Russian Fed. **75 L5** 43.46N135.14E

Ölgod Denmark **46 B3** 55.49N 8.39E
Olhão Portugal **50 B2** 37.01N 7.50W
Olifants r. Namibia **106 B2** 25.28S 19.23E
Olivares Spain **50 D3** 39.45N 2.21W
Olney England **15 B3** 52.09N 0.42W
Ölögey Mongolia **74 E6** 48.54N 90.00E
Olomouc Czech. **57 E4** 49.36N 17.16E
Olonets Russian Fed. **59 C6** 61.00N 32.59E
Oloron France **48 C2** 43.12N 0.35W
Olot Spain **50 G5** 42.11N 2.30E
Olpe Germany **47 F3** 51.02N 7.52E
Olsztyn Poland **57 G6** 53.48N 20.29E
Olteniţa Romania **56 H6** 44.05N 26.31E
Olteţ r. Romania **56 G6** 44.13N 24.28E
Olympus, Mt. Cyprus **68 D4** 34.55N 32.52E
Olympus, Mt. Greece **56 F4** 40.04N 22.20E
Omagh N. Ireland **23 B1** 54.35N 7.20W
Omaha U.S.A. **87 G5** 41.15N 96.00W
Oman Asia **105 H4** 22.30N 57.30E
Oman, G. of Asia **69 J2** 25.00N 58.00E
Ombrone r. Italy **54 C5** 42.40N 11.00E
Omdurman Sudan **105 F3** 15.37N 32.59E
Ommen Neth. **47 E4** 52.32N 6.25E
Omolon r. Russian Fed. **61 N4** 68.50N158.30E
Omono r. Japan **76 D6** 39.44N140.05E
Omsk Russian Fed. **60 G3** 55.00N 73.22E
Omulew r. Poland **57 G6** 53.05N 21.32E
Omuta Japan **76 A3** 33.02N130.26E
Oña Spain **50 D5** 42.44N 3.25W
Onda Spain **50 E3** 39.58N 0.16W
Onega, L. Russian Fed. **60 D3** 62.00N 35.30E
Onitsha Nigeria **108 C2** 6.10N 6.47E
Onstwedde Neth. **47 F5** 53.04N 7.02E
Ontaki san mtn. Japan **76 C4** 35.55N137.29E
Ontario d. Canada **91 J3** 52.00N 86.00W
Ontario, L. N. America **87 K5** 43.40N 78.00W
Oosterhout Neth. **47 C3** 51.38N 4.50E
Oosthuizen Neth. **47 C4** 52.33N 5.00E
Oostmalle Belgium **47 C3** 51.18N 4.45E
Opole Poland **57 E5** 50.40N 17.56E
Oporto Portugal **50 A4** 41.09N 8.37W
Oradea Romania **57 G3** 47.03N 21.55E
Oran Algeria **104 B5** 35.45N 0.38W
Orange Australia **80 D2** 33.19S149.10E
Orange France **48 F3** 44.08N 4.48E
Orange r. R.S.A. **106 B2** 28.43S 16.30E
Orangeburg U.S.A. **87 J3** 33.28N 80.53W
Orange, C. Brazil **96 D8** 4.25N 51.32W
Orchies France **47 B2** 50.28N 3.15E
Orchila i. Venezuela **95 F3** 11.52N 66.10W
Ordu Turkey **68 E6** 41.00N 37.52E
Orduña Spain **50 D5** 43.00N 3.00W
Örebro Sweden **58 C2** 59.17N 15.13E
Oregon d. U.S.A. **86 B5** 44.00N120.00W
Öregrund Sweden **58 D3** 60.20N 18.30E
Orekhovo-Zuyevo Russian Fed. **59 D5** 55.47N 39.00E
Orel Russian Fed. **59 D4** 52.58N 36.04E
Ore Mts. Europe **40 H5** 50.30N 12.50E
Orenburg Russian Fed. **60 E2** 51.50N 55.00E
Orense Spain **50 B5** 42.20N 7.52W
Ore Sund str. Denmark **46 F3** 55.40N 12.40E
Orford England **15 D3** 52.06N 1.31E
Orford Ness c. England **15 D3** 52.05N 1.36E
Orgeyev Moldavia **59 B3** 47.24N 28.50E
Oriental, Cordillera mts. Colombia **94 E1** 5.00N 74.30W
Orihuela Spain **50 E3** 38.05N 0.56W
Orinduik Guyana **95 G1** 4.41N 60.01W
Orinoco r. Venezuela **95 G2** 9.00N 61.30W
Orinoco Delta f. Venezuela **95 G2** 9.00N 61.30W
Orissa d. India **71 E4** 20.15N 84.00E
Oristano Italy **54 B3** 39.53N 8.36E
Oristano, G. of Med. Sea **54 B3** 39.50N 8.30E
Orivesi l. Finland **58 G3** 62.20N 29.30E
Orizaba Mexico **92 E3** 18.51N 97.08W
Orkney Is. d. Scotland **24 E5** 59.00N 3.00W
Orlando U.S.A. **87 J2** 28.33N 81.21W
Orléans France **48 D4** 47.54N 1.54E
Ormiston Scotland **27 F2** 55.55N 2.56W
Ormskirk England **20 C2** 53.35N 2.53W
Orne r. France **48 C5** 49.17N 0.10W
Örnsköldsvik Sweden **58 D3** 63.19N 18.45E
Orona i. Kiribati **82 I7** 4.29S172.10W
Oronsay i. Scotland **26 B3** 56.01N 6.14W
Orosei Italy **54 B4** 40.23N 9.40E
Orosei, G. of Med. Sea **54 B4** 40.15N 9.45E
Orosháza Hungary **57 G3** 46.34N 20.40E
Oroville U.S.A. **86 C6** 48.57N119.27W
Orsha Belorussia **59 C4** 54.30N 30.23E
Orsk Russian Fed. **60 E2** 51.13N 58.35E
Orşova Romania **57 H2** 44.42N 22.22E
Orthez France **48 C2** 43.29N 0.46W
Örum Denmark **46 D4** 56.27N 10.41E
Oruro Bolivia **96 C6** 18.05S 67.00W
Orust i. Sweden **46 E6** 58.08N 11.30E
Oryakhovo Bulgaria **56 F5** 43.42N 23.58E
Osaka Japan **76 C4** 34.40N135.30E
Osa Pen. Costa Rica **94 C2** 8.20N 83.30W
Osh Kirgizia **60 G2** 40.37N 72.49E
Oshawa Canada **91 K2** 43.53N 78.51W
Oshima i. Hokkaido Japan **76 D7** 41.40N139.40E
Oshima i. Tosan Japan **76 D4** 34.40N139.28E
Oshogbo Nigeria **108 B2** 7.50N 4.35E
Osijek Yugo. **56 D6** 45.35N 18.43E
Oskarshamn Sweden **58 D2** 57.16N 16.25E
Oslo Norway **58 B2** 59.56N 10.45E
Oslofjorden est. Norway **58 B2** 59.30N 10.30E
Osmancik Turkey **68 D6** 40.58N 34.50E
Osmaniye Turkey **68 E5** 37.04N 36.15E
Osnabrück Germany **47 G4** 52.17N 8.03E
Osorno Spain **50 C5** 42.24N 4.22W
Oss Neth. **47 D3** 51.46N 5.31E
Ossa mtn. Greece **56 F3** 39.47N 22.41E
Ossa, Mt. Australia **80 D1** 41.52S146.04E
Osse r. Nigeria **108 C2** 5.55N 5.15E
Ossett England **21 D2** 53.40N 1.35W
Ostashkov Russian Fed. **59 C5** 57.09N 33.10E
Ostend Belgium **47 A3** 51.13N 2.55E
Österdal r. Sweden **58 C3** 61.03N 14.30E
Österö i. Faroe Is. **58 L9** 62.10N 7.00W
Östersund Sweden **58 C3** 63.10N 14.40E
Östhammar Sweden **58 D3** 60.15N 18.25E
Ostrava Czech. **57 F4** 49.50N 18.15E
Ostroleka Poland **57 G6** 53.06N 21.34E
Ostrov Russian Fed. **59 B5** 57.22N 28.22E
Ostrowiec-Swietokrzyski Poland **57 G5** 50.57N 21.23E
Ostrów Mazowiecka Poland **57 G6** 52.50N 21.56E
Ostrów Wielkopolski Poland **57 E5** 51.39N 17.49E
Osŭm r. Bulgaria **56 G5** 43.41N 24.51E
Osumi gunto is. Japan **76 A2** 30.30N131.00E
Osumi kaikyo str. Japan **76 A2** 31.30N131.00E
Osuna Spain **50 C2** 37.14N 5.06W
Oswestry England **16 A2** 52.52N 3.03W
Otaru Japan **76 D8** 43.14N140.59E
Oti r. Ghana **108 B2** 8.43N 0.10E
Otley England **20 D2** 53.54N 1.41W
Otra r. Norway **58 A2** 58.10N 8.00E
Otranto Italy **54 G4** 40.09N 18.30E
Otranto, Str. of Med. Sea **56 D4** 40.10N 19.00E
Otta Norway **58 B3** 61.46N 9.33E
Ottawa Canada **91 K2** 45.25N 75.43W
Ottawa r. Canada **91 K2** 45.23N 73.55W
Ottawa Is. Canada **91 J3** 59.50N 80.00W
Otterburn town England **22 B2** 55.14N 2.10W
Otterup Denmark **46 D3** 55.31N 10.25E
Ottery St. Mary England **13 D2** 50.45N 3.16W
Ouachita r. U.S.A. **87 H3** 33.10N 92.10W
Ouachita Mts. U.S.A. **87 H3** 34.40N 94.30W
Ouagadougou Burkina Faso **104 B3** 12.20N 1.40W
Ouargla Algeria **104 C5** 32.00N 5.16E
Oudenarde Belgium **47 B2** 50.50N 3.37E
Oudtshoorn R.S.A. **106 C1** 33.35S 22.12E
Ouessant, Île d' i. France **48 A5** 48.28N 5.05W
Oughter, Lough Rep. of Ire. **28 D4** 54.01N 7.28W
Oujda Morocco **104 B5** 34.41N 1.45W
Oulu Finland **58 F4** 65.02N 25.27E
Oulu r. Finland **58 F4** 65.04N 25.23E
Oulujärvi l. Finland **58 F4** 64.30N 27.00E
Ounas r. Finland **58 F4** 66.33N 25.37E
Oundle England **17 D2** 52.28N 0.28W
Our r. Lux. **47 E1** 49.53N 6.16E
Ourthe r. Belgium **47 D2** 50.38N 5.36E
Ouse r. E. Sussex England **15 C1** 50.46N 0.03E
Ouse r. Humber. England **21 E2** 53.41N 0.42W
Outer Hebrides is. Scotland **24 A4** 57.40N 7.35W
Outwell England **15 C3** 52.36N 0.15E
Overath Germany **47 F2** 50.56N 7.18E
Overflakkee i. Neth. **47 C3** 51.45N 4.08E
Overijssel d. Neth. **47 E4** 52.25N 6.30E
Overton England **14 A2** 51.15N 1.15W
Overton Wales **18 D2** 52.58N 2.56W
Overuman l. Sweden **58 C4** 66.06N 14.40E
Oviedo Spain **50 C5** 43.21N 5.50W
Ovruch Ukraine **59 B4** 51.20N 28.50E
Owase Japan **76 C4** 34.04N136.12E
Owel, Lough Rep. of Ire. **28 D3** 53.34N 7.24W
Owen Falls Dam Uganda **106 D5** 0.30N 33.05E
Owenkillew r. N. Ireland **23 B1** 54.43N 7.22W
Owen Sound town Canada **91 J2** 44.34N 80.56W
Owen Stanley Range mts. P.N.G. **80 D5** 9.30S148.00E
Owerri Nigeria **108 C2** 5.29N 7.02E
Owo Nigeria **108 C2** 7.10N 5.39E
Oxelösund Sweden **58 D2** 58.40N 17.10E
Oxford England **14 A2** 51.45N 1.15W
Oxfordshire d. England **14 A2** 51.46N 1.10W
Oxted England **15 C2** 51.16N 0.01E
Oyapock r. Guiana **95 I1** 4.10N 51.40W
Oykel r. Scotland **24 D4** 57.52N 4.22W
Oymyakon Russian Fed. **61 L3** 63.30N142.44E
Oyo Nigeria **108 B2** 7.50N 3.55E
Ozamiz Phil. **79 G5** 8.09N123.59E
Ozark Plateau U.S.A. **87 H4** 36.00N 93.35W
Ozersk Russian Fed. **57 H7** 54.26N 22.20E

P

Paamiut see Frederikshåb Greenland **91**
Pabna Bangla. **71 F4** 24.00N 89.15E
Pachuca Mexico **92 E4** 20.10N 98.44W
Pacific-Antarctic Basin Pacific Oc. **112 E1** 62.00S 98.00W
Pacific-Antarctic Ridge Pacific Oc. **112 B2** 57.00S145.00W
Pacific Ocean 83
Padang Indonesia **78 C3** 0.55S100.21E
Padangpanjang Indonesia **78 C3** 0.30S100.26E
Padangsidempuan Indonesia **78 B4** 1.20N 99.11E
Padborg Denmark **46 C2** 54.50N 9.22E
Paddock Wood England **15 C2** 51.11N 0.23E
Paderborn Germany **52 D4** 51.43N 8.44E
Padre I. U.S.A. **87 G2** 27.00N 97.20W
Padstow England **12 C2** 50.33N 4.57W
Padua Italy **54 C6** 45.27N 11.52E
Pag i. Yugo. **56 B6** 44.28N 15.00E
Pagadian Phil. **79 G5** 7.50N123.30E
Pagai Selatan i. Indonesia **78 C3** 3.00S100.18E
Pagai Utara i. Indonesia **78 C3** 2.42S100.05E
Pagan i. Mariana Is. **79 L7** 18.08N145.46E
Pahala Hawaii U.S.A. **86 O8** 19.12N155.28W
Paible Scotland **24 A4** 57.35N 7.28W
Päijänne l. Finland **58 F3** 61.30N 25.30E
Paimboeuf France **48 B4** 47.14N 2.01W
Painswick England **13 E3** 51.47N 2.11W
Paisley Scotland **26 D2** 55.50N 4.26W
Pais Vasco d. Spain **50 D5** 43.00N 2.30W
Pakanbaru Indonesia **78 C4** 0.33N101.20E
Pakaraima Mts. Guyana **95 G2** 5,30N 60.00W
Pakistan Asia **70 C5** 30.00N 70.00E
Pak Lay Laos **78 C7** 18.10N101.24E
Pakse Laos **78 D7** 15.05N105.50E
Pakwach Uganda **106 D5** 2.17N 31.28E
Palana Russian Fed. **61 N3** 59.05N159.59E
Palangkaraya Indonesia **78 E3** 2.16S113.56E
Palawan i. Phil. **78 F5** 9.30N118.30E
Palembang Indonesia **78 C3** 2.59S104.50E
Palencia Spain **50 C5** 42.01N 4.34W
Palenque Mexico **92 F3** 17.32N 91.59W
Palermo Italy **54 D3** 38.09N 13.22E
Palit, C. Albania **56 D4** 41.24N 19.23E
Palk Str. India / Sri Lanka **71 E2** 10.00N 79.40E
Palma Spain **51 G3** 39.36N 2.39E
Palma, B. of Spain **51 G3** 39.30N 2.40E
Palma del Río Spain **50 C2** 37.43N 5.17W
Palmas, C. Liberia **104 B2** 4.30N 7.55W
Palmas, G. of Med. Sea **54 B3** 39.00N 8.30E
Palmerston Atoll Cook Is. **82 J6** 18.04S163.10W
Palmerston North New Zealand **80 G1** 40.21S175.37E
Palmi Italy **54 E3** 38.22N 15.50E
Palmira Colombia **94 D1** 3.33N 76.17W
Palm Springs town U.S.A. **86 C3** 33.49N116.34W
Palmyra Syria **68 E4** 34.36N 38.15E
Palmyra I. Pacific Oc. **82 J8** 5.52N162.05W
Palmyras Pt. India **71 F4** 20.40N 87.00E
Paloh Indonesia **78 D4** 1.46N109.17E
Palopo Indonesia **79 G3** 3.01S120.12E
Palos, C. Spain **40 E2** 37.38N 0.41W
Pamekasan Indonesia **78 E2** 7.11S113.50E
Pamiers France **48 D2** 43.07N 1.36E
Pamirs mts. Tajikistan **74 B4** 37.50N 73.30E
Pampa U.S.A. **86 F4** 35.32N100.58W
Pampas f. Argentina **97 C4** 35.00S 63.00W
Pamplona Colombia **94 E2** 7.24N 72.38W
Pamplona Spain **50 E5** 42.49N 1.39W
Panama C. America **94 C2** 9.00N 80.00W
Panama Canal Panama **94 D2** 9.21N 79.54W
Panama City Panama **94 D2** 8.57N 79.30W
Panama City U.S.A. **87 I3** 30.10N 85.41W
Panama, G. of Panama **94 D2** 8.30N 79.00W
Panay i. Phil. **79 G6** 11.10N122.30E
Panevežys Lithuania **58 F1** 55.44N 24.24E
Pangkalpinang Indonesia **78 D3** 2.05S106.09E
Pangnirtung Canada **91 L4** 66.05N 65.45W
Pantano del Esla l. Spain **50 C4** 41.40N 5.50W
Pantelleria i. Italy **54 D2** 36.48N 12.00E
Paola Italy **54 F3** 39.21N 16.03E
Pápa Hungary **57 E3** 47.19N 17.28E
Papeete Tahiti **83 L6** 17.32S149.34W
Papenburg Germany **47 F5** 53.05N 7.25E
Paphos Cyprus **68 D4** 34.45N 32.25E
Paps of Jura mts. Scotland **26 C2** 55.55N 6.00W
Papua, G. of P.N.G. **79 L2** 8.50S145.00E
Papua New Guinea Austa. **80 D5** 6.00S143.00E
Papun Myanma **78 B7** 18.05N 97.26E
Paracel Is. S. China Sea **78 E7** 16.20N112.00E
Paraguaná Pen. Venezuela **94 E3** 12.00N 70.00W
Paraguay r. Argentina **97 D5** 27.30S 58.50W
Paraguay S. America **97 D5** 23.00S 58.00W
Parakou Benin **108 B2** 9.23N 2.40E
Paramaribo Surinam **95 H2** 5.52N 55.14W
Paraná Argentina **97 C4** 31.45S 60.30W
Paraná r. Argentina **97 D4** 34.00S 58.30W
Parczew Poland **57 H5** 51.39N 22.54E
Pardubice Czech. **57 D5** 50.03N 15.45E
Parepare Indonesia **80 A5** 4.03S119.40E
Paria, G. of Venezuela **95 G3** 10.30N 62.00W
Pariaman Indonesia **78 C3** 0.36S100.09E
Paria Pen. Venezuela **95 G3** 10.45N 62.30W
Parigi Indonesia **79 G3** 0.49S120.10E
Parika Guyana **95 H2** 6.50N 58.24W
Paris France **48 E5** 48.52N 2.20E
Parkano Finland **58 E3** 62.03N 23.00E
Parker Dam U.S.A. **86 D3** 34.25N114.05W
Parma Italy **54 C6** 44.48N 10.18E
Parnaíba r. Brazil **96 E7** 3.00S 42.00W
Parnassós mtn. Greece **56 F3** 38.33N 22.35E
Pärnu Estonia **58 F2** 58.28N 24.30E
Pärnu r. Estonia **58 F2** 58.23N 24.32E
Páros i. Greece **56 G2** 37.04N 25.11E
Parral Mexico **92 C5** 26.58N105.40W
Parrett r. England **13 E3** 51.10N 3.00W
Parry, C. Greenland **91 K5** 76.50N 71.00W
Parry Is. Canada **91 H5** 76.00N102.00W
Parseta r. Poland **57 D7** 54.12N 15.33E
Partabpur India **71 E4** 23.28N 83.15E
Parthenay France **48 C4** 46.39N 0.14W
Partry Mts. Rep. of Ire. **28 B3** 53.40N 9.30W
Pasadena U.S.A. **86 C3** 34.10N118.09W
Pasay Phil. **79 G6** 14.30N120.54E
Paso de Bermejo f. Argentina **97 C4** 32.50S 70.00W
Paso Socompa f. Chile **97 C5** 24.27S 68.18W
Passau Germany **52 F3** 48.35N 13.28E
Passero, C. Italy **54 E2** 36.40N 15.08E
Pasto Colombia **94 D1** 1.12N 77.17W
Pasuruan Indonesia **78 E2** 7.38S112.44E
Pasvik r. Norway **58 G5** 69.45N 30.00E
Patagonia f. Argentina **97 C3** 45.00S 68.00W
Pateley Bridge town England **20 D3** 54.05N 1.45W
Paterson U.S.A. **87 L5** 40.55N 74.10W
Pathfinder Resr. U.S.A. **86 E5** 42.25N106.55W
Patía r. Colombia **94 D1** 1.54N 78.30W
Patiala India **71 D5** 30.21N 76.27E
Patkai Hills Myanma **71 G5** 26.30N 95.40E
Patna India **71 F4** 25.37N 85.12E
Patna Scotland **26 D2** 55.22N 4.30W
Patos, L. Brazil **97 D4** 31.00S 51.10W
Pátras Greece **56 E3** 38.15N 21.45E
Patras, G. of Med. Sea **56 E3** 38.15N 21.35E
Patrickswell Rep. of Ire. **28 C2** 52.34N 8.42W
Patrington England **21 E2** 53.41N 0.02W
Patuca r. Honduras **94 C4** 15.50N 84.25W
Pau France **48 C2** 43.18N 0.22W
Pauillac France **48 C3** 45.12N 0.44W
Pavia Italy **54 B6** 45.10N 9.10E
Pavlodar Kazakhstan **60 G3** 52.21N 76.59E
Pavlograd Ukraine **59 D3** 48.34N 35.50E
Pavlovo Russian Fed. **59 E5** 55.58N 43.05E
Pavlovskaya Russian Fed. **59 D3** 46.18N 39.48E
Peace r. Canada **90 G3** 59.00N111.26W
Peace River town Canada **90 G3** 56.15N117.18W
Peale, Mt. U.S.A. **86 E4** 38.26N109.14W
Pearl r. U.S.A. **87 I3** 30.15N 89.25W
Peć Yugo. **56 E5** 42.40N 20.17E
Pechenga Russian Fed. **58 G5** 69.28N 31.04E
Pechora r. Russian Fed. **60 E4** 68.10N 54.00E
Pechora G. Russian Fed. **60 E4** 69.00N 56.00E
Pecos U.S.A. **86 F3** 31.25N103.30W
Pecos r. U.S.A. **86 F2** 29.45N101.25W
Pécs Hungary **57 F3** 46.05N 18.14E
Peebles Scotland **27 E2** 55.39N 3.12W
Peel r. Canada **90 E4** 68.13N135.00W
Peel I.o.M. **20 A3** 54.14N 4.42W
Peel f. Neth. **47 D3** 51.30N 5.50E
Peel Fell mtn. England / Scotland **27 F2** 55.17N 2.35W
Peene r. Germany **52 F5** 53.53N 13.49E
Pegu Myanma **71 H3** 17.18N 96.31E
Pegu Yoma mts. Myanma **71 G3** 18.40N 96.00E
Pegwell B. England **15 D2** 51.18N 1.25E
Peipus, L. Europe **58 F2** 58.30N 27.30E
Pekalongan Indonesia **78 D2** 6.54S109.37E
Pelat, Mont mtn. France **48 G3** 44.17N 6.41E
Peleng i. Indonesia **79 G3** 1.30S123.10E
Pelly r. Canada **90 E4** 62.50N137.35W
Pelotas Brazil **97 D4** 31.45S 52.20W
Pematangsiantar Indonesia **78 B4** 2.59N 99.01E
Pemba Mozambique **106 E3** 13.02S 40.30E
Pemba I. Tanzania **106 D4** 5.10S 39.45E
Pembridge England **16 B2** 52.13N 2.54W
Pembroke Wales **18 B1** 51.41N 4.57W
Peñaranda de Bracamonte Spain **50 C4** 40.54N 5.13W
Penarth Wales **18 C1** 51.26N 3.11W
Peñas, Cabo de c. Spain **50 C5** 43.42N 5.52W
Pendine Wales **18 B1** 51.44N 4.33W
Pendle Hill England **20 C2** 53.52N 2.18W
Penganga r. India **71 E3** 18.52N 79.56E
Penicuik Scotland **27 E2** 55.49N 3.13W
Penistone England **20 D2** 53.31N 1.38W
Penmaenmawr Wales **18 C3** 53.16N 3.54W
Pennsylvania d. U.S.A. **87 K5** 41.00N 78.00W
Penny Highland mtn. Canada **91 L4** 67.10N 66.50W
Penonomé Panama **94 C2** 8.30N 80.20W
Penrhyn Atoll Cook Is. **83 K7** 9.00S158.00W
Penrhyndeudraeth Wales **18 B2** 52.56N 4.04W
Penrith England **22 B1** 54.40N 2.45W
Penryn England **12 B2** 50.10N 5.07W
Pensacola U.S.A. **87 I3** 30.30N 87.12W
Penticton Canada **90 G2** 49.29N119.38W
Pentire Pt. England **12 C2** 50.35N 4.55W
Pentland Firth str. Scotland **24 E5** 58.40N 3.00W
Pentland Hills Scotland **27 E2** 55.50N 3.20W
Pen-y-ghent mtn. England **20 C3** 54.10N 2.14W
Pen-y-groes Wales **18 B3** 53.03N 4.18W
Penza Russian Fed. **59 E4** 53.11N 45.00E
Penzance England **12 B2** 50.07N 5.32W
Penzhina, G. of Russian Fed. **61 N3** 61.00N163.00E
Peoria U.S.A. **87 I5** 40.43N 89.38W
Perabumulih Indonesia **78 C3** 3.29S104.14E
Pereira Colombia **94 D1** 4.47N 75.46W
Peribonca r. Canada **91 K2** 48.50N 72.00W
Périgueux France **48 D3** 45.12N 0.44E
Perija, Sierra de mts. Venezuela **94 E2** 9.00N 73.00W
Perim i. Yemen **105 G3** 12.40N 43.24E
Perito Moreno Argentina **97 B3** 46.35S 71.00W
Perm Russian Fed. **60 E3** 58.01N 56.10E
Péronne France **47 A1** 49.56N 2.57E
Perpignan France **48 E2** 42.42N 2.54E
Perranporth England **12 B2** 50.21N 5.09W
Persepolis ruins Iran **69 I3** 29.55N 53.00E
Pershore England **16 B2** 52.07N 2.04W
Perth Australia **80 A2** 31.58S115.49E
Perth Scotland **27 E3** 56.24N 3.28W
Peru S. America **96 B7** 10.00S 75.00W
Peru Basin Pacific Oc. **112 E4** 19.00S 96.00W
Peru-Chile Trench Pacific Oc. **97 B5** 23.00S 71.30W
Perugia Italy **54 D5** 43.06N 12.24E
Péruwelz Belgium **47 B2** 50.32N 3.36E
Pervomaysk Ukraine **59 C3** 48.03N 30.50E
Pervouralsk Russian Fed. **60 E3** 56.59N 59.58E
Pesaro Italy **54 D5** 43.54N 12.54E
Pescara Italy **54 E5** 42.27N 14.13E
Pescara r. Italy **54 E5** 42.28N 14.13E
Peshawar Pakistan **71 C6** 34.01N 71.40E
Petare Venezuela **95 F3** 10.31N 66.50W
Petatlán Mexico **92 D3** 17.31N101.16W
Peterborough England **15 B3** 52.35N 0.14W
Peterhead Scotland **24 G4** 57.30N 1.46W
Peterlee England **22 C1** 54.45N 1.18W
Petersfield England **15 B2** 51.00N 0.56W
Petra ruins Jordan **68 D3** 30.19N 35.26E
Petrich Bulgaria **56 F4** 41.25N 23.13E
Petropavlovsk Kazakhstan **60 F3** 54.53N 69.13E
Petropavlovsk Kamchatskiy Russian Fed. **61 N3** 53.03N158.43E
Petrópolis Brazil **97 E5** 22.30S 43.02W
Petrovsk Zabaykal'skiy Russian Fed. **61 J2** 51.20N108.55E
Petrozavodsk Russian Fed. **60 C3** 61.46N 34.19E

Rwanda Africa **106 D4** 2.00S 30.00E
Ryan, Loch Scotland **26 C1** 54.56N 5.02W
Ryazan Russian Fed. **59 D4** 54.37N 39.43E
Ryazhsk Russian Fed. **59 E4** 53.40N 40.07E
Rybachi Pen. Russian Fed. **58 H5** 69.45N 32.30E
Rybinsk Resr. Russian Fed. **59 D5** 58.30N 38.25E
Rybnik Poland **57 F5** 50.06N 18.32E
Ryde England **14 A1** 50.44N 1.09W
Ryder's Hill England **13 D2** 50.31N 3.53W
Rye England **15 C1** 50.57N 0.46E
Rye *r.* England **21 E3** 54.10N 0.44W
Rye B. England **15 C1** 50.53N 0.48E
Ryki Poland **57 G5** 51.39N 21.56E
Ryton England **22 C1** 54.59N 1.47W
Ryukyu Is. Japan **75 J2** 26.00N 126.00E
Ryukyu Is. Trench Pacific Oc. **82 C10** 25.00N 129.00E
Rzeszów Poland **57 G5** 50.04N 22.00E
Rzhev Russian Fed. **59 C5** 56.15N 34.18E

S

Saale *r.* Germany **52 E4** 51.58N 11.53E
Saar *r.* Germany **47 E1** 49.43N 6.34E
Saarbrücken Germany **52 C3** 49.15N 6.58E
Saarburg Germany **47 E1** 49.36N 6.33E
Saaremaa *i.* Estonia **58 E2** 58.30N 22.30E
Saarijärvi Finland **58 F3** 62.44N 25.15E
Saarland *d.* Germany **52 C3** 49.20N 7.00E
Saba *i.* Leeward Is. **93 L3** 17.42N 63.26W
Šabac Yugo. **56 D6** 44.45N 19.41E
Sabadell Spain **50 G4** 41.33N 2.07E
Sabah *d.* Malaysia **78 F5** 5.00N 117.00E
Sabana, Archipiélago de Cuba **93 H4** 23.30N 80.00W
Sabanalarga Colombia **94 E3** 10.38N 75.00W
Sabinas Mexico **92 D5** 27.51N 101.10W
Sabinas Hidalgo Mexico **92 D5** 26.33N 100.10W
Sabine *r.* U.S.A. **87 H2** 29.40N 93.50W
Sable, C. Canada **91 L2** 43.30N 65.50W
Sable, C. U.S.A. **84 L4** 25.00N 81.20W
Sable I. Canada **91 M2** 44.00N 60.00W
Sacedón Spain **50 D4** 40.29N 2.44W
Sachsen *d.* Germany **52 F4** 50.45N 13.00E
Sachsen-Anhalt *d.* Germany **52 E4** 52.00N 11.30E
Sacramento U.S.A. **86 B4** 38.32N 121.30W
Sacramento *r.* U.S.A. **86 B4** 38.05N 122.00W
Sacramento Mts. U.S.A. **86 E3** 33.10N 105.50W
Sádaba Spain **50 E5** 42.19N 1.10W
Saddleworth Moor *hills* England **20 D2** 53.32N 1.55W
Sadiya India **71 G5** 27.49N 95.38E
Sado *i.* Japan **76 D6** 38.00N 138.20E
Saeby Denmark **46 D5** 57.20N 10.30E
Safaha *des.* Saudi Arabia **68 E2** 26.30N 39.30E
Safaniya Saudi Arabia **69 H3** 28.00N 48.48E
Säffle Sweden **58 C2** 59.08N 12.55E
Saffron Walden England **15 C3** 52.02N 0.15E
Safi Morocco **104 B5** 32.20N 9.17W
Safonovo Russian Fed. **59 C5** 55.08N 33.16E
Saga Japan **76 A3** 33.08N 130.30E
Sagaing Myanma **71 G4** 22.00N 95.56E
Sagamihara Japan **76 D4** 35.35N 139.30E
Sagar India **71 E4** 23.50N 78.44E
Saglouc Canada **91 K4** 62.10N 75.40W
Sagua la Grande Cuba **93 H4** 22.55N 80.05W
Sagunto Spain **50 E3** 39.40N 0.17W
Sahagún Spain **50 C5** 42.23N 5.02W
Sahara *des.* Africa **104 D3** 18.00N 12.00E
Saharan Atlas *mts.* Algeria **104 C5** 34.20N 2.00E
Saharanpur India **71 D5** 29.58N 77.33E
Sahba, Wadi *r.* Saudi Arabia **69 H2** 24.05N 51.30E
Sahiwal Pakistan **71 D5** 30.40N 73.06E
Saïda Lebanon **68 D4** 33.32N 35.22E
Saidabad Iran **69 I3** 29.28N 55.43E
Saidpur Bangla. **71 F4** 25.48N 89.00E
Saimaa *l.* Finland **58 F3** 61.20N 28.00E
Saimbeyli Turkey **68 E5** 38.07N 36.08E
St. Abb's Head Scotland **27 F2** 55.54N 2.07W
St. Agnes England **12 B2** 50.18N 5.13W
St. Albans England **15 B2** 51.46N 0.21W
St. Alban's Head England **13 E2** 50.35N 2.04W
St. Aldhelm's Head England **13 E2** 50.35N 2.04W
St. Amand France **47 B2** 50.27N 3.26E
St. Amand-Mont-Rond *town* France **48 E4** 46.43N 2.29E
St. Andrews Scotland **27 F3** 56.20N 2.48W
St. Andrews B. Scotland **27 F3** 56.23N 2.43W
St. Ann's Bay *town* Jamaica **93 I3** 18.26N 77.12W
St. Ann's Head Wales **18 A1** 51.41N 5.11W
St. Anthony Canada **91 M3** 51.24N 55.37W
St. Augustine U.S.A. **87 J2** 29.54N 81.19W
St. Austell England **12 C2** 50.20N 4.48W
St. Austell B. England **12 C2** 50.16N 4.43W
St. Barthelemy *i.* Leeward Is. **93 L3** 17.55N 62.50W
St. Bees England **22 A1** 54.29N 3.36W
St. Bees Head England **22 A1** 54.31N 3.39W
St. Blazey England **12 C2** 50.22N 4.48W
St. Boniface Canada **91 I2** 49.54N 97.07W
St. Brides B. Wales **18 A1** 51.48N 5.03W
St. Brieuc France **48 B5** 48.31N 2.45W
St. Catharines Canada **91 K2** 43.10N 79.15W
St. Céré France **48 D3** 44.52N 1.53E
St. Clears Wales **18 B1** 51.48N 4.30W
St. Cloud U.S.A. **87 H6** 45.34N 94.10W
St. Columb Major England **12 C2** 50.26N 4.56W
St. Croix *i.* U.S.V.Is. **93 L3** 17.45N 64.35W
St. David's Wales **18 A1** 51.54N 5.16W
St. David's Head Wales **18 A1** 51.55N 5.19W
St. Denis France **48 E5** 48.56N 2.21E
St. Dié France **48 G5** 48.17N 6.57E
St. Dizier France **48 F5** 48.38N 4.58E
St. Elias, Mt. U.S.A. **90 D4** 60.20N 141.00W
Sainte Marie, Cap *c.* Madagascar **106 G6** 25.34S 45.10E
Saintes France **48 C3** 45.44N 0.38W
St. Étienne France **48 F3** 45.26N 4.26E
St. Feliu de Gixols Spain **51 G4** 41.47N 3.02E
Saintfield N. Ireland **23 D1** 54.28N 5.50W
St. Fillans Scotland **26 D3** 56.24N 4.07W
St. Flour France **48 E3** 45.02N 3.05E
St. Gallen Switz. **52 D2** 47.25N 9.23E
St. Gaudens France **48 D2** 43.07N 0.44E
St. George's Grenada **93 L2** 12.04N 61.44W
St. Georges Guiana **95 I1** 3.54N 51.48W
St. George's Channel U.K./Rep. of Ire. **28 E1** 52.00N 6.00W
St. Germain France **48 E5** 48.53N 2.04E
St. Gilles-sur-Vie France **48 C4** 46.42N 1.56W
St. Girons France **48 D2** 42.59N 1.08E
St. Gotthard Pass Switz. **52 D2** 46.30N 8.55E
St. Govan's Head Wales **18 B1** 51.36N 4.55W
St. Helena *i.* Atlantic Oc. **114 I4** 16.00S 6.00W
St. Helena B. R.S.A. **106 B1** 32.35S 18.00E
St. Helens England **20 C2** 53.28N 2.43W
St. Helier Channel Is. **48 B5** 49.12N 2.07W
St. Hubert Belgium **47 D2** 50.02N 5.22E
St. Hyacinthe Canada **91 K2** 45.38N 72.57W
St. Ives Cambs. England **15 B3** 52.20N 0.05W
St. Ives Cornwall England **12 B2** 50.13N 5.29W
St. Ives B. England **12 B2** 50.14N 5.26W
St. Jean Pied-de-Port France **48 C2** 43.10N 1.14W
St. John Canada **91 L2** 45.16N 66.03W
St. John *r.* Canada **91 L2** 45.30N 66.05W
St. John's Antigua **93 L3** 17.07N 61.51W
St. John's Canada **91 M2** 47.34N 52.41W
St. John's Pt. N. Ireland **23 D1** 54.13N 5.39W
St. Joseph Mo. U.S.A. **87 H4** 39.45N 94.51W
St. Just England **12 B2** 50.07N 5.41W
St. Keverne England **12 B2** 50.03N 5.05W
St. Kitts-Nevis Leeward Is. **93 L3** 17.20N 62.45W
St. Lawrence *r.* Canada/U.S.A. **91 L2** 48.45N 68.30W
St. Lawrence, G. of Canada **91 L2** 48.00N 62.00W
St. Lawrence I. U.S.A. **90 A4** 63.00N 170.00W
St. Lô France **48 C5** 49.07N 1.05W
St. Louis Senegal **104 A3** 16.01N 16.30W
St. Louis U.S.A. **87 H4** 38.40N 90.15W
St. Lucia Windward Is. **93 L2** 14.05N 61.00W
St. Maixent France **48 C4** 46.25N 0.12W
St. Malo France **48 B5** 48.39N 2.00W
St. Malo, Golfe de *g.* France **48 B5** 49.20N 2.00W
St. Marc Haiti **93 J3** 19.08N 72.41W
St. Margaret's at Cliffe England **15 D2** 51.10N 1.23E
St. Margaret's Hope Scotland **24 F5** 58.50N 2.57W
St. Martin *i.* Leeward Is. **93 L3** 18.05N 63.05W
St. Mary's *i.* England **12 A1** 49.55N 6.16W
St. Mary's Loch Scotland **27 E2** 55.29N 3.12W
St. Maurice *r.* Canada **91 K2** 46.20N 72.30W
St. Mawes England **12 B2** 50.10N 5.01W
St. Moritz Switz. **52 D2** 46.30N 9.51E
St. Nazaire France **48 B4** 47.17N 2.12W
St. Neots England **15 B3** 52.14N 0.16W
St. Nicolas Belgium **47 C3** 51.10N 4.09E
St. Omer France **48 E6** 50.45N 2.15E
St. Paul France **48 E2** 42.49N 2.29E
St. Paul U.S.A. **87 H6** 45.00N 93.10W
St. Peter Port Channel Is. **48 B5** 49.27N 2.32W
St. Petersburg Russian Fed. **59 C5** 59.55N 30.25E
St. Petersburg U.S.A. **87 J2** 27.45N 82.40W
St. Pierre and Miquelon *is.* N. America **91 M2** 47.00N 56.15W
St. Polten Austria **57 D4** 48.13N 15.37E
St. Quentin France **47 B1** 49.51N 3.17E
St. Thomas *i.* U.S.V.Is. **93 L3** 18.22N 64.57W
St. Trond Belgium **47 D2** 50.49N 5.11E
St. Tropez France **48 G2** 43.16N 6.39E
St. Vallier France **48 F3** 45.11N 4.49E
St. Vincent and the Grenadines C. America **95 G3** 13.10N 61.15W
St. Vincent, C. Portugal **50 A2** 37.01N 8.59W
St. Vith Belgium **47 E2** 50.15N 6.08E
St. Wendel Germany **47 F1** 49.27N 7.10E
St. Yrieix France **48 D3** 45.31N 1.12E
Saipan *i.* Mariana Is. **79 L7** 15.12N 145.43E
Sakai Japan **76 C4** 34.37N 135.28E
Sakaka Saudi Arabia **68 F3** 29.59N 40.12E
Sakarya *r.* Turkey **68 C6** 41.08N 30.36E
Sakata Japan **76 D6** 38.55N 139.51E
Sakété Benin **108 B2** 6.45N 2.45E
Sakhalin *i.* Russian Fed. **61 L2** 50.00N 143.00E
Sakskõbing *d.* Denmark **46 E2** 54.48N 11.42E
Sal *r.* Russian Fed. **59 E3** 47.33N 40.40E
Sala Sweden **58 D2** 59.55N 16.38E
Salado *r.* La Pampa Argentina **97 C4** 36.15S 66.45W
Salado *r.* Santa Fé Argentina **97 C4** 31.40S 60.41W
Salado *r.* Mexico **92 E5** 26.46N 98.55W
Salala Oman **105 H3** 17.00N 54.04E
Salamanca Spain **50 C4** 40.58N 5.40W
Salamina Colombia **94 D2** 5.24N 75.31W
Salar de Uyuni *l.* Bolivia **97 C5** 20.30S 67.45W
Salatiga Indonesia **78 E2** 7.15S 110.34E
Salavat Russian Fed. **60 E3** 53.22N 55.50E
Sala y Gomez *i.* Pacific Oc. **83 P5** 26.28S 105.28W
Salbris France **48 E4** 47.26N 2.03E
Salcombe England **13 D2** 50.14N 3.47W
Sale England **20 C2** 53.26N 2.19W
Salekhard Russian Fed. **60 F4** 66.33N 66.35E
Salem India **71 E2** 11.38N 78.08E
Salen Strath. Scotland **26 C3** 56.31N 5.56W
Salerno Italy **54 E4** 40.41N 14.45E
Salerno, G. of Med. Sea **54 E4** 40.30N 14.45E
Salford England **20 C2** 53.30N 2.17W
Salgótarján Hungary **57 F4** 48.07N 19.48E
Salima Malaŵi **106 D3** 13.46S 34.26E
Salina Cruz Mexico **92 E3** 16.11N 95.12W
Salins France **48 F4** 46.56N 5.53E
Salisbury England **13 F3** 51.04N 1.48W
Salisbury Md. U.S.A. **87 K4** 38.22N 75.37W
Salisbury Plain *f.* England **13 F3** 51.15N 1.55W
Salmas Iran **69 G5** 38.13N 44.50E
Salmon *r.* U.S.A. **86 C6** 45.50N 116.50W
Salmon River Mts. U.S.A. **86 D5** 44.30N 114.30W
Salo Finland **58 E3** 60.23N 23.10E
Salobreña Spain **50 D2** 36.45N 3.35W
Salon France **48 F2** 43.38N 5.06E
Salsk Russian Fed. **59 E3** 46.30N 41.33E
Salso *r.* Italy **54 D2** 37.07N 13.57E
Salt Jordan **68 D4** 32.03N 35.44E
Salta Argentina **97 C5** 24.46S 65.28W
Saltash England **12 C2** 50.25N 4.13W
Saltburn-by-the-Sea England **22 D1** 54.35N 0.58W
Saltcoats Scotland **26 D2** 55.37N 4.47W
Saltee Is. Rep. of Ire. **28 E2** 52.08N 6.36W
Saltfleet England **17 E3** 53.25N 0.11E
Saltillo Mexico **92 D5** 25.30N 101.00W
Salt Lake City U.S.A. **86 D5** 40.45N 111.55W
Salton Sea *l.* U.S.A. **86 C3** 33.25N 115.45W
Salûm Egypt **68 B3** 31.31N 25.09E
Salvador Brazil **96 F6** 12.58S 38.20W
Salwa Qatar **69 H2** 24.44N 50.50E
Salween *r.* Myanma **78 B7** 16.30N 97.33E
Salyany Azerbaijan **69 H5** 39.36N 48.59E
Salzach *r.* Austria **57 C4** 48.35N 13.30E
Salzburg Austria **57 C3** 47.54N 13.03E
Salzburg *d.* Austria **57 C3** 47.25N 13.15E
Salzgitter Germany **52 E5** 52.02N 10.22E
Samana Dom. Rep. **93 K3** 19.14N 69.20W
Samana Cay *i.* Bahamas **93 J4** 23.05N 73.45W
Samar *i.* Phil. **79 H6** 11.45N 125.15E
Samara Russian Fed. **59 G4** 53.10N 50.15E
Samarinda Indonesia **78 F3** 0.30S 117.09E
Samarkand Uzbekistan **60 F1** 39.40N 66.57E
Samarra Iraq **69 F4** 34.13N 43.52E
Samawa Iraq **69 G3** 31.18N 45.18E
Sambalpur India **71 F4** 21.28N 84.04E
Sambor Ukraine **57 H4** 49.31N 23.10E
Sambre *r.* Belgium **47 C2** 50.29N 4.52E
Sam Neua Laos **78 C8** 20.25N 104.04E
Samoa Is. Pacific Oc. **113 S4** 13.00S 171.00W
Sámos *i.* Greece **68 B5** 37.44N 26.45E
Samothráki *i.* Greece **56 G4** 40.26N 25.35E
Sampit Indonesia **78 E3** 2.34S 112.59E
Samrong Cambodia **78 C6** 14.12N 103.31E
Samsö *i.* Denmark **46 D3** 55.50N 10.35E
Samsö Baelt *str.* Denmark **46 D3** 55.50N 10.50E
Samsun Turkey **68 E6** 41.17N 36.22E
Samui, Ko *i.* Thailand **78 C5** 9.30N 100.00E
San Mali **104 B3** 13.21N 4.57W
San'a Yemen **105 G3** 15.23N 44.14E
Sana *r.* Yugo. **56 C6** 45.03N 16.22E
Sana *r.* Yugo. **56 C6** 45.03N 16.23E
Sanaga *r.* Cameroon **104 C2** 3.35N 9.40E
San Ambrosio *i.* Chile **97 B5** 26.28S 79.53W
Sanandaj Iran **69 G4** 35.18N 47.01E
San Andrés, I. de Colombia **94 C3** 12.35N 81.42W
San Antonio U.S.A. **86 G2** 29.25N 98.30W
San Antonio, C. Cuba **93 H4** 21.50N 84.57W
San Antonio, Punta *c.* Mexico **92 A5** 29.45N 115.41W
San Bernardino U.S.A. **86 C3** 34.07N 117.18W
San Blas, C. U.S.A. **87 I2** 29.40N 85.25W
San Carlos Luzon Phil. **79 G7** 15.59N 120.22E
San Carlos Venezuela **95 F2** 9.39N 68.35W
San Carlos de Bariloche Argentina **97 B3** 41.11S 71.23W
San Carlos del Zulta Venezuela **94 E2** 9.01N 71.55W
San Cristóbal Dom. Rep. **93 J3** 18.27N 70.07W
San Cristóbal Venezuela **94 E2** 7.46N 72.15W
Sancti Spiritus Cuba **93 I4** 21.55N 79.28W
Sanda *i.* Scotland **26 C2** 55.17N 5.34W
Sandakan Malaysia **78 F5** 5.52N 118.04E
Sanday *i.* Scotland **24 F6** 59.15N 2.33W
Sandbach England **20 C2** 53.09N 2.23W
Sandbank Scotland **26 D2** 55.59N 4.58W
Sande Germany **46 B2** 54.44N 8.58E
Sandgate England **15 D2** 51.05N 1.09E
San Diego U.S.A. **86 C3** 32.45N 117.10W
Sandnes Norway **58 A2** 58.51N 5.45E
Sandness Scotland **24 G7** 60.19N 1.40W
Sandö *i.* Faroe Is. **58 M8** 61.50N 6.45W
Sandoway Myanma **71 G3** 18.28N 94.20E
Sandpoint *town* U.S.A. **86 C6** 48.17N 116.34W
Sandringham England **15 C3** 52.50N 0.30E
Sandviken Sweden **58 D3** 60.38N 16.50E
Sandwich England **15 D2** 51.16N 1.21E
Sandy England **15 B3** 52.08N 0.18W
San Felipe Colombia **95 F1** 1.55N 67.06W
San Felipe Mexico **92 B6** 31.03N 114.52W
San Felipe Venezuela **94 F3** 10.25N 68.40W
San Félix *i.* Chile **97 A5** 26.23S 80.05W
San Fernando Phil. **79 G7** 16.39N 120.19E
San Fernando Spain **50 B2** 36.28N 6.12W
San Fernando Trinidad **93 L2** 10.16N 61.28W
San Fernando de Apure Venezuela **95 F2** 7.53N 67.15W
San Fernando de Atabapo Venezuela **95 F1** 4.03N 67.45W
San Francisco U.S.A. **86 B4** 37.45N 122.27W
San Francisco, C. Ecuador **96 A8** 0.38N 80.08W
San Francisco de Macorís Dom. Rep. **93 J3** 19.19N 70.15W
Sanggan He *r.* China **75 I5** 40.23N 115.18E
Sangha *r.* Congo **106 B4** 1.10S 16.47E
Sangi *i.* Indonesia **79 H4** 3.30N 125.30E
Sangihe Is. Indonesia **79 H4** 2.45N 125.20E
San Gil Colombia **94 E2** 6.35N 73.08W
Sangli India **71 D3** 16.55N 74.37E
Sangonera *r.* Spain **50 E2** 37.58N 1.04W
Sangre de Cristo Mts. U.S.A. **86 E4** 37.30N 106.00W
Sanjo Japan **76 D5** 37.37N 138.57E
San Jordi, G. of Spain **50 F4** 40.50N 1.10E
San Jorge *r.* Colombia **94 E2** 9.10N 74.40W
San Jorge, G. of Argentina **97 C3** 46.00S 66.00W
San José Costa Rica **93 H1** 9.59N 84.04W
San José Guatemala **92 F2** 13.58N 90.50W
San Jose U.S.A. **86 B4** 37.20N 121.55W
San José de Guanipa Venezuela **95 G2** 8.54N 64.09W
San José del Guaviare Colombia **94 E1** 2.35N 72.38W
San Juan Argentina **97 C4** 31.33S 68.31W
San Juan *r.* Costa Rica **93 H2** 10.50N 83.40W
San Juan Puerto Rico **93 K3** 18.29N 66.08W
San Juan *r.* U.S.A. **86 D4** 37.20N 110.05W
San Juan del Norte Nicaragua **93 H2** 10.58N 83.40W
San Juan de los Morros Venezuela **95 F2** 9.53N 67.23W
San Juan Mts. U.S.A. **86 E4** 37.30N 107.00W
Sankt Peter Germany **46 B2** 54.19N 8.38E
San Lázaro, C. Mexico **92 B4** 24.50N 112.18W
San Leonardo Spain **50 D4** 41.49N 3.04W
Sanlúcar de Barrameda Spain **50 B2** 36.46N 6.21W
San Lucas, C. Mexico **92 C4** 22.50N 110.00W
San Luis Cuba **93 I4** 20.13N 75.50W
San Luis Obispo U.S.A. **86 B4** 35.16N 120.40W
San Luis Potosi Mexico **92 D4** 22.10N 101.00W
San Luis Potosí *d.* Mexico **92 D4** 23.00N 100.00W
San Marino Europe **54 D5** 43.55N 12.27E
San Marino *town* San Marino **54 D5** 43.55N 12.27E
San Matias, G. of Argentina **97 C3** 41.30S 64.00W
Sanmenxia China **75 H4** 34.46N 111.17E
San Miguel El Salvador **93 G2** 13.28N 88.10W
San Miguel de Tucumán Argentina **97 C5** 26.47S 65.15W
San Miguelito Panama **94 D2** 9.02N 79.30W
San Pablo Phil. **79 G6** 13.58N 121.10E
San Pedro Dom. Rep. **93 K3** 18.30N 69.18W
San Pedro Mexico **92 D5** 25.50N 102.59W
San Pedro, Punta *c.* Costa Rica **94 C2** 8.30N 83.30W
San Pedro, Sierra de *mts.* Spain **50 B3** 39.20N 6.20W
San Pedro Sula Honduras **93 G3** 15.26N 88.01W
San Pietro *i.* Italy **54 B3** 39.09N 8.16E
Sanquhar Scotland **27 E2** 55.22N 3.56W
San Remo Italy **54 A5** 43.48N 7.46E
San Salvador *i.* Bahamas **93 J4** 24.00N 74.32W
San Salvador El Salvador **93 G2** 13.40N 89.10W
San Sebastián Spain **50 E5** 43.19N 1.59W
San Severo Italy **54 E4** 41.40N 15.24E
Santa Ana El Salvador **93 G2** 14.00N 89.31W
Santa Ana U.S.A. **86 C3** 33.44N 117.54W
Santa Barbara Mexico **92 C5** 26.48N 105.49W
Santa Barbara U.S.A. **86 C3** 34.25N 119.41W
Santa Clara Cuba **94 C5** 22.25N 79.58W
Santa Cruz Bolivia **96 C6** 17.58S 63.14W
Santa Cruz Canary Is. **104 A4** 28.27N 16.14W
Santa Cruz Is. Solomon Is. **80 F4** 10.30S 166.00E
Santa Elena, C. Costa Rica **93 G2** 10.54N 85.56W
Santa Fé Argentina **97 C4** 31.38S 60.43W
Santa Fe U.S.A. **86 E4** 35.41N 105.57W
Santa Maria Brazil **97 D5** 29.40S 53.47W
Santa Maria U.S.A. **86 B3** 34.56N 120.25W
Santa Maria di Leuca, C. Italy **54 G3** 39.47N 18.24E
Santa Marta Colombia **94 E3** 11.18N 74.10W
Santander Colombia **94 D1** 3.00N 76.25W
Santander Spain **50 D5** 43.28N 3.48W
Santañy Spain **51 G3** 39.20N 3.07E
Santarém Brazil **96 D7** 2.26S 54.41W
Santarém Portugal **50 A3** 39.14N 8.40W
Santa Rosa Argentina **97 C4** 36.00S 64.40W
Santa Rosa Honduras **93 G2** 14.47N 88.46W
Santa Rosa de Cabal Colombia **94 D1** 4.52N 75.37W
Santa Rosalia Mexico **92 B5** 27.20N 112.20W
Santiago Chile **97 B4** 33.30S 70.40W
Santiago Dom. Rep. **94 E4** 19.30N 70.42W
Santiago Panama **93 H1** 8.08N 80.59W
Santiago de Compostela Spain **50 A5** 42.52N 8.33W
Santiago de Cuba Cuba **94 D5** 20.00N 75.49W
Santiago del Estero Argentina **97 C5** 27.48S 64.15W
Santo Domingo Dom. Rep. **93 K3** 18.30N 69.57W
Santoña Spain **50 D5** 43.27N 3.26W
Santos Brazil **97 E5** 23.56S 46.22W
Santo Tomé de Guayana Venezuela **95 G2** 8.22N 62.40W
San Valentin, Cerro *mtn.* Chile **97 B3** 46.33S 73.20W
San Vicente El Salvador **93 G2** 13.38N 88.42W
São Francisco *r.* Brazil **96 F6** 10.10S 36.40W
São Francisco do Sul Brazil **97 E5** 26.17S 48.39W
São José do Rio Prêto Brazil **97 E5** 20.50S 49.20W
São Luís Brazil **96 E7** 2.34S 44.16W
Saona *i.* Dom. Rep. **93 K3** 18.09N 68.42W
Saône *r.* France **48 F3** 45.46N 4.52E
São Paulo Brazil **97 E5** 23.33S 46.39W
São Paulo de Olivença Brazil **96 C7** 3.34S 68.55W
São Roque, C. Brazil **96 F7** 5.00S 35.00W
São Tomé *i.* São Tomé & Príncipe **104 C2** 0.19N 6.43E
São Tomé & Príncipe Africa **104 C2** 1.00N 7.00E
Sapporo Japan **76 E8** 43.05N 141.21E
Sapri Italy **54 E4** 40.04N 15.38E
Saqqiz Iran **69 G5** 36.14N 46.15E
Sarab Iran **69 G5** 37.56N 47.35E
Sara Buri Thailand **78 C6** 14.32N 100.53E

Sarajevo Yugo. 56 D5 43.52N 18.26E
Sarangarh India 71 E4 21.38N 83.09E
Saransk Russian Fed. 59 F4 54.12N 45.10E
Saratov Russian Fed. 59 F4 51.30N 45.55E
Saratov Resr. Russian Fed. 41 O5 51.00N 46.00E
Sarawak d. Malaysia 78 E4 3.00N 114.00E
Sarbaz Iran 69 K2 26.39N 61.20E
Sardinia i. Italy 54 B4 40.00N 9.00E
Sarek mtn. Sweden 58 D4 67.10N 17.45E
Sargodha Pakistan 71 D6 32.01N 72.40E
Sarh Chad 104 D2 9.08N 18.22E
Sarigan i. Mariana Is. 79 L7 16.43N 145.47E
Sarikei Malaysia 78 E4 2.07N 111.31E
Sarisbury England 14 A1 50.52N 1.17W
Sark i. Channel Is. 48 B5 49.26N 2.22W
Sarmi Indonesia 79 J3 1.51S 138.45E
Sarmiento Argentina 97 C3 45.38S 69.08W
Särna Sweden 58 C3 61.40N 13.10E
Sarny Ukraine 59 B4 51.21N 26.31E
Saros, G. of Turkey 68 B6 40.32N 26.25E
Sarpsborg Norway 58 B2 59.17N 11.06E
Sarrebourg France 48 G5 48.43N 7.03E
Sarria Spain 50 B5 42.47N 7.25W
Sarthe r. France 48 C4 47.29N 0.30W
Sarur Oman 69 J1 23.25N 58.10E
Sasebo Japan 76 A3 33.10N 129.42E
Saskatchewan d. Canada 90 H3 55.00N 105.00W
Saskatchewan r. Canada 91 H3 53.25N 100.15W
Saskatoon Canada 90 H3 52.10N 106.40W
Sasovo Russian Fed. 59 E4 54.21N 41.58E
Sassandra Côte d'Ivoire 104 B2 4.58N 6.08W
Sassari Italy 54 B4 40.43N 8.33E
Sassnitz Germany 52 F6 54.32N 13.40E
Satara India 71 D3 17.43N 74.05E
Satpura Range mts. India 71 D4 21.50N 76.00E
Satrup Germany 46 C2 54.41N 9.38E
Satu Mare Romania 57 H3 47.48N 22.52E
Sauda Norway 58 A2 59.38N 6.23E
Saudi Arabia Asia 105 G4 26.00N 44.00E
Saulieu France 48 F4 47.17N 4.14E
Sault Sainte Marie Canada 91 J2 46.32N 84.20W
Saumlaki Indonesia 79 I2 7.59S 131.22E
Saumur France 48 C4 47.16N 0.05W
Saundersfoot Wales 18 B1 51.43N 4.42W
Sava r. Yugo. 56 E6 44.50N 20.26E
Savai'i I. W. Samoa 82 I6 13.36S 172.27W
Savannah U.S.A. 87 J3 32.09N 81.01W
Savannah r. U.S.A. 87 J3 32.10N 81.00W
Savannakhet Laos 78 C7 16.34N 104.55E
Savé Benin 108 B2 8.04N 2.37E
Save r. Mozambique 106 D2 21.00S 35.01E
Saveh Iran 69 H4 35.00N 50.25E
Savona Italy 54 B6 44.18N 8.28E
Savonlinna Finland 58 G3 61.52N 28.51E
Savu Sea Pacific Oc. 79 G2 9.30S 122.30E
Sawbridgeworth England 15 C2 51.50N 0.09E
Sawston England 15 C3 52.07N 0.11E
Sawu i. Indonesia 79 G1 10.30S 121.50E
Saxmundham England 15 D3 52.13N 1.29E
Saxthorpe England 15 D3 52.50N 1.09E
Sayan Mts. Russian Fed. 74 F7 51.30N 102.00E
Saynshand Mongolia 75 H6 44.58N 110.10E
Sayula Mexico 92 D3 19.52N 103.36W
Săzava r. Czech. 57 D4 49.53N 14.21E
Scafell Pike mtn. England 22 A1 54.27N 3.12W
Scalasaig Scotland 26 B3 56.04N 6.12W
Scalby England 21 E3 54.18N 0.26W
Scalloway Scotland 24 G7 60.09N 1.13W
Scammon Bay town U.S.A. 90 B4 61.50N 165.35W
Scandinavia f. Europe 113 J8 65.00N 18.00E
Scapa Flow str. Scotland 24 E5 58.53N 3.05W
Scarba i. Scotland 26 C3 56.11N 5.42W
Scarborough England 21 E3 54.17N 0.24W
Scarborough Tobago 95 G3 11.11N 60.44W
Scarinish Scotland 26 B3 56.30N 6.48W
Schaffhausen Switz. 52 D2 47.42N 8.38E
Schagen Neth. 47 C4 52.47N 4.47E
Schefferville Canada 91 L3 54.50N 67.00W
Schelde r. Belgium 47 C3 51.13N 4.25E
Scheveningen Neth. 47 C4 52.07N 4.16E
Schiedam Neth. 47 C3 51.55N 4.25E
Schiermonnikoog i. Neth. 47 E5 53.28N 6.15E
Schlei est. Germany 46 C2 54.38N 9.55E
Schleiden Germany 47 E2 50.32N 6.29E
Schleswig Germany 52 D6 54.32N 9.34E
Schleswig-Holstein d. Germany 52 D6 54.00N 10.00E
Schouten Is. Indonesia 79 J3 0.45S 135.50E
Schouwen i. Neth. 47 B3 51.42N 3.45E
Schwandorf Germany 52 F3 49.20N 12.08E
Schwaner Mts. Indonesia 78 E3 0.45S 113.20E
Schwedt Germany 52 G5 53.04N 14.17E
Schweinfurt Germany 52 E4 50.03N 10.16E
Schwelm Germany 47 F3 51.17N 7.18E
Schwerin Germany 52 E5 53.38N 11.25E
Sciacca Italy 54 D2 37.31N 13.05E
Scilly, Isles of England 12 A1 49.55N 6.20W
Scotland U.K. 24 D4 55.30N 4.00W
Scottsbluff U.S.A. 86 F5 41.52N 103.40W
Scourie Scotland 24 C5 58.20N 5.09W
Scranton U.S.A. 87 K5 41.25N 75.40W
Scridain, Loch Scotland 26 B3 56.22N 6.06W
Scunthorpe England 21 E2 53.35N 0.38W
Seaford England 15 C1 50.46N 0.08E
Seaham England 22 C1 54.52N 1.21W
Seahouses England 22 C2 55.35N 1.38W
Seal r. Canada 91 I3 59.00N 95.00W
Seamill Scotland 26 D2 55.41N 4.52W
Seascale England 22 A1 54.24N 3.29W
Seaton Cumbria England 22 A1 54.41N 3.31W
Seaton Devon England 13 D2 50.43N 3.05W
Seaton Delaval England 22 C2 55.05N 1.31W
Seattle U.S.A. 86 B6 47.35N 122.20W
Sebastian Vizcaino B. Mexico 92 B5 28.20N 114.45W
Sebha Libya 104 D4 27.04N 14.25E
Sebinkarahisar Turkey 68 E6 40.19N 38.25E
Sêda r. Portugal 50 A3 38.55N 7.30W
Sedan France 47 C1 49.42N 4.57E
Sedbergh England 22 B1 54.20N 2.31W
Sedgefield England 22 C1 54.40N 1.27W
Segovia Spain 50 C4 40.57N 4.07W
Segre r. Spain 50 F4 41.25N 0.21E
Segura r. Spain 50 E3 38.07N 0.14W
Segura, Sierra de mts. Spain 50 D2 38.00N 2.50W
Seil i. Scotland 26 C3 56.18N 5.33W
Seiland i. Norway 58 E5 70.30N 23.00E
Seinäjoki Finland 58 E3 62.45N 22.55E
Seine r. France 48 D5 49.28N 0.25E
Seistan f. Iran 70 B5 31.00N 61.15E
Sekondi-Takoradi Ghana 108 A1 4.59N 1.43W
Selaru i. Indonesia 79 I2 8.15S 131.00E
Selatan, Tanjung c. Indonesia 78 E3 4.20S 114.45E
Selby England 21 D2 53.47N 1.05W
Sele r. Italy 54 E4 40.30N 14.50E
Selebi-Pikwe Botswana 106 C2 22.01S 27.50E
Selenga r. Mongolia/Russian Fed. 74 G7 52.20N 106.20E
Sélestat France 48 G5 48.16N 7.28E
Selkirk Scotland 27 F2 55.33N 2.51W
Selkirk Mts. Canada/U.S.A. 90 G2 49.00N 116.00W
Selsey England 15 B1 50.44N 0.47W
Selsey Bill c. England 15 B1 50.44N 0.47W
Selston England 16 C3 53.04N 1.19W
Selvas f. Brazil 96 C7 9.00S 68.00W
Selwyn Mts. Canada 90 E4 63.00N 130.00W
Seman r. Albania 56 D4 40.53N 19.25E
Semarang Indonesia 78 E2 6.58S 110.29E
Seminoe Resr. U.S.A. 86 E5 42.05N 106.50W
Semipalatinsk Kazakhstan 60 G2 50.26N 80.16E
Semmering Pass Austria 57 D3 47.40N 16.00E
Semois r. France 47 C1 49.53N 4.45E
Sendai Kyushu Japan 76 A2 31.49N 130.18E
Sendai Tofuku Japan 76 D6 38.20N 140.50E
Senegal Africa 104 A3 14.15N 14.15W
Sénégal r. Senegal/Mauritania 104 A3 16.00N 16.28W
Sengkang Indonesia 78 G3 4.09S 120.02E
Senigallia Italy 54 D5 43.42N 13.14E
Senja i. Norway 58 D5 69.20N 17.30E
Senlis France 48 E5 49.12N 2.35E
Sennar Sudan 105 F3 13.31N 33.38E
Sennen England 12 B2 50.04N 5.42W
Senneterre Canada 91 K2 48.24N 77.16W
Sennybridge Wales 18 C1 51.57N 3.35W
Sens France 48 E5 48.12N 3.18E
Seoul S. Korea 75 K4 37.30N 127.00E
Sepik r. P.N.G. 79 K3 3.54S 144.30E
Sept Îles town Canada 91 L3 50.13N 66.22W
Seraing Belgium 47 D2 50.37N 5.33E
Serang Indonesia 78 D2 6.07S 106.09E
Seremban Malaysia 78 C4 2.42N 101.54E
Sergach Russian Fed. 59 F5 55.32N 45.27E
Seria Brunei 78 E4 4.39N 114.23E
Serian Malaysia 78 E4 1.10N 110.35E
Sermate i. Indonesia 79 H2 8.30S 129.00E
Serov Russian Fed. 60 F3 59.42N 60.32E
Serowe Botswana 106 C2 22.25S 26.44E
Serpa Portugal 50 B2 37.56N 7.36W
Serpent's Mouth str. Venezuela 95 G2 9.50N 61.00W
Serpukhov Russian Fed. 59 D4 54.53N 37.25E
Sérrai Greece 56 F4 41.04N 23.32E
Serra Môco mtn. Angola 102 D3 12.30S 15.00E
Serre r. France 47 B1 49.40N 3.22E
Serui Indonesia 79 J3 1.53S 136.15E
Sesimbra Portugal 50 A3 38.26N 9.06W
Sète France 48 E2 43.25N 3.43E
Setif Algeria 104 C5 36.09N 5.26E
Settat Morocco 104 B5 33.04N 7.37W
Settle England 20 C3 54.05N 2.18W
Setúbal Portugal 50 A3 38.31N 8.54W
Setúbal, B. of Portugal 50 A3 38.20N 9.00W
Sevan, L. Armenia 69 G6 40.22N 45.20E
Sevastopol' Ukraine 59 C2 44.36N 33.31E
Sevenoaks England 15 C2 51.16N 0.12E
Sévérac France 48 E3 44.20N 3.05E
Severn r. Canada 91 J3 56.00N 87.40W
Severn r. England 13 E3 51.50N 2.21W
Severnaya Zemlya is. Russian Fed. 61 H5 80.00N 96.00E
Severnyy Donets r. Ukraine/Russian Fed. 59 D3 49.08N 37.28E
Severodvinsk Russian Fed. 60 D4 64.35N 39.50E
Seville Spain 50 C2 37.24N 5.59W
Sèvre Niortaise r. France 48 C4 46.35N 1.05W
Seward U.S.A. 90 D4 60.05N 149.34W
Seward Pen. U.S.A. 90 B4 65.00N 164.10W
Seychelles Indian Oc. 115 L4 5.00S 55.00E
Seydhisfjördhur Iceland 58 K7 65.16N 14.02W
Sézanne France 48 E5 48.44N 3.44E
Sfântu-Gheorghe Romania 56 G6 45.52N 25.50E
Sfax Tunisia 104 D5 34.45N 10.43E
'sGravenhage see The Hague Neth. 47
Shaanxi d. China 75 H4 35.00N 109.00E
Shache China 74 B5 38.27N 77.16E
Shaftesbury England 13 E3 51.00N 2.12W
Shahjahanpur India 71 E5 27.53N 79.55E
Shahr-i-Babak Iran 69 I3 30.08N 55.04E
Shahr Kord Iran 69 H4 32.40N 50.52E
Shaib al Qur r. Saudi Arabia 68 F3 31.02N 42.00E
Shakhty Russian Fed. 59 E3 47.43N 40.16E
Shamiya Desert Iraq 69 G3 30.30N 45.30E
Sham, Jebel mtn. Oman 69 J1 23.14N 57.17E
Shandong d. China 75 I4 35.45N 117.30E
Shandong Peninsula China 75 J4 37.00N 121.30E
Shanghai China 75 J3 31.13N 121.25E
Shangrao China 75 I3 28.28N 117.54E
Shangshui China 75 I4 33.33N 114.38E
Shannon r. Rep. of Ire. 28 C2 52.39N 8.43W
Shannon, Mouth of the est. Rep. of Ire. 28 B2 52.29N 9.57W
Shantar Is. Russian Fed. 61 L3 55.00N 138.00E
Shantou China 75 I2 23.23N 116.39E
Shanxi d. China 75 H4 36.45N 112.00E
Shaoguan China 75 H2 24.54N 113.33E
Shaoxing China 75 J3 30.02N 120.35E
Shaoyang China 75 H3 27.43N 111.24E
Shap England 22 B1 54.32N 2.40W
Shapinsay i. Scotland 24 F6 59.03N 2.51W
Shapur ruins Iran 69 H3 29.42N 51.30E
Shaqra Saudi Arabia 69 G2 25.17N 45.14E
Sharjah U.A.E. 69 I2 25.20N 55.26E
Shashi China 75 H3 30.16N 112.20E
Shasta, Mt. U.S.A. 86 B5 41.35N 122.12W
Shatt al Arab r. Iraq 69 H3 30.00N 48.30E
Shebelle r. Somali Rep. 105 G2 0.30N 43.10E
Shebshi Mts. Nigeria 108 D2 8.30N 11.45E
Sheeffry Hills Rep. of Ire. 28 B3 53.45N 9.40W
Sheelin, Lough Rep. of Ire. 28 D3 53.48N 7.20W
Sheerness England 15 C2 51.26N 0.47E
Sheffield England 21 D2 53.23N 1.28W
Shefford England 15 B3 52.02N 0.20W
Shelby U.S.A. 86 D6 48.30N 111.52W
Shelikof Str. U.S.A. 90 C3 58.00N 153.45W
Shëngjin Albania 56 D4 41.49N 19.33E
Shengze China 75 J3 30.55N 120.39E
Shenyang China 75 J5 41.50N 123.26E
Shepetovka Ukraine 59 B4 50.12N 27.01E
Shepparton Australia 80 D2 36.25S 145.26E
Sheppey, Isle of England 15 C2 51.24N 0.50E
Shepshed England 16 C2 52.46N 1.17W
Shepton Mallet England 13 E3 51.11N 2.31W
Sherborne England 13 E2 50.56N 2.31W
Sherbrooke Canada 91 K2 45.24N 71.54W
Sheridan U.S.A. 86 E5 44.48N 107.05W
Sheringham England 15 D3 52.56N 1.11E
Sherkin I. Rep. of Ire. 28 B1 51.28N 9.27W
Sherman U.S.A. 87 G3 33.39N 96.35W
Sherridon Canada 91 H3 57.07N 101.05W
'sHertogenbosch Neth. 47 D3 51.42N 5.19E
Sherwood Forest f. England 16 C3 53.10N 1.05W
Shetland Is. d. Scotland 24 G7 60.20N 1.15W
Shevchenko Kazakhstan 60 E2 43.37N 51.11E
Shiel, L. Scotland 24 C3 56.50N 5.35W
Shifnal England 16 B2 52.40N 2.23W
Shijiazhuang China 75 I5 38.04N 114.28E
Shikarpur Pakistan 70 C5 27.58N 68.42E
Shikoku d. Japan 76 B3 33.30N 133.00E
Shikoku i. Japan 76 B3 33.30N 133.00E
Shikoku sanchi mts. Japan 76 B3 34.00N 134.00E
Shikotsu ko l. Japan 76 E8 42.50N 141.26E
Shilbottle England 22 C2 55.22N 1.43W
Shildon England 22 C1 54.37N 1.39W
Shilka Russian Fed. 75 I7 51.55N 116.01E
Shilka r. Russian Fed. 75 J7 53.20N 121.10E
Shillong India 71 G4 25.34N 91.53E
Shimizu Japan 76 D4 35.08N 138.38E
Shimoga India 71 D2 13.56N 75.31E
Shimo jima i. Japan 76 A3 32.10N 130.30E
Shimonoseki Japan 76 A4 34.02N 130.58E
Shinano r. Japan 76 D5 37.58N 139.02E
Shingu Japan 76 C3 33.44N 135.59E
Shin, Loch Scotland 24 D5 58.06N 4.32W
Shiono misaki c. Japan 76 C3 33.28N 135.47E
Shipka Pass Bulgaria 56 G5 42.45N 25.25E
Shipley England 20 D2 53.50N 1.47W
Shipston on Stour England 16 C2 52.04N 1.38W
Shipton England 21 D3 54.01N 1.09W
Shiqian China 75 H3 27.30N 108.20E
Shirakawa Japan 76 D5 37.10N 140.15E
Shirak Steppe f. Georgia 69 G6 41.40N 46.20E
Shirane san mtn. Japan 76 D4 35.42N 138.12E
Shiraz Iran 69 I3 29.36N 52.33E
Shire r. Mozambique 106 D3 17.44S 35.17E
Shirebrook England 16 C3 53.14N 1.16W
Shiriya saki c. Japan 76 E7 41.24N 141.30E
Shizuishan China 74 G5 39.17N 106.52E
Shizuoka Japan 76 D4 35.02N 138.28E
Shkodër Albania 56 D5 42.03N 19.30E
Shkoder, L. Albania/Yugo. 56 D5 42.10N 19.18E
Shoeburyness England 15 C2 51.31N 0.49E
Sholapur India 71 D3 17.43N 75.56E
Shoreham-by-Sea England 15 B1 50.50N 0.17W
Shostka Ukraine 59 C4 51.53N 33.30E
Shotts Scotland 27 E2 55.49N 3.48W
Shpola Ukraine 59 C3 49.00N 31.25E
Shreveport U.S.A. 87 H3 32.30N 93.46W
Shrewsbury England 16 B2 52.42N 2.45W
Shrewton England 13 F3 51.11N 1.55W
Shropshire d. England 16 B2 52.35N 2.40W
Shu'aiba Iraq 69 G3 30.30N 47.40E
Shuangliao China 75 J5 43.30N 123.29E
Shuangyashan China 75 K6 46.37N 131.22E
Shumagin Is. U.S.A. 90 C3 55.00N 160.00W
Shunde China 75 H2 22.50N 113.16E
Shur r. Iran 69 I3 28.00N 55.45E
Shushtar Iran 69 H4 32.04N 48.53E
Shuya Russian Fed. 59 E5 56.49N 41.23E
Shwebo Myanma 71 G4 22.35N 95.42E
Sialkot Pakistan 71 D6 32.29N 74.35E
Siargao i. Phil. 79 H5 9.55N 126.05E
Siauliai Lithuania 58 E1 55.51N 23.20E
Šibenik Yugo. 56 B5 43.45N 15.55E
Siberia f. Asia 113 O8 62.00N 104.00E
Siberut i. Indonesia 78 B3 1.30S 99.00E
Sibi Pakistan 70 C5 29.31N 67.54E
Sibiu Romania 56 G6 45.47N 24.09E
Sibolga Indonesia 78 B4 1.42N 98.48E
Sibu Malaysia 78 E4 2.18N 111.49E
Sichuan d. China 74 G3 30.30N 103.00E
Sicily i. Italy 54 E2 37.30N 14.00E
Sidi Barrani Egypt 68 B3 31.38N 25.58E
Sidi-bel-Abbès Algeria 104 B5 35.15N 0.39W
Sidlaw Hills Scotland 27 E3 56.31N 3.10W
Sidmouth England 13 D2 50.40N 3.13W
Siedlce Poland 57 H6 52.10N 22.18E
Sieg r. Germany 47 F2 50.49N 7.11E
Siegburg Germany 47 F2 50.48N 7.13E
Siegen Germany 47 G2 50.52N 8.02E
Siena Italy 54 C5 43.19N 11.20E
Sierpc Poland 57 F6 52.52N 19.41E
Sierra Leone Africa 104 A2 8.30N 12.00W
Sighişoara Romania 56 G7 46.13N 24.49E
Sighty Crag mtn. England 22 B2 55.07N 2.38W
Siglufjördhur Iceland 58 J7 66.09N 18.55W
Signy France 47 C1 49.42N 4.25E
Sigüenza Spain 50 D4 41.04N 2.38W
Siirt Turkey 68 F5 37.56N 41.56E
Sikar India 71 D5 27.33N 75.12E
Sikasso Mali 104 B3 11.18N 5.38W
Sikhote-Alin Range mts. Russian Fed. 61 L2 45.20N 136.50E
Sikkim d. India 71 F5 27.30N 88.30E
Sil r. Spain 50 B5 42.24N 7.15W
Silchar India 71 G4 24.49N 92.47E
Sileby England 16 C2 52.44N 1.06W
Silesian Plateau mts. Poland 57 F5 50.30N 19.30E
Silgarhi Nepal 71 E5 29.14N 80.58E
Silifke Turkey 68 D5 36.22N 33.57E
Siliguri India 71 F5 26.42N 88.30E
Siling Co l. China 74 D3 31.40N 88.30E
Silistra Bulgaria 59 B2 44.07N 27.17E
Siljan l. Sweden 58 C3 60.50N 14.40E
Silkeborg Denmark 46 C4 56.10N 9.39E
Silloth England 22 A1 54.53N 3.25W
Silsden England 20 D2 53.55N 1.55W
Silver City U.S.A. 86 E3 32.47N 108.16W
Silverstone England 16 C2 52.05N 1.03W
Silverton England 13 D2 50.49N 3.29W
Simanggang Malaysia 78 E4 1.10N 111.32E
Simeulue i. Indonesia 78 B4 2.30N 96.00E
Simferopol' Ukraine 59 C2 44.57N 34.05E
Simla India 71 D5 31.07N 77.09E
Simmern Germany 47 F1 49.59N 7.32E
Simo r. Finland 58 F4 65.38N 24.57E
Simonsbath England 13 D3 51.07N 3.45W
Simplon Pass Switz. 52 C2 46.15N 8.03E
Simplon Tunnel Italy/Switz. 54 B7 46.20N 8.05E
Simrishamn Sweden 58 C1 55.35N 14.20E
Sinai pen. Egypt 68 D3 29.00N 34.00E
Sinaloa d. Mexico 92 C4 25.00N 107.30W
Sinan China 75 H3 27.56N 108.22E
Sincelejo Colombia 94 D2 9.17N 75.23W
Sindal Denmark 46 D5 57.29N 10.12E
Sines Portugal 50 A2 37.58N 8.52W
Singapore Asia 78 C4 1.20N 103.45E
Singapore town Singapore 78 C4 1.20N 103.45E
Singaraja Indonesia 78 F2 8.06S 115.07E
Singitikos G. Med. Sea 56 F4 40.12N 24.00E
Singkawang Indonesia 78 D4 0.57N 108.57E
Singkep i. Indonesia 78 C3 0.30S 104.20E
Sinj Yugo. 56 C5 43.42N 16.38E
Sinop Turkey 68 D6 42.02N 35.09E
Sintang Indonesia 78 E4 0.03N 111.31E
Sint Eustatius i. Leeward Is. 93 L3 17.33N 63.00W
Sint Maarten i. Neth. Antilles 95 G4 18.05N 63.05W
Sinuiju N. Korea 75 J5 40.04N 124.25E
Sion Mills N. Ireland 23 B1 54.47N 7.30W
Sioux City U.S.A. 87 G5 42.30N 96.28W
Sioux Falls town U.S.A. 87 G5 43.34N 96.42W
Sioux Lookout town Canada 91 I3 50.07N 91.54W
Siping China 75 J5 43.15N 124.25E
Sipora i. Indonesia 78 B3 2.10S 99.40E
Sira r. Norway 58 A2 58.13N 6.13E
Siracusa Italy 54 E2 37.05N 15.17E
Siret r. Romania 59 B3 45.28N 27.56E
Sirhan, Wadi f. Saudi Arabia 68 E3 31.00N 37.30E
Sirra, Wadi r. Saudi Arabia 69 G1 23.10N 44.22E
Sirte Libya 104 D5 31.10N 16.39E
Sirte, G. of Libya 104 D5 31.45N 17.50E
Sisak Yugo. 56 C6 45.30N 16.21E
Sishen R.S.A. 106 C2 27.48S 22.59E
Sisophon Cambodia 78 C6 13.37N 102.58E
Sisteron France 48 F3 44.16N 5.56E
Sitka U.S.A. 90 E3 57.05N 135.20W
Sittang r. Myanma 71 H3 17.30N 96.53E
Sittard Neth. 47 D3 51.00N 5.52E
Sittingbourne England 15 C2 51.20N 0.44E
Sivas Turkey 68 E5 39.44N 37.01E
Sivrihisar Turkey 68 C5 39.29N 31.32E
Siwa Egypt 68 B3 29.11N 25.31E
Siwa Oasis Egypt 68 B3 29.10N 25.45E
Sixmilecross N. Ireland 23 B1 54.33N 7.08W
Sjöbo Sweden 46 G3 55.39N 13.44E
Skaelskör Denmark 46 E3 55.15N 11.18E
Skaerbaek Denmark 46 B3 55.09N 8.47E
Skagen Denmark 46 D5 57.44N 10.37E
Skagerrak str. Denmark/Norway 58 B2 57.45N 8.55E
Skagway U.S.A. 90 E3 59.23N 135.20W
Skaill Scotland 24 F5 58.57N 2.43W
Skälderviken b. Sweden 46 F4 56.20N 12.40E
Skalintyy mtn. Russian Fed. 61 K3 56.00N 130.40E
Skals Denmark 46 C4 56.33N 9.23E
Skanderborg Denmark 46 C4 56.01N 9.53E
Skanör Sweden 46 F3 55.25N 12.50E
Skara Sweden 58 C2 58.23N 13.25E
Skarzysko-Kamienna Poland 57 G5 51.08N 20.53E
Skeena r. Canada 90 F3 54.10N 129.08W
Skegness England 17 E3 53.09N 0.20E
Skellefte r. Sweden 58 E4 64.44N 21.07E
Skellefteå Sweden 58 E4 64.45N 21.00E
Skelmersdale England 20 C2 53.34N 2.49W
Skelmorlie Scotland 26 D2 55.51N 4.52W

Sunda Str. Indonesia 78 C2 6.00S105.50E
Sunderland England 22 C1 54.55N 1.22W
Sundsvall Sweden 58 D3 62.22N 17.20E
Sungaipenuh Indonesia 78 C3 2.00S101.28E
Sungguminasa Indonesia 78 F2 5.14S119.27E
Sungurlu Turkey 68 D6 40.10N 34.23E
Sunninghill *town* England 15 B2 51.24N 0.39W
Sunwu China 75 K6 49.40N127.10E
Sunyani Ghana 108 A2 7.22N 2.18W
Suomussalmi Finland 58 G4 64.52N 29.10E
Suonada *str.* Japan 76 A3 33.45N131.30E
Suonenjoki Finland 58 F3 62.40N 27.06E
Superior U.S.A. 87 H6 46.42N 92.05W
Superior, L. N. America 87 I6 48.00N 88.00W
Süphan Dağlari *mtn.* Turkey 68 F5 38.55N 42.55E
Sur Oman 69 J1 22.23N 59.32E
Sura Russian Fed. 59 F4 53.52N 45.45E
Sura *r.* Russian Fed. 41 O6 56.10N 46.00E
Surabaya Indonesia 78 E2 7.14S112.45E
Surakarta Indonesia 78 E2 7.32S110.50E
Surat India 71 D4 21.10N 72.54E
Sûre *r.* Lux. 47 E1 49.43N 6.31E
Surgut Russian Fed. 60 G3 61.13N 73.20E
Surigao Phil. 79 H5 9.47N125.29E
Surin Thailand 78 C6 14.53N103.29E
Surinam S. America 95 H1 4.00N 56.00W
Suriname *r.* Surinam 95 H2 5.52N 55.14W
Surrey *d.* England 15 B2 51.16N 0.30W
Surtsey *i.* Iceland 58 I6 63.18N 20.37W
Sutlej *r.* Pakistan 71 C5 29.26N 71.09E
Sutton G.L. England 15 B2 51.22N 0.12W
Sutton Bridge England 17 E2 52.46N 0.12E
Sutton Coldfield England 16 C2 52.33N 1.50W
Sutton in Ashfield England 16 C3 53.08N 1.16W
Sutton on Sea England 17 E3 53.18N 0.18E
Suva Fiji 82 H6 18.08S178.25E
Suwałki Poland 57 H7 54.07N 22.56E
Suwon S. Korea 75 K4 37.16N126.59E
Suzhou China 75 J3 31.21N120.40E
Suzu misaki *c.* Japan 76 C5 37.30N137.21E
Svartisen *mtn.* Norway 58 C4 66.30N 14.00E
Svedala Sweden 46 G3 55.30N 13.11E
Sveg Sweden 58 C3 62.02N 14.20E
Svendborg Denmark 46 D3 55.04N 10.38E
Svenstrup Denmark 46 C4 56.58N 9.52E
Svetogorsk Russian Fed. 58 G3 61.07N 28.50E
Svishtov Bulgaria 56 G5 43.36N 25.23E
Svitavy Czech. 57 E4 49.45N 16.27E
Svobodnyy Russian Fed. 75 K7 51.24N128.05E
Svolvaer Norway 58 C5 68.15N 14.40E
Swadlincote England 16 C2 52.47N 1.34W
Swaffham England 15 C3 52.38N 0.42E
Swains I. Samoa 82 I6 11.03S171.06W
Swale *r.* England 21 D3 54.05N 1.20W
Swanage England 13 F2 50.36N 1.59W
Swan Is. Honduras 94 C4 17.25N 83.55W
Swanley England 15 C2 51.24N 0.12E
Swanscombe England 15 C2 51.26N 0.19E
Swansea Wales 18 C1 51.37N 3.57W
Swansea B. Wales 18 C1 51.33N 3.50W
Swaziland Africa 106 D2 26.30S 31.30E
Sweden Europe 58 C2 63.00N 16.00E
Sweetwater U.S.A. 86 F3 32.37N100.25W
Swift Current *town* Canada 90 H3 50.17N107.49W
Swilly, Lough Rep. of Ire. 28 D5 55.10N 7.32W
Swindon England 13 F3 51.33N 1.47W
Świnoujście Poland 57 D6 53.55N 14.18E
Switzerland Europe 52 D2 47.00N 8.00E
Syderö *i.* Faroe Is. 58 M8 61.30N 6.50W
Sydney Australia 80 E2 33.55S151.10E
Sydney Canada 91 L2 46.10N 60.10W
Syktyvkar Russian Fed. 60 E3 61.42N 50.45E
Sylhet Bangla. 71 G4 24.53N 91.51E
Sylt *i.* Germany 52 D6 54.50N 8.20E
Syracuse U.S.A. 87 K5 43.03N 76.10W
Syr Darya *r.* Asia 60 F2 46.00N 61.12E
Syria Asia 68 E4 35.00N 38.00E
Syriam Myanma 78 B7 16.45N 96.17E
Syrian Desert Asia 68 E4 32.00N 39.00E
Syzran Russian Fed. 59 F4 53.10N 48.29E
Szczecin Poland 57 D6 53.25N 14.32E
Szczecinek Poland 57 E6 53.42N 16.41E
Szeged Hungary 57 G3 46.16N 20.08E
Székesfehérvár Hungary 57 F3 47.12N 18.25E
Szekszárd Hungary 57 F3 46.22N 18.44E
Szombathely Hungary 57 E3 47.12N 16.38E

T

Tabasco *d.* Mexico 92 F3 18.30N 93.00W
Tábor Czech. 57 D4 49.25N 14.41E
Tabora Tanzania 106 D4 5.02S 32.50E
Tabriz Iran 69 G5 38.05N 46.18E
Tabūk Saudi Arabia 68 E3 28.25N 36.35E
Tacloban Phil. 79 G6 11.15N124.59E
Tacoma U.S.A. 86 B6 47.16N122.30W
Tacuarembó Uruguay 97 D4 31.42S 56.00W
Tadcaster England 21 D2 53.53N 1.16W
Tademait Plateau Algeria 104 C4 28.45N 2.10E
Taegu S. Korea 75 K4 35.52N128.36E
Taejon S. Korea 75 K4 36.20N127.26E
Taganrog Russian Fed. 59 D3 47.14N 38.55E
Taganrog, G. of Ukraine/Russian Fed. 59 D3 47.00N 38.30E
Tagaytay City Phil. 79 G6 14.07N120.58E
Tagbilaran Phil. 79 G5 9.38N123.53E
Tagus *r.* Portugal 50 A3 39.00N 8.57W
Tahat, Mt. Algeria 102 C7 23.20N 5.40E
Tahiti *i.* Îs. de la Société 83 L6 17.37S149.27W
Taibei Taiwan 75 J2 25.05N121.32E
Taidong Taiwan 75 J2 22.49N121.10E
Taima Saudi Arabia 68 E2 27.37N 38.30E
Tain Scotland 24 D4 57.49N 4.02W
Tainan Taiwan 75 J2 23.01N120.14E
Taiping Malaysia 78 C4 4.54N100.42E
Taivalkoski Finland 58 G4 65.35N 28.20E
Taiwan Asia 75 J2 23.30N121.00E
Taiwan Str. China/Taiwan 75 I2 25.00N120.00E
Taiyuan China 75 H4 37.50N112.30E
Taizhong Taiwan 75 J2 24.09N120.40E
Taizhou China 75 I4 32.30N119.50E
Ta'izz Yemen 105 G3 13.35N 44.02E
Tajan Indonesia 78 E3 0.02S110.05E
Tajikistan Asia 74 A5 39.00N 70.30E
Tajrish Iran 69 H4 35.48N 51.20E
Tajuna *r.* Spain 50 D4 40.10N 3.35W
Tak Thailand 78 B7 16.47N 99.10E
Takalar Indonesia 78 F2 5.29S119.26E
Takamatsu Japan 76 B4 34.28N134.05E
Takaoka Japan 76 C5 36.47N137.00E
Takasaki Japan 76 D5 36.20N139.00E
Takestan Iran 69 H5 36.02N 49.40E
Takht-i-Suleiman *mtn.* Iran 69 H5 36.30N 50.58E
Taklimakan Shamo *des.* China 74 C5 38.10N 82.00E
Talasskiy Ala Tau *mts.* Kirgizia 74 B5 42.20N 73.20E
Talaud Is. Indonesia 79 H4 4.20N126.50E
Talavera de la Reina Spain 50 C3 39.58N 4.50W
Talca Chile 97 B4 35.28S 71.40W
Talcahuano Chile 97 B4 36.40S 73.10W
Taldom Russian Fed. 59 D5 56.49N 37.30E
Talgarth Wales 18 C1 51.59N 3.15W
Taliabu *i.* Indonesia 79 G3 1.50S124.55E
Talkeetna U.S.A. 90 D4 62.20N150.09W
Tallahassee U.S.A. 87 J3 30.28N 84.19W
Tallinn Estonia 58 F2 59.22N 24.48E
Tamale Ghana 108 A2 9.26N 0.49W
Tamanrasset Algeria 104 C4 22.50N 5.31E
Tamar *r.* England 12 C2 50.28N 4.13W
Tamaulipas *d.* Mexico 92 E4 24.00N 98.20W
Tambacounda Senegal 104 A3 13.45N 13.40W
Tambov Russian Fed. 59 E4 52.44N 41.28E
Tambre *r.* Spain 50 A5 42.50N 8.55W
Tâmega *r.* Portugal 50 A4 41.04N 8.17W
Tamil Nadu *d.* India 71 E2 11.15N 79.00E
Tampa U.S.A. 87 J2 27.58N 82.38W
Tampere Finland 58 E3 61.32N 23.45E
Tampico Mexico 92 E4 22.18N 97.52W
Tamsag Bulag Mongolia 75 I6 47.10N117.21E
Tamworth Australia 80 E2 31.07S150.57E
Tamworth England 16 C2 52.38N 1.42W
Tana *r.* Kenya 106 E4 2.32S 40.32E
Tana Norway 58 G5 70.26N 28.14E
Tana *r.* Norway 58 G5 69.45N 28.15E
Tana *i.* Vanuatu 82 G6 19.30S169.20E
Tanacross U.S.A. 90 D4 63.12N143.30W
Tanahmerah Irian Jaya Indonesia 79 K2 6.08S140.18E
Tana, L. Ethiopia 105 F3 12.00N 37.20E
Tanana U.S.A. 90 C4 65.11N152.10W
Tanaro *r.* Italy 54 B6 45.01N 8.46E
Tanderagee N. Ireland 23 C1 54.21N 6.26W
Tanega shima *i.* Japan 76 A2 30.32N131.00E
Tanga Tanzania 106 D4 5.07S 39.05E
Tanganyika, L. Africa 106 C4 5.37S 29.30E
Tanggula Shan *mts.* China 74 E4 32.40N 92.30E
Tangier Morocco 104 B5 35.48N 5.45W
Tangshan China 75 I5 39.37N118.05E
Tanimbar Is. Indonesia 79 I2 7.50S131.30E
Tanjay Phil. 79 G5 9.31N123.10E
Tanjungbalai Indonesia 78 B4 2.59N 99.46E
Tanjungkarang Indonesia 78 D2 5.28S105.16E
Tanjungpandan Indonesia 78 D3 2.44S107.36E
Tanjungredeb Indonesia 78 F4 2.09N117.29E
Tannis Bugt *b.* Denmark 46 D5 57.40N 10.10E
Tannu Ola Range *mts.* Russian Fed. 61 H2 51.00N 93.30E
Tano *r.* Ghana 108 A2 5.07N 2.54W
Tanta Egypt 68 C3 30.48N 31.00E
Tanzania Africa 106 D4 5.00S 35.00E
Tao'an China 75 J6 45.25N122.46E
Tapachula Mexico 92 F2 14.54N 92.15W
Tapajós *r.* Brazil 96 D7 2.40S 55.30W
Tapti *r.* India 71 D4 21.05N 72.45E
Tara *r.* Russian Fed. 60 G3 56.30N 74.40E
Tara *r.* Yugo. 56 D5 43.23N 18.47E
Tarakan Indonesia 78 F4 3.20N117.38E
Tarancón Spain 50 D4 40.01N 3.01W
Taranto Italy 54 F4 40.28N 17.14E
Taranto, G. of Italy 54 F4 40.00N 17.20E
Tarawa *i.* Kiribati 82 H8 1.25N173.00E
Tarbagatay Range *mts.* Kazakhstan 74 C6 47.00N 83.00E
Tarbat Ness *c.* Scotland 24 E4 57.52N 3.46W
Tarbert Rep. of Ire. 28 B2 52.33N 9.24W
Tarbert Strath. Scotland 26 C2 55.51N 5.25W
Tarbert W.Isles Scotland 24 B4 57.55N 6.50W
Tarbes France 48 D2 43.14N 0.05E
Tarbolton Scotland 26 D2 55.31N 4.29W
Tardoire *r.* France 48 C3 45.57N 1.00W
Tarifa Spain 50 C2 36.01N 5.36W
Tarija Bolivia 97 C5 21.33S 64.45W
Tarim Basin *f.* Asia 113 N6 40.00N 83.00E
Tarim He *r.* China 74 C5 41.00N 83.30E
Tarkwa Ghana 108 A2 5.16N 1.59W
Tarlac Phil. 79 G7 15.29N120.35E
Tarleton England 20 C2 53.41N 2.50W
Tarm Denmark 46 B3 55.54N 8.31E
Tarn *r.* France 48 D3 44.15N 1.15E
Tarnica *mtn.* Poland 57 H4 49.05N 22.44E
Tarnów Poland 57 G5 50.01N 20.59E
Tarporley England 20 C2 53.10N 2.42W
Tarragona Spain 50 F4 41.07N 1.15E
Tarrasa Spain 50 F4 41.34N 2.00E
Tarsus Turkey 68 D5 36.52N 34.52E
Tartary, G. of Russian Fed. 61 L2 47.40N141.00E
Tartu Estonia 58 F2 58.20N 26.44E
Tarutung Indonesia 78 B4 2.01N 98.54E
Tashkent Uzbekistan 74 A5 41.16N 69.13E
Tasiilaq *see* Ammassalik Greenland 91
Tasikmalaya Indonesia 78 D2 7.20S108.16E
Tasinge *i.* Denmark 46 D2 54.58N 10.38E
Tasmania *d.* Australia 80 D1 42.00S147.00E
Tasman Sea Pacific Oc. 80 E2 38.00S162.00E
Tåstrup Denmark 46 F3 55.39N 12.28E
Tatarsk Russian Fed. 60 G3 55.14N 76.00E
Tatnam, C. Canada 91 I3 57.00N 91.00W
Tatvan Turkey 68 F5 38.31N 42.15E
Taung-gyi Myanma 71 H4 20.49N 97.01E
Taunton England 13 D3 51.01N 3.07W
Taunus *mts.* Germany 52 D4 50.07N 8.10E
Taurus Mts. Turkey 68 D5 37.15N 34.15E
Tavira Portugal 50 B2 37.07N 7.39W
Tavistock England 12 C2 50.33N 4.09W
Tavoy Myanma 78 B6 14.07N 98.18E
Taw *r.* England 13 C3 51.05N 4.05W
Tawau Malaysia 78 F4 4.16N117.54E
Tawe *r.* Wales 18 C1 51.38N 3.56W
Tay *r.* Scotland 27 E3 56.21N 3.18W
Tay, Loch Scotland 26 D3 56.32N 4.08W
Taylor, Mt. U.S.A. 86 E4 35.14N107.36W
Taymyr, L. Russian Fed. 61 I4 74.20N101.00E
Taymyr Pen. Russian Fed. 61 I4 75.30N 99.00E
Taynuilt Scotland 26 C3 56.26N 5.14W
Tayport Scotland 27 F3 56.27N 2.53W
Tayshet Russian Fed. 61 I3 55.56N 98.01E
Tayside *d.* Scotland 27 E3 56.35N 3.28W
Taytay Palawan Phil. 78 F6 10.47N119.32E
Taz *r.* Russian Fed. 60 G4 67.30N 78.50E
Tbilisi Georgia 69 G6 41.43N 44.48E
Tebingtinggi Indonesia 78 B4 3.20N 99.08E
Tebingtinggi Indonesia 78 C3 3.37S103.09E
Tees *r.* England 22 C1 54.35N 1.11W
Tees B. England 22 C1 54.40N 1.07W
Teesdale *f.* England 22 B1 54.38N 2.08W
Tegal Indonesia 78 D2 6.52S109.07E
Tegucigalpa Honduras 93 G2 14.05N 87.14W
Tehran Iran 69 H4 35.40N 51.26E
Tehuacán Mexico 92 E3 18.30N 97.26W
Tehuantepec Mexico 92 E3 16.21N 95.13W
Tehuantepec, G. of Mexico 92 F3 16.00N 95.00W
Teifi *r.* Wales 18 B2 52.05N 4.41W
Teignmouth England 13 D2 50.33N 3.30W
Teith *r.* Scotland 27 D3 56.09N 4.00W
Tekirdag Turkey 68 B6 40.59N 27.30E
Tela Honduras 93 G3 15.56N 87.25W
Telavi Georgia 69 G6 41.56N 45.30E
Tel-Aviv-Yafo Israel 68 D4 32.05N 34.46E
Telford England 16 B2 52.42N 2.30W
Telgte Germany 47 F3 51.59N 7.46E
Tel Kotchek Syria 68 F5 36.48N 42.04E
Tell Atlas *mts.* Algeria 104 C5 36.10N 4.00E
Telukbetung Indonesia 78 D2 5.28S105.16E
Teluk Intan Malaysia 78 C4 4.00N101.00E
Tema Ghana 108 A2 5.41N 0.01W
Teme *r.* England 16 B2 52.10N 2.13W
Temirtau Kazakhstan 60 G2 50.05N 72.55E
Tempio Italy 54 B4 40.54N 9.06E
Temple U.S.A. 87 G3 31.06N 97.22W
Temple Ewell England 15 D2 51.09N 1.16E
Templemore Rep. of Ire. 28 D2 52.48N 7.51W
Temuco Chile 97 B4 38.45S 72.40W
Tenasserim Myanma 78 B6 12.05N 99.00E
Tenbury Wells England 16 B2 52.18N 2.35W
Tenby Wales 18 B1 51.40N 4.42W
Ten Degree Channel Indian Oc. 78 A5 10.00N 92.30E
Tendrara Morocco 104 B5 32.50N 1.40W
Tenerife *i.* Canary Is. 104 A4 28.10N 16.30W
Tengchong China 74 F2 25.02N 98.28E
Tengiz, L. Kazakhstan 60 F2 50.30N 69.00E
Teng Xian Shandong China 75 I4 35.10N117.14E
Tenke Zaïre 106 C3 10.34S 26.12E
Tennessee *d.* U.S.A. 87 I4 36.00N 86.00W
Tennessee *r.* U.S.A. 87 I4 37.10N 88.25W
Tenterden England 15 C2 51.04N 0.42E
Teófilo Otoni Brazil 97 E6 17.52S 41.31W
Tepic Mexico 92 D4 21.30N104.51W
Teplice Czech. 57 C5 50.40N 13.50E
Ter *r.* Spain 51 G5 42.02N 3.10E
Tera *r.* Portugal 50 A3 38.55N 8.01W
Teramo Italy 54 D5 42.40N 13.43E
Teresina Brazil 96 E7 4.50S 42.50W
Termez Uzbekistan 60 F1 37.15N 67.15E
Termini Italy 54 D2 37.59N 13.42E
Terminos Lagoon Mexico 92 F3 18.30N 91.30W
Termoli Italy 54 E4 41.58N 14.59E
Ternate Indonesia 79 H4 0.48N127.23E
Terneuzen Neth. 47 B3 51.20N 3.50E
Terni Italy 54 D5 42.34N 12.44E
Ternopol Ukraine 59 B3 49.35N 25.39E
Terre Haute U.S.A. 87 I4 39.27N 87.24W
Terschelling *i.* Neth. 47 D5 53.25N 5.25E
Teruel Spain 50 E4 40.21N 1.06W
Teslin *r.* Canada 90 E4 62.00N135.00W
Test *r.* England 14 A1 50.55N 1.29W
Têt *r.* France 48 E2 42.43N 3.00E
Tetbury England 13 E3 51.37N 2.09W
Teterev *r.* Ukraine 59 C4 51.03N 30.30E
Tetney England 17 D3 53.30N 0.01W
Tetuan Morocco 104 B5 35.34N 5.22W
Teviotdale *f.* Scotland 27 F2 55.26N 2.46W
Teviothead Scotland 27 F2 55.20N 2.56W
Tewkesbury England 13 E3 51.59N 2.09W
Texarkana U.S.A. 87 H3 33.28N 94.02W
Texas *d.* U.S.A. 86 G3 32.00N100.00W
Texel *i.* Neth. 47 C5 53.05N 4.47E
Texoma, L. U.S.A. 87 G3 34.00N 96.40W
Tezpur India 71 G5 26.38N 92.49E
Thabana Ntlenyana *mtn.* Lesotho 102 E2 29.30S 29.10E
Thailand Asia 78 C7 16.00N101.00E
Thailand, G. of Asia 78 C6 11.00N101.00E
Thai Nguyen Vietnam 78 D8 21.31N105.55E
Thale Luang *l.* Thailand 78 C5 7.30N100.20E
Thame England 15 B2 51.44N 0.58W
Thame *r.* England 14 A2 51.38N 1.10W
Thames *r.* England 15 C2 51.30N 0.05E
Thames Haven England 15 C2 51.31N 0.31E
Thana India 71 D3 19.14N 73.02E
Thanh Hoa Vietnam 78 D7 19.50N105.48E
Thanjavur India 71 E2 10.46N 79.09E
Thar Desert India 71 C5 28.00N 72.00E
Tharrawaddy Myanma 74 E1 17.37N 95.48E
Tharthar Basin *f.* Iraq 68 F4 33.56N 43.16E
Tharthar, Wadi *r.* Iraq 68 F4 34.18N 43.07E
Thásos *i.* Greece 56 G4 40.40N 24.39E
Thaton Myanma 78 B7 16.56N 97.20E
Thaungdut Myanma 71 G4 24.26N 94.45E
Thaxted England 15 C2 51.57N 0.21E
Thayetmyo Myanma 71 G3 19.20N 95.18E
Thebes *ruins* Egypt 68 D2 25.41N 32.40E
The Cherokees, L. O' U.S.A. 87 H4 36.45N 94.50W
The Cheviot *mtn.* England 22 B2 55.29N 2.10W
The Everglades *f.* U.S.A. 87 J2 26.00N 80.30W
The Fens *f.* England 15 C3 52.32N 0.13E
The Glenkens *f.* Scotland 26 D2 55.10N 4.13W
The Gulf Asia 69 H2 27.00N 50.00E
The Hague Neth. 47 C4 52.05N 4.16E
The Little Minch *str.* Scotland 24 B4 57.40N 6.45W
Thelon *r.* Canada 91 I4 64.23N 96.15W
The Long Mynd *hill* England 16 B2 52.33N 2.50W
The Machers *f.* Scotland 26 D1 54.45N 4.28W
The Marsh *f.* England 17 E2 52.50N 0.10E
The Minch *str.* Scotland 24 C5 58.10N 5.50W
The Mumbles Wales 18 C1 51.34N 4.00W
The Naze *c.* England 15 D2 51.53N 1.17E
The Needles *c.* England 14 A1 50.39N 1.35W
Theodore Roosevelt L. U.S.A. 86 D3 33.30N111.10W
The Pas Canada 91 H3 53.50N101.15W
The Pennines *hills* England 20 C3 54.40N 2.20W
The Potteries *f.* England 16 B2 53.00N 2.10W
The Rhinns *f.* Scotland 26 C1 54.50N 5.02W
Thermopylae, Pass of Greece 56 F3 38.47N 22.34E
The Six Towns *town* N. Ireland 23 C1 54.46N 6.53W
The Skerries *is.* Wales 18 B3 53.27N 4.35W
The Snares *is.* New Zealand 82 G3 48.00S166.30E
The Solent *str.* England 14 A1 50.45N 1.20W
Thessaloniki Greece 56 F4 40.38N 22.56E
Thessaloniki, G. of Med. Sea 56 F4 40.10N 23.00E
The Swale *str.* England 15 C2 51.22N 0.58E
Thetford England 15 C3 52.25N 0.44E
The Trossachs *f.* Scotland 26 D3 56.15N 4.25W
The Wash *b.* England 17 E2 52.55N 0.15E
The Weald *f.* England 15 C2 51.05N 0.20E
The Wrekin *hill* England 16 B2 52.40N 2.33W
Thiers France 48 E3 45.51N 3.33E
Thiès Senegal 104 A3 14.48N 16.56W
Thimbu Bhutan 71 F5 27.29N 89.40E
Thionville France 48 G5 49.22N 6.11E
Thíra *i.* Greece 56 G2 36.24N 25.27E
Thirsk England 21 D3 54.15N 1.20W
Thisted Denmark 46 B4 56.58N 8.42E
Thitu Is. S. China Sea 78 E6 10.50N114.20E
Thjórsá *r.* Iceland 58 I6 63.53N 20.38W
Tholen *i.* Neth. 47 C3 51.34N 4.07E
Thomasville U.S.A. 87 J3 30.50N 83.59W
Thonburi Thailand 78 C6 13.43N100.27E
Thornaby-on-Tees England 22 C1 54.34N 1.18W
Thornbury England 13 E3 51.36N 2.31W
Thorne England 21 E2 53.36N 0.56W
Thorney England 15 B3 52.37N 0.08W
Thornhill Scotland 27 E2 55.15N 3.46W
Thornton England 20 C2 53.53N 3.00W
Thorpe-le-Soken England 15 D2 51.50N 1.11E
Thorshavn Faroe Is. 58 M9 62.02N 6.47W
Thouars France 48 C4 46.59N 0.13W
Thrapston England 17 D2 52.24N 0.32W
Three Kings Is. New Zealand 82 H4 34.09S172.09E
Thuin Belgium 47 C2 50.21N 4.20E
Thuingen *d.* Germany 52 E4 51.00N 10.45E
Thule Greenland 91 L5 77.30N 69.29W
Thun Switz. 52 C2 46.46N 7.38E
Thunder Bay *town* Canada 91 J2 48.25N 89.14W
Thuringian Forest *mts.* Germany 52 E4 50.40N 10.50E
Thurles Rep. of Ire. 28 D2 52.41N 7.50W
Thurnscoe England 21 D2 53.31N 1.19W
Thursby England 22 A1 54.40N 3.03W
Thursday I. Australia 79 K1 10.45S142.00E
Thurso Scotland 24 E5 58.35N 3.32W
Thyborön Denmark 46 B4 56.42N 8.12E
Tianjin China 75 I5 39.08N117.12E
Tian Shan *mts.* Asia 74 C5 42.00N 80.30E
Tianshui China 74 G4 34.25N105.58E
Tibati Cameroon 104 D2 6.25N 12.33E
Tiber *r.* Italy 54 D4 41.45N 12.16E
Tiberias, L. Israel 68 D4 32.49N 35.36E
Tibesti Mts. Chad 104 D4 21.00N 17.30E
Tibet *d.* China 74 D4 32.20N 86.00E
Tibetan Plateau *f.* China 74 D4 34.00N 86.15E
Tiburon I. Mexico 92 B5 29.00N112.25W
Ticehurst England 15 C2 51.02N 0.23E
Ticino *r.* Italy 54 B6 45.09N 9.12E
Tickhill England 21 D2 53.25N 1.08W
Tidjikdja Mauritania 104 A3 18.29N 11.31W
Tiel Neth. 47 D3 51.53N 5.26E
Tielt Belgium 47 B3 51.00N 3.20E
Tierra Blanca Mexico 92 E3 18.28N 96.12W

Unye Turkey 68 E6 41.09N 37.15E
Unza *r.* Russian Fed. 41 N6 57.40N 43.30E
Upata Venezuela 95 G2 8.02N 62.25W
Upavon England 13 F3 51.17N 1.49W
Upernavik Greenland 91 M5 72.50N 56.00W
Upolu *i.* W. Samoa 82 I6 13.55S171.45W
Upper Egypt *f.* Egypt 68 D2 26.00N 32.00E
Upper Lough Erne N. Ireland 23 B1 54.13N 7.32W
Upper Taymyr *r.* Russian Fed. 61 I4 74.10N 99.50E
Upper Tean England 16 C2 52.57N 1.59W
Uppingham England 16 D2 52.36N 0.43W
Uppsala Sweden 58 D2 59.55N 17.38E
Upton upon Severn England 16 B2 52.04N 2.12W
Ur *ruins* Iraq 69 G3 30.55N 46.07E
Uraba, G. of Colombia 94 D2 8.30N 77.00W
Uracoa Venezuela 95 G2 9.03N 62.27W
Ural *r.* Russian Fed./Kazakhstan 60 E2 47.00N 52.00E
Ural Mts. Russian Fed. 60 E3 60.00N 59.00E
Ural'sk Kazakhstan 59 G4 51.19N 51.20E
Uranium City Canada 90 H3 59.32N108.43W
Urbino Italy 54 D5 43.43N 12.38E
Ure *r.* England 21 D3 54.05N 1.20W
Uren Russian Fed. 59 F5 57.30N 45.50E
Urfa Turkey 68 E5 37.08N 38.45E
Urgench Uzbekistan 60 E2 41.35N 60.41E
Ürgup Turkey 68 D5 38.39N 34.55E
Urlingford Rep. of Ire. 28 D2 52.43N 7.35W
Urmia, L. Iran 69 G5 37.40N 45.28E
Urmston England 20 C2 53.28N 2.22W
Uruapan Mexico 92 D3 19.26N102.04W
Uruguaiana Brazil 97 D5 29.45S 57.05W
Uruguay S. America 97 D4 33.00S 55.00W
Uruguay *r.* Uruguay 97 D4 34.00S 58.30W
Ürümqi China 74 D5 43.43N 87.38E
Uryu ko *l.* Japan 76 E9 44.22N142.15E
Uşak Turkey 68 C5 38.42N 29.25E
Ushant *i. see* Ouessant, Île d' *i.* France 48
Ushnuiyeh Iran 69 G5 37.03N 45.05E
Usk Wales 18 D1 51.42N 2.53W
Usk *r.* Wales 18 D1 51.34N 2.59W
Üsküdar Turkey 68 C6 41.00N 29.03E
Ussuriysk Russian Fed. 75 K5 43.48N131.59E
Ustica *i.* Italy 54 D3 38.42N 13.11E
Usti nad Labem Czech. 57 D5 50.41N 14.00E
Ust'kamchatsk Russian Fed. 61 N3 56.14N162.28E
Ust-Kamenogorsk Kazakhstan 60 G2 50.00N 82.40E
Ust Kut Russian Fed. 61 I3 56.40N105.50E
Ust'Maya Russian Fed. 61 L3 60.25N134.28E
Ust Olenëk Russian Fed. 61 J4 72.59N120.00E
Ust'Tsilma Russian Fed. 60 E4 65.28N 53.09E
Ust Urt Plateau *f.* Asia 59 E2 43.30N 55.00E
Utah *d.* U.S.A. 86 D4 39.00N112.00W
Utica N.Y. U.S.A. 87 K5 43.06N 75.05W
Utiel Spain 50 E3 39.33N 1.13W
Utrecht Neth. 47 D4 52.04N 5.07E
Utrecht *d.* Neth. 47 D4 52.04N 5.10E
Utrera Spain 50 C2 37.10N 5.47W
Utsunomiya Japan 76 D5 36.40N139.52E
Uttaradit Thailand 78 C7 17.20N100.05E
Uttar Pradesh *d.* India 71 E5 27.40N 80.00E
Uttoxeter England 16 C2 52.53N 1.50W
Uusikaupunki Finland 58 E3 60.48N 21.30E
Uwaina Saudi Arabia 69 H2 26.46N 48.13E
Uwajima Japan 76 B3 33.13N132.32E
Uyo Nigeria 108 C2 5.01N 7.56E
Uyun Saudi Arabia 69 F2 26.32N 43.41E
Uyuni Bolivia 97 C5 20.28S 66.47W
Uzbekistan Asia 60 E2 42.00N 63.00E
Uzda Belorussia 59 B4 53.28N 27.11E
Uzhgorod Ukraine 57 H4 48.38N 22.15E

V

Vaagö *i.* Faroe Is. 58 L9 62.03N 7.14W
Vaal *r.* R.S.A. 102 E2 29.04S 23.37E
Vaasa Finland 58 E3 63.06N 21.36E
Vác Hungary 57 F3 47.49N 19.10E
Vadodara India 71 D4 22.19N 73.14E
Vaduz Liech. 52 D2 47.08N 9.32E
Vaggeryd Sweden 58 C2 57.30N 14.10E
Váh *r.* Czech. 57 F3 47.40N 18.09E
Vaitupu *i.* Tuvalu 82 H7 7.28S178.41E
Valdai Hills Russian Fed. 59 C5 57.10N 33.00E
Valday Russian Fed. 59 C5 57.59N 33.10E
Valdemarsvik Sweden 58 D2 58.13N 16.35E
Valdepeñas Spain 50 D3 38.46N 3.24W
Valdez U.S.A. 90 D4 61.07N146.17W
Valdivia Chile 97 B4 39.46S 73.15W
Valença Portugal 50 A5 42.02N 8.38W
Valence France 48 F3 44.56N 4.54E
Valencia Spain 50 E3 39.29N 0.24W
Valencia *d.* Spain 50 E3 40.00N 0.40W
Valencia Venezuela 95 F3 10.14N 67.59W
Valencia de Alcántara Spain 50 B3 39.25N 7.14
Valencia, G. of Spain 50 F3 39.38N 0.20W
Valencia, L. Venezuela 95 F3 10.09N 67.30W
Valenciennes France 47 B2 50.22N 3.32E
Vale of Berkeley *f.* England 13 E3 51.42N 2.25W
Vale of Evesham *f.* England 16 C2 52.05N 1.55W
Vale of Gloucester *f.* England 13 E3 51.54N 2.15W
Vale of Kent *f.* England 15 C2 51.08N 0.38E
Vale of Pewsey *f.* England 13 F3 51.21N 1.45W
Vale of Pickering *f.* England 21 E3 54.11N 0.45W
Vale of White Horse *f.* England 14 A2 51.38N 1.32W
Vale of York *f.* England 21 D3 54.12N 1.25W
Valera Venezuela 94 E2 9.21N 70.38W
Valga Estonia 58 F2 57.44N 26.00E
Valinco, G. of Med. Sea 49 H1 41.40N 8.50E
Valjevo Yugo. 56 D6 44.16N 19.56E
Valkeakoski Finland 58 F3 61.17N 24.05E
Valkenswaard Neth. 47 D3 51.21N 5.27E
Valladolid Spain 50 C4 41.39N 4.45W
Valle de la Pascua Venezuela 95 F2 9.15N 66.00W
Valledupar Colombia 94 E3 10.10N 73.16W
Valletta Malta 54 E1 35.53N 14.31E
Valley City U.S.A. 86 G6 46.57N 97.58W
Valmiera Latvia 58 F2 57.32N 25.29E
Valnera *mtn.* Spain 50 D5 43.10N 3.40W
Valognes France 48 C5 49.31N 1.28W
Valparaíso Chile 97 B4 33.05S 71.40W
Vals, C. Indonesia 79 J2 8.30S137.30E
Valverde Dom. Rep. 93 J3 19.37N 71.04W
Valverde del Camino Spain 50 B2 37.35N 6.45W
Van Turkey 68 F5 38.28N 43.20E
Vancouver Canada 90 F2 49.13N123.06W
Vancouver I. Canada 90 F2 50.00N126.00W
Vänern *l.* Sweden 58 C2 59.00N 13.15E
Vänersborg Sweden 58 C2 58.23N 12.19E
Vanimo P.N.G. 79 K3 2.40S141.17E
Van, L. Turkey 68 F5 38.35N 42.52E
Vännäs Sweden 58 D3 63.56N 19.50E
Vannes France 48 B4 47.40N 2.44W
Vanua Levu *i.* Fiji 82 H6 16.33S179.15E
Vanuatu Pacific Oc. 80 F4 16.00S167.00E
Var *r.* France 48 G2 43.39N 7.11E
Varanasi India 71 E4 25.20N 83.00E
Varangerfjorden *est.* Norway 58 G5 70.00N 29.30E
Varaždin Yugo. 56 C7 46.18N 16.20E
Varberg Sweden 58 C2 57.06N 12.15E
Vardar *r.* Greece 56 F4 40.31N 22.43E
Varde Denmark 46 B3 55.37N 8.29E
Varel Germany 47 G5 53.24N 8.08E
Varennes France 48 E4 46.19N 3.24E
Varkaus Finland 58 F3 62.15N 27.45E
Varna Bulgaria 59 B2 43.13N 27.57E
Varnaes Denmark 46 C3 55.01N 9.34E
Värnamo Sweden 58 C2 57.11N 14.03E
Várpalota Hungary 57 F3 47.12N 18.09E
Vasilkov Ukraine 59 C4 50.12N 30.15E
Vaslui Romania 59 B3 46.38N 27.44E
Västerås Sweden 58 D2 59.36N 16.32E
Västerdal *r.* Sweden 58 C3 60.32N 15.02E
Västervik Sweden 58 D2 57.45N 16.40E
Vatnajökull *mts.* Iceland 58 J7 64.20N 17.00W
Vättern *l.* Sweden 58 C2 58.30N 14.30E
Vaughn N.Mex. U.S.A. 86 E3 34.35N105.14W
Vavuniya Sri Lanka 71 E2 8.45N 80.30E
Växjö Sweden 58 C2 56.52N 14.50E
Vaygach *i.* Russian Fed. 60 F4 70.00N 59.00E
Vecht *r.* Neth. 47 E4 52.39N 6.01E
Vega *i.* Norway 58 B4 65.40N 11.55E
Vejen Denmark 46 C3 55.29N 9.10E
Vejlby Denmark 46 D4 56.11N 10.14E
Vejle Denmark 46 C3 55.43N 9.33E
Vejle *d.* Denmark 46 C3 55.50N 9.20E
Vélez Málaga Spain 50 C2 36.48N 4.05W
Velikaya *r.* Russian Fed. 58 G2 57.54N 28.06E
Velikiye-Luki Russian Fed. 59 C5 56.19N 30.31E
Velikiy Ustyug Russian Fed. 59 F6 60.48N 45.15E
Velletri Italy 54 D4 41.41N 12.47E
Vellinge Sweden 46 G3 55.28N 13.01E
Vellore India 71 E2 12.56N 79.09E
Velsen Neth. 47 C4 52.28N 4.39E
Velsk Russian Fed. 59 E6 61.05N 42.06E
Veluwe *f.* Neth. 47 D4 52.17N 5.45E
Venachar, Loch Scotland 26 D3 56.13N 4.19W
Vendas Novas Portugal 50 A3 38.41N 8.27W
Vendôme France 48 D4 47.48N 1.04E
Venezuela S. America 95 F2 7.00N 65.20W
Venezuela, G. of Venezuela 94 E3 11.30N 71.00W
Veniaminof Mt. U.S.A. 90 C3 56.05N159.20W
Venice Italy 54 D6 45.26N 12.20E
Venice, G. of Med. Sea 54 D6 45.20N 13.00E
Venlo Neth. 47 E3 51.22N 6.10E
Venraij Neth. 47 D3 51.32N 5.58E
Venta *r.* Latvia 58 E2 57.22N 21.31E
Ventspils Latvia 58 E2 57.22N 21.31E
Ventuari *r.* Venezuela 95 F1 4.00N 67.35W
Vera Argentina 97 C5 29.31S 60.30W
Vera Spain 50 E2 37.15N 1.51W
Veracruz Mexico 92 E3 19.11N 96.10W
Veracruz *d.* Mexico 92 E3 18.00N 95.00W
Veraval India 71 C4 20.53N 70.28E
Vercelli Italy 54 B6 45.19N 8.26E
Verdon *r.* France 48 F2 43.42N 5.39E
Verdun France 48 F5 49.10N 5.24E
Vereeniging R.S.A. 106 C2 26.41S 27.56E
Verín Spain 50 B4 41.55N 7.26W
Verkhniy Baskunchak Russian Fed. 59 F3 48.14N 46.44E
Verkhoyansk Russian Fed. 61 L4 67.25N133.25E
Verkhoyansk Range *mts.* Russian Fed. 61 K4 66.00N130.00E
Vermont *d.* U.S.A. 87 L5 44.00N 72.30W
Verona Italy 54 C6 45.27N 10.59E
Versailles France 48 D5 48.48N 2.08E
Vert, Cap *c.* Senegal 104 A3 14.45N 17.25W
Verviers Belgium 47 D2 50.36N 5.52E
Vervins France 47 B1 49.50N 3.55E
Verwood England 13 F2 50.53N 1.53W
Vesoul France 48 G4 47.38N 6.09E
Vesterålen *is.* Norway 58 C5 68.55N 15.00E
Vestfjorden *est.* Norway 58 C4 68.10N 15.00E
Vestjaellands *d.* Denmark 46 E3 55.30N 11.30E
Vestmanna Is. Iceland 58 I6 63.30N 20.20W
Vesuvius *mtn.* Italy 54 E4 40.48N 14.25E
Vesyegonsk Russian Fed. 59 D5 58.38N 37.19E
Vetlanda Sweden 58 C2 57.26N 15.05E
Vetluga *r.* Russian Fed. 59 F5 56.18N 46.19E
Vettore, Monte *mtn.* Italy 54 D5 42.50N 13.18E
Vézère *r.* France 48 D3 44.53N 0.55E
Viana do Castelo Portugal 50 A4 41.41N 8.50W
Viborg Denmark 46 C4 56.28N 9.25E
Viborg *d.* Denmark 46 C4 56.40N 9.00E
Vicenza Italy 54 C6 45.33N 11.32E
Vichada *r.* Colombia 95 F1 4.58N 67.35W
Vichuga Russian Fed. 59 E5 57.12N 41.50E
Vichy France 48 E4 46.07N 3.25E
Victoria *d.* Australia 80 D2 37.20S144.10E
Victoria Canada 90 F2 48.26N123.20W
Victoria de las Tunas Cuba 93 I4 20.58N 76.59W
Victoria Falls *f.* Zimbabwe/Zambia 106 C3 17.58S 25.45E
Victoria I. Canada 90 G5 71.00N110.00W
Victoria, L. Africa 102 F4 1.00S 33.00E
Vidin Bulgaria 56 F5 43.58N 22.51E
Viedma Argentina 97 C3 40.45S 63.00W
Vienna Austria 57 E4 48.13N 16.22E
Vienne France 48 F3 45.32N 4.54E
Vienne *r.* France 48 C4 47.13N 0.05W
Vientiane Laos 78 C7 18.01N102.48E
Vieques *i.* Puerto Rico 93 K3 18.08N 65.30W
Vierwaldstätter *l.* Switz. 52 D2 47.10N 8.50E
Vierzon France 48 E4 47.14N 2.03E
Vietnam Asia 78 D6 15.00N108.00E
Vigan Phil. 79 G7 17.35N120.23E
Vignemale, Pic de *mtn.* France 48 C2 42.46N 0.08W
Vigo Spain 50 A5 42.15N 8.44W
Vijayawada India 71 E3 16.34N 80.40E
Vijosë *r.* Albania 56 D4 40.39N 19.20E
Vikna *i.* Norway 58 B4 64.59N 11.00E
Vila Vanuatu 82 G6 17.44S168.19E
Vila Franca Portugal 50 A3 38.57N 8.59W
Vilaine *r.* France 48 B4 47.30N 2.25W
Vilanova la Geltrú Spain 50 F4 41.13N 1.43E
Vila Real Portugal 50 B4 41.17N 7.45W
Vila Real de Santo António Portugal 50 B2 37.12N 7.25W
Vilhelmina Sweden 58 D4 64.38N 16.40E
Viljandi Estonia 58 F2 58.22N 25.30E
Villablino Spain 50 B5 42.57N 6.19W
Villacañas Spain 50 D3 39.38N 3.20W
Villach Austria 57 C3 46.37N 13.51E
Villagarcía Spain 50 A5 42.35N 8.45W
Villahermosa Mexico 92 F3 18.00N 92.53W
Villajoyosa Spain 50 E3 38.31N 0.14W
Villa María Argentina 97 C4 32.25S 63.15W
Villanueva de la Serena Spain 50 C3 38.58N 5.48W
Villaputzu Italy 54 B3 39.28N 9.35E
Villarrica Paraguay 97 D5 25.45S 56.28W
Villarrobledo Spain 50 D3 39.16N 2.36W
Villavicencio Colombia 94 E1 4.09N 73.38W
Villefranche France 48 F3 46.00N 4.43E
Villena Spain 50 E3 38.39N 0.52W
Villeneuve France 48 D3 44.25N 0.43E
Villeneuve d'Ascq France 47 B2 50.37N 3.10E
Villeurbanne France 48 F3 45.46N 4.54E
Vilnius Lithuania 58 F1 54.40N 25.19E
Vilvoorde Belgium 47 C2 50.56N 4.25E
Vilyuy *r.* Russian Fed. 61 K4 64.20N126.55E
Vilyuysk Russian Fed. 61 K3 63.46N121.35E
Vimmerby Sweden 58 C2 57.40N 15.50E
Viña del Mar Chile 97 B4 33.02S 71.35W
Vindel *r.* Sweden 58 D3 63.56N 19.54E
Vinderup Denmark 46 B4 56.30N 8.48E
Vindhya Range *mts.* India 71 D4 22.55N 76.00E
Vinh Vietnam 78 D7 18.42N105.41E
Vinh Loi Vietnam 78 D5 9.17N105.44E
Vinnitsa Ukraine 59 B3 49.11N 28.30E
Vire France 48 C5 48.50N 0.53W
Vire *r.* France 48 C5 49.20N 0.53W
Virgin Gorda *i.* B.V.Is. 93 L3 18.30N 64.26W
Virginia *d.* U.S.A. 87 K4 37.30N 79.00W
Virgin Is. (British) C. America 95 G4 18.30N 64.30W
Virgin Is. (U.S.A.) C. America 95 F4 18.30N 65.00W
Virovitica Yugo. 56 C6 45.51N 17.23E
Virton Belgium 47 D1 49.35N 5.32E
Vis *i.* Yugo. 56 C5 43.03N 16.10E
Visby Sweden 58 D2 57.37N 18.20E
Viscount Melville Sd. Canada 90 H5 74.30N104.00W
Visé Belgium 47 D2 50.44N 5.42E
Višegrad Yugo. 56 D5 43.47N 19.20E
Viseu Portugal 50 B4 40.40N 7.55W
Vishakhapatnam India 71 E3 17.42N 83.24E
Viso, Monte *mtn.* Italy 54 A6 44.38N 7.05E
Vistula *r.* Poland 57 F7 54.23N 18.52E
Vitebsk Belorussia 59 C5 55.10N 30.14E
Viterbo Italy 54 D5 42.26N 12.07E
Viti Levu *i.* Fiji 82 H6 18.00S178.00E
Vitim *r.* Russian Fed. 61 J3 59.30N112.36E
Vitoria Spain 50 D5 42.51N 2.40W
Vitória da Conquista Brazil 96 E6 14.53S 40.52W
Vitória Espírito Santo Brazil 97 E5 20.19S 40.21W
Vittoria Italy 54 E2 36.57N 14.21E
Vizianagaram India 71 E3 18.07N 83.30E
Vlaardingen Neth. 47 C3 51.55N 4.20E
Vladikavkaz Russian Fed. 59 E2 43.02N 44.43E
Vladimir Russian Fed. 59 E5 56.08N 40.25E
Vladivostok Russian Fed. 75 K5 43.09N131.53E
Vlieland *i.* Neth. 47 D5 53.15N 5.00E
Vlorë Albania 56 D4 40.28N 19.27E
Vltava *r.* Czech. 57 D5 50.22N 14.28E
Vogelkop *f.* Indonesia 79 I3 1.10S132.30E
Voghera Italy 54 B6 44.59N 9.01E
Voil, Loch Scotland 26 D3 56.21N 4.26W
Voiron France 48 F3 45.22N 5.35E
Vojens Denmark 46 C3 55.15N 9.20E
Volcano Is. Japan 82 E10 25.00N141.00E
Volga *r.* Russian Fed. 59 F3 45.45N 47.50E
Volga Uplands *hills* Russian Fed. 59 F4 53.15N 45.45E
Volgograd Russian Fed. 59 E3 48.45N 44.30E
Volgograd Resr. Russian Fed. 59 F4 51.00N 46.05E
Volkhov *r.* Russian Fed. 59 C6 60.15N 32.15E
Vologda Russian Fed. 59 D5 59.10N 39.55E
Vólos Greece 56 F3 39.22N 22.57E
Volsk Russian Fed. 59 F4 52.04N 47.22E
Volta *r.* Ghana 108 B2 5.50N 0.41E
Volta, L. Ghana 108 A2 7.00N 0.00
Volta Redonda Brazil 97 E5 22.31S 44.05W
Volterra Italy 54 C5 43.24N 10.51E
Volturno *r.* Italy 54 D4 41.02N 13.56E
Volzhskiy Russian Fed. 59 E3 48.48N 44.45E
Voorburg Neth. 47 C4 52.05N 4.22E
Vopnafjördhur *est.* Iceland 58 K7 65.50N 14.30W
Vorarlberg *d.* Austria 57 A3 47.15N 9.55E
Vordingborg Denmark 46 E3 55.01N 11.55E
Vorkuta Russian Fed. 60 F4 67.27N 64.00E
Voronezh Russian Fed. 59 D4 51.40N 39.13E
Vosges *mts.* France 48 G5 48.10N 7.00E
Voss Norway 58 A3 60.38N 6.25E
Vostok I. Kiribati 83 K6 10.05S152.23W
Vouga *r.* Portugal 50 A4 40.41N 8.38W
Voves France 48 D5 48.16N 1.37E
Voznesensk Ukraine 59 C3 47.34N 31.21E
Vranje Yugo. 56 E5 42.34N 21.52E
Vratsa Bulgaria 56 F5 43.12N 23.33E
Vrbas *r.* Yugo. 56 C6 45.06N 17.29E
Vršac Yugo. 56 E6 45.08N 21.18E
Vung Tau Vietnam 78 D6 10.21N107.04E
Vyatka *r.* Russian Fed. 41 P6 55.40N 51.40E
Vyatskiye Polyany Russian Fed. 59 G5 56.14N 51.08E
Vyazma Russian Fed. 59 C5 55.12N 34.17E
Vyazniki Russian Fed. 59 E5 56.14N 42.08E
Vyborg Russian Fed. 59 B5 60.45N 28.41E
Vyrnwy *r.* Wales 18 C2 52.45N 3.01W
Vyrnwy, L. Wales 18 C2 52.46N 3.30W
Vyshniy-Volochek Russian Fed. 59 C5 57.34N 34.23E
Vytegra Russian Fed. 59 D6 61.04N 36.27E

W

Wa Ghana 108 A3 10.07N 2.28W
Waal *r.* Neth. 47 C3 51.45N 4.40E
Waalwijk Neth. 47 D3 51.42N 5.04E
Wabag P.N.G. 79 K2 5.28S143.40E
Wabash *r.* U.S.A. 87 I4 38.25N 87.45W
Wabush City Canada 91 L3 53.00N 66.50W
Waco U.S.A. 87 G3 31.33N 97.10W
Wad Pakistan 70 C5 27.21N 66.30E
Wadden Sea Neth. 47 D5 53.15N 5.05E
Waddesdon England 15 B2 51.50N 0.54W
Waddington, Mt. Canada 90 F3 51.30N125.00W
Wadebridge England 12 C2 50.31N 4.51W
Wadhurst England 15 C2 51.03N 0.21E
Wadi Halfa Sudan 105 F4 21.55N 31.20E
Wad Medani Sudan 105 F3 14.24N 33.30E
Wafra Kuwait 69 G3 28.39N 47.56E
Wageningen Neth. 47 D3 51.58N 5.39E
Wager Bay *town* Canada 91 I4 65.55N 90.40W
Wagga Wagga Australia 80 D2 35.07S147.24E
Wah Pakistan 71 D6 33.50N 72.44E
Wahpeton U.S.A. 87 G6 46.16N 96.36W
Waigeo *i.* Indonesia 79 I3 0.05S130.30E
Wainfleet All Saints England 17 E3 53.07N 0.16E
Waingapu Indonesia 79 G2 9.30S120.10E
Wainwright U.S.A. 90 B5 70.39N160.00W
Wajir Kenya 106 E5 1.46N 40.05E
Wakasa wan *b.* Japan 76 C4 35.50N135.40E
Wakayama Japan 76 C4 34.12N135.10E
Wakefield England 21 D2 53.41N 1.31W
Wake I. Pacific Oc. 82 G9 19.17N166.36E
Wakkanai Japan 76 E9 45.26N141.43E
Wałbrzych Poland 57 E5 50.48N 16.19E
Walbury Hill England 14 A2 51.21N 1.30W
Walcheren *f.* Neth. 47 B3 51.32N 3.35E
Wales *d.* U.K. 18 C2 52.30N 3.45W
Wallasey England 20 B2 53.26N 3.02W
Wallingford England 14 A2 51.36N 1.07W
Wallis, Îles *is.* Pacific Oc. 82 I6 13.16S176.15W
Wallsend England 22 C1 55.00N 1.31W
Walmer England 15 D2 51.12N 1.23E
Walney, Isle of England 22 A1 54.05N 3.12W
Walsall England 16 C2 52.36N 1.59W
Waltham Abbey England 15 C2 51.42N 0.01E
Waltham on the Wolds England 16 D2 52.49N 0.49W
Walton on the Naze England 15 D2 51.52N 1.17E
Walvis Bay *town* R.S.A. 106 B2 22.50S 14.31E
Wamba Nigeria 108 C2 8.57N 8.42E
Wanderup Germany 46 C2 54.43N 9.22E
Wangeroog *i.* Germany 47 F5 53.50N 7.50E
Wangford Fen *f.* England 15 C3 52.25N 0.31E
Wantage England 14 A2 51.35N 1.25W
Wanxian China 75 H3 30.54N108.20E
Warangal India 71 E3 18.00N 79.35E
Ward Rep. of Ire. 28 E3 53.25N 6.21W
Wardha India 71 E4 20.41N 78.40E
Ward's Stone *mtn.* England 20 C3 54.03N 2.36W
Ware England 15 B2 51.49N 0.02W
Wareham England 13 E2 50.41N 2.08W
Warendorf Germany 47 G3 51.57N 8.00E
Wark Forest *hills* England 22 B2 55.06N 2.24W
Warley England 16 B2 52.29N 2.02W
Warminster England 13 E3 51.12N 2.11W
Warnemünde Germany 46 F2 54.11N 12.05E
Warrenpoint N. Ireland 23 C1 54.06N 6.15W
Warri Nigeria 108 C2 5.36N 5.46E
Warrington England 20 C2 53.25N 2.38W
Warrnambool Australia 80 D2 38.23S142.03E
Warsaw Poland 57 G6 52.15N 21.00E
Warsop England 16 C3 53.13N 1.08W
Warta *r.* Poland 57 D6 52.45N 15.09E
Warwick England 16 C2 52.17N 1.36W
Warwickshire *d.* England 16 C2 52.13N 1.30W

X

Y